Religion as a Public Good

Religion as a Public Good

Jews and Other Americans on Religion in the Public Square

EDITED BY ALAN MITTLEMAN

ROWMAN & LITTLEFIELD PUBLISHERS, INC.
Lanham • Boulder • New York • Toronto • Oxford

ROWMAN & LITTLEFIELD PUBLISHERS, INC.

Published in the United States of America
by Rowman & Littlefield Publishers, Inc.
A wholly owned subsidary of The Rowman & Littlefield Publishing Group, Inc.
4501 Forbes Boulevard, Suite 200, Lanham, Maryland 20706
www.rowmanlittlefield.com

PO Box 317
Oxford
OX2 9RU, UK

British Library Cataloguing in Publication Information Available

Library of Congress Cataloging-in-Publication Data

Religion as a public good : Jews and other Americans on religion in the public square /
edited by Alan Mittleman.
    p. cm.
Includes bibliographical references and index.
    ISBN 0-7425-3124-4 (cloth : alk. paper) — ISBN 0-7425-3125-2 (pbk. : alk. paper)
1. Judaism—Social aspects—United States. 2. Judaism and state—United States. 3.
Jews—United States—Politics and government. 4. Judaism and politics—United
States. 5. Religion and sociology—United States. 6. Religious pluralism—United
States. 7. United States—Politics and government—1993—Philosophy. I. Mittleman,
Alan.

BM205.R42 2003
296.3'82'0973—dc21   2003052433

Printed in the United States of America

♾ The paper used in this publication meets the minimum requirements of American
National Standard for Information Sciences—Permanence of Paper for Printed Library
Materials, ANSI/NISO Z39.48-1992.

Managing Editor: Mark Ami-El
Typesetting: Ami-El Applications, Jerusalem, Israel

This volume is dedicated to the memory of
Professor Daniel J. Elazar,
founding president of the
Center for Jewish Community Studies
and the Jerusalem Center for Public Affairs,
scholar, and friend.
This project began under his inspiration and guidance.
May his memory be a blessing.

Jews and the American Public Square is a three-year project of communal dialogue, research, and publication devoted to exploring the relationship between the faith and culture of American Jews and their civic engagement. Initiated by a major grant from the Pew Charitable Trusts, the project seeks to foster greater understanding among both Jews and non-Jews of the role of religion in American public life.

Also available:

Jewish Polity and American Civil Society: Communal Agencies and Religious Movements in the American Public Sphere, edited by Alan Mittleman, Jonathan D. Sarna, and Robert Licht (2002).

Jews and the American Public Square: Debating Religion and Republic, edited by Alan Mittleman, Jonathan D. Sarna, and Robert Licht (2002).

Contents

Introduction

Alan Mittleman

For modern Jews seeking their bearings in the vexed domain of how religion should relate to American public life *The Origins of Republican Form of Government*, by Oscar Straus, would be an instructive place to begin. Straus was a leading figure in nineteenth- and early-twentieth-century American Jewry. His book originated in a series of lectures that the young, thirty-five-year-old Columbia University educated lawyer delivered at the Brooklyn Historical Society in 1885. Straus's task was to locate the intellectual impetus for republican government in the United States. He argued that almost nothing in the political experience and conceptual range of the American Founders predisposed them to democratic republicanism. From their study of history, the Founders were well aware of the weaknesses of the ancient Greek and Roman republics, as well as the Venetian republic. Furthermore, the British experience under Cromwell was hardly inspiring. The origin of republicanism, Straus argued, was to be found in the Puritan reading of the Hebrew scriptures. It was the Bible that taught the early Americans the paths and virtues of self-rule. As Straus marshals evidence for his thesis, he attempts to delineate incipiently republican forms of polity and political practice in the Bible and, indeed, in subsequent Jewish tradition. He argues that the Hebrew Commonwealth was, as he puts it, "the first Federal Republic." Thus Straus insinuates the Jewish political tradition into the American Founding.

Straus also insinuated core American principles into his own life. Although an immigrant from the Rhineland, he became thoroughly

1

American. When appointed by Grover Cleveland to serve as ambassador to Turkey, his highest priority was to work for the religious
liberties of American Protestant missionaries in the Ottoman Empire. Straus was also the first American Jew to rise to a seat in a
presidential cabinet; he was Theodore Roosevelt's Secretary of
Commerce and Labor. Perhaps nothing, however, attests to the
depth of his embrace of American values than the name that he gave
to his firstborn son—Roger Williams Straus. Thus an immigrant of
humble German-Jewish stock came to live an American-Jewish
dream of profound affinity between the Jewish and the American
traditions.

Straus's book has fallen into almost complete neglect. The major
historians of the American Founding, such as Gordon Wood, take no
notice of it. Indeed, despite an enviable level of erudition, Straus's
work falls far short of credible, contemporary historiography. Although, in fairness to him, the problem with which he grappled—the
role of religion in informing and stimulating republican thought in
America—is once again on the front burner of the historiography of
the Founding.[1] He has fared no better among Jewish historians, who
dismiss his book as apologetic literature. Naomi Cohen, who has
written the authoritative biography of Straus, passes over this youth-
ful book without evaluating its worth.[2] More recently, Jonathan
Sarna treats the book as part of what he calls the American Jewish
"cult of synthesis." By cult of synthesis Sarna refers to a protracted
effort by American Jews, beginning in the early nineteenth century
and extending into the 1960s, to celebrate the alleged inner unity of
Judaism and Americanism. In Sarna's view, works such as Straus's
are based on an abiding Jewish anxiety about fitting in, about being
accepted. At the point where American Jews gain acceptance and
their anxiety fades, their interest in the cult of synthesis subsides.
On this analysis, the dearth of apologetic literature about Judaism
and Americanism in our time attests to the maturity and normalcy of
the American Jewish community.[3]

Given the harsh judgment of history on *The Origin of Republican
Form of Government*, what does Straus have to offer a twenty-first-
century reader? Although there is much truth in the critical judgment against him, I find it hard to believe that it is the last word to
be said about works such as Straus's. Does a concept as negative as
anxiety explain everything? Is the desire to know how Judaism,
Jewishness, and American democracy fit together only a form of
angst-ridden public relations? Dated as it is, Straus's work speaks to
a perennial and compelling intellectual problem. How does Judaism,

which is of ultimate importance for serious Jews, relate to the duties of American citizenship and to the consciousness of civic belonging? What is the nature of the covenant between American Jews and America? How should American Jews think about their obligations, duties, and dissents vis-à-vis their country? What contribution can Judaism make to a decent politics? To the virtues required by democratic citizens? To the moral discourse that impinges upon our more contentious public policy debates? To the ennobling of our much coarsened culture? These, it seems to me, are recurrent, foundational, and serious questions. They are ill served by facile sermonizing and shallow apologetics. Perhaps the earlier works in this genre, Straus excepted, were marred by those faults. We can be more circumspect today, but we dare not be more aloof. The urgency of these questions is not dissipated by either assimilation or acceptance. Nor is it well served by preformed political ideologies, either of the left or the right.

In an ever more diverse society, Americans grapple—especially after September 11, 2001—with the vexing question of what, if anything, does or should unite them. The great consensus historians of the 1950s, such as Louis Hartz, could confidently assert that liberal ideas, drawn from canonical figures such as John Locke, ran through the American experience like a red thread. Our nation was founded on a set of self-evident truths; our politics and common life, however dimly, expressed them. Those days are gone, perhaps forever. For decades we have had an open-ended contestation over whether any truths are normative for us. Does our polity need a consensual public philosophy or does proceduralism—a commitment to certain rules of the game—suffice? At either end of this spectrum, elite opinion often presumed that we could agree on at least one thing: religion was not a proper source for either a public philosophy or a canon of democratic rules of the road. Religion was properly a private matter, a source of comfort and guidance for those in need of such things. It was not in any sense a "public good." Jews, as a small minority of distinctively liberal political orientation, were vigorous advocates for this view.

As with so much else in American life, the once regnant faith in secularity has come under constant and growing assault. As mentioned above, recent historiography of the American Founding gives new emphasis to the role of religion in shaping revolutionary, republican, and constitutional currents of thought. Public philosophy has hammered away at what, in retrospect, appear as naïve or wishful assumptions that only secular epistemological and moral claims are fit expressions of "public reason." Public policy has come to a belated awareness of the enormous role that faith-based organizations play in healing our distressed civil society. Political theory looks to religious traditions, more so than at any time since the seventeenth century, as sources of political teaching and perhaps even of political wisdom. For their part, religious thinkers, responding to the new curiosity toward their traditions in American intellectual circles, are renegotiating the boundaries between the spheres of the once allegedly private and the public.

Jewish intellectuals such as Michael Walzer, Amitai Etzioni, and Michael Sandel have had a great deal to do with revising liberalism, advocating for a public philosophy, rediscovering the importance of community, and calling for a renewal of civil society. With the exception of Walzer, they have done so, however, as thinkers who happen to be Jews rather than as Jewish thinkers. Attempts to bring Jewish religious texts and traditions into a fertile philosophical dialogue with American public life have been infrequent. Perhaps the reflexive commitment of most of the Jewish community to secular liberalism, and to a Judaism read through secular and liberal spectacles, has stunted or scanted the effort. Perhaps the absence of a broad receptive audience for such an effort has relegated it to the stratosphere of academic discourse. At any rate, American Jewry is overdue for a renewal of Oscar Straus's project: a serious yet accessible consideration of how Jews and Judaism, religion in America, and the American public square interact.

This book is a contribution to that project. It originated in a three-year program, initiated by the Pew Charitable Trusts and the Center for Jewish Community Studies, which aimed to reintroduce a dialogue about faith and public affairs into the American Jewish community. The program, entitled "Jews and the American Public Square," was to have culminated in a national conference in Washington, D.C., on September 12, 2001. As the extent of the catastrophe of September 11 was becoming clear, that conference was canceled. Most of the chapters in this book were originally prepared for the conference which was to have addressed the theme "Religion as a Public Good: Jews and Other Americans in the Public Square." Although conceived as a dialogue that included Christian panelists and audience members as well, the main thrust of the conference, as of this volume, was on Jewish contributions to an intra-Jewish conversation.

Rather than see Straus's topic as passé, the organizers thought it urgent, for both Jewish and general reasons. The Jewish reasons have to do with the inward turn of the American Jewish community. Over the past decade, the Jewish community has become painfully aware of the mounting toll of unbridled assimilation. To combat this, it has sought to increase Jewish commitment, learning, and identification. Focused on its own survival (euphemistically dubbed "continuity" and then "renaissance"), there has been a shift from a civic or social activist Judaism to an interior, spiritualized Judaism. Since the late 1960s, American Jews lived out their Judaism, as one scholar put it, as a civil religion of "sacred survival." The focus was activism on behalf of Soviet Jewry and Israel, as well as Holocaust remembrance. The civic structures of the Jewish polity, such as the federations and defense agencies, had higher salience in the minds of many Jewish leaders than the synagogues. Little emphasis attached to Hebrew and Jewish literacy or Jewish observance. That situation changed dramatically by the early 1990s when, as a result of new findings about a more than 50 percent intermarriage rate, real concerns for American Jewish survival emerged. The resultant shift in communal priorities has given the traditional foci of Jewish religion a higher profile in American Jewish life than they have had in a century. Yet what are the public consequences of this new stress on religious observance, learning and tradition? Will the larger American public sphere be depleted of significance by an inward turn? Will Jews retreat to their own spiritual gardens, following countless other Americans out of engagement with political and public life? That would be a historic break with prior Jewish practice, as well as a betrayal of a very this-world religious tradition.

It is all to the good that American Jewry is concentrating on enriching and deepening Jewish knowledge and commitment. Certainly a religion that exhausted itself in political activism, "social justice," and "sacred survival" left much to be desired. For too long much of American Judaism seemed to be synonymous with the public policy platforms of the left wing of the Democratic Party. It is well to have moved beyond that. But if one temptation of religion in America was a social gospel progressivism, the other is a romantic and Gnostic spirituality. Jews must resist that too. They must remain anchored in the real worlds of history and politics, leavening them with transcendence, truth, and Torah.

Although there is little evidence for a Jewish abandonment of the American public sphere, there has been a drift of American Jews toward privatized spirituality and alienation from the Jewish communal and institutional sphere. This takes place against a larger American pattern of weakening loyalty to civil (including religious) and political institutions. We have become, in Robert Wuthnow's phrase, a nation of "seekers" rather than "dwellers."[4] Americans have become increasingly concerned about the decline in civil and political engagement—to use an older term, "civic virtue"—in American life. Talk of renewing civil society and of citizenship education is all the rage. Americans have begun to think anew about the necessary connections between social institutions, morals, common purposes, and the public sphere. The role of religious communities and traditions looms large in this reconsideration. For many observers, religion is an engine of civic engagement, a crucial source of moral orientation, and a generator of social capital. Religion, if surveys are to be believed, is for many Americans a "public good." Yet this kind of thinking remains threatening for many American Jews. American Jews have a well-developed discourse on the constitutional dimensions, the legal dimensions, of the problem of the relation of church and state. They are less adept, however, at doing what Oscar Straus did over a century ago: articulating the proper public role of religion in the ongoing democratic project. That is where this volume hopes to make a contribution.

The contributors to this book agree on little. Their diverse religious and political positions reflect the sturdy pluralism of the American Jewish community. This author cannot even say that they agree on the need to rethink the public role of religion in American society. Two of them offer powerful arguments, entirely typical of many American Jews, for why religion should remain out of the public sphere to the greatest practicable extent. Others show a tentative if greater openness to renegotiating the boundaries that liberals once thought fixed. Others enthusiastically subvert the "wall of separation between church and state" as Jews have heretofore understood it (that is, quite strictly). Nor do the contributors come from a single disciplinary perspective. They include historians, political scientists, legal scholars, political philosophers, and theologians. Some of the contributors have made their distinguished careers as Jewish thinkers, others as scholars who are Jews. In this volume, however, all of them, with three exceptions, try to situate themselves—some intensively, others less so—as American Jews. The three exceptions consist of sympathetic friends who were invited to join the dialogue: two American Christian scholars and one Jewish observer from abroad.

The volume begins with a philosophical essay by Professor Jean Bethke Elshtain, one of the nation's leading voices on the moral and religious dimensions of our politics. Elshtain describes the complex process by which nascent liberal politics, both European and American, came to marginalize religion and treat it as little better than a public nuisance rather than a public good. Her essay suggests that for liberalism to fulfill its promise it must become capacious rather than monistic, pluralist rather than fretful where religion is concerned.

Against this general background, the next two chapters describe the historical and philosophical context for American Jews today. Professor Marc Dollinger begins by exploring the paradoxes immanent in the American Jewish relationship with the federal government. Since colonial times, Jews have cherished the autonomy of their communities, particularly their institutions of mutual assistance. With the New Deal, however, Jews came to accept, at first tentatively then enthusiastically, an increasing government role in the provision of social welfare. Dollinger analyzes the conflicts within American Jewish political culture that resulted from this settlement. Jews want governmental involvement and autonomy, universalist liberalism and group survival, individual rights and collective identity. He discusses the possibility of a greater public role for religion and the complexity of the Jewish response to this possibility.

In chapter 3 I analyze the philosophical consequences of liberalism for primordial groups such as the Jews. By "liberalism" is meant that system of rights-oriented political thought reaching back to the seventeenth century that puts individuals at the center of the normative universe. I consider the appeal of liberal ideas of freedom for a formerly oppressed people, and analyze the tensions between Jewish and liberal convictions about the uses of freedom. I argue that the renewal of civil society can only come about through a new empowerment of religious and other communities. The implications of this view at the level of policy are that Jews will need to invest more trust in local rather than national solutions in cases where local solutions are appropriate.

The next section articulates what might be called the mainstream view within the Jewish community, as well as the dissent from that view. The mainstream view is pervasively liberal. As Professor Kenneth D. Wald puts it, "many American Jews regard liberalism as applied Judaism." Wald argues that the creedal element of a religious tradition, in this case Jewish beliefs, has less to do with social and political action than do communal experiences, memories, and self-interest. There is a vast gap between religious beliefs and their translation into meaningful political guidance. Affirming the wis-

dom of keeping religion private, Wald doubts whether there is anything to be gained by urging that religion take on a greater role in
public life. Arguing in a legal key, Professor Erwin Chemerinsky
studies and decries the weakening of the wall of separation between
church and state. He analyzes the rise of the "equal treatment" theory of the establishment clause and decisively rejects it in favor of a
strict version of neutrality, that is, of no aid to religion. Chemerinsky recounts the benefits of this position for American Jews offering, with great expertise, what might be called the normative
American Jewish narrative of church-state relations. Finally, the
distinguished historian Gertrude Himmelfarb weighs in with a critique of these typically liberal views. Himmelfarb argues that Jews
underestimate both the extent to which a decent society requires
moral underpinnings and the contribution of religion to that public
morality. She argues for a remoralization of society, nurtured by the
virtues that traditional religions promote. The three authors have
very different appraisals of what the Jewish interest is and of what
sort of society is most conducive to Jewish flourishing. That my
sympathies lean more toward the view of Professor Himmelfarb detracts not at all from the importance of Wald's and Chemerinsky's
perspectives.

   The third section focuses on how tradition-minded Jews ought to
think about and act within the American public square. In chapter 7,
leading political theorist Professor William Galston delineates and
analyzes the tensions between the Jewish political tradition and the
American constitutional tradition. He argues that the former tradition can affirm the latter because Judaism has a tradition of legiti-
mizing secular authority. Given the legitimacy of secular authority,
he argues in favor of religious participation in the secular sphere in
such a way that both religious authenticity and secular legitimacy
may be preserved. He evokes authoritative moral norms by means of
which this balance can be effectuated. The next chapter, by the emi-
nent Jewish public theologian David Novak, argues for a religiously
informed Jewish public thought and practice based on a shared
"Judeo-Christian ethic" and a natural law conception of the common
good. Novak believes that humans share a moral commonality and
that all members of American society have a duty to enhance that
commonality. He proposes a sort of Jewish "Lemon test" with three
prongs: Jewish public policy should satisfy the interests of Torah, of
the common good, and of the Jewish people. He argues that policies
such as state-funded tuition vouchers for use in religious schools,
decried by liberals as subversive of a common culture, in fact en-

hance moral commonality properly understood. Finally, Michael J. Broyde, a professor of law and judge on the Orthodox Beth Din (Court) of America, uses the same concepts as Novak to reach a diametrically opposed conclusion. Utilizing the idea of the Noahide Laws, the "moral commonality" binding both Jews and non-Jews, Broyde finds no obligation for Jews to teach non-Jews Noahide law and morals. Consequently, Jews have no obligation to advocate that secular government enforce Noahide standards of behavior, for example, by proscribing polytheism, abortion, or homosexual acts. All of these matters are subject not to clear Torah duties but to a calculus of political gain or loss. Although Jews should rather live in a society where infractions of Jewish law principles do not occur, in our society this is unrealistic. Jews therefore should be on the side of maximum liberty so that their own practices—in their own enclaves—will be permitted. While Novak draws socially conservative lessons from his commitment to traditional Judaism, Broyde derives libertarian ones. The dilemma posed by Wald, of how religious teachings can be translated into effective public philosophy and action, returns. Fortunately, these authors, despite their considerable differences, believe that the dilemma is far from insuperable.

In the fourth section, the emphasis is on how religious views, including Jewish views, might be expressed in a society of marked social and religious pluralism. The well-known sociologist, Professor Alan Wolfe, analyzes the changes in the composition of American religion since the founding period. Given the shift from de facto Protestant establishment to "Judeo-Christian" civil religion to vast and incommensurable pluralism, Wolfe rejects the idea that America requires some shared religio-moral underpinnings. He claims that it is time to admit that founders such as George Washington were simply wrong. We have more freedom today than we did in the eighteenth century and, just as importantly, the habits of liberty are deeply engrained in Americans' souls. If we look to how Americans actually live rather than to the anxieties of public intellectuals, we come away with confidence that American morals and American religion are healthy. Michael Gottsegen, while not disputing that religion can serve as a public good, questions whether it actually does in the here and now. He asks whether religious groups educate Americans for an expansive conception of the common good, for placing the whole political community before the needs of their own religious circle. Gottsegen calls for religion to exercise its traditional "prophetic" role with a twist: to help renew American civic life within a religiously pluralistic public square. Professor Elliot

Dorff, a prominent social ethicist and leader of the Conservative movement in Judaism, recounting his years of service on government ethics commissions, rehearses the principles that he discovered for advocating religiously grounded views in a pluralistic setting. Dorff advocates a practical ethic of epistemological modesty and moral restraint by the religious. He develops guidelines for how religiously based views can be articulated in the public sphere. He attempts to draw lines between domains in which religion can serve the common good, such as in the burgeoning discussion about bioethical problems, and domains where religious expression is, in his view, divisive, for example, in public schools. Dorff captures the mood of some sectors of the Jewish community. Some have moved beyond the "strict separationist" position embraced by Wald and Chemerinsky and show greater openness to a role for religion in public discourse. They stop short, as does Dorff, of weakening the "wall of separation," however. Professor Carl Raschke, a scholar whose range embraces both evangelicalism and postmodernism, argues that, in the wake of the September 11 catastrophe, Americans need to rethink their openness to religious pluralism. He suggests that the affirmation of boundless religious pluralism is paired with a presumption of secularity of the sort: because the modern world is basically secular religion doesn't much matter and therefore religious differences are noninvidious. After September 11, however, religious differences appear highly consequential. Not all forms of religion are acceptable under the pluralist umbrella. Raschke, addressing American Jews, calls for a renewal of the "Judeo-Christian tradition" as a defining feature of American identity.

The last section features two "practitioners." Congressman Mickey Edwards, an eight-term representative from Oklahoma and, after his retirement from the House, a lecturer at Harvard's Kennedy School of Government, reflects on how Judaism, religion, and politics converged in his career as an elected official. Edwards, a conservative, is ambivalent about the public dimensions of religion. His ambivalence illustrates how even those Jews identified with the Republican Party and with a conservative political orientation remain cautious about the proper place of religion in the public square. Kevin "Seamus" Hasson is the founder and president of the Becket Fund for Religious Liberty, a law firm and research institute dedicated to advancing the cause of religious liberty at home and abroad. Hasson writes from a perspective informed by Catholic natural law theory, arguing that nothing short of a profound appreciation of human dignity can ground the right of religious liberty.

The fact that humans seek transcendence implies that a decent politics must accommodate our transcendence-seeking natures. The public square should not lie to us about who we are but reflect the great diversity of ways in which we seek the truth.

In the afterword, the chief rabbi of Britain, Professor Jonathan Sacks, continues the long tradition of outside observers who take a deep interest in the religious life of the American people and who see it as crucial to the health of their (our) democracy. Sacks argues for a public philosophy and a politics guided by Judaic convictions rather than by a purely pragmatic and political construal of Jewish interests.

These essays should provide much food for thought. Although the excitement of having many of these thinkers in the same room was not to be, this book is a credible substitute. My hope is that it can advance a conversation that was delayed by 9/11 but must not be stopped by it.

The editor wishes to acknowledge that chapter 1, "The Liberal Social Contract and the Privatization of Religion," was first published in *The Republic of Faith*, Carl Raschke and William Dean, editors, The Davies Group Publishers, 2002. It is reprinted by permission.

Notes

1. For a survey of contemporary approaches to the Founding, including those that emphasize religion, see Robert Booth Fowler, *Enduring Liberalism: American Political Thought since the 1960s* (Lawrence: University Press of Kansas, 1999), 88-97. An excellent, detailed treatment of the theme may be found in James H. Hutson, *Religion and the Founding of the American Republic* (Washington, D.C.: Library of Congress, 1998).

2. Naomi Cohen, *A Dual Heritage: The Public Career of Oscar Straus* (Philadelphia: Jewish Publication Society, 1969).

3. Jonathan Sarna, "The Cult of Synthesis in American Jewish Culture," *Jewish Social Studies: New Series* 5, nos. 1-2 (Fall 1998-Winter 1999): 52-79.

4. See Robert Wuthnow, *Loose Connections: Joining Together in America's Fragmented Communities* (Cambridge, Mass.: Harvard University Press, 1998).

1

The Liberal Social Contract and the Privatization of Religion

Jean Bethke Elshtain

The standard treatment of the history of liberalism's relationship to religion is that liberalism saved religion from itself, that is, from its bloodcurdling excesses and absolutist demands. By forcing a regime of "toleration" on religion, liberalism in its constitutional forms demanded that religion act more tolerantly. And so it came to pass that both sectarian groups (that means religion, of course) and nonsectarian groups (all the others organized along the lines of the liberal mandate) learned to live happily, or at least safely, with and among one another. But this truce is insistently represented as a rather fragile one. If religion threatens to get "out of hand," it must be beaten back. At this point, the wars of religion and even the Spanish Inquisition get trotted out in argument as if they were serious historic possibilities in late-twentieth-century American democracy, as if the return of the Spanish Inquisition—perhaps under the auspices of the notorious "Christian Right"—were the greatest danger we faced from a resurgent and, by definition, intolerant and absolutist religiosity.

This is the regnant story of liberalism's triumph in relation to religion—that triumph, remember, being in large part the way liberalism rescued religion from its endemic horrors. But surely there must

be other ways to tell the tale even though those alternative explana-
tory and historic frameworks never acquired the self-evident status
of the narrative described above, probably because the difficulties
are so daunting. Liberalism and religion are such protean topics,
having so many possible shapes, permutations, twists, and turns,
that one embarks on the task of beating this material into shape with
some trepidation. Too much that is too important could be left out.

Let us rummage in the preliberal past for a moment or two. Before the emergence of those social contract theories associated with
liberalism (though not liberalism exclusively), assumptions about
governance and rule held that government's legitimacy turned on a
divine mandate. This need not mean that a ruler reigned absolutely
or tyrannically; indeed, a ruler could violate the office which was
his sacred trust, go from being king to being tyrant, and be openly
chastised, even punished with tyrannicide as a kind of emergency
escape valve. The major point is that rulers were beholden to a
power outside themselves for the office they held in trust. The theory was that this would stay the hand of those rulers tempted by ex-
cess, overtaken by what St. Augustine called the *libidi dominandi*,
or a lust to dominate. The historic record is uneven, of course, as to
just how much restraint was afforded by the fact that a ruler was not
the judge of his own legitimacy. But it is important to note that premodern societies in Europe—and that is my focus—were honey-
combed with communal and corporate bodies functioning autono-
mously. The university, an invention of the Middle Ages, is a good
example of an autonomous communal institution into which the
king's writ did not run. Families were intergenerational and extended, and this afforded a good measure of social power and protection. Guilds set standards for skilled trades and crafts. Most importantly, no doubt, religion and civic standing were tethered
together. You could not be a subject in good standing unless you
were a communicant in good standing.

All of this was to change. With the coming of greater commerce,
the breakup of medieval Christendom, the centralization and solidi-
fication of monarchies and principalities, and, in 1555 the Peace of
Augsburg with its enshrining of the *cuius regio* rule—namely, that
the faith of the ruler was the faith of his kingdom—Western Europe
moved decisively into a new era. Religious adherence and standing
as a political subject remained mutually constitutive. But this too
changed dramatically with the dissolution of the once familiar political and social world. Powerful new sources of legitimation were
located and proclaimed for earthly rule: legitimation lies with the

people, with subjects who have contracted for that purpose—that was one startling idea that traced its lineage back to the *populus romanus* and was brought forward by legists in the service of the centralizing monarchy par excellence, that of the Capetians in France.

Skip ahead several centuries and the social contract thinkers appear upon the historic stage. To lump, as we do, Hobbes, Locke, and Rousseau together as social contract thinkers is not that helpful because their differences are far more interesting than their similarities. Hobbes is too idiosyncratic, so for our purposes, Locke and Rousseau are, and remain, important. Locke, associated famously with his Letter on Toleration as well as his treatises on government, insisted, as a precondition for civil government, that religion and government had to be distinguished and lines drawn between them. The seeds of the privatization of religion were to germinate most powerfully and completely in our own time.

Locke drew up a rigid civic map with religion within one sphere and government in another. A person could be a citizen of each, so long as that citizen never attempted to merge and to blend those two aspects of *himself.* And it was a "him" self in this era as women lacked civic standing. Herein lies a tale in itself. My hunch as to the reluctance of Western polities to grant women the vote is far more complex than simple gender discrimination, as it is now called; rather, women were feared as being a "backward" element, that is, women remained more wedded to their faith and were more pious. Certainly the radical laicism of the postrevolutionary French Republics regarded women as suspect characters mired in "Catholic superstition" and somehow under the control of their parish priests: women did not get the vote in France until after World War II—the last major Western democracy to grant women the franchise. But this is a story in itself.

In the religious domain, one answered God's call. But step out of that domain and take one step into the civic realm and God does not and must not figure directly any more. One's fidelity is pledged to the magistrate and to the proper business of governing. If the magistrate should egregiously overstep its bounds, there is always the "appeal to heaven" and the possibility of revolution. All religions—save atheism and Roman Catholicism—are to be tolerated. (Atheists could not be trusted, Locke argued, because they would not take an oath on the Bible; Catholics could not be trusted because they had a double loyalty—a political theology at odds with constitutive liberal principles.) Disobedience must take place only in the most extreme situations with the "appeal to heaven" that violates the separation doctrine quite explicitly. But once God is appealed to in extremis, God must retreat. Most of the time—the norm—holds that religion and government need not meet one another directly. Religion is located as irrelevant in a strong public sense. Note here that, in the words of constitutional scholar Michael McConnell: "Locke's exclusion of atheists and Catholics from toleration cannot be dismissed as a quaint exception to his beneficent liberalism; it follows logically from the ground on which his argument for toleration rested. If religious freedom meant nothing more than that religion should be free so long as it is irrelevant to the state, it does not mean very much." Why? Because religion has been privatized and its meaning reduced to the subjective spiritual well-being of religious practitioners.

James Madison picked up on certain aspects of Locke, whereas Thomas Jefferson looked to others. Locke was certainly *primus inter pares* of social contractarians for the founders of the American republic, some of whom (Jefferson most notably) held views about the salutary nature of religious indifference not embraced by the vast majority of his fellow countrymen and women. But the Lockean formula had finessed as many problems as it attempted to solve, presuming, as it did, that human beings could seal themselves off into compartments and be believers one moment, good subjects of the king the next, even though the categories necessarily bleed into one another. But the "separate spheres" argument persisted, tethered to a wildly optimistic view that religious and governmental jurisdiction would rarely conflict. The only sure guarantee of that would be to render religion utterly privatized and publicly irrelevant—something Locke did not preach, but he helped to pave the way.

Here Rousseau enters as a shadow around the liberal disestablishmentarian project. For Rousseau understood that you couldn't demarcate spheres so tidily. In fact, Rousseau argues, what all governments and polities require, especially at their founding, is a civil religion of some sort or another so that religion constantly buttresses the legitimacy and authority of the civic entity in question. This civil religion was not a take it or leave it free-for-all. Civil religion welded together the different parts of the polity and demanded that citizens, through a form of civic membership in which religion was subordinated to the good of the polity, make manifest their devotion to public life. Rousseau even wrote up a constitution for Poland in which he spoke keenly of civic games, quasi-religious rituals, and the need for public displays of patriotism. Any person who was divided in his loyalty and allegiance could never be a full-fledged participant in the *patrie*. A form of enlightened, reasonable civil religion was the glue that held the polity together. No one was exempted from this civil religion—loyalty to the state was the ultimate loyalty that trumps all other forms of fidelity. Rousseau moves with vehemence against strong forms of Christianity, like Catholicism, because this form of faith inevitably puts a man at odds with himself. Believers are easily confused as to where their allegiances lie. They are placed, intolerably, under a dual obligation. Rousseau describes this situation with contempt, Catholicism taking the major beating as a religion so manifestly hideous he couldn't understand why it persisted. But, one way or the other, Catholicism's mere presence as an institutional form that could buttress and sustain loyalty and commitment to something other than the state led Rousseau to attack it in order to redirect all loyalty to the state. There can be no "private religion" in Rousseau's ideal polity. There is only civil religion or no religion at all—though Rousseau makes it clear that civil religion is a necessary buttress to government and rule.

It is a short distance from Rousseau's declaration that the only good religion is a civil religion to the very different pronouncements of John Stuart Mill in his classic, *On Liberty*. Mill is adamantly opposed to civil religions: that would be an intolerable fusion of power. But he extends his animus to religion in general. Religion plays to the "worse" rather than the "better" parts of human nature. Religion has always been a retrograde force, standing in the way of reason, progress, and enlightenment. Religion survives now as an atavism but it is living on borrowed time. One day soon, in the wake of spreading enlightenment, unreasoning *Instinct* will eventually be supplanted by *Reason*. In fact, Mill assumes a sharing or unity of moral and political beliefs among those individuals who are dominated by reason. For ultimately, according to Mill, reason must speak in one voice. In practice this meant that the ignorant or the irrational must defer to those who have attained enlightenment and learned to speak in the voice of reason. Given Mill's bifurcated understanding of mind that dictated one must attain an "apotheosis of Reason" and utterly reject the "idolatry" of Instinct, religion is not only privatized, but it is also saddled with the burden of being responsible for most of history's horrors. Finally, only the weak require superstition. The strong do not need religious milk with their enlightened tea. This Millian backdrop helps to make intelligible a lecture I attended thirty-five or so years ago as an undergraduate, delivered by one Sir Julian Huxley, who announced in booming stentorian tones that by the year 2000 the remaining atavisms and superstitions would all have vanished in the cool, clear light of reason. The two most important slated for obliteration? Religion and nationalism. This is what one calls a failed prognostication.

How did things fare on America's shores? How far did the writ of Locke, Rousseau, or Mill run? There are several analytic and historic tracks down which one must move simultaneously in this matter. Let us call them the "constitutional" and the "popular." The constitutional track is powerfully defined by the First Amendment's protection against establishment and guarantee of free exercise. One could make the case that the astonishing evidence of Americans exercising religions freely, from the inception to the present, turns precisely on nonestablishment. This may not have been what the framers expected to happen. But it does show that nonestablishment of religion is not necessarily deadly to religion; indeed, it may actually help religion to flourish.

But there are tensions and strains in this picture that draw together the popular and constitutional tracks. They help account for the fact that so many American citizens who are religious believe that their society has acted in ways that betray its commitment to free exercise in any robust sense. And free exercise is what America means in this matter. From the inception of settlement on these new shores, American democracy has been premised on the enactment of projects that were a complex intermingling of religious and political imperatives. The majority of Americans were religious seekers and believers who saw in communal liberty a freedom for religion rather than a freedom from religion. It is, therefore, not surprising that such a huge chunk of American juridical life has been devoted to sorting out the often ineptly named church-state debate. In a less churched society this would be a far less salient issue.

In a way, it is moot to argue that America embodies the best of what the West in general deeded to future generations in this matter: a refusal of theocracy; a proliferation of religion. A differentiation between politics and religion was sown early on in Western culture with the emergence of various forms of papal doctrine distinguishing the *regnum* from *sacerdotium*, roughly marking the sword of the earthly and spiritual kingdoms respectively. The two got all tangled up with one another, to be sure, but they were nonetheless distinct. What Rousseau attempted to do was to fuse politics and religion into one in the service of politics. What Locke attempted to do was to drive politics and religion apart in order to promote "toleration," but at the price of privatizing religion over time. What American

citizens did under the umbrella of nonestablishment was to prolifer-
ate churches all over the country as public institutions that, rather
than challenging government routinely, instead reminded people of
what membership in a body requires, thereby sustaining those civic
habits Tocqueville extolled in his classic work.

Ever present, of course, was the possibility that the church or
churches might be a locus for dissent—for religious believers did
claim a dual citizenship that theoretically could conflict. Indeed,
such conflict would be nigh inevitable as too much of the same territory is claimed by both politics and religion. Thus for Tocqueville,
religion in general contributes to the maintenance of a democratic
republic by directing the mores and helping, thereby, to regulate
political life. In fact, Tocqueville insisted that the ideas of Christianity and liberty are so completely intermingled that if you tried to
sever religion from democracy in America you would wind up de-
stroying democracy. Democracy, he further claimed, needs the sort
of transcendent justification that religion helps to provide; thus, the
eighteenth-century philosophers were wrong about the weakening of
religion. "It is tiresome," notes Tocqueville ironically, "that the
facts do not fit their theory at all." Surprisingly, the separation of
church and state—a secular state—had led to a society that was anything but secular. Perhaps, deep down, Americans understood that
religion feeds hope and is thus attached to a constitutive principle of
human nature. Amidst the flux and tumult of a rambunctious democratic politics, religion shaped and mediated these passions. Were
the day to come when they would be unleashed upon the world unrestrained, then we would arrive at an unhappy moment indeed, a
dreary world Tocqueville called democratic despotism.

So where is the problem? How does state-sponsored irreligion, if
not atheism, make its moves? Over the last half century during
which religious belief and church attendance have waxed and
waned—they are now at huge, if not record highs—constitutional
law has moved to privatize religion altogether. The strong separationists have held sway at many points in ongoing constitutional adjudication. A "strong separationist" means one who seeks not only a
properly secular state, but a thoroughly secularized society—one
stripped of any and all public markers and reminders of religion.
Religion must be thoroughly privatized. It must become invisible to
public life. There is, in this position, a built-in animus against the
determination by religious denominations to sustain their own network of schools, welfare provision, political advocacy, and so on. A
harsh opposition between enlightenment values and religious faith is

presupposed. Because there is a wall of separation between them on the level of what holds a democratic society together, a unity that religion always threatens to disrupt, the secular state goes on a rampage and gobbles up society so that it, too, might be thoroughly secularized. That, at least, is the dream of ardent separationists. For some reason, members of this school of liberal analysis can get misty-eyed at any mention of the "marginalized" or "subaltern groups," but can then turn terminator and chomp at the bit with ferocious enthusiasm at the prospect of shutting up "religious people." The bright line separating church and state must now extend to religion and politics generally. Religion, cut off from any supply lines, goes on life support and then eventually fulfills Julius Huxley's dream: first it will be privatized and then it will disappear.

To be sure, in *Agostini v. Felton* (June 23, 1997), the Supreme Court may have signaled a mild turning away from such holdings as the one that prompted the challenge and which dictated that federally funded programs providing supplemental, remedial instruction to disadvantaged children could not be administered by "sectarian schools" without violating the establishment clause. This had led, in practice, to the spectacle of mobile units perched outside parochial and other religious schools as children, even children with severe disabilities, in weather fair or foul, were removed from their school buildings and taken to these units in order to receive instruction. The Court (5-4) no longer believes that the mere physical placement of public employees on parochial school grounds "inevitably results in the impermissible effect of state-sponsored indoctrination or constitutes a symbolic union between government and religion."

Still, the general drive along the constitutional track is not limited to decisions made by courts. What has emerged as a hallmark of liberal political philosophy is a position I call liberal monism, by which is meant the view that all institutions internal to a democratic society must conform to a single authority principle (one person, one vote, or some such); a single standard of what counts as reason and deliberation (here Mill and later Millians); and a single vocabulary of political discussion (John Rawls.) Democracy is defined in such a way that religion must be kept marginalized. Reason is defined in such a way that faith is discounted as something else, whether irrationalism or a peculiar atavism, or a form of private solace that must be kept utterly privatized. Those who adhere to this position, or a version of it, begin with the menace of establishment or the specter of advancing hordes of priests and televangelists as backdrop. Then they go on to construct their "bright line" form of defense. This powerful, contemporary school, associated with the work of John Rawls (but not he alone), holds that when religious persons enter the public sphere they are obliged to do so in a secular civic idiom short of any explicit reference to religious commitment and belief. Christians, Jews, Muslims, as citizens, are not permitted to give reasons for why they favor or oppose a public policy measure in any way that is explicitly religious. If you cannot translate the position into a language proclaimed to be both civic and neutral, you should keep quiet rather than enter public life on illegitimate terms that might threaten America's ostensible working consensus.

Rather than acknowledging and even celebrating religious plurality and diversity, the liberal monist stance repudiates them in any robust sense. In practice, it means that the free exercise clause can be interpreted out of existence as an unfortunate glitch in the totally secular framework the framers actually intended to set up. All this in the name of a purported neutrality that inescapably values certain aspects and features of the human condition and despises and belittles others.

There are many straws in the wind where the matter of liberalism and its betrayal of religion is concerned. Fundamental to monistic liberalism, in principle and in practice, is that anything that presents itself as religious in any public way must have the last breath of life squeezed out of it. A more capacious liberalism, aware of life's variability and nuance, aware that any endorsement of rules and procedures is a substantive one that tacitly embraces some version of a good life by contrast to some other, that understands that self-governance requires real social locations where people can learn what it means to act and to be acted upon and what membership and responsibility entail—that sort of liberalism would not be driven to and would never support the intolerances of liberal monism. That more capacious liberalism is protective, not destructive, of plurality and understanding. Pluralism is an empty word unless there are real social institutions and spaces that enable persons to keep alive their own traditions, habits, and preciously held beliefs.

That more general model—one that is within our historic reach—seems to have faded from the scene as claims about what it takes to create social harmony and make citizens embrace more of the coloration of the liberal monist posture. In his last major address before his death in 1996, Joseph Cardinal Bernardin spoke at Georgetown University of the role of religion in American society. He pointed out the incoherence of claiming to respect religious belief but insisting that people keep it to themselves—precisely what a devout per-

son cannot do. For religious faith isn't a private matter, it is constitutive of membership in a particular body—the church, the temple,
the mosque, the synagogue. Persons of faith cannot bracket their
beliefs out when they enter the public square.

In viewing religious belief as a civic peril, we invite irony. We
fret about belief that is too ardent but also about the loss of belief in
America at present—the loss of democratic faith. If we push the notion too far that in order to be acceptable public fare, all religious
claims and categories must be secularized, we wind up depluralizing
our polity and endangering our democracy.

Cardinal Bernardin's reaction to these specific concerns was to
insist that the logic of church-state separation—"narrow, juridical
and institution in character"—should not be extended to encompass
religion and politics in a democratic civil society. Civil society involves the many networks, institutions, associations, and relationships that lie beyond the purview of the state's writ. It is a terrible
mistake to carry the logic of church-state separation over into this
realm. Were such separation to be fully effected, "we would be a
poorer culture and society." To skeptics, Bernardin submitted three
ways in which religion has a necessarily public role: in articulating
a consistent ethic of life against reckless maniacs like Dr. Kevorkian
(as but one example); in contributing in civil society through religiously based institutions in education, health care, family service,
and "direct outreach to the poorest parts of our society"; and finally,
in the realm of civil and moral formation, as religion teaches service
to one's neighbor and a sense of civic stewardship. Real pluralism
gives all religious believers the space to be Catholic and American,
Jewish and American, evangelical and American, Muslim and
American. Through relentless privatization, real pluralism is precisely what liberal monism would eliminate. Perhaps the constitutional lawyers will hear the message. Perhaps many already have.
But at the moment, going far beyond anything we have seen thus
far, there are forms of the most extreme separationism, published in
prestigious law journals, which aim precisely to curb free exercise.
They are awaiting their chance to erupt and to drive, at long last, the
stake into the heart of religion. Something that one version of liberalism believes should have happened long ago.

Lest anyone think these arguments are exclusively elite contesta-
tions with little or no effect on a free-exercising people, the warning
must be that many Americans themselves have accepted without a
whimper the privatizing of religion as the basis for tolerance in contrast to robust pluralism. The incessant hammering on religion as

private has been absorbed as civic gospel truth, perhaps by a wide majority at this juncture. In his recent book, *One Nation After All*, sociologist Alan Wolfe surveys the attitudes of middle-class Americans from different regions of the country. He wonders if what is being displayed really counts as "tolerance" although he does not suggest an alternative. Wolfe's middle-class respondents simply assume that religion is a private matter to be discussed only reluctantly.

What is disquieting about the words of many of Wolfe's respondents is the undercurrent of brittle fearfulness—fearfulness of the open expression of serious disagreement and religious difference. The general view goes like this: If I am quiet about what I believe and everybody else is quiet about what he or she believes, then nobody interferes with the rights of anybody else. But this is precisely what real believers, whether political or religious or both, cannot do: keep quiet. Silence is simply not an option for those struggling against the current regime: whether that be a struggle to establish Martin Luther King's "beloved community," or a fight against economic inequality and injustice, or active opposition to abortion or capital punishment. To tell religious believers to keep quiet or else they will interfere with my rights by definition simply by speaking out is an intolerant idea. It is, in effect, to tell folks they cannot really believe what they believe or be who they are.

The grand liberal metanarrative of the terrible and ever present danger posed to liberalism by religion has worked. Beneath every expression of religious differences lies lurking, if we believe Wolfe's respondents, a fear of religious intolerance and even religious warfare. So Wolfe's middle classers are disturbed when religion is inserted into the public sphere. But a private religion, as they surely know, makes no sense. One must have public expression of a faith in order for it to be faith. That is, religion either expresses itself in social, communal, public meetings, rules, or symbols, or strives for such modes of expression in situations where these are forbidden. To a good many of the middle classers in Wolfe's book who have not read John Rawls, public expression of religious beliefs and religiously based arguments are already crossing the ("bright") line and somehow "forcing" something on somebody else.

Consider the remarks of "Jody Fields," one of Wolfe's respondents: "If you are a Hindu and you grew up being a Hindu, keep it to yourself. Don't impose your religion, and don't make me feel bad because I do this and you do that." I submit that this is not tolerance at all, but rather an intolerance of religious pluralism. If one transposes Hindu for Jew in the above comment it becomes clearer. Telling a Hindu to hide their Hinduism is scarcely a picture of liberal pluralism. There are others in Wolfe's study who venture toward robust tolerance because they endorse robust public expression of religious belief. They want to learn more about "what Muslims do," so "don't wipe out culture, add to it." Religious freedom by no means requires such a thoroughgoing privatization of religion that it becomes intolerable for religion to present any public face to the world. But overall, Wolfe's work suggests that the continuing privatization of religion within constitutional law has helped to fuel and solidify a privatization within the culture. Religion becomes one of the things it is best not to talk about.

Stephen Carter, in his recent book, *The Dissent of the Governed*, reflects on the trends here noted. His primary target is the courts and the ways in which any notion of disobedience to judicial decrees has come to seem un-American. In Carter's view, part of the reason for this is that the secular liberals who dominate law find it almost impossible to imagine that "there are people to whom faith is more important than particular political ends." The upshot is the alienation of tens of millions of voters. But they have not gone easily into that privatized silence. They are angry and feel as if they are somehow unwelcome in America. What Carter calls "liberal constitutionalism" and I call "liberal monism" has played a huge role in the presumption that America could and should create a nationwide "single community" with "enforceable understandings" of how everything is to be organized. Families, as a result, have been stripped of religious freedom in many concrete ways, including freedom to educate their children in a faith tradition. Here so many costly barriers are placed in the pathways of parents that most acquiesce and send their children to public schools.

"Tolerance," Carter reminds us, "is not simply a willingness to listen to what others have to say. It is also a resistance to the quick use of state power—the exclusive prerogative of violent force—to force dissenters and the different to conform." Carter points to chapter and verse in the pro-life protest and the ways in which attempts to quash this form of public advocacy have proceeded apace with the blessing of the courts. By setting up as paradigmatic the view that the nation must be morally more or less the same, plurality is denied and community autonomy is eroded by force of law. All of this going back to the notion, monistic at base, that a human being cannot serve simultaneously two masters or handle two complex and at times, perhaps, conflicting sets of claims. This view gives democratic citizens little credit and equates democracy with one strand of liberalism. That strand is the one that most assiduously pushes for acceptance of the view that it, and it alone, is in a neutral position, permitting all others to flourish, when it is, in fact, a highly ideological position that compels others to shut up or disappear.

With law professors arguing we need more, not less, government regulation of sectarian bodies, the presence of religion in public expression is seen as anomalous in any case. And with some feminist jurisprudentialists insisting that in fact every single institution in American society should be compelled legally to conform to standard liberal modes of representation and legitimation in their internal organization (all associations must look alike and sprout analogous forms of administration), it is perhaps not too much to fret about a future moment in which authentic religious toleration, dependent on robust pluralism, is a thing of the past. That would indeed be a sorry spectacle. A worst-case scenario would see Orthodox Jews compelled in every "public" venue to give up the external insignia of their faith. Catholic hospitals and doctors would be forced to perform abortions on pain of punitive measures and the Catholic Church, additionally, not in its time but in a court's time, would be required to ordain women priests. All Christian schools and academies would face a mandated national agenda from which none was permitted to waver. Loss of free exercise is the full implication of a strong juridical liberalism (in the philosophic sense). Genuine religious liberty, free exercise that pertains to bodies of the faithful and the institutions needed to sustain faithfulness, would be lost as one standard triumphed. At that point we would be in a world different from the one we now inhabit in the thoroughgoingness of it all. America would no longer be a liberal democracy but, rather, a betrayer of liberalism's most capacious premises and promises.

2

"A Proper Blessing?": The Jew and the American Public Square

Marc Dollinger

At the height of Franklin D. Roosevelt's popularity, Judge Jonah Goldstein observed that Jews lived in three *velten* (worlds); *die velt* (this world), *yene velt* (the world to come), and Roosevelt. In the 1932 presidential election that catapulted the former New York governor to the White House, the Democratic standard-bearer earned over 80 percent of the American Jewish vote. In the elections that followed, Jewish support for FDR would skyrocket to an astronomical 90 percent.[1]

The New Deal marked a major turning point in the American Jewish community's relationship to the public square. For the first time on this nation's shores, policy-makers, social workers, economists, and labor leaders joined federal government agencies as respected experts and trusted advisors. In an arena once reserved for the nation's Protestant elite, Jews benefited from Roosevelt's pragmatic approach to public policy. While recent historiographic analyses have deflated much of the enthusiasm once reserved for FDR, his decision to dismantle the federal government's glass ceiling catapulted American Jews into unprecedented positions of influence.

27

Three generations later, Jewish leaders have paused to reconsider their community's relationship to American public life. President Bush's faith-based initiative enjoys the support of a growing minority of American Jewish leaders, including of course former Indianapolis mayor and current presidential advisor Stephen Goldsmith. The Anti-Defamation League's national director, Abraham Foxman, offered conditional support for charitable choice while Harvey Blitz of the Union of Orthodox Jewish Congregations of America declared the Orthodox Jewish community "pleased that President Bush is committed to increasing the partnership between government and faith- and community-based institutions." Even Connecticut senator and former Democratic vice-pesidential nominee Joseph Lieberman, while not endorsing the specifics of the Bush plan, welcomed a larger public role for religion and accepted the president's invitation to join him when he launched his program at a Christian family and social service center.

The trusting relationship that has developed between American Jews and the federal government stands in sharp contrast to most diaspora Jewish history. For much of their European experience, Jews endured marginalization at the hands of unsympathetic central powers. At their worst, medieval governments created isolated ghettos, imposed "Jew taxes," and eliminated any chance for social mobility. Jewish communities learned to fear government and sought to limit its influence whenever possible. As a mythical character in one famous Broadway play (*Fiddler on the Roof*) once asked, "Is there a proper blessing for the czar?" The reply, known to virtually every American Jew, communicates a strong communal distrust of authority: "May God bless and keep the czar far away from us!"

The ease with which Jews embraced this nation's federal authority raises fascinating questions about the legacy of the European Enlightenment, the seminal event that liberated Jews from the ghettos and promised full civil equality. With the arrival of Jewish immigrants to this country, whether among Sephardic colonial settlers, nineteenth-century German Jews, or turn-of-the-century eastern Europeans, communal leaders questioned the federal government's ability to translate constitutional ideals into reality. Over the past three hundred and fifty years, Jewish leaders have alternated between particularist calls for governments to protect Jews as a persecuted minority vulnerable to anti-Semitic outbursts and universalist appeals for Washington to celebrate Judaism as a religious faith consistent with broad-based American ideals.

Against this backdrop, the twentieth-century American Jewish love affair with the federal government conveys a far different political reality than experienced by most modern European Jews. In the past seventy years, the Jewish community's relationship to the public square has forced us to reconsider the most basic assumptions about centralized power, authority, and its meaning for Jews.

We stand today before a benevolent government where Jews enjoy status, power, and privilege. Jewish legislators draft laws. Jewish judges interpret them in courtrooms filled with Jewish attorneys on both sides of the aisle. The admonition given by Anatevka's spiritual leader could only resonate within the fictional and idealized world of the musical stage. In Washington, D.C., and across the nation, American Jews blessed and wanted to keep government as close as they possibly could.

This chapter will examine the relationship between the organized Jewish community and the public square between the New Deal years, when most American Jews joined the political mainstream, and the late 1960s, when Johnsonian liberalism challenged Jewish leaders to reevaluate their public policy assumptions. During this pivotal generation, Jewish leaders rallied in support of broad new governmental powers designed to lift the nation out of the Great Depression only to turn away from centralized authority when it meant acceptance of Great Society-era race-based quota programs. Government, interpreted through the New Deal and early postwar years as the guarantor of individual rights, embraced a new wave of sociological research that acknowledged the ravaging impact of racism, focused federal programs on specific underserved groups, and splintered FDR's New Deal coalition.

The question of the Jewish community's relationship to the American public square has challenged generations of American Jewish historians. Early studies searching for the root causes of American Jewish political activism pointed to prophetic Judaism, a history of oppression, and a desire to unite the particular needs of a Jewish minority with the universal claims of civil equality. Moses Rischin, Irving Howe, Lawrence Fuchs, and Henry Feingold all embraced this classical approach.[2]

In more recent years, studies of Jews and American politics have examined the breakup of the black/Jewish alliance and the Jewish community's apparent retreat from public life. Murray Friedman, head of Temple University's Center for the Study of American Jews and a former member of President Ronald Reagan's Civil Rights Commission, lamented the Jewish retreat by asking "What Went

Wrong?" in relations between blacks and Jews. Others, such as Seth Forman, criticized Jewish leaders for devoting too much time to the public square at the expense of Jewish interests. The "long-standing differences over such issues as community control of school districts, racial preferences, the role of Israel in world politics, open admissions at universities and the anti-Semitism of some controversial Black leaders," Forman explained, "began to outweigh the mutually perceived common interests that had for decades worked to cement cooperation between significant segments of both groups." Similar theses defined other works in the field.[3]

Even as historians of the American Jewish experience have chronicled the last generation's apparent retreat from liberalism, they have missed important challenges to accepted church/state separation wisdom. The organized Jewish community's rock-solid commitment to a high and impenetrable barrier between church and state cracked along several well-defined fault lines. In a variety of places and times, Jewish leaders mediated between a fear of centralized authority and their desire to realize Jewish communal goals. Most of the time, that required the filing of amicus briefs in favor of a strict constitutional interpretation. Other times, though, it mandated Jewish organizational acceptance of government monies for social welfare, relief, and other operations. And for one particular American Jewish constituency, the Orthodox, the debate over church/state separation rarely provoked the sort of interest and passion it generated among less traditional Jews. Orthodox groups often backed a larger public profile for religion hoping it would help achieve their Jewish educational goals.

The modern debate over Jews and church/state separation began during the nation's worst economic depression and proved beneficial for Jews and their relationship to government. Between 1933 and 1941, Jewish social workers led the charge for federal intervention and often requested that the government fund religious-based organizations. With unemployment hovering at 25 percent and breadlines forming in major American cities, social workers from both the public and private spheres understood the need for fast, effective action. Since religious-based social welfare agencies boasted years of experience, bureaucratic infrastructure, and an established record of high-quality care, the pragmatic Roosevelt turned to them as an obvious quick fix. Jewish social workers, for their part, could ensure continued service to their clients without fear of bankrupting their cash-strapped institutions.

Jewish leaders addressed church/state concerns by separating the secular aspects of their work from the religious. Since the nation's high unemployment rate grew from systemic weaknesses in the international economy rather than individual vice, the dean of the Graduate School for Jewish Social Work explained, the Jewish poor "should be aided by the government whose duty it is to care for its citizens." In Boston, the executive director of the city's Jewish Philanthropies called for the creation of "an elaborate program of public social work, particularly in the field of relief" while the leader of Omaha's Jewish community argued that "it is totally illogical . . . to hold ourselves aloof as a special and segregated group and to refuse to accept . . . aid and assistance . . . from the public agencies." Jewish social workers, many of whom grew up in the labor union movement, demanded that the U.S. government abandon its voluntaristic approach to social welfare in favor of state-sponsored programs typical throughout western Europe. President Roosevelt proved willing to experiment with new ideas and, unlike many of his predecessors, welcomed Jewish advisors into his administration.[4]

The Jewish community did not have to wait long to test the new waters of affirmative government. Within eight weeks of his inauguration, Roosevelt secured passage of the Federal Emergency Relief Act (FERA), which allocated an initial five hundred million dollars "to provide for cooperation by the federal government with the several states . . . in relieving the hardships and suffering caused by unemployment." Before passage of the Social Security Act prompted FDR to phase it out in December 1935, the FERA committed four billion dollars to some twenty million Americans.[5]

The FERA's effect on the Jewish community proved immediate and profound. Within months, Jewish social service agencies relinquished the vast majority of their case loads to public agencies. By 1934, Jewish agencies cut their welfare budgets in half. While Jewish social workers celebrated the government's newfound commitment to social welfare, they still worried that the public agencies would not deliver high-quality care or serve the special needs of Jewish clients. Whenever and wherever possible, they sought cooperative arrangements with government. In some cases, they encouraged the public agencies to hire Jewish communal professionals to work with their coreligionists. At other times, FDR funded Jewish agencies themselves. In Atlanta, for example, the Jewish community managed to retain its case load after arguing for the special religious needs of its clients. In Baltimore, Birmingham, Cleveland, Pittsburgh, and St. Louis, Jewish agencies maintained their operational autonomy because public agencies could not be found or did not dispense relief. The New Deal taught American Jews the wisdom of accommodation and compromise. "The most important lesson coming out of this emergency," a leader of Cleveland's Jewish community concluded, "is the fact that an unwilling Jewish community has come to realize that relief work can, under proper safeguards, be financed by public funds without detriment to the Jewish families thus served."[6]

Roosevelt's social welfare support offered Jews an unintended benefit: the strengthening of Jewish social, cultural, and educational programming. By taking over financial responsibility for the secular aspects of welfare reform, the New Deal allowed Jewish agencies to refocus their limited resources on programs for Jewish cultural survival and redefine the relationship between an activist government and its religious minorities. Within just two years of FDR's inauguration, the executive director of New York City's Jewish Federation announced that Jewish educational and cultural programs commanded over 60 percent of their budget and had developed into "large and growing fields." In 1937, Jewish educators reported "marked improvements" in school classrooms, buildings, and decorations. In Los Angeles, over half of the 1938 United Jewish Welfare Fund budget for local activities paid for educational programs. At a time when the Great Depression united all Americans under the same economic umbrella, Jewish communal leaders managed to shape the federal government into a powerful agent for Jewish ethnic continuity.[7]

Throughout the New Deal era, Jewish leaders approached their entry into the American public square as evidence of their emerging status as full and equal citizens. One's Jewishness promised not to compromise civil rights as communal leaders called on government to protect all its citizens, regardless of race, religion, or national origin. In the postwar years, this individualist orientation encouraged Jewish leaders to press for heightened church/state separation. Jewish organizations, led by the American Jewish Committee (AJC) and American Jewish Congress (AJCongress) lobbied for strict legal guarantees of civil rights and civil liberties. They pressed for passage of a federal anti-lynching law, a fair employment practices commission, implementation of the Supreme Court's Brown decision, and the landmark Civil Rights Act of 1964 and Voting Rights Act of 1965.

Despite the impressive gains made during the New Deal years, American Jews still struggled on the margins of society. Restrictive quotas limited Jewish matriculation at the leading graduate schools, employment in many major corporations, and membership in elite social clubs as Jewish leaders turned to the government to flex its considerable muscle in defense of full civil and religious equality.

Jewish organizations held competing ideas about the best approach to postwar church/state issues. The American Jewish Congress demanded a strict sense of church/state separation. Its leaders pointed to the divisive effects of religious incursions on Jewish students and held to the principle that all citizens enjoyed the right to a public education free of religious interference. For the American Jewish Committee (AJC), by contrast, social integration entailed continuing dialogue with less emphasis on judicial intervention. It favored an accommodationist approach that gave greater priority to interfaith dialogue and educational programs. By teaching Christians about Jewish observance and by showing Jews the ties they shared with Christians, the AJC believed that it could find common ground to bind all Americans without strident constitutional appeals.

Jewish communal discord over the church/state question intensified in 1947 when the U.S. Congress considered legislation to provide federal funding for private and parochial schools. While the relationship between Washington and both public and private universities strengthened throughout the postwar period, almost all in the Jewish community opposed any alliance between the national government and private religious primary and secondary schools. Most Jews feared that government support of private schools would create an educational system divided along religious, ethnic, and economic lines. Only public education, credited with bringing diverse Americans together in the same classroom, could create a pluralist nation receptive to its Jewish citizens. A viable public school system, Jewish leaders believed, demanded a strict funding monopoly.

Jewish groups opposed federal aid to private education because they feared it might one day challenge the integrity of public schools. Release time programs, which permitted students to be "released" from their regular studies in order to participate in private sectarian religious study, threatened Jewish social acceptance in a more immediate and profound way. Under the terms of these programs, teachers would be permitted to lead a daily class in Christian theology. In some cases, Jewish students would be permitted to excuse themselves to the school library for the duration of the lesson. At other times, teachers demanded that they participate in the class religious study. Both scenarios alienated Jewish students from their peers and inspired Jewish communal leaders to petition the nation's judicial authorities for redress.[8]

Maintaining a strict interpretation of the Constitution furthered postwar Jewish efforts to protect public schools and guarded against anti-Jewish activities. Yet, a heroic defense of church/state separation did not always serve Jewish interests. To the surprise of most national Jewish leaders, many local Jewish parents adopted an alternative interpretation of the religious freedom question. These middle-class Jews reveled in the glory of their consensus-era social integration and did not want to participate in political campaigns which distinguished them from their Christian neighbors. What appeared a principled defense of strict constitutional interpretation actually masked a deeper and more important priority: the successful integration of Jewish children into the social world of their new suburban communities.

For them, successful acculturation to American life could best be guaranteed by demonstrating the inherent compatibility between Judaism and Christianity. Learning about Christian holidays, even allowing time for religious instruction and observance, illustrated the highest ideals of pluralism, tolerance, and understanding. American Jews would be most secure in a community that understood and accepted the religious diversity of its population. In an argument typical of many supporters of Catholic parochial schools, some Jews argued that as long as government refrained from endorsing a particular point of view, no constitutional promise had been breached. Their confidence in the worthiness of interfaith understanding and dialogue outweighed concerns that minority religious rights might be compromised.[9]

While the American Jewish Congress and AJC opposed joint holiday observances in public schools, the Anti-Defamation League (ADL) gave conditional support. Instead of opposing religious activities outright, the ADL distinguished between exclusive religious programs, which were not acceptable, and inclusive ones, which were encouraged as a means of promoting interfaith understanding. Many Jews agreed with the ADL position. In Chelsea, Massachusetts, Jewish parents who objected to singing Christmas carols in school faced resistance from some other Jewish parents who wanted their children to participate. In Cleveland, the local Jewish Community Relations Council opposed a plan to celebrate both Christmas and Hanukkah in the public schools. When Jewish parents expressed their support of the dual celebration, the JCRC reconsidered and reversed its stance.[10]

This new minority view differed from the Jewish community's traditional position on church/state separation. In the nineteenth century, Reform Jews from Germany and central Europe cherished the legal distinction between religion and nation. They hoped that constitutional protection of religious rights would realize the post-Emancipation vision of civil equality lacking in Europe. With the rapid immigration of Jews from eastern Europe at the turn of the twentieth century, separation of church and state gained greater importance. The new immigrants, their children and grandchildren, embraced the American educational system. With the exception of some in the Orthodox community, American Jews resisted the temptation to establish their own private schools. For most, public schools offered not only a free education, but the opportunity to become American. Students learned to speak unaccented English, studied the history of their new country, and received lessons in civics. At a time when Jews searched for ways to resolve conflicts between their brand of Judaism and their vision of what it meant to be American, the clear delineation between church and state in the public schools offered the best chance for rapid and successful adaptation to American life.[11]

By the mid-1960s, the American Jewish community's relationship to the public square endured its greatest test. With his Great Society, LBJ lobbied Congress and the American people for specific commitments to affirmative action, community action programs, and recognition that racism acted as the most destructive social force in American society.

By most accounts, the Great Society failed. In the 1966 midterm election, millions of white ethnic Americans, though few Jews, bolted from the Democratic Party and began a neoconservative realignment that brought Richard Nixon to the White House in 1969. The New Deal coalition, constructed by FDR to include the northern white working class, southern blacks, and Midwestern farmers, disintegrated in the midst of an unpopular domestic policy and growing opposition to U.S. foreign policy in Southeast Asia.

Jewish leaders reacted to the changing public square with grave concerns over the viability of Johnsonian liberalism and its perceived threat to American Jewish life. As the federal government began to focus its impressive strength on challenging the white elite power structure that defined American political and social life, Jews once again saw themselves on the losing side.

Jewish opposition to the Great Society first emerged when the Johnson administration employed racial criteria in its reform programs. Under that binary system, Jews became, in terms of federal public policy, part of the white privileged class and, by extension some believed, responsible for participating in the subjugation of African Americans. As historian Seth Forman argued, efforts to "normalize" or "whiten" American Jewry ended with "a series of interpretations that redefine[d] benevolent Jewish attitudes toward Blacks as primarily motivated by self-interest and, to that extent, not markedly distinct from the racist attitudes of the larger white society." Jewish leaders could point to a host of polls to demonstrate their community's disproportionate commitment to liberal ideals. They prided themselves on their exceptionalism and criticized President Johnson for understating what they perceived as the precarious position of Jews within the larger white Christian society.[12]

The whitening of Jewish America clashed with Johnsonian liberalism when the president excluded the Jewish poor from some of his Great Society programs. Contemporary sociological studies, most notably the famous Moynihan Report, linked racial oppression, the instability of the black family, and the legacy of slavery, with perpetuation of a "culture of poverty" in America's inner cities. "At the heart of the deterioration of the fabric of Negro society is the deterioration of the Negro family," Moynihan argued, "it is the fundamental source of the weakness of the Negro community at the present time." By pouring government resources into specific African American populated neighborhoods, Johnson hoped to minimize the effects of institutional racism and open new doors of opportunity in education, local political control, and job placement.[13]

Unfortunately, 15 percent of American Jewish families struggled to survive on annual incomes less than $3,000, the amount Johnson defined as the nation's poverty level. Most did not live in one of the president's designated poverty zones, excluding them from many benefits of the War on Poverty. "This approach," the AJCongress concluded in a 1971 study, "is unfair, unjust, and inequitable." Report authors Naomi Levine and Martin Hochbaum wanted poverty "defined by need, not geography" and criticized Johnson for excluding "the Jewish poor from participating in the anti-poverty program." The AJCongress officials explained that their concern was "with the Jewish poor" and "in this regard, we can say unequivocally that, in spite of the billions of dollars spent in fighting poverty, . . . little of this money has gone to alleviate the plight of the

Jewish poor. Indeed, the war against Jewish poverty has not yet begun."[14]

When affirmative action test cases worked their way through the court system in the late 1960s and early 1970s, many Jewish organizations supported the white plaintiffs. Only two national Jewish organizations, the Reform movement's Union of American Hebrew Congregations and the National Council of Jewish Women, defended the affirmative action policies of the University of California, Davis, Medical School in the famed *Bakke* case. In St. Louis, the Jewish Federation's executive director announced that "it is not the responsibility of a Jewish agency to meet Negro *needs unless it* [*sic*] *also serves the total general community*" (emphasis his). Another observer noted, "It has become increasingly apparent that the community's selfish interests diverge significantly from the dictates of abstract universalism."[15]

The threat of court-ordered busing in the North inspired Jewish "white flight" to local private schools. "Jews are human too," Shad Polier of the AJCongress explained, "They often act out of selfish motives." Polier pointed out that "education has been the key to the Jew's success in America and when busloads of Negro children are sent into their school, Jews are frightened." Even though the National Jewish Community Relations Advisory Council supported school integration, it argued in a 1964 position paper that it "regard[ed] the neighborhood school as having important educational values" and wanted to preserve it from the threat of busing. Midge Decter, in a *Commentary* article the same year, put the issue in stark simplicity: "white parents do not want their children sent daily and alone to face the dangers—many imagined, some perhaps real—in Negro and Puerto Rican slums." As Leo Pfeffer of the AJCongress explained in testimony before the New Jersey Senate Committee on Education, Jews "go there [day schools] not because they love God but because they are afraid of the Negro." Four years later, Daniel Elazar observed that "the all-day school movement was clearly strengthened by the fact that many Jews were caught in changing neighborhoods where the public schools deteriorated before they were ready to move." The Jewish community's "romance with the public school," Milton Himmelfarb predicted in 1960, "is beginning to cool."[16]

Tensions between the American Jewish leadership and federal policy makers peaked when the government adopted quotas as a possible remedy for past racial injustices. When government, educational institutions, and industry employed strict quotas in the 1920s to limit the influence of the nation's new immigrant classes, Jews suffered. In the 1960s, government switched course, endorsing quotas as a tool for once-marginal groups to gain greater power and influence. Unfortunately for American Jews enjoying the newfound rewards of middle-class status, the new quotas threatened to undo two generations of Jewish social mobility. A government that had, in the recent past, represented tremendous opportunity for American Jews appeared to change course, marginalizing Jews for being too powerful, too privileged, and too "white."

Jews celebrated the liberal ideals of Franklin D. Roosevelt, who opened the government to Jews, and Martin Luther King, Jr., who demanded that Congress and the courts protect the constitutional rights of each individual citizen. President Johnson, on the other hand, appealed to group status, alienating Jewish leaders who feared a return to more anti-Semitic times. As the associate director of the AJC explained in 1964, the American Jew, once committed to such traditional liberal causes as unionization, had lost his political bearings. "While in the 1930s he more or less subscribed to the notion that what was good for labor was good for the country," he explained, "he now finds that his principles are at odds with any such doctrine in relation to the Negro."[17]

From most outward appearances, the group-centered approach of LBJ's Great Society programs soured Jews on greater civil involvement. For the first time since entering the American mainstream, Jews faced marginalization based on their religious affiliation. While most Jews remained committed Democratic voters, their disillusionment with the new approach to American liberalism forever changed the fabric and texture of their political culture.

Yet, despite the organized Jewish community's opposition to many federal programs, the highly charged political events of the 1960s did not hasten a Jewish retreat from the new ethnic-conscious American public square. When LBJ acknowledged group-based inequality, he handed the Jewish community an unintended gift—the ability to express a more public form of Judaism without fear of mainstream American opposition. Jews, who shied away from public displays of their Judaism during the consensus 1950s, awoke in the late 1960s to find an American culture that actively encouraged, and even rewarded, ethnic difference. Jewish leaders harnessed the new pluralistic group-centered liberalism to build Jewish educational institutions, combat assimilation, and revive American Jewish identity on a national scale. In a debate all too often dominated by discussion of what Jonathan Kaufman called the "balkanization" of

America, the meaningful parallels between group-based liberal policies and the political culture of American Jews have been overlooked.[18]

What seemed a rapid retreat from American public life was actually an embrace of the era's new self-directed credo. Between 1964, when passage of the Civil Rights Act marked the symbolic end of one liberal epoch, and 1980, when Ronald Reagan's election ushered in an era of conservative politics, Jews fashioned ethnic nationalism into a powerful tool for American Jewish continuity. As they had in both the New Deal and the civil rights movement, Jews accommodated to the realities of a new and different public square in a bid to promote their own social mobility. In the 1930s, that meant support of FDR's New Deal liberal programs. A generation later, it joined blacks and Jews in an alliance to end segregation. By the mid-1960s, the politics of liberal accommodation changed yet again, this time encouraging Jews to focus on the particular needs of their own community.[19]

Jewish leaders reinvented themselves as an inspired diaspora community committed to Jewish survival in the United States, emancipation for their coreligionists in the Soviet Union, and a new form of American Zionism almost immune from historic concerns over dual loyalty. Hundreds of Jewish day schools, many from the once assimilationist Reform movement, opened their doors. The Habad movement welcomed thousands of ba'alei tshuvah (masters of the return to tradition). Synagogues revitalized their worship services with gender-inclusive liturgy, guitar music, and even an occasional drum for added spiritual effect. Throughout the country and across all denominational lines, a new generation of Jewish youth emerged with few of the inhibitions that inspired their parents and grandparents to keep their Judaism private.

During the turn-of-the-century era of massive Jewish immigration to the United States, communal leaders enjoyed a population with a high level of Jewish education but struggled with social discrimination and lack of resources. In the immediate postwar years, Jews began to enjoy material prosperity but often subsumed their distinctive Jewish identities in an effort to acculturate to the consensus mentality of the time. By the late 1960s, middle-class status mixed with group-based liberalism to offer Jewish leaders the perfect recipe for strengthening Jewish identity. While Jews of the 1930s could take comfort and satisfaction in knowing that they were safe in America because their president welcomed them, Jews in the 1960s and 1970s reveled in the knowledge that they could focus their considerable resources on Jewish continuity without fear of reprisal. As Rabbi Dov Peretz Elkins stated, our "commandment for the 1970s must be, 'Thou shalt be a Proud Jew!' A Jew with dignity and self respect and knowledge and commitment."[20]

Despite concerns expressed by Jewish leaders fearful of ethnic splintering, the embrace of group-based liberalism did not translate into a departure from old style consensus politics. In many ways, Jewish attitudes toward public education, busing, and private Jewish day schools reflected the very accommodationist values Jews thought they lost at the end of the civil rights movement. In the 1950s and early 1960s, civil rights liberalism joined blacks and Jews in a common struggle for legal enfranchisement. By the mid-1960s, Great Society liberalism rallied blacks and Jews around a new set of political ground rules: group status mattered, distinctive ethnic culture should be encouraged, and power should be shared more equitably among social groups. For Jews, Johnsonian liberalism legitimized their own particularist approach to ethnic politics just as it offered a link to the ideology and strategies employed by black nationalists.

By emphasizing the similarities between accommodationist liberalism and its group-based cousin, Jews identified as consensus Americans even as they embraced a public Jewish posture. The newfound religious life of the *ba'al tshuvah*, for example, reflected Americanism as much as it demonstrated a return to tradition. Only in a pluralist United States could a young Jew in search of meaning know that public expression of Judaism would be respected. The Soviet Jewry movement, as well, revealed a similar affinity for mainstream American political culture. Calling on the patriotic themes of the Cold War, these American activists felt confident making particularist appeals to Congress, the president, and the American people. For American Zionists, the rise of group consciousness advanced a powerful model of ethnic activism that legitimated Jewish appeals for *aliyah* and inspired a stronger ideological connection to the State of Israel. Jewish New Leftists, calling on lessons they learned in the Free Speech and anti-Vietnam War protest movements, created a Jewish social reform movement that sought to internalize the most important elements of the secular American counterculture. Jewish feminists, as well, invoked themes from the larger American movement for gender equality in their critique of traditional Jewish life.

Despite its Americanist orientation, the new Jewish activism still signaled a communal retreat from the universalist ideals of classical

Enlightenment liberalism. As Rabbi Schulweis explained, "The Enlightenment vision of a constantly progressing universal society calling for Jews to involve themselves in the battle for social justice is now interpreted as suicidal."[21] The tension between ethnic particularism and civil equality threw American Jews into political limbo. While the organized Jewish community could celebrate its newfound programmatic successes, it also had to face painful new questions about the role of the Jew in the American public square. Communal leaders began to wonder if Jews were "primarily members of a tribe, Americans, or 'citizens of the world'?" Even the Reform movement's Central Conference of American Rabbis, well-known for its activist liberalism in the civil rights movement era, could not reject the new ethos: "until the recent past," it explained with some ambivalence in 1976, "our obligations to the Jewish people and to all humanity seemed congruent. At times now these two perspectives appear to conflict."[22]

The rise of group-based liberalism proved a mixed blessing for the Jewish community. Only by rejecting their historic affinity for classical liberal individualism could Jews fully enjoy the benefits of a new group-conscious American culture. Yet, they feared that their newfound embrace of ethnic self-interest would undermine the individualist protections that made America exceptional. For American Jews, the emergence of identity politics created a powerful and complex paradox that challenged historic allegiances and confused conventional political logic.

As we labor to understand the complex, ironic, and seemingly contradictory nature of American Jewish political culture between the 1930s and 1960s, we must ease our traditional definitions of liberalism and conservatism. These terms, slippery as they are, have conflicted and alternating historical meanings. Some Jewish neoconservatives claim the mantle of an earlier brand of individualist liberalism while many Jews who remained within the Democratic Party have made special efforts to distinguish their brand of liberal politics from those espoused by group-conscious leftists. With recent calls for voucher programs and increased funding for faith-based institutions, Jewish leaders from across the political spectrum have reexamined accepted wisdom and wondered if "religious communities contain powerful resources for the renewal of American democracy."[23]

Those on both the left and the right have borrowed basic political assumptions from one another without acknowledgment or apology. This has been especially true as Jewish leaders struggle to define the proper role of religion in American public life. An examination of these ill-defined political boundaries sharpens our understanding of the church/state dilemma and helps us discover the core issues involved.

In modern America, liberals have tended to trust government and, in the New Deal spirit, looked to Washington as a powerful positive force for social change. Passage of the Civil Rights Act of 1964 and the Voting Rights Act of 1965 provided ample evidence for the liberal contention that a loose interpretation of federal constitutional authority offered government the latitude it needed to solve problems. Even though the modern Democratic Party traces itself to the Jeffersonian ideals of the early republic, contemporary liberals fear abuse by local authorities and trust the federal government with important discretionary power to preserve a fair and just society.

When advocates of a greater public religious profile raise the issue of church/state separation, most liberals transform themselves into strict constructionists, distrusting government, fearing latitude, and embracing Ronald Reagan's contention that government was the problem rather than the solution. They raise age-old concerns over how an unsympathetic Christian-run nation can compromise the religious freedom of its Jewish minority and laud Thomas Jefferson's distrust of federal authority as both appropriate and needed. The barrier between religion and the state needed to remain high and impenetrable.

Two issues complicate this classic Jewish defense of church/state separation: it fails to account for massive government subsidies already undergirding the American Jewish communal infrastructure and it ignores the ways Johnsonian liberalism employed elasticity in the establishment clause to promote Jewish life by encouraging public expression of difference. While much attention has been paid to Jewish organizational opposition to government funding for Christian parochial schools, few have examined Jewish liberal attitudes toward the tax deductibility of donations to Jewish nonprofit organizations, synagogues, and community centers. Without the ability to encourage philanthropic donations through this tax vehicle, American Jewish leaders would face dire economic circumstances. Among temple board members and the rabbis and cantors they hire, few voices have been heard raising objections to the parsonage, an impressive form of income tax relief extended to clergy of all faiths by a sympathetic federal government interested in raising the profile of organized religion. Contrary to conventional understanding, even the strictest of Jewish legal interpreters have permitted and benefited from state-sponsored support of American Jewish religious life.

Jews on the right of the political spectrum have engaged in the same sort of creative argumentation. Conservatives often decry federal intervention and lobby against increased spending on social programs. "Tax and spend liberals," they complain, think they can solve problems by throwing money at them. By interpreting constitutional questions narrowly, conservatives hope to respect the founding fathers' fear of centralized power and keep authority in the hands of local officials closest to their constituents and their needs.

Yet, the distrust of authority does not extend to a government that wishes to promote a more public religious role. At a time when strict construction remains the legal philosophy of choice for most conservatives, more and more Jewish Republicans are calling for a loose interpretation of the church/state clause. In a modern-day illustration of Hamiltonian means to Jeffersonian ends, conservatives seek a more powerful federal government to realize their national vision of a pious nation rooted in religious ethics.

These apparent contradictions unearth important and powerful impulses that have been buried just beneath the surface of the political landscape. They ask us to pause and question when government authority undermines American democracy and when it serves a social good.

Among those who seek a larger public role for Jews, a loose interpretation of the church/state clause acknowledges the Jewish community's entry into the American mainstream and reaffirms Judaism's critical place in the Protestant-Catholic-Jew triad described a generation ago by Will Herberg. By opening up government to greater religious expression, Jews achieve a greater voice in American cultural life.

For those who wish to preserve the barrier between church and state, a strict constitutional interpretation seeks to limit government in the area most vital for American Jews: religious autonomy. While liberals may trust government on issues of civil rights, affirmative action, and even group-based ethnic consciousness, the same does not hold true for public religion. They view the constitutional safeguard of individual rights as a key principle to ensure that Jews remain equal citizens in a Christian-dominated society.

While Jewish responses to government authority have spanned the political continuum, each held to the same basic tension: mediating between government power, social inclusion, and how American

Jews could achieve the one goal missing from two thousand years of Jewish diaspora living: a benevolent civil authority, run by Christians, yet friendly to Jews. With this standard, the political lines dividing American Jews blur. Jewish Republicans who support a larger public voice for organized religion share common ground with Jewish Democrats interested in modeling their own ethnic revival after the ones pioneered in the African American, Latino, and women's communities. Jewish radicals alienated from the anti-Semitic New Left have been able to communicate with centrist community leaders on the need for Jewish primacy in political debate. Even Reform movement Jews, reared in the liberal civil rights movement and committed to a secular universalist interpretation of American life, now share a common bond with their Orthodox co-religionists, the desire to maintain a strong network of Jewish day schools.

Despite the allure of government dollars and the Jewish community's newfound position of power and influence in the public square, the majority of Jews will remain cautious and skeptical on the question of church/state separation. Born of FDR's optimism, challenged by the contradictions of postwar middle-class suburban life, and even antagonistic to LBJ's version of activist government, American Jews continue to view a strict separation of church and state as their best guarantor of civil equality. They believe that a narrow constructionist argument brought Jews to the public square in the last generation and a loose interpretation threatens the Jewish community's minority voice.

Most Jews have not joined the public religion celebration because it conflicts with the belief that religious freedom is best protected by a government that keeps out of the way and lets the nation's faith communities develop as they see fit. With this concern, mainstream Jewish organizations have created an unlikely political alliance with several fundamentalist Christian groups who have expressed similar reservations. Whether on the left or right, secular or faith based, American Jews have experienced a church/state debate that complicates conventional wisdom and would confound even the chief rabbi of Anatevka.

Notes

1. Evelyn Lewis, "The Jewish Vote" (Ph.D. dissertation, Ball State University, 1976); and Marc Dollinger, *Quest for Inclusion: Jews and Lib-*

eralism in Modern America (Princeton, N.J.: Princeton University Press, 2000).

2. Moses Rischin, *The Promised City: New York's Jews, 1870-1914* (Cambridge, Mass.: Harvard University Press, 1962); Irving Howe, *World of Our Fathers* (New York: Galahad Books, 1976); Lawrence Fuchs, *The Political Behavior of American Jews* (Glencoe, Ill.: Free Press, 1956); and Henry Feingold, "A Midrash on American Jewish History," in Murray Friedman, ed., *Utopian Dilemma: New Political Directions for American Jews* (Washington, D.C.: Ethics and Public Policy Center, 1985).

3. Seth Forman, *Blacks in the Jewish Mind: A Crisis of Liberalism* (New York: New York University Press, 1998), 1. See, for example, Jonathan Rieder, *Canarsie: The Jews and Italians of Brooklyn against Liberalism* (Cambridge, Mass.: Harvard University Press, 1985).

4. *Proceedings, National Conference of Jewish Social Service, 1931,* 25, 54-55. *American Jewish Year Book* 34 (1932-1933), 68-69. *Proceedings, National Conference of Jewish Social Service, 1932,* 99. For an expanded discussion of FERA and its relationship to the New Deal, see Dollinger, *Quest for Inclusion,* ch. 1.

5. *1935 Yearbook of Jewish Social Work,* Part I, 22, 20, *Proceedings, National Conference of Jewish Social Welfare, 1935,* 26.

6. *Proceedings: National Conference of Jewish Social Service, 1934,* 7-8, *Proceedings, National Conference of Jewish Social Welfare, 1935,* 26. *Proceedings, National Council of Jewish Social Service, 1931,* 27.

7. *Proceedings, National Conference Of Jewish Welfare, 1935,* 1, *Jewish Social Work, 1935,* 20, *Proceedings, National Conference of Jewish Social Service, 1935,* 104. *Proceedings, National Conference of Jewish Social Welfare, 1937,* 53, 12, 60. *United Jewish Welfare Fund Yearbook, 1938,* 32-33, *United Jewish Welfare Fund Yearbook, 1939,* 48-49.

8. William W. Brickman, *Chronology and Bibliography of Church-State-School Relations* (New York: National Society of Hebrew Day Schools, 1970), as well as the yearly summary of *The Civil Rights and Civil Liberties Decisions of the United States Supreme Court: A Summary and Analysis* (New York: Commission on Law and Social Action, 1950-1960). For more on church/state separation in postwar America, see Dollinger, *Quest for Inclusion,* ch. 6.

9. Philip Gleason, *Speaking of Diversity* (Baltimore, Md.: Johns Hopkins University Press, 1992), chs. 8, 10, and 11.

10. "Religious Holiday Observances in the Public Schools, NCRAC, Report of the Eighth Plenary Session," 25-28 May 1950, 24, 32-33, 35. Manuscript Collection 202, box 51, folder 3, AJA. See also Charles Sherman, *The Jew within American Society* (Detroit: Wayne State University Press, 1965), 183-89.

11. Michael Meyer, *Response to Modernity: A History of the Reform Movement in Judaism* (New York: Oxford University Press, 1988). The Jewish experience in eastern Europe taught American Jews not to trust state-controlled churches. See Robert T. Gan, "The Jews and the Problem

of Separation of Church and State, 1960-1965," box 2654, AJA. As early
as 1925, the United Synagogue of America opposed "any effort to introduce religious instruction into the public schools, and reiterate[d] strongly
its absolute disapproval of any effort to introduce religious instruction of
any nature into the public school system." *Justice, Justice, You Shall Pursue,* 55. See also Friedman, *Utopian Dilemma,* 28-31. See also, Jonathan
D. Sarna and David G. Dalin, *Religion and State in the American Jewish
Experience: A Documentary History* (South Bend, Ind.: University of
Notre Dame Press, 1997); and Naomi Cohen, *Jews in Christian America:
The Pursuit of Religious Equality* (New York: Oxford University Press,
1992).

12. Forman, *Blacks in the Jewish Mind,* 2. See also Marc Dollinger,
"The Other War: American Jews, Lyndon Johnson, and the Great Society,"
American Jewish History, 89, no. 4 (December 2001): 437-61.

13. William Brink and Louis Harris, *Black and White: A Study of US
Racial Attitudes Today* (New York: Simon and Schuster, 1966), 144.

14. Naomi Levine and Martin Hochbaum, "The Jewish Poor and the
Anti-Poverty Program: A Study of the Economic Opportunity Act, Its
Failure to Help the Jewish Poor, and Recommendations for Its Revision So
That All of This Nation's Poor May Share More Equitably in Its Program
and Assistance," 33, Commission on Urban Affairs, American Jewish
Congress, New York, November 1971. See also Dollinger, "The Other
War."

15. Herman L. Kaplow, Executive Director, Jewish Federation of St.
Louis, "Jewish Federations: Their Agencies and the Integration Struggle,"
5, August 26, 1964, SC Box A-89 247, Klau Library, Hebrew Union Col-
lege-Jewish Institute of Religion, Cincinnati, Ohio. Gordon Lafter, "Universalism and Particularism," in *Jewish Identity,* David Theo Goldberg and
Michael Krausz, eds. (Philadelphia: Temple University Press, 1993), 180.
See also Dollinger, *Quest for Inclusion,* ch. 8.

16. Statement by Shad Polier, A Symposium on Negro-Jewish Tensions, April 7, 1966, 1, New York, folder "Black Jewish Tensions 1961-
1966," box 14, collection *P-572, Papers of Shad Polier, American Jewish
Historical Society, New York. "De facto Segregation in Public Schools: A
Position Paper for the Guidance of Jewish Communities and Agencies," 3,
adopted in substance by the plenary session of the NJCRAC in June 1964
and in its final form by the executive committee of the NJCRAC on October 17, 1964, Small collections, Correspondence file, Clarence Israel,
AJA, Cincinnati, Ohio. Midge Decter, "The Negro and New York
Schools," *Commentary* 38 (1964): 31. Eugene Rothman, "Whither the He-
brew Day School," *Midstream* 17 (June/July 1971): 20. Daniel Elazar,
"The Institutional Life of American Jewry," *Midstream* 17 (June/July
1971): 47. Milton Himmelfarb, "Reflections on the Jewish Day School,"
Commentary 30 (July 1960): 30.

17. David Danzig, "Rightists, Racists, and Separatists: A White Bloc in
the Making?" *Commentary* 38 (1964): 32.

18. Jonathan Kaufman, *Broken Alliance: The Turbulent Times between Blacks and Jews in America* (New York: Scribner, 1995), 13.

19. Other American ethnic groups shared in the new activism. The renamed SNCC (Student National Coordinating Committee), for example, labored to reduce economic inequality among the nation's urban African Americans. NOW (National Organization for Women) led the call for gender equality, AIM (American Indian Movement) demanded greater recognition of American Indian rights and claims, while Mecha organized as a political voice for Mexican-American students.

20. Rabbi Dov Peretz Elkins, "Commandments for Our Day," delivered Shavuot morning, May 30, 1971, *A Tradition Reborn: Sermons and Essays on Liberal Judaism* (South Brunswick, N.J.: A.S. Barnes, 1973), 68.

21. Harold Schulweis, "The New Jewish Right," *Moment* 1 (May/June 1975): 57.

22. Lafter, "Universalism and Particularism in Jewish Law: Making Sense of Political Loyalties," 180.

23. "Jews and the American Public Square: A Project of the Center for Jewish Community Studies, Initiated by the Pew Charitable Trusts," 1.

3

The Theological-Political Predicament of American Jewry

Alan Mittleman

Leo Strauss, in an autobiographical aside, spoke of being in the grip of a "theological political predicament" as a young man. He meant by this something like the following. For modern Jews the constellation of religious beliefs that seems to them reasonable and compelling—the theological horizon, so to speak—is constrained by the political horizon. They are spiritually indebted, to the point of dependency, on the values of the political system, which, for the lucky ones at least, derive from the Enlightenment. Judaism therefore depends on the Enlightenment. But what happens when confidence in the Enlightenment begins to wobble and Judaism, now weakened by its dependency, lacks the strength to make up the difference?

In Strauss's day, this predicament took a particular form. Jews were wedded to a liberal solution to the Jewish problem: equal citizenship under the law was to have solved the perennial problem of Jewish suffering. They turned in hope to the realization of this ideal not in messianic time, but in their time. They had accommodated their religion, their traditional way of life, to suit the requirements of a liberal era. Their theological imagination had become liberal to its core. In the process, they lost the ability and the readiness to endure suffering as their ancestors had done. Jewish suffering became

49

an anomaly for liberal Jews, an aberration in a liberal era rather than a metaphysical constant. The beliefs of the ancestors had become implausible, but the beliefs of the moderns, of the liberals, were also becoming implausible, and more so every day. Hence the predicament: with weakened faith in both traditional Judaism and in the possibility of a liberal solution there was almost nowhere to turn.

For American Jews, the theological-political predicament is much less dire but it does nonetheless involve their long-term viability as a community. For many American Jews, no less than for German Jews, liberal norms, hopes, and convictions have become the substance and limit of their theological imagination. Let me illustrate this with two homey examples. Every semester at least one of my students wants to write a research paper on intermarriage. Typically, this student has a good Jewish upbringing and active Jewish involvement. Most likely the student has told her friends that she will only date other Jews and hopes someday to marry a Jew. Her friends then chastise her, implying that she is guilty of prejudice or bigotry for discriminating against non-Jews as potential dates or mates. The student is now confused and wants to work through her conflicted values, her theological-political predicament writ small, in a paper.

Although this predicament sometimes takes the form of adolescent peers asserting, in the name of personal freedom, their right to date whomever they wish, this is not always the case. What is at stake is not liberty or autonomy or expressive individualism, but a specific worry about discrimination. Choosing to date only Jews seems to violate a deep-seated taboo. It makes a distinction, thought to be invidious, between persons on the basis of religion or ethnicity. One might ascribe this to adolescent zealotry or confusion, but adult Jews appear to be no less zealous or confused. In a 2000 American Jewish Committee survey, 47 percent of American Jews answered that it was "racist" to insist that Jews marry only other Jews. This and other recent surveys show an erosion of resistance to the very idea of intermarriage. Not only has intermarriage lost its taboo quality, but many American Jews seem to affirm it as a triumph of open-mindedness and liberty over a discredited tribalism. American Jews seamlessly transfer liberal norms of conduct, fully appropriate to law and to civil society, to the Jewish sphere without hesitation. The theological horizon is constrained by the political imagination.

My second example is drawn from an interview in the *Forward* (November 2, 2001) with *Playboy*'s Miss November, Lindsey

Vuolo. Ms. Vuolo is a proud Reform Jew and chose to include a photo of her Bat Mitzvah in the montage of nude pictures. When asked about the compatibility of her *Playboy* exposure with her Judaism, she reflected: "Some people will look up to this as a positive thing. With all the Chandra Levy and Monica Lewinsky talk, it's a bit weird. But I think what I'm doing is positive. I'm not doing anything religiously wrong. I'm not being exploited—it's my choice."

Although she began to have some qualms during Yom Kippur, she managed to quiet her conscience. As the *Forward* explains: "When she heard that her rabbi knew about the [photo] shoot, [she said] 'Watching him deliver the sermon, I almost felt wrong. I was there atoning for my sins, but I don't feel like I've sinned [with *Playboy*]. I'm not hurting anyone.'"

For Ms. Vuolo, what constitutes the categories of the "religiously wrong" or "sin"? It would be religiously wrong for someone to exploit—to use or take unfair advantage of—someone else. It would be a sin to hurt, which apparently means to infringe on the freedom of action of someone else. But since, on her account, she hasn't done either of these things her moral conscience is clear. Perhaps her rabbi, whose sermons she watches rather than hears, never preached on *tzniyut* (modesty). Most likely the Judaism articulated in her temple makes no room for *tzniyut* because, in terms of the prevailing liberal paradigm, it would be a personal lifestyle choice rather than a feature of a Jewish public morality. The very idea of a public morality would appear to violate the liberal respect for the privacy and autonomy of persons. And so two millennia of Jewish law and custom drop from view, as religious rights and wrongs, sins and virtues are reconstituted along the moral lines of a competing, virtually hegemonic liberal culture.

We are now in a better position to get an idea of the American Jewish version of the theological-political predicament. Liberalism, deeply felt although perhaps poorly understood, has moved from the political sphere to the religious one. It has colonized the Jewish religious and moral imagination. The liberalism to which this author refers here is not contemporary liberalism, in the sense of that set of ideas and values to which contemporary conservatism is opposed. Rather, the author refers to the ancestor of both contemporary liberalism and contemporary conservatism in all their variations—that stream of political thought that places individuals and their liberty, equality, and agency at the normative center.[1] There is much to celebrate in the liberal tradition. We are all its beneficiaries and almost no one, Jew or gentile, wishes to live under a nonliberal regime when he has a choice in the matter. Nonetheless, liberalism becomes a predicament or crisis for American Jews when its premises and cultural effects subvert or imperil the continued existence of the Jews themselves. Were the views of those Jews who believe that Jewish endogamy is racist or that Judaism is an afterthought of the principle of noninterference to become truly dominant, then it would be difficult to see what future American Jewry could have, or deserve.

The task then is to reconfigure the relationship between the liberal tradition and the Jewish tradition such that their respective spheres of influence achieve a proper relationship. In the past, this relationship has often been styled as one of universalism versus particularism. This author believes that this is profoundly misleading. As if we were not already sufficiently aware of it, the events of September 11 remind us that the liberal tradition is also a particularism. Other streams of civilization, such as Islam, do not share its anthropological, political, and normative assumptions. Both liberalism and Judaism are particularisms with universal aspirations. As particularisms, they ought to be able to find a mutually enriching co-existence. It is only when the universal intention of liberalism seeks to overwhelm Jewish particularism that trouble—both for the Jews and for liberalism itself—ensues. Or, alternately, trouble ensues when Jews equate the universal intention of liberalism with the universal intention of Judaism.

In the following, I will attempt to analyze how that co-existence has gone awry and how it might be made to work. My assumption is that the theological-political nexus of Judaism and liberalism cannot be severed, nor should it be. We must work from within the connection. Given the theological-political predicament, Jews are dependent upon liberalism. This author argues that they must resist that upon which they depend and that liberalism will become more capacious and less monistic—to use Jean Bethke Elshtain's terms—through the force of their resistance.[2] In resisting monistic liberalism, Jews can draw on the resources of their own political tradition and perhaps enrich the liberal tradition in the process.

The liberal tradition is about liberty. There were, as Quentin Skinner points out, traditions of liberty before liberalism.[3] Liberty before liberalism was grounded in Roman republican thought and appropriated by Renaissance neo-Roman thinkers such as Machiavelli. Such British thinkers as Milton, Harrington, and Sidney were advocates of liberty without being in the precise sense liberals. A tradition of liberty is also found in the Jewish political tradition.

The Israelites are liberated from Egypt to serve God and to govern themselves or, at least immediately, to be governed by Him through His prophet. In both traditions of liberty, the emphasis is positive: self-rule and shared forms of life orient persons toward a common good. In the liberal tradition as such, liberty extends to individuals who are perfectly free to separate themselves from shared forms of life, public ideas of the good, and thick bonds of solidarity and sentiment. The idea of negative liberty, always in some state of tension with earlier republican currents of positive liberty, infiltrates the liberal tradition.[4]

Although Judaism seems plighted to a positive conception of liberty such that it could be on a collision course with liberalism, there is nothing in the liberal tradition that is necessarily subversive of Judaism. The liberal tradition, at least in the United States, mitigates its own emphasis on individual autonomy by constitutional protections of freedom of association. That is, liberalism understands that human sociality is not incidental to human individuality. Humans are radically social. The Constitution takes the freedom to associate with one another, and by implication, with one's kind as a natural right. Nonetheless, the agents who are free to associate with one another are individuals. The Constitution does not take notice of primordial groups, of collectivities as the building blocks of political society. If there are such collectivities, they are, in the Constitution's universe, the states. But the states are also unions of individuals. Nor does the Constitution have regard for the civil society institutions such as schools, families, and churches that generate the virtues which a democratic citizenry requires. The Constitution does not consider those forms of spiritual cement that weld individuals into a democratic political community. Thus, despite a generous space that American liberalism gives to religious and other primordial communities there is an underlying bias built in to the system in favor of the individual—the free, reasonable moral agent over the encumbered and implicated member of a primordial group.

The liberal ontology, which places individuals at the center, animates one of the canonical texts of the liberal tradition, Locke's *Letter Concerning Toleration*. In this text, we can find that bias in favor of the individual, which eventually creates a problem for groups like the Jews. In the *Letter* Locke finds a parallel between the church and the state. The church, he writes, is a "free and voluntary association of individuals."[5] Constituting a church is directly parallel to constituting a political community: it is an act of free and consenting adults. Both kinds of community are governed by a purposive rationality (*Zweckrationalität*, as Weber calls it). The aim of the political community is civil peace; the aim of the religious community is the public worship of God for the end of the salvation of the individual soul. Individuals are free to judge whether the religious community suits their spiritual needs or not. If they remain within it, they are subject to its laws and discipline, although these have no positive or negative relevance to their civil status as citizens. The religious community is as easily entered as left. The free, rational person judges whether the community's reasonableness is compatible with his own.

Locke's construction of the religious community requires a sweeping de-emphasis on those bonds of sociality that are more primordial than rational assent alone. He is suspicious of loyalty and friendship; he sees them as potential allies of subservience.[6] The idea that religious community might claim us before we as conscious agents choose it provokes anxiety. Locke's treatment of Islam in the Letter—Muslims are not just men of faith but servants of the Ottoman sultan and therefore sources of sedition within the state—suggests that religious communities which do not fit his secularized Protestant model of gathered community need not be tolerated. The Jews resemble Locke's Muslims more than his Protestant sectaries. Although neither then nor now citizens or subjects of a foreign sovereign, Jews nonetheless participate in an older, more metaphysically encumbering form of theological-political community than Locke would allow for. Participation in the Jewish covenantal polity precedes the entry of individual Jews into civil society and carries its own set of obligations.

As an example of this claim, consider Locke's statement in *An Essay Concerning Human Understanding* (Book II, Chapter XXI, para. 56) regarding one's choice of diet.

All men seek happiness, but not of the same sort. The mind has a different relish, as well as the palate; and you will as fruitlessly endeavour to delight all men with riches or glory (which yet some men place their happiness in) as you would to satisfy all men's hunger with cheese or lobsters; which, though very agreeable and delicious fare to some, are to others extremely nauseous and offensive: and many persons would with reason prefer the griping of an hungry belly to those dishes which are a feast to others.

Locke writes about lobsters as if they were an illustration of the principle of "de gustibus non est disputandum." It is merely a matter of taste in which reason has no share. The observation is part of a larger argument that deprives the classical, primarily Aristotelian, claim that there is a single standard of eudaemonia of its sense. There is no summum bonum, Locke assures us, no way of human flourishing common to us all. There are only particular goods or individual versions of happiness based on idiosyncratic choices. Some find lobsters and cheese tasty while others do not. The idea that God might prohibit us from tasting lobsters in the first place and that this prohibition binds us even before we were born, as it were, would strike him as bizarre. It is a "speculative opinion" about something that is at best "indifferent." Jewish worship is, as he elsewhere puts it, "false" and "abominable."[7]

Of less concern than Locke's anti-Judaism is his construction of religious community as a purely consensual association of like-minded individuals. Since early modernity, Jews have attempted the transformation of the Jewish polity, with its covenantal dimensions of reciprocity, obligation and law, into a Lockean-liberal church. Beginning with Moses Mendelssohn, they have subtly replaced the language of covenant with its secular descendant, social contract, effacing although never quite obliterating the older political resonances of Jewish national solidarity. At the dawn of the liberal order, the choice was between remaining within an integral *kehillah* (Jewish community)—the misnamed "state within a state"—or assuming the rights and duties of citizenship in a state that was supposed to transcend religious and ethnic particularities. That project is now complete, at least in the United States. Jews reconstituted their diaspora polity as a voluntary community, a free association of citizens of Jewish affiliation, with remarkable success. To the extent that pervasive anti-Semitism encompassed the liberal creation of a voluntaristic community, a certain continuity with older lines of group consciousness endured. With the welcome decline of anti-Semitism, however, the voluntarist project of diaspora Jewry is left on its own to compete with other forms of private association in which persons may find satisfaction. It is not that Jewish life is a poor competitor—far from it. It is that Jewish life must continuously redefine itself in terms adopted from liberalism in order to appear intelligible and appealing to the denizens of a liberal order. The appearance of paid advertisements on the Op-Ed page of the *New York Times* in which prominent figures gave personal answers to the question "Why be Jewish?" is a sign of the times.

As Steven Cohen and Arnold Eisen have essayed in their recent book, *The Jew Within*, the emphasis on voluntarism, individual choice, personal as opposed to public standards of meaning has eroded loyalty to communal institutions, indeed, to Israel, the most powerful symbolic locus of Jewish national solidarity.[8] Contemporary Jews are increasingly drawn to an inward-looking, self-oriented search for meaning rather than to communal engagement and Jewish civic participation. The focus of their study is the private spiritual journey of what the authors call the "sovereign self." The sovereign self is not animated by duties to other humans or to God, or by the aspiration to achieve what T. H. Green called the "best self." It is merely an expressive self, in love with its own depths and fascinated by its own protean contours. The project of making this self is an end in itself. It signifies the ultimacy of freedom or, more precisely, the inability or unwillingness to posit a goal beyond freedom. Freedom is not to be ordered by higher goods. Rather, freedom, in the sense of the negative freedom to act without coercion, has become the highest good.

The Jewish tradition, as mentioned above, is no stranger to the value of freedom. Nonetheless, in the Jewish tradition there is a strong bias toward freedom as a positive and instrumental value. Freedom facilitates the pursuit of collective and individual holiness. Freedom allows for self-rule, for the project of creating a just and holy commonwealth. These ideas are resisted and—for the sake of civil peace in a pluralistic society—properly so by liberalism. Liberalism in its origins overcame both an aristocratic and a republican tradition that saw politics as a means to the achievement of public virtue. In the American version of liberal origins, the Puritan covenantal tradition was overcome in favor of an Enlightenment social contractarianism. American Jews, despite the bias of the Jewish political tradition in favor of positive liberty, came to share in the liberal disregard for aims allegedly higher than negative liberty. The bulk of their political engagement, advocacy for Israel excepted, has been devoted to projects of negative liberty, such as fighting discrimination and clearing the public square of the last vestiges of the Puritan covenantal tradition. American Jews have been piously devoted to what Richard John Neuhaus famously called the "naked public square." By working to strip public discourse and civic life of older, republican, and religious expressions of solidarity, Jews helped to advance a version of liberalism that valorizes individual autonomy, rights, and freedom of choice over community, obligation, and prudence. Nonetheless, were it not for older countervailing forms of group solidarity, such as tzedakah (charity, an inadequate but serviceable translation), Jewish communities would not, most likely, have endured under the centrifugal forces of liberalism.

Tzedakah is a project of positive liberty. It presupposes that individuals are encumbered rather than self-possessed; that they have duties to a collectivity that significantly impinge on their freedom of choice and their discretion over their possessions. The continued Jewish embrace of *tzedakah* is an example of how Jews resist assimilation to a purely liberal pattern of life without being aware of it.

The transformations that have given us Cohen and Eisen's impoverished "sovereign self" need not be seen as the simple outcome of a clash of cultures, of liberalism versus Judaism. On the contrary, they track a movement within liberalism itself, on which Judaism, caught in a theological-political predicament, depends. The transformation within liberalism has to do with the loss of liberalism's republican heritage, with an undue emphasis on individual rights and negative liberty, with a decline of civic participation and social trust, as well as overreliance on government and the courts to solve social problems. It also has to do with the increasing secularization of American society and the privatization of religion, processes which the Jewish community has done much to advance. These factors have had a leveling effect, which has diminished the moral authority of the liberal tradition and the Jewish tradition as well. The way back from this mutual diminution requires moral and spiritual renewal. It requires a new appreciation for the sources of moral and spiritual renewal, those local communities, especially religious ones, and the virtuous selves that they nurture. It requires a new appreciation of how the moral formation of citizens occurs in communities and in families, as well as for those thick traditions of moral life without which moral formation cannot occur.

For Jews this renewal will require a retrieval of older and more complex moral constitutions of selfhood and community than contemporary liberal doctrines of rights, agency, and voluntarism allow for. Such concepts as covenantal liberty (as opposed to liberal natural liberty) and divine ownership of our persons (as opposed to liberal autonomy) will have to get a contemporary, morally cogent articulation. Politically, Jews need to resist the leveling influence of liberal political culture by advocating those policies that strengthen communities and reverse the privatization of religion. This will cut against the grain of previous Jewish public policy advocacy.

Let us focus for the moment on a constitutional issue in which the Jewish community has been heavily invested: religious liberty and the separation of church and state. Michael Sandel calls our attention to the modern misreading of the religion clauses of the Constitution. On Sandel's account, the Founders based the right to religious liberty on the freedom of conscience while the moderns have transformed this into a freedom of choice. By "freedom of conscience" Sandel means the duty to worship God in a manner free from external coercion. In both Locke and Madison and Jefferson, religious liberty is necessary because conscience imposes duties on us that are prior to the claims of civil society. "Religious liberty," Sandel writes, "addressed the problem of encumbered selves, claimed by duties they cannot renounce, even in the face of civil obligations that may conflict."[9] To the greatest extent possible, a decent and liberal politics requires that persons not be forced to violate their deepest, most constitutive convictions. For many, the conviction of faith is not chosen or willed: it is given by grace or, in the normal Jewish case, given by birth. Religious liberty is the acknowledgment that duties to God must be accommodated. It grows, as in Locke's "Letter" or Madison's "Memorial and Remonstrance," out of a consciousness still stirred by religion in which the advocate of toleration or of liberty understands that our duties to God are radical, real, and unique. The self is not sovereign; it is "encumbered." It does not fully possess itself. It is possessed by God, to whom it must give fealty.

By contrast, the modern, fully secularized approach to religious liberty treats it as a sign of respect for a species of personal choice. What religious liberty accommodates on the modern, voluntarist account is not duty but autonomy. What it preserves is not freedom of conscience, which can be the most demanding master, but freedom of choice, which seldom aspires to moral austerity. In Sandel's view, the transformation in our understanding of religious liberty is ultimately subversive of religious liberty. It is one thing for the state to have to accommodate the patterned duties of historic religious communities and their adherents. (The law, for example, eventually made room for conscientious objector status in order to accommodate Mennonites and other traditional pacifists.) It is another thing for the state to have to respect individual choices. On the former account, the state allows for religious exemptions precisely because they are religious. The state recognizes the importance of religious communities and their adherents for civil society. On the latter account, the state presumes a neutral stance between religion and non-religion. It forbears from recognizing religion as a public good. It aspires to a neutrality that respects persons irrespective of the content of their choices and beliefs. As such, it recasts the demands of religious conscience into mere personal choice. Since one person's choice is not necessarily more worthy of accommodation than another's, religion becomes just another lifestyle option, with no more compelling claim on the state for accommodation than trout fishing.

When the state of Connecticut sought to accommodate the religious beliefs of sabbatarians by allowing them, alone among all employees, to choose their day off, the Supreme Court overruled the statute on the grounds that Sabbath observers should not be given choices that others do not have. The law allowing Sabbath observers to choose Saturday as their day off unfairly discriminated against others who were not given the right to choose. So too, Captain Simcha Goldman was not allowed to wear distinctive headgear if all others lacked a similar right. Nor were Native Americans allowed to use peyote in defiance of otherwise valid drug laws. In every case, what was formerly thought a duty of conscience properly protected by the Free Exercise clause became a personal choice that can neither confer "special rights" on a few nor trump generally applicable law. The reduction of conscience to choice, of religious liberty to a species of freedom of expression erodes our cultural understanding of what religious liberty is for and imperils our support for it over the long term. The welcome reversal by the Court of some of these trends in 2001, in *Good News Club v. Milford School District*, was decided more on free speech than free exercise grounds. Free exercise since *Smith* is an endangered right; free speech has more plausibility in contemporary jurisprudence. Indeed it has more of a "plausibility structure" beneath it than free exercise. The scanting and deformation of free exercise, abetted by a five-decade-long emphasis on unrealistically stringent establishment standards, serves neither the aims of liberalism nor of American Jews. The very existence of the Free Exercise clause and of the singular and distinctive position that religious liberty occupies in the Constitution should signal to us that religion does play a crucial role in civil society; that it must not be reduced to a lifestyle option or to the mere choice of private persons.

Senator Joseph Lieberman, during the election campaign of 2000, called attention to this fact, quite controversially in the eyes of many Jewish leaders, when he said that the Constitution gives us freedom for religion rather than freedom from religion. Lieberman was, in his own way, resisting political theorist Jean Bethke Elshtain's liberal monism. By liberal monism, she refers to a drive within liberal societies to bring discrepant standards of authority, reason, and moral language under a single norm. A monistic approach to authority, for example, would force the Catholic Church, perhaps through legal challenges, to accept women as priests. It would force an Orthodox institution, such as a college of Yeshiva University, to accommodate gay partners as a married couple. A monistic approach to reason reads religious moral reasoning out of the public conversation as a defective, regressive, or merely idiosyncratic expression. A monistic approach to moral language reduces all normative discourse to what Mary Ann Glendon calls rights talk, to claims and counterclaims of rights unmitigated by such frameworks as duty or aspiration. Monistic liberalism, on Elshtain's account, receives powerful support from the intellectuals and the media. It is also the preference of American Jews. It is this preference that Jews must learn to discern and resist.

Taking a cue from Sandel, American Jews need to recover the original liberal concept of the duties of conscience, which is not far removed from the Jewish concept of *mitzvot bein adam l'makom* (commandments between man and God). It is out of respect for the duties that man has toward God that the liberal, constitutional state first circumscribed its own power. To take such duties seriously, as duties that claim us rather than as choices that we elect, reveals our embeddedness in an order that is metaphysically prior to the liberal order in which we dwell. It qualifies and relativizes our belonging to the polity. Alternately, it makes us morally serious and responsible persons who can serve the liberal polity with our learned habits of both loyalty and criticism. To retrieve a doctrine of the duties of conscience or of the *mitzvot bein adam l'makom* will help rescue contemporary Judaism from the platitudes of liberalism on the one side and the temptations of otherworldly or Gnostic spiritualism on the other. It would rescue Judaism from becoming a distinction without a difference. Here is a current example of how to assert a distinction, based on conscience, and resist monistic liberalism at the same time.

The Orthodox Jewish community of Tenafly, New Jersey was ordered by the municipality and, on August 9, 2001, the U.S. District court, to remove an *eruv* (a symbolic boundary transforming a public space into a private one where carrying on the Sabbath is permissible) that it had erected with the help of Verizon and a local cable company.[10] Needless to say, some of the members of the borough council were Jewish. They took the liberal monist view that for the state to endorse the *eruv* would be an impermissible violation of the Establishment clause. (Given the current state of Establishment clause jurisprudence, this may not be far-fetched.) Whether this constitutional quibble is a fig leaf for a darker bias against Orthodox

Jews is unclear. At any rate, the Jewish members of the borough council who are Reform Jews were quite surprised when the Commission on Social Action of Reform Judaism filed a brief on the side of the *eruv* proponents, who have now brought the case to an appeals court. No one was surprised that the Orthodox Union or the Agudah filed amicus briefs but Reform's deviation from strict separationist dogmatism took the Jewish politicians off guard. This seems to me a salutary case of a religious movement almost wholly identified with contemporary liberalism stepping back from redundancy. In advocating a position that honors religious liberty and affirms that Shabbat observance, which is enhanced by an *eruv*, is a duty of Jewish conscience, the Reform movement resisted monistic liberalism.[11]

The Jewish self, possessed by the *mitzvot* of Shabbat, is surely more complex and possibly more conflicted than the autonomous, expressive self of contemporary liberalism. It is precisely such a self that liberalism needs if it is to become, in Elshtain's words, more capacious. Liberalism needs communities where such morally complex selves are formed. These are the so-called "seedbeds of virtue" where the habits of the heart, the habits of loyalty, respect for legitimate social authority, perseverance, altruism, and independence are cultivated. Liberalism, as William Galston reminds us, needs its own virtues. A healthy liberal society cultivates virtues in its citizens. American Jews need to ask themselves whether the laws and policies they advocate cultivate the virtues and strengthen the communities that nurture them. The Jewish community's recent performance during the debate on faith-based initiatives is not encouraging in this regard.

The Jewish community first tacked in the strict separationist direction: public funding to social services delivered by houses of worship would violate the Establishment clause. Insofar as there already were four years of experimentation under prior law, however, the community began to back away from this strategy last winter. (The endorsement by both Gore and Lieberman of some version of charitable choice also complicated the mainstream Jewish approach to the problem.) The next stratagem stressed the potential for discrimination against religious, ethnic, or sexual minorities. The Title VII exemption permitting religious bodies to hire only their own members, if extended under charitable choice, would amount to state-sponsored discrimination. The prospect of religious ministries refusing to hire persons of other faiths or disapproved sexual orientation was thought to trump all other considerations. Additionally, the fear that Jewish agencies might face increased competition for funds also played a role. In sum, Jewish groups, with the exception of the Orthodox, opposed charitable choice out of a mix of high principle and interest politics.

Throughout the long and at this point quite transformed debate, a clarifying moment for me occurred one evening on a news program where the anchor was interviewing David Saperstein and a black minister, who was—like many blacks—an advocate for charitable choice. At one point in their debate, the interviewer interrupted and observed that there was a striking asymmetry in their positions. The minister was talking about urgent and debilitating human need and what could be done to alleviate it while the rabbi was talking about abstract constitutional principles. Even she felt a jarring disjunction between the worlds that the two sides represented.

This disjunction is emblematic of how the Jewish community often treats such matters. It is so wedded to the liberal monist imperative of keeping religion private that it is unwilling to experiment with promising new possibilities for alleviating the misery of our most neglected citizens. While I would never fault the Jewish community for its philanthropy, its covenantal habits of *tzedakah*, or for its publicmindedness, it is wrong on charitable choice and on a kindred idea, tuition vouchers. In both of these cases, community-serving ministries and community-enhancing schools might well be strengthened by an infusion of public funds. The long-term interest of the Jewish community as well as that of American liberalism lies in strengthening the institutions of civil society, both general and Jewish. Jews should seek alternatives to state monopolies; they should be on the side of local control and participatory democracy. There were, of course, good reasons for turning to the state and the courts, particularly in the 1960s. But do we not face a different set of problems today?

The way out of the theological-political predicament of American Jews lies in a double movement of retrieval. Not only Jews but all Americans must retrieve a fuller range of liberal possibilities than contemporary, anemic liberalism provides. For their part, Jews must also retrieve older ideas of Jewish selfhood, virtue, and polity; of the liberty that Judaism celebrated long before liberalism.

Notes

1. David Johnston, *The Idea of a Liberal Theory* (Princeton, N.J.: Princeton University Press, 1994), 17.

2. Jean Bethke Elshtain, "The Liberal Social Contract and the Privatization of Religion," in this volume.

3. Quentin Skinner, *Liberty before Liberalism* (Cambridge: Cambridge University Press, 1998), ch. 1, passim.

4. Isaiah Berlin, *Four Essays on Liberty* (New York: Oxford University Press, 1969), ch. 3. For the best recent exposition of this often caricatured concept, see John Gray, *Isaiah Berlin* (Princeton, N.J.: Princeton University Press, 1996), ch. 1.

5. John Locke, "A Letter Concerning Toleration," in *Treatise of Civil Government* (New York: Appleton-Century-Crofts, 1939), 175.

6. Douglas Kries, *Piety and Humanity* (Lanham, Md.: Rowman & Littlefield, 1997).

7. Locke, "Letter Concerning Toleration," 218.

8. Steven M. Cohen and Arnold Eisen, *The Jew Within* (Bloomington: Indiana University Press, 2001).

9. Michael Sandel, *Democracy's Discontent: America in Search of a Public Philosophy* (Cambridge, Mass.: Harvard University Press, 1996), 66.

10. *Forward*, November 16, 2001.

11. In late 2002, the Third Circuit Court issued an injunction barring Tenafly from removing the *eruv*. As of this writing, the constitutionality of the *eruv* has been upheld.

4

The Probable Persistence of American Jewish Liberalism

Kenneth D. Wald

At a *havurah* meeting some years ago, a rabbi recounted how he explained the Jewish position on abortion to an anxious congregant. Confronted with a request to tell his congregant "what Jews believe" about abortion, the rabbi tried hard to provide an answer that captured the subtlety and ambiguity of Jewish thinking on this perplexing topic. Eventually, the congregant lost patience with fine-grained Talmudic exegesis and pressed the rabbi to cut to the chase. Determined to stick to his guns, the rabbi proceeded to a carefully worded and nuanced conclusion. Judaism does not endow the fetus with full humanity prior to birth, the rabbi announced, but rather gives precedence to the mother and thus considers abortion morally permissible under certain circumstances. At this point, the rabbi said, the congregant breathed an audible sigh of relief, saying how happy he was to learn that Judaism supported his pro-choice position on abortion.

I have deployed this anecdote for two reasons. First, the story underscores a central claim of the chapter: the manner in which Jews engage the American public square has relatively little to do with Jewish religious beliefs per se. Accordingly, attempts to reorient that behavior via reinterpretations of the tradition are unlikely to produce much change in how Jews confront public life. Second, the anecdote illustrates the danger of approaching any religious tradition with an eye toward extracting clear political lessons on contemporary issues. Ransacking a religious tradition for post-hoc justification of a political position is known in theological circles as "proof-texting" and is properly derided. It is one thing to ask with an open mind if one's faith contains helpful perspectives on a contentious political subject, quite another to shake that faith until it yields support for a position that was reached on essentially secular grounds. Yet that is an ever-present danger when believers seek to extract political lessons from religious texts.[1]

This inquiry is apposite because a growing chorus of voices within the Jewish community contends that American Jews need to reorient their thinking about religion in the public square. When Senator Joseph Lieberman proclaimed his belief in the need for a religious voice in the public realm during the 2000 campaign, some Jews who had been thrilled by Lieberman's nomination for vice president were alarmed and confused. Lieberman appeared to suggest that Jews abandon their traditional resistance to religious definitions of the American state, and to welcome both theological discourse about public issues and state subsidies for religious institutions that provide public services within a distinctively religious context. The reflexive Jewish embrace of a "high wall of separation" between church and state has been labeled anachronistic if not counterproductive. While I remain unpersuaded of the need for Jews to revise their core beliefs, the fundamental concern of this chapter is the likelihood of such a development and the sheer difficulty of bringing Jewish religious values into contemporary political debate in a meaningful way.

This chapter begins with a review of the political behavior of contemporary Jewry in the United States, compressing a half century of research into a concise accounting. "Political behavior" means the focus is primarily on the attitudes and actions of rank-and-file members of the Jewish community rather than the positions of communal leaders and elites. Then I will suggest why the source of Jewish political behavior is to be found less in the "creedal" aspect of Judaism and more in the institutional and cultural aspects of the Jewish experience. Though true to some degree of most religions, there is reason to believe that the barriers to a religiously based political ethic are particularly severe in the case of Judaism.

American Jews: A Brief Political Portrait

After more than half a century of careful empirical research with sophisticated quantitative tools, scholars continue to grapple with a central puzzle about the political behavior of American Jewry. Milton Himmelfarb posed the underlying question in a stark if politically incorrect form: Why do Jews earn like Episcopalians but vote like Puerto Ricans?[2] As the question implies, the persistence of Jewish liberalism flies in the face of conventional wisdom about the economic origins of political sympathies. Scholars have no difficulty explaining the Democratic tilt among Hispanics and African Americans, groups that benefit directly from the social programs and tax policies of that party. Because they enjoy much higher levels of income and status, the same calculus of self-interest does not account for persistent Jewish support of the Democratic Party and its agenda.

The evidence for the persistence of Jewish political liberalism emerges from a diverse group of studies—ecological analyses of election results, intensive analysis of Jewish respondents in surveys of the general population, special polls of American Jewry, and elite samples with a substantial Jewish representation. These diverse sources converge in their portrait of a population that is both economically affluent and anchored to the left side of the political continuum in the United States.[3] Of course, because this conclusion speaks of central tendencies, it leaves plenty of room for individual exceptions. Yet even allowing for the inevitable diversity that characterizes any large group of individuals, what statisticians call "variance," the pattern is fairly stark.[4]

Voting in presidential elections offers one useful benchmark of core political loyalties. In the period since the 1960 election, when reliable public opinion data first became available, Jewish voters have generally voted 15 to 25 percent more Democratic than the electorate as a whole. According to exit polls from the 2000 election, Jews voted almost four to one in favor of Al Gore while the rest of the electorate was split almost exactly down the middle. In congressional elections, the partisan skew among Jews has often been even larger than in presidential contests. This pattern seems to have been set early in the New Deal, when Jews flocked to the Democratic banner in solidarity with Franklin D. Roosevelt, and it has persisted for all but a few elections until the present day.[5]

The sheer magnitude of Jewish Democratic support becomes even more striking in comparison with other groups. Looking at congressional elections since 1990, Greenberg and Wald found a very even partisan division of the vote among the white middle-class citizens who resemble Jews in socioeconomic status.[6] By contrast, Jews voted roughly three to one in favor of Democratic candidates during the same period. Jews even stand out from the other stalwarts in the Democratic coalition by their loyalty and participation. Among groups with the highest aggregate levels of Democratic attachment, Jews report roughly the same levels of Democratic self-identification as African Americans. As politicians understand well, not all partisans show up on election day or vote consistently with their self-described political identity. Because of their high turnout and sustained loyalty, Leege, et al., found that Jews—despite their smaller numbers—frequently matched or exceeded African Americans in their net contribution to Democratic electoral support.[7]

If the depth of Jewish affinity for the Democratic Party is impressive, the breadth of that commitment is equally arresting. Many religious groups are politically divided by internal cleavages. Among Catholics and Protestants, for example, scholars have reported substantial partisan variation associated with age, education, income, residence, gender, and religious commitment. These patterns, while present to some degree in the Jewish community, are much less salient. Consider generational and gender differences in partisanship. Like young people in other religious traditions, young Jews are less Democratically inclined than their elders. By the same token, scholars have reported a Jewish gender gap with women more Democratically inclined than men. But in both cases, younger Jews and Jewish men do not actually cross party lines. Rather, they are more likely to declare themselves Independent than to embrace the Republican label. Moreover, in the voting booth, they often behave in a manner that is barely distinguishable from their older or female coreligionists. So, unlike the pattern for Roman Catholics, the underlying age and gender differences in party attachment among Jews do not translate into much greater Jewish support for the Republican Party.

This highly partisan behavior rests on a Jewish commitment to liberalism or what is more commonly described as a progressive political ethic. Compared to non-Jews in general or gentiles with high levels of education, Jews are more likely to pick the "liberal" label and appreciably less likely to identify themselves as conservatives. On specific issues, Jews do not invariably select the preference that is associated with the liberal political orientation. This has led some observers to note that while Jews may be irredeemably Democratic, they are not inevitably liberal. Steven M. Cohen and Charles Lieb-man have taken this claim one step further, contending that Jewish liberalism is limited to a relatively small set of issues.[8] However, unlike Europe, where terms like "left wing" and "right wing" refer to a specific set of preferences on public issues, the equivalent labels in the United States tend to suggest an affinity with some groups and distaste for others rather than a syndrome of positions that cover the entire political agenda.[9] That is, liberals and conservatives in the United States are polarized more consistently by the groups they favor and oppose than by stands on all the issues that dominate the political agenda. For many Americans, picking a side in a political debate is largely a matter of identifying the groups engaged in conflict and then rooting for the side championed by one's friends.[10] On this dimension, American Jews are distinctive in their sense of closeness to groups such as feminists, racial minorities, and environmentalists and causes such as reproductive freedom and civil rights. Compared to other Americans, Jews are notably cooler to religious conservatives, gun owners, the pro-life movement, and other political objects associated with conservatism. By the measure that defines liberalism and conservatism as understood in the United States, Jews are central components of the liberal alliance.

Apart from this general disposition, the Jewish political ethos does manifest itself on a large number of specific issues. First, Jews are generally more sympathetic than non-Jews to an activist role for government. In practice, they tend to support high levels of government spending on social services and aggressive state efforts to root out discrimination. Measured by a wide range of indicators—political attitudes, voting, participation—Jews have remained distinctive among whites in their commitment to the traditional goals of the civil rights movement.[11] Jews have thus aligned on the Democratic side of the issues that largely defined American political life from the New Deal through the Great Society.

Second, on many of the "social" issues that defined partisan conflict from the 1960s through the 1980s, Jews also exhibited a distinctive profile. Compared to non-Jews, Jewish respondents were much more sympathetic to the goals of groups such as women, gays, and the pro-choice movement. In terms of tangible issues, Jews were notably on the side of liberal abortion laws, gay rights provisions, expanding opportunities for women, strong civil liberties protection for unpopular groups and views, and other such positions.

Finally and perhaps least surprisingly, Jews remain stalwart advocates of the legal doctrine known as separationism and resolute opponents of its opposite number, accommodationism.[12] This set of attitudes, more commonly known as church-state separation, refers principally to debate over the first of the two religion clauses in the First Amendment to the U.S. Constitution.[13] Whether compared to the rest of the population or just to their socioeconomic equivalents, Jews stand out by their resistance to any state action that appears to encourage or endorse religion. When it comes to school prayer, moments of silence, religious devotions at athletic events, graduation prayers, or other such initiatives, Jews have long led the effort to prohibit such acts as unconstitutional "establishment" of religion. The more recent debate over school vouchers has yielded a similar pattern among Jewish elites but with less clear tendencies among the rank and file. Apart from this one exception, Jews tend to be on the forefront of efforts to maintain a high wall of separation between church and state.

The positions that distinguish Jews from other Americans are not manifested on isolated clusters of issues. There is an inner logic that connects these issues. Jews cohere around a set of issue positions that mark them off as a small minority group that sympathizes with the plight of other minorities. The support for civil rights is one obvious example. Jews see themselves as past and potentially future victims of irrational discrimination who require the patronage of the state as legal protection from prejudice. But the same attitude appears to underpin the Jewish support for civil liberties and for progressive orientations on social issues. In these cases, Jews side with minorities that seek state support as they face the brunt of majoritarian hostility. Unpopular minorities—whether defined by race, extreme political views, or "deviant" sexual orientation—are the major beneficiaries of state protection from oppression and legally enforced disadvantage. Commitment to activist government can be understood in the same terms. In the eyes of many Jews, government is the engine of social progress and the guarantor of fundamental freedoms.

The separationist ethic of American Jewry must be understood as a central element of this political syndrome or what William Galston recently described as "the grain of sand in the oyster of politics around which the pearl of liberalism gradually formed."[14] Indeed, there is some evidence that commitment to a "high wall of separation" may be the underlying factor that promotes Jewish liberalism in other domains.[15] Religious minorities are likely to resist state efforts that appear to give official sanction to corporate religion and that seem likely to restrict the religious freedom of individuals. In practice, Jews thus call on the courts to minimize public, state-sanctioned displays of religion under the establishment clause but they read the free exercise clause broadly, as protecting all manner of individual religious expression from state sanction. The apparent contradiction dissolves when we recognize that both positions are natural for religious minorities. When laws give official recognition to religion, it is likely to be the religion of the majority. Similarly, as a long history of free exercise jurisprudence makes clear, the state is most likely to burden the religious freedom of religious minorities rather than dominant or mainstream traditions. On this issue, like the others that distinguish Jews from their fellow Americans, Jews take their political cue from their precarious status as a very small minority. Hence, in characterizing of Jews as liberal or as carriers of a liberal political ethic, I use the term expansively to include separationism as a core component.

From time to time, political activists have asserted that the Jewish political syndrome described above is destined to disappear. Indeed, anticipating the end of Jewish political distinctiveness has almost become a cottage industry. Such reports are fueled by surges in Jewish support for this or that Republican candidate or movement or some apparent attitude shift in the Jewish community at large. Of late, reports from this perspective have highlighted Jewish support for Republican mayoral candidates such as Richard Riordan of Los Angeles or New York's Rudy Giuliani, extrapolating from these races to an imminent realignment of the Jewish vote in presidential elections.[16] On closer inspection, however, these transformations often prove ephemeral as analysts confuse a temporary attraction or antipathy to a particular candidate based on very specific causes with a deep-seated change in political allegiance.[17] More commonly, as in the case of the Riordan candidacy in Los Angeles, the analyst fails to compare Jews with relevant control groups. When employed properly in multivariate models, the data sustain the traditional view of Jewish political distinctiveness. Despite these sometimes breathless declarations, there is precious little evidence that Jews are poised for a major political realignment in the foreseeable future.

Due to constraints of time and space, I have painted the case for Jewish political liberalism with a broad brush, omitting some nuances and shadings that a fuller discussion would allow. For example, differences between Jews and other respondents may be attributable to economic and educational differences rather than to any inherent qualities of Judaism itself. Jews are disproportionately represented in what sociologists call the "New Class," highly educated

and affluent professionals who specialize in the creation and ma-
nipulation of symbols. Jewish politics may seem exceptional only
because Jews share the political sentiments of this particular stra-
tum, which are strikingly different from the views of the general
population on certain issues.[18] Indeed, when Jews are compared with
non-Jews who possess comparable social profiles, the attitude differences often narrow. As recent research has suggested, however,
the differences do not disappear and frequently retain statistical significance.

By characterizing Jews as part of the Democratic and progressive
coalition in American public life, it is not meant to overlook a pal-
pable conservative and Republican presence in the Jewish community. The survey data, Jewish political elites, and the universe of
Jewish organizations all include vigorous representatives of right-
wing perspectives. Indeed, the very conference that originally commissioned this paper would have been unlikely had it not been for
the efforts of Jewish neoconservatives to raise alarm about the implications for Jews of Father Neuhaus's "naked public square."[19]
While individual Jews may have moved into the Republican coalition, sometimes attaining positions of considerable influence, they
have not heralded a mass movement among their coreligionists.
What Irving Kristol recently and somewhat petulantly called "The
Political Stupidity of the Jews"—meaning their stubborn adherence
to liberal values and the Democratic Party—continues unabated.[20]

As a final qualification, it is important to remember that Jews are
not altogether immune to the same considerations that prompt other
Americans to take stands on various political issues. The dominant
models of political behavior in the social sciences assign a major
role to the individual's perception of his or her self-interest. On occasion, self-interest blunts the general thrust of Jewish liberalism.
For example, Jewish enthusiasm for Democratic candidates wanes
when the party's nominee is held responsible for mishandling the
economy or taking the wrong position on a salient issue such as Israel, race relations, or church and state.[21] A recent survey illustrated
the power of self-interest on the question of publicly funded vouchers for attendance at private schools.[22] Consistent with their separationist tendencies, Jews were generally cool to vouchers. However,
closer inspection revealed that Jewish attitudes on the subject bore
the strong imprint of age. Vouchers commanded (bare) majority
support among people in the 18-44 age range but decreasing levels
of support across older cohorts. The most plausible explanation for
this pattern, that it reflects an opportunity for parents of young chil-

dren to reduce the financial cost of educating their children privately, falls squarely within the self-interest model.

The Sources of Jewish Political Orientations

If we are to judge the prospects for the development of a new political ethic among Jews, one with a somewhat different understanding of the role of religion in society, it is essential to understand the process by which members of a religious group attain a degree of political cohesion. As we shall see, the sources of political cohesion are not likely to be found in the content of the religious tradition but rather in the social situation that confronts adherents of the tradition.

In understanding the political distinctiveness of any religious group, scholars generally invoke one of the three human "faces" presented by the social phenomenon of religion.[23] The first component, creed, refers to the belief system of the religious group. Creeds are typically enshrined in sacred writings, interpreted by a priesthood or caste-like elite with charismatic authority (in the Weberian sense), and acted out through rituals and ceremonies. Creeds may speak to politics explicitly or may provide broad guidelines that are studied for political guidance. By community, the second aspect of religion with political relevance, scholars emphasize the social reality of religious collectivities. The social traits and situation shared by members of a religious group—their size, geographical distribution, economic resources, educational attainments, racial and ethnic identity, subjective social status—may play an important role in sensitizing individuals to certain political positions.[24] Finally, political scientists have given particular attention to the organizational component of religion. Religious groups, made tangible in the form of congregations and denominations, develop formal organizations that may attain extraordinary breadth and articulation. Like other institutions, these organizations develop interests that may be pursued and defended through political action.

Although these three components can be isolated for analytic purposes, they often cohere in ways that reinforce a common political orientation. Consider the overwhelming support for Israel in the American Jewish community. This support draws on creedal, communal, and institutional factors. From a creedal viewpoint, Israel represents the embodiment of a longing for a return to Zion, the ancient homeland. Among religious Jews, settling in Jerusalem is a sacred obligation, a *mitzvah*. For many secular Jews, it may also constitute an opportunity to realize Jewish social values in a concrete way. From a communal perspective, Israel also represents an important focus of Jewish identity and self-esteem, an effective counterpoint to the Holocaust for a population that continues to see itself as socially marginal. From a self-interest perspective, the existence of Israel can be justified as a guarantee of Jewish continuity and a safe haven for Jews whose existence is threatened by adverse social conditions and persecution. After all, what could be a stronger interest than self-preservation?

The three components have also been invoked to account for the general pattern of Jewish support for liberal values and the Democratic Party. From a creedal perspective, Jewish liberalism seems to draw on religious tradition, mining the prophetic motif in general and specific *mitzvot*. In the earliest and fullest statement of this approach, Lawrence Fuchs attributed Jewish political orientations to the creedal emphasis on *tzedakah* and respect for learning.[25] Jews embraced the American welfare state, Fuchs argued, because they saw it as a realization of traditional emphases on helping one's neighbor through philanthropy. Given their respect for education, Jews had few philosophical differences with the idea of harnessing state power and expertise to promote the public welfare. Even Jewish openness to a foreign policy that engaged the world was said by Fuchs to be rooted in the internationalist ethos that had long characterized the tradition.

Advocates of the communal interpretation emphasized the Jewish experience of oppression as the major causal source of Jewish political behavior in the United States. Jews carried with them on their migration to America a personal history that associated conservatism with xenophobia and, at the other end of the spectrum, linked liberalism with Jewish emancipation. The association was reinforced by the initial American experience in which Jews were residentially segregated, denied full opportunities for social advancement, and forced to work in industries that denied basic rights. Not surprisingly, they embraced the American Left and reacted to Roosevelt's New Deal almost as manna from heaven. Even as they gradually overcame the barriers to full participation in American society, Jews retained a perspective that regarded liberal values, oppressed minorities, and Democratic politicians as their major allies. As Mark Dolgin demonstrates elsewhere in this volume, that pattern began to weaken in the late 1960s and 1970s as the Democratic and liberal turn to identity politics prompted a Jewish reassessment of political alliances. Yet in the end, the Jewish commitment to progressive politics was sustained by the actions of political elites. Following Watergate, the Republicans attempted to gain majority status by detaching evangelical Protestants from their Democratic moorings, offering policies that Jews saw as dangerously sectarian and likely to diminish the religious neutrality of the state. Democrats gained renewed support among Jews by resisting these policies and by their decision in 2000 to confer the vice presidential nomination upon an observant Jew. At century's end, Jews were voting much as they had in the 1930s.

Because we are so accustomed to claims that Jewish liberalism contradicts Jewish self-interest, it is surprising to learn that some scholars explain that liberalism precisely from a self-interest perspective. In the views of Leonard Fein and Benjamin Ginsberg, Jews embrace liberalism because liberalism has been good for the Jews.[26] The Democratic Party and the welfare state it built were the chief conduits by which many Jews attained high levels of political access and manifold employment opportunities. The early civil rights legislation championed by Democrats and opposed by the bulk of Republicans provided Jews with protection from egregious discrimination and helped dismantle the edifice of quotas, restrictive covenants, and other devices that had handicapped Jews in their competition for success. By helping blacks in their struggle for equality, Ginsberg insisted, Jews were helping themselves. A liberal society, so Fein argued, mutes the intense economic and social strains that elsewhere have proven fertile grounds for the growth of anti-Semitism. Not by coincidence, Jews have enjoyed some of their most productive and safe periods of existence in multinational states like the Habsburg Monarchy and the Ottoman Empire.[27]

If asked to indicate which of these three factors—creed, communal experience, or institutional interest—best accounts for their distinctive political orientation, Jews would no doubt select the first. That conclusion emerges from a series of surveys in which Jews were asked to define the essence of Judaism.[28] To the dismay, no doubt, of rabbis and other educators, Jewish responses in these surveys generally suggested that fidelity to the tradition had less to do with ritual observance or support for Israel and was, instead, largely a matter of supporting worthy social causes. Though rarely stated as such, it seems that many American Jews regard liberalism as applied Judaism. In their support for state funding of social services, antidiscrimination legislation, strong civil liberties policies, and strict church-state separation, Jews often believe that they are actualizing the ethical imperatives embedded in the Jewish tradition.

Despite the intuitive appeal of the creedal approach and its apparent embrace by Jews themselves, scholars have gradually lost faith in the causal role of religious values as sources of mass political behavior. Consider Fuchs's claim that something in Judaism, essentially the prophetic tradition, inclined Jews to adopt political positions that set them apart from other Americans. If, as Fuchs contended, political liberalism was inherent in Jewish religious values, then liberalism should have been strongest among Jews with the greatest attachment to Judaism. But in fact, there was compelling evidence of just the reverse. The most religious Jews, presumably those most attuned to the secular values embedded in Jewish tradition, have been more politically conservative than their coreligionists.[29] The pattern should not be overstated to suggest a massive "devotional divide" among Jews. Nonetheless, scholars have found that Jewish commitment to liberalism and the Democratic Party is either unrelated to or negatively related to Jewish religious involvement. In the face of this finding, it is hard to claim that Judaism per se has a clear liberal ethic. Using Paula Hyman's language, scholars have moved away from "cultural" explanations of Jewish politics in favor of interpretations that stress "situational" factors such as communal experience and self-interest.[30]

Some critics have taken another tack, assailing the very notion that Judaism should be understood to support the progressive political agenda. The neoconservatives who dominated *Commentary* since the 1970s led the way with claims that many features of Judaism, rightly understood, are in fact more compatible with right-wing than left-wing political causes. Focusing on *tzedakah*, for example, they called attention to the Maimonidean concept of levels of charity. The highest form of philanthropy obtained when the donor enabled the recipient to achieve self-reliance rather than prolonging dependency. Applied to contemporary politics, this perspective suggested that the welfare state subsidized dependency by providing funds without regard for the recipient's willingness to work or to undertake self-improvement. "Workfare programs," the centerpiece of welfare reform during the Clinton era, would seem more compatible with philanthropy as understood in the Jewish tradition. More generally, the critics of Judaism as liberalism contend, liberal Jews have embraced the prophetic motif selectively, choosing to overlook its explicitly religious aspects.

Creeds and Political Behavior

Why is it that scholars place so little confidence in creedal explanations of Jewish political behavior? This section considers factors that inhibit the use of the Jewish tradition as a source of guidance in contemporary political battles.

In emphasizing the barrier to using Judaism as a source of public philosophy, I am most emphatically not asserting a post-modernist position that the tradition is without meaning or relevance to contemporary issues. I recognize the existence of a tradition with certain norms and prescriptions that were meant to be understood in a certain way. Contrary to the spirit of the age, Judaism is not whatever any Jew happens to say or believe about it. The tradition has integrity precisely because it has meaning, difficult though it may be to discern the message.

Nor do I wish to deny that value of investigating Judaism from a political perspective. In a number of productive efforts, scholars have used political frameworks to make sense of the Jewish experience. From very different theoretical starting points, Ira Sharkansky and Steven Brams have delved into the Hebrew Bible to illuminate the nature of political life among Jews in both ancient and modern times.[31] Aaron Wildavsky distilled a number of models of leadership from the history of Jewish civilization.[32] In numerous scholarly publications he both produced and inspired, Daniel Elazar demonstrated the contribution of covenantal thinking to the evolution of Western political thought.[33] A recent volume by Michael Walzer and colleagues attempted, as a reviewer put it, to "think politically about Judaism and to think Jewishly about politics."[34] As such studies indicate, there is much to be gained by exploring the political terrain from a Jewish perspective and understanding how the tradition has helped Jews cope with questions of governance. This is not a call against serious moral reflection about politics.

Notwithstanding the value of these efforts, they must necessarily fall short of extracting a coherent or systematic political orientation that will provide substantial guidance as Jews consider contemporary political controversies. Developing a religiously grounded vision of the public square is challenging for all faith traditions but even more complicated in Judaism because of several unique aspects of the tradition. This section will identify both the general and specific barriers to that project.

The major religious traditions that have persisted in the modern era acquire their staying power from the breadth and richness of their beliefs. Religious systems command our attention because they confront the fundamental existential dilemmas of human life. As Aaron Wildavsky reminded us in an influential essay, cultural systems such as religions provide answers to such basic questions as "Who am I?" and "What shall I do?"[35] They help us understand our place in the universe and our purpose on earth. These traditions influence the social order primarily by constructing "moral universes" that contain standards of behavior and social norms—Thou shalt not kill, I am thy brother's keeper, etc.[36] Religious elites draw on these standards and norms in formulating guidance for their adherents.

The very qualities that empower religious traditions—breadth and depth—make it exceptionally difficult to interrogate these traditions for their political meaning. How do we "translate" general concepts into concrete laws or specific policies that are consistent with the overarching moral imperative from which they derive?

Consider the sixth commandment in the Decalogue. For Albert Schweitzer, the prohibition on killing was literal, forbidding the extermination not just of humans but also of insects, animals, and pests. That interpretation gained great respect but few followers. Following Cardinal Bernardin's "seamless garment" approach, the National Conference of Catholic Bishops has proscribed the taking of life through capital punishment or abortion and put severe limits on the acceptable use of force during wartime. The bishops' contemporary understanding of the sixth commandment has not commanded much behavioral conformity among the rank and file, nor, if some critics are to be believed, have the bishops themselves always acted consistently with it.[37] At other times and places, the commandment has been read rather narrowly, permitting a wide range of violence against wartime enemies and the application of capital punishment. Indeed, although Judaism and Christianity have no formal doctrines of jihad or holy war, wartime has often produced a level of clerical nationalism among ministers that strikingly resembles such a position.

The central problem, it seems to me, is that the issues that dominate political debate seldom present simple or clear moral imperatives. The changing public attitudes to the civil rights movement are particularly instructive. Many Americans of diverse religious faith reached the conclusion that segregation, embodied in de jure restrictions on African Americans, was morally unacceptable.[38] Many in the religious community enlisted enthusiastically in the campaign to register black voters, pass civil rights laws, and otherwise promote full citizenship for racial minorities. In this relatively brief phase of the civil rights movement, the moral imperative seemed clear and unambiguous. But once the civil rights debate shifted from de jure to de facto segregations, raising disturbing questions about white privilege and invisible racism, calling forth demands for affirmative action, community control and, more recently, reparations, many Americans had considerable difficulty locating the appropriate moral compass. The problem is not any weakness in public attitudes about the role of religious thinking or justification in the public square. Rather, the challenge inheres in the way that public issues present very specific challenges that may not be addressed by religious tradition or may raise a host of considerations that suggest different and conflicting theological imperatives. Given the nature and function of religious language, it is no easy task—nor necessarily a possible one—to identify how a tradition might speak to these concrete political debates.

The same "translation" problem arises in the secular context of constitutional interpretation. The Bill of Rights boldly declares the unfettered freedom of speech, the free exercise of religion, the right to a trial by a jury of one's peers, and so forth. In principle, we have little difficulty understanding these as natural rights, whether divinely ordained or inherent in human agency. But what do these concepts mean in practice? Does the right of free speech include burning a symbol of the Republic and is polygamy protected under the free exercise clause? Does the guarantee of a "fair" trial require that juries include citizens who resemble the defendant in racial and socioeconomic traits? Is my car, my daughter's high school locker, and my computer's hard drive subject to or exempt from search and seizure? These are not easy issues to resolve because of the inherent gap between constitutional language and the more focused world of public policy. To answer each question, we must debate the language, meaning, intent, and relevance of constitutional concepts formulated two centuries ago. As the vigorous debates among constitutional scholars attest, it is no simple task to find a position that commands consensus as constitutionally authentic.

Even if it might be possible to develop a meaningful political position rooted in a religious ethic, it is not clear that our political system can make effective use of such insights. Consider the intriguing experience of "Just Life," an attempt in the 1980s by some Protestant evangelicals and Roman Catholics to develop a political movement devoted to their understanding of biblical principles. Dismayed by the polarization between pro-life and social justice agendas, this group pledged to support financially political candidates of any party who adhered in practice to Cardinal Bernardin's "seamless ethic" of life. Accordingly, support was limited to candidates who opposed abortion, war, and capital punishment, and favored generous social welfare policies. Just Life folded, a victim of the very polarization it wanted to heal. Although grounded in a theological position with integrity and sincerity, there were simply few viable candidates who fit the profile and therefore qualified for funding. In normal times, political elites seek to divide the public and attract majority support to their position. In such a polarized environment, delicate shadings of opinion are not likely to be heard.

The translation gap between broad religious language and the messy particularity of policy debates complicates efforts to extract political guidance from a religious tradition. That is as true for Lutheranism as much as Catholicism or Buddhism. The process of utilizing a religious tradition for political guidance, difficult enough in general, is further challenged by two additional barriers in Judaism.[39] The starting point for any such effort in Judaism, the written and oral laws, do not lend themselves easily to systematic exposition. As a religious tradition, Judaism has been deeply marked by the concrete circumstances of Jewish existence. The classic Jewish tradition confronts questions of governance not with an eye on universals or systematic theory but with a "contextual, idiographic, juridically concrete discourse that rarely departs from the life-world in which it is embodied."[40] From the perspective of developing perspectives on politics, the two most salient aspects of that life-world were (1) diaspora and (2) lack of agency. Because of these realities, Judaism has seldom devoted much effort to developing systematic political theory.

By virtue of their dispersion across the globe, Jews developed a remarkably decentralized tradition largely lacking in central authority. The religious tradition enshrined in Jewish sacred texts and commentary is neither static nor closed. The Hasidic movement emerged early in the nineteenth century as a revivalist protest against what it claimed was the excessive legalism and formalism of mainstream Judaism. The possibilities of adaptation and evolution further increased following the emancipation of European Jewry in the mid- to late-nineteenth century. As Jews emerged from ghettos to participate more fully in European societies, Judaism itself was recast and reformulated to meet the new situation.[41] Challenged by the emergence of Reform and then Conservative variants of Judaism, the embattled upholders of tradition adopted the mantle of Orthodoxy. Each stream developed its own understanding of Jewish law and reinterpreted the tradition according to its principles and needs.

The elasticity of the Jewish tradition facilitated Jewish political pluralism, permitting communities to develop political cultures that responded to local factors. From the mid-nineteenth century to the Holocaust, Jonathan Frankel argues, the political systems of European Jewry were determined by "the particular political system prevailing at any given moment."[42] Paula Hyman's study of Western Europe during this period affirmed that Jewish political behavior responded to situational factors, foremost among them the openness of the state to Jews in the wake of emancipation.[43] Where Jews were admitted to full citizenship, they divided among a wide range of parties. But in societies that offered only a restricted political role to them, Jews tended to cluster in parties of the left. In the post-Holocaust era, Rubinstein maintains, Jews moved to the right in response both to their economic gains and the growth of anti-Semitism on the left.[44] In another variant of the situational perspective, Ginsberg holds that Jewish politics are driven largely by the imperatives of safety and security.[45] Thus Jews have embraced regimes and politicians of whatever ideological stripe who promised them access to power, opportunity, and protection from anti-Semitism.

This transformation exemplifies a general pattern of religious evolution. Katz maintains that religious communities transplanted from a core to a peripheral setting engage in creative reinterpretation of tradition better to adapt to the host culture.[46] This takes the form of highlighting or "foregrounding" those aspects of the tradition that resonate with the indigenous culture and deemphasizing ("backgrounding") discordant components that make adaptation more difficult. The form of Judaism that emerged in Cochin India, for example, was built on a foundation myth that paralleled Hindu legend, imposed what amounted to a caste system, and embraced, Jewish analogs to Hindu ritual acts and symbols of purity. Because such syncretism is common, the spread of Judaism across the globe did not produce a uniform transnational religion but rather a set of "national" religions sharing a family name but varying significantly from one another in matters of style and practice. Unlike Catholicism, a tradition with a transnational hierarchy and the legitimate teaching authority to impose a uniform understanding of the faith, Judaism had few mechanisms to promote such standardization.

Liebman and Cohen have argued strongly that such national differentiation now divides the American and Israeli forms of Juda-

ism.[47] Although they do not offer a complete theory to explain the
process, they contend that Judaism has evolved to fit the situation of
the Jewish communities in the two countries. Each has interpreted
Judaism and Jewish symbols in very distinct ways. American Jews
have been westernized and exist as a minority in a diverse, multicultural liberal state. Politically, this experience has taught them to
value the tradition of tolerance and to develop strong support for
minority civil liberties. As noted above, this includes unyielding
opposition to state-supported expressions of religiosity, which Jews
understand will inevitably mean Christianity, the religious faith of
the majority.[48] Sympathy with underdogs has also translated into a
high level of support for activist government intended to promote
economic equality among groups. By contrast, Israeli Jews have
adapted to the eastern character of their environment and, more con-
cretely, to the experience of being the dominant majority in a Jewish
state. This has produced less sensitivity to abridgement of minority
civil liberties and a much-diminished commitment to the goal of
social equality between Jew and non-Jew. Unlike American Jews,
who firmly believe the state should make no recognition of religion,
Israeli Jews exhibit a greater tolerance for religious expression by
the state, confident that such expression will take the form of Jewish
observance. If not two Judaisms, this social evolution has produced
what Liebman and Cohen describe as two worlds of Judaism.

The reality of diaspora has thus rendered it difficult if not
impossible to develop a universal Jewish ethic of the public square.
Even if such an enterprise were possible, it would be difficult due to
the other violent reality of Jewish history, lack of sovereignty. For
most of their history, Jews have been a subject people. The task of
politics was to buffer the small and beleaguered community from
the harsh treatment of its religious enemies. Although one can iso-
late a recognizably "Jewish" style of politics in this period, few
would describe this syndrome as a full-fledged theory about how
Jews should participate in a democratic political state that accords
them full citizenship.[49] Jews did not develop such a doctrine because
it was not necessary and Jewish law, as argued, responded to the
concrete historical circumstances of the community.

The lack of much guidance on such matters from the Jewish tradition has been a perennial problem in the State of Israel. Before the
state was created, a delegation from the Orthodox community appeared before the British Commission that was preparing plans for
the partition of Palestine. They insisted that the Jewish State created
by partition be designed so it accorded with Jewish law. Yeshayahu

Leibowitz imagined the questions that well-meaning commissioners might have asked in response to such a demand:

> What do you mean by a state according to the Torah, and what will its legal system be? Will this be a democratic state, in which political authority derives ultimately from the people who confer it upon their leadership, or will it be a state in which political authority flows down from the apex of a political pyramid? Will office holders be elected or appointed, and by whom? Will this be a state that maintains an army and weaponry and includes the conduct of war, when necessary, among its legitimate functions, or will it be a neutral and pacifist state that does not acknowledge war at all as an instrument of policy? Will the economy of the state be based on private enterprise, each person doing as he pleased with his own property, with production based on the institutions of hired labor, or will it be a socialist or communist economy?[50]

Had these questions been raised, Leibowitz speculated, they would have been met with silence. The delegation equated Torah with the Shulhan Arukh "which does not and could not deal with even one of the political and social questions of an independent Jewish society in the present, since none of these questions were relevant either in Safed where Rabbi Joseph Caro resided, or in Cracow, the home of Rabbi Moses Isserles."

While diaspora has fractured the unity of the Jewish people, robbing the community of a central authority with the legitimacy to issue binding interpretations of Jewish law, the historical experience of the Jewish people has meant that concrete questions of governance received little attention from the tradition. These two factors, coupled with the intrinsic difficulty of applying religious insights to public policy, make it unlikely that Judaism will yield a coherent public philosophy that commands widespread support among Jews.

The Persistence of Jewish Liberalism

If Judaism lacks a defining political ethic, why do American Jews believe they are acting out the authentic tradition by their current political position? By answering that question, we will obtain further insight into the difficulties of developing religiously based approaches to the public square. The answer will also help us understand why Jews are not likely soon to shed their classic liberalism in matters of religion and state.

Given the conceptual distance between religious principle and political position, how do people attempt to link the two domains? Without intermediaries, individual congregants are unlikely to draw much in the way of political insight from their religious tradition. As noted elsewhere, religious language seldom offers specific guidance on questions of public policy. Religion undergirds "moral universes" that emphasize broad principles such as justice and equality. But the "translation gap" between such considerations and the particular political issues of the day makes it difficult for individuals to work out connections on their own.

The answer, provided by a large body of empirical research, is that individuals learn how to correlate their religious and political positions via cues from religious and political elites. Clergy and fellow congregants may offer some guidance about how to understand the political relevance of the community's religious tradition. This may be communicated implicitly, via powerful symbols, rich language, and social interaction, or even explicitly by guidelines from the pulpit or in the classroom. The religious congregation turns out to be an exceptionally powerful potential environment for political learning.[51] The addition of "potential" as a qualifier is meant to recognize that many religious groups avoid trying to engage in political socialization. Yet in many congregations, the informal political learning may well operate in spite of a manifest strategy to avoid taking sides on contentious issues.

As mentioned above, the linkage between religious and political views is also reinforced by the actions of political and religious elites. In attempting to build majority coalitions, political parties target religious groups as electoral constituencies. They may choose to emphasize certain issues or positions on these issues as a means of attracting support. Electoral appeals are framed in the context of moral universes by deploying powerful symbols that are expected to resonate with specific denominations or traditions.[52] In the 1980s, for example, the Republicans attempted to increase their support among white evangelical Protestants, a predominantly Democratic constituency, by utilizing potent symbols of marriage, the family, and a host of traditional values. They embraced certain policies consistent with this perspective and painted the Democrats as the enemies of religious tradition. The effort succeeded, as white Evangelicals became the largest and most reliable component of the Republican electoral coalition.

The correlation between religious values and political positions is just that, a correlation. The causal element is not religious values per se. Individuals learn which political choices accord with their religious values but the political values may well come first and the religious justifications develop afterwards.

If Jewish political liberalism does not rest in a causal sense upon Jewish religious values, it is more likely to reflect the influence of communal and organizational factors. The intensification of Jewish commitment to the Democratic Party in the 1990s, wholly unexpected by most analysts, seems especially likely to have been generated by such considerations. Perhaps the most powerful inducement was the embrace of the Republican Party by evangelical Protestants, a strategy pursued conscientiously by GOP elites throughout the 1980s.[53] Although they once shared a strong loyalty to the Democratic Party, Jews and evangelicals have moved in different directions since the New Deal.[54] For many Jews, Christian conservatism presents a direct challenge to their own political integration. Jews believe they have thrived in what the Lubavitcher rabbi once called the "Kingdom of Kindness" precisely because the state takes no official notice of religious claims or religious traits. They regard the Christian Right as a threat to a liberal political system because the movement appears determined to reverse this norm.

This perception of the Christian Right has been the object of some debate, with neoconservative Jews generally defending the political aspirations of Evangelicals as compatible with Jewish interests.[55] Nonetheless, data about the political perspectives of the rank-and-file supporters of the Christian Right suggest that Jews have reasons to worry about the movement's political aspirations. Compared to other Americans, those who most strongly identify with the Christian Right "give strong expression to what might be termed 'Christian nationalism'—the idea that America's political troubles can be alleviated by making a Christian outlook more central to government."[56] This includes the belief that the United States should be declared a Christian nation by constitutional amendment, that the religious views of politicians are relevant in determining fitness for office, and that organized prayer should be permitted in public schools. None of these policies is likely to facilitate the continued integration of Jews into the American polity. Recalling that ideology in the United States is often a matter of group affinity, the base constituency for the Christian Right is demonstrably more hostile to groups with which Jews sympathize—religious and sexual minorities in particular. These data suggest that Jewish concern about the movement has an empirical foundation and is likely to continue to keep Jews from enlisting wholeheartedly in the faith-based campaign or the Republican Party.

Given the anchoring of Jewish liberalism (including separationism) in communal perceptions of self-interest, it is unlikely that Jews will depart from that position in the near future. Even if they do, the path of change is unlikely to run through reinterpretation of the Jewish sources. Extracting political guidance from religious sources, an inherently difficult enterprise to begin with, is especially difficult because of the unique developmental experience of Jewish law. Those who anticipate a reorientation of Jews toward the public square will not find much hope in creedal, communal, or organizational factors.

Notes

1. This discussion is largely limited to domestic issues because there is relatively little hard data on how Jews compare to other Americans in their foreign policy attitudes. Even on Israel, the principal difference is that Jews exhibit higher levels of salience and knowledge than other Americans. For detailed information on American attitudes to Israel, see Eytan Gilboa, *American Public Opinion toward Israel and the Arab-Israeli Conflict* (Lexington, Mass.: D.C. Heath, 1987).

2. Milton Himmelfarb, "Another Look at the Jewish Vote," *Commentary* 80 (December 1985): 39.

3. This discussion is largely limited to domestic issues because there is relatively little hard data on how Jews compare to other Americans in their foreign policy attitudes. Even on Israel, the principal difference is that Jews exhibit higher levels of salience and knowledge than other Americans. For detailed information on American attitudes to Israel, see Gilboa, *American Public Opinion toward Israel.*

4. The principal source of data referred to in this chapter is the Jewish Political Behavior Study, a survey of approximately 500 Jews and 500 non-Jews conducted by the Knowledge Networks organization in the summer of 2000. For information about this study, see Anna Greenberg and Kenneth D. Wald, "Still Liberal after All These Years? The Contemporary Political Behavior of American Jewry," in *Jews in American Politics*, Sandy Maisel and Ira N. Forman, eds. (Lanham, Md.: Rowman & Littlefield, 2001), 167-99. The major source of data on group voting patterns comes from the election day exit polls conducted by a consortium of news organizations under the direction of Voter News Service.

5. The principal exception was 1980 when Jewish doubts about Jimmy Carter's commitment to Israel prompted widespread Democratic defections. Even in that contest, however, many of the Jews who left the

Democratic Party supported the independent John Anderson rather than cast a Republican presidential vote.

6. Greenberg and Wald, "Still Liberal after All These Years?"

7. David C. Leege, et al., *The Political Mobilization of Cultural Differences: Social Change and Voter Mobilization Strategies in the Post-New Deal Period* (Princeton, N.J.: Princeton University Press, 2002).

8. Steven M. Cohen and Charles S. Liebman, "American Jewish Liberalism: Unraveling the Strands," *Public Opinion Quarterly* 61 (Fall 1997): 405-30.

9. Pamela Johnson Conover and Stanley Feldman, "The Origins and Meaning of Liberal/Conservative Self-Identifications," *Journal of Politics* 25 (November 1981): 617-45.

10. David O. Sears, et al., "Self-Interest vs. Symbolic Politics in Policy Attitudes and Presidential Voting," *American Political Science Review* 74 (September 1980): 670-84. This stream of research, known more generally as social heuristics, recognizes that most citizens invest little effort in comprehending the political world and develop cognitive shortcuts to help them select a political identity. It is less helpful for understanding the political thinking of elites and intellectuals.

11. James M. Glaser, "Toward an Explanation of the Racial Liberalism of American Jews," *Political Research Quarterly* 50 (June 1997): 437-58.

12. Steven M. Cohen, "Religion and the Public Square: Attitudes of American Jews in Comparative Perspective—Part One," *Jerusalem Letter* 434 (July 16, 2000).

13. Most studies of religion and state focus on the establishment clause. As argued below, Jewish views are distinctive on both religion clauses.

14. William Galston, "Who's a Liberal?" *Public Interest* (Summer 2001): 100.

15. Kenneth D. Wald and Lee Sigelman, "Romancing the Jews: The Christian Right in Search of Strange Bedfellows," in *Sojourners in the Wilderness: The Religious Right in Comparative Perspective*, Corwin Smidt and James Penning, eds. (Lanham, Md.: Rowman & Littlefield, 1997), 139-68.

16. Peter Beinart, "New Bedfellows: The New Latino-Jewish Alliance," *New Republic* 217 (August 11, 1997): 22-6; Murray Friedman, "Are American Jews Moving to the Right?" *Commentary* 109 (April 2000): 50-52.

17. Raphael J. Sonenshein and Nicholas A. Valentino, "The Distinctiveness of Jewish Voting: A Thing of the Past?" *Urban Affairs Review,* 35 (January 2000): 358-89.

18. Steven Brint, *In an Age of Experts: The Changing Role of Professionals in Politics and Public Life* (Princeton, N.J.: Princeton University Press, 1994). In his careful exposition of the attitudinal differences between New Class and other citizens, Brint shows that the distinctiveness of

the New Class is limited to social liberalism. On economic issues, the "New Class" is either indistinguishable or quite conservative.

19. Richard Neuhaus, *The Naked Public Square: Religion and Democracy in America* (Grand Rapids, Mich.: Eerdmans, 1984). For a similar perspective, see Stephen L. Carter, *The Culture of Disbelief: How American Law and Politics Trivialize Religious Devotion* (New York: Basic Books, 1993).

20. Irving Kristol, "On the Political Stupidity of the Jews," *Azure,* no. 8 (1999).

21. Lee Sigelman, "If You Prick Us, Do We Not Bleed? If You Tickle Us, Do We Not Laugh?" *Journal of Politics* 53 (November 1991): 977-92.

22. Greenberg and Wald, "Still Liberal after All These Years?" 180-82.

23. Kenneth D. Wald, *Religion and Politics in the United States,* 3rd ed. (Washington, D.C.: Congressional Quarterly, 1997).

24. These two approaches, creedal and communal, are sometimes equated with a continuum that has "believing" at one end and "behaving" at the other. The former attributes the greatest significance to the content of a religious tradition while the latter tends to emphasize the consequences of interaction with fellow group members in a congregational milieu. See Kenneth D. Wald and Corwin E. Smidt, "Measurement Strategies in the Study of Religion and Politics," in *Rediscovering the Religious Factor in American Politics,* David C. Leege and Lyman E. Kellstedt, eds. (Armonk, N.Y.: M.E. Sharpe, 1993), 26-49.

25. Lawrence H. Fuchs, *Political Behavior of American Jews* (Glencoe, Ill.: Free Press, 1956).

26. Leonard Fein, *Where Are We? The Inner Life of America's Jews* (New York: Harper and Row, 1988); Benjamin Ginsberg, *The Fatal Embrace: Jews and the State* (Chicago: University of Chicago Press, 1993).

27. Marsha L. Rozenblit, *Reconstructing a National Identity: The Jews of Habsburg Austria during World War I* (New York: Oxford University Press, 2000).

28. See Marshall Sklare and Joseph Greenblum, *Jewish Identity on the Suburban Frontier* (New York: Basic Books, 1967).

29. Steven M. Cohen, *American Modernity and Jewish Identity* (New York: Tavistock, 1983).

30. Paula E. Hyman, "Was There a 'Jewish Politics' in Western and Central Europe?" in *The Quest for Utopia: Jewish Political Ideas and Institutions through the Ages,* Zvi Gitelman, ed. (Armonk, N.Y.: M.E. Sharpe, 1992), 105-18.

31. Ira Sharkansky, *Israel and Its Bible: A Political Analysis* (New York: Garland, 1996); Steven J. Brams, *Biblical Games: A Strategic Analysis of Stories in the Old Testament* (Cambridge, Mass.: MIT Press, 1980).

32. Aaron B. Wildavsky, *The Nursing Father: Moses As a Political Leader* (University: University of Alabama Press, 1984); *Assimilation ver-*

sus Separation: Joseph the Administrator and the Politics of Religion in Biblical Israel (New Brunswick, N.J.: Transaction Publishers, 1993).

33. Daniel J. Elazar and John Kincaid, eds., *Covenant, Polity, and Constitutionalism* (Lanham, Md.: University Press of America, 1980); Alan L. Mittleman, *The Politics of Torah: The Jewish Political Tradition and the Founding of Agudat Israel* (Albany: SUNY Press, 1996).

34. Michael Walzer, et al., *The Jewish Political Tradition,* vol. 1, *Authority* (New Haven, Conn.: Yale University Press, 2000).

35. Aaron Wildavsky, "Choosing Preferences by Constructing Institutions: A Cultural Theory of Preference Formation," *American Political Science Review* 81 (March 1987): 6.

36. Robert Wuthnow, *Meaning and Moral Order: Explorations in Cultural Analysis* (Berkeley: University of California Press, 1987).

37. J. Stephen Cleghorn, "Respect for Life: Research Notes on Cardinal Bernardin's 'Seamless Garment'," *Review of Religious Research* 28 (December 1986): 129-41; Timothy Byrnes and Mary C. Segers, *The Catholic Church and the Politics of Abortion* (Boulder, Colo.: Westview, 1992).

38. Charles Marsh, *God's Long Summer: Stories of Faith and Civil Rights* (Princeton, N.J.: Princeton University Press, 1997). Marsh demonstrates convincingly that there was no moral consensus among Protestant evangelicals whose attitudes to civil rights ranged from virulent racism to intense commitment with a midpoint of indifference.

39. This section draws heavily on Kenneth D. Wald and Michael D. Martinez, "The Transnational Nexus of Religion and Politics: Jewish Religiosity and Political Behavior in the United States and Israel," presented to the annual meeting of the Society for the Scientific Study of Religion, Houston, Texas, 2000.

40. Bernard Susser, "On the Reconstruction of Jewish Political Theory," in *Public Life in Israel and the Diaspora,* Sam N. Lehman-Wilzig and Bernard Susser, eds. (Ramat Gan, Israel: Bar-Ilan University Press, 1981), 13-22. One could argue that the concreteness of Jewish law, compared to the abstraction of many Christian traditions, makes it easier to apply the Jewish tradition to tangible political issues.

41. Pierre Birnbaum and Ira Katznelson, eds., *Paths of Emancipation: Jews, States, and Citizenship* (Princeton, N.J.: Princeton University Press, 1995).

42. Jonathan Frankel, "Modern Jewish Politics: East and West (1840-1939)," in *The Quest for Utopia: Jewish Political Ideas and Institutions,* Zvi Gitelman, ed. (Armonk, N.Y.: M.E. Sharpe, 1992), 86.

43. Hyman, "Was There a 'Jewish Politics'?"

44. W. D. Rubinstein, *The Left, the Right, and the Jews* (London: Croom Helm, 1982).

45. Ginsberg, *The Fatal Embrace.*

46. Nathan Katz, "Understanding Religion in Diaspora: The Case of the Jews of Cochin," *Religious Studies and Theology* 15 (1996): 5-17.

47. Charles S. Liebman and Steven M. Cohen, *Two Worlds of Judaism: The Israeli and American Experiences* (New Haven, Conn.: Yale University Press, 1990).

48. Naomi Cohen, *Jews in Christian America* (New York: Oxford University Press, 1992).

49. Alan Dowty, *The Jewish State a Century Later* (Berkeley: University of California Press, 1998).

50. Yeshayahu Leibowitz, *Judaism, Human Values, and the Jewish State*, Eliezer Goldman, ed. (Cambridge, Mass.: Harvard University Press, 1992), 153.

51. Christopher P. Gilbert, *The Impact of Churches on Political Behavior: An Empirical Study* (Westport, Conn.: Greenwood, 1993); Ted Jelen, "Political Christianity: A Contextual Analysis," *American Journal of Political Science* 36 (August 1992): 692-714; Kenneth D. Wald, Dennis E. Owen, and Samuel S. Hill, Jr., "Churches as Political Communities," *American Political Science Review* 82 (June 1988): 531-48.

52. Leege, et al., *The Political Mobilization*. A recent *New York Times* article quoted a senior Bush adviser's offhand allusion to the "character and values stuff," a shorthand designation for the programs and themes that resonated with religious traditionalists.

53. Duane Oldfield, *The Right and the Righteous* (Lanham, Md.: Rowman & Littlefield, 1996).

54. Wesley Allinsmith and Beverly Allinsmith, "Religious Affiliation and Politico-Economic Attitudes: A Study of Eight Major U.S. Religious Groups," *Public Opinion Quarterly* 12 (Autumn 1948): 377-89.

55. For an early attempt, see Merrill Simon, *Jerry Falwell and the Jews* (Middle Village, N.Y.: Jonathan David, 1984).

56. Tom W. Smith, *A Survey of the Religious Right: Views on Politics, Society, Jews, and Other Minorities* (New York: American Jewish Committee, 1996), 1.

5

The Need for a Wall Separating Church and State: Why the Establishment Clause Is So Important for Jews and Why Jews Are So Important for the Establishment Clause

Erwin Chemerinsky

Every year, when I teach the part of constitutional law concerning the establishment clause, the class discusses whether Christmas pageants in public schools are constitutionally permissible. Inevitably, the class divides along religious lines. The majority of Christian students don't see any problem with it and, in fact, many express the view that Christmas is a national holiday celebrated by all and school assemblies with nativity scenes and everyone singing Christmas carols are part of the celebration. Always many non-Christian students express their discomfort with such assemblies containing religious symbols, like a nativity scene, and explicitly religious carols. Some of the students speak forcefully of their own experience as children and being made to feel like outsiders and how uncomfortable they were during the Christmas celebrations in their schools. Given the demographics of the schools where I have taught, usually these students are Jewish, though occasionally there are Muslim, Buddhist, or atheist students to express the same views.

This annual occurrence is a simple example of why the establishment clause matters so much for Jews and why Jews are so important for the establishment clause. The establishment clause, above all, is meant to ensure a secular government. In an overwhelmingly Christian society, this is of enormous importance to minority religions in allowing them to avoid their feeling outsiders to their government or coerced to participate in religions they don't believe in. Although there has been anti-Semitism throughout American history, Jews have lived in peace and prosperity for a longer time in the United States than in virtually any place since the destruction of the Temple. It is not coincidental that it is in a place where there is a constitution that prevents government from establishing religion and that ensures the free exercise of religion.

The benefits of the establishment clause for minority religions, of course, are not limited to Jews. The United States is incredibly religiously diverse and all minority religions benefit from the establishment clause. Jews, however, by virtue of their success in professions such as law, play a key role in expressing and enforcing the establishment clause to the benefit of all religions. Jews definitely are not unique in this role. For example, many of the most important free speech cases were litigated on behalf of Jehovah's Witnesses. But there is also no doubt that in both public discourse and litigation, Jews are important in maintaining a secular government.

As the simple example from my class illustrates, it generally must be those of minority religions to object to the presence of religion in government or government involvement with religion. Those of the majority religion often just don't experience any problems with its presence.

This chapter develops three points. First, it explains why the establishment clause should be interpreted as mandating a separation of church and state. This is the view traditionally taken by most Jewish groups and this section of the chapter explains why the establishment clause matters so much for Jews. Second, it discusses how the separation of church and state is under attack—both politically and within the Supreme Court. There already has been great erosion of the wall separating church and state and there is the prospect, with future appointments to the Court, that the wall could be eliminated. This section also explains why the approach favored by conservatives—treating religious beliefs and groups equally with nonreligious beliefs and groups—is undesirable in terms of the central purposes of the establishment clause. Finally, the chapter considers the danger of this to Jews and other minority religions in terms of the issues likely to come up in the next few years.

Why Separate Church and State?

The Futility of a Historical Inquiry

As with all constitutional provisions, some look to history as a guide to the meaning of the religion clauses. This is particularly difficult for these provisions because there is no apparent agreement among the framers as to what they meant. Justice Brennan expressed this well when he stated: "A too literal quest for the advice of the Founding Fathers upon the issues of these cases seems to me futile and misdirected for several reasons. . . . [T]he historical record is at best ambiguous, and statements can readily be found to support either side of the proposition."[1]

Yet, justices on all sides of the issue continue to invoke history and the framers' intent to support their position. Chief Justice Rehnquist has remarked that "[t]he true meaning of Establishment Clause can only be seen in its history."[2] In *Rosenberger v. Rector and Visitors of the University of Virginia*, which concerned whether a public university could deny student activity funds to a religious group, both Justice Thomas in a concurring opinion and Justice Souter dissenting focused at length on James Madison's views of religious freedom.[3]

As Professor Laurence Tribe has cogently summarized, there were at least three main views of religion among key framers:

[A]t least three distinct schools of thought . . . influenced the drafters of the Bill of Rights: first, the evangelical view (associated primarily with Roger Williams) that "worldly corruptions . . . might consume the churches if sturdy fences against the wilderness were not maintained"; second, the Jeffersonian view that the church should be walled off from the state in order to safeguard secular interests (public and private) "against ecclesiastical depredations and incursions"; and, third, the Madisonian view that religious and secular interests alike would be advanced best by diffusing and decentralizing power so as to assure competition among sects rather than dominance by any one.[4]

These are quite distinct views of the proper relationship between religion and the government. Roger Williams was primarily concerned that government involvement with religion would corrupt and undermine religion, whereas Thomas Jefferson had the opposite fear that religion would corrupt and undermine the government. James Madison saw religion as one among many types of factions that existed and that needed to be preserved. He wrote that "[i]n a free government the security for civil rights must be the same as that for religious rights. It consists in the one case in the multiplicity of interests, and the other in the multiplicity of sects. The degree of security in both cases will depend on the number of interests and sects."[5]

The problem of using history in interpreting the religion clauses is compounded by the enormous changes in the country since the First Amendment was adopted. The country is much more religiously diverse in the 1990s than it was in 1791. Justice Brennan observed that "our religious composition makes us a vastly more diverse people than were our forefathers. They knew differences chiefly among Protestant sects. Today the nation is far more heterogeneous religiously, including as it does substantial minorities not only of Catholics and Jews but as well of those who worship according to no version of the Bible and those who worship no God at all."[6]

Also, as discussed below, a significant number of cases involving the establishment clause have arisen in the context of religious activities in connection with schools. But public education, as it exists now, did not exist when the Bill of Rights was ratified and it is inherently difficult to apply the framers' views to situations that they could not have imagined. Justice Brennan also remarked that "the structure of American education has greatly changed since the First Amendment was adopted. In the context of our modern emphasis upon public education available to all citizens, any views of the eighteenth century as to whether the exercises at bar are an 'establishment' offer little aid to decision."[7]

The reality is that the divergence of views among the framers, and the abstractness with which they were stated, makes it possible for those on all sides of the debate to invoke history in support of their positions.[8] I do not believe that the framers' intent should be controlling in constitutional interpretation, even if it could be known,[9] and in the area of religion I don't think there ever will be more than each side finding apt quotations to support its position.

Religion Is Different

Those who oppose a separation of church and state emphasize that religion should not be treated any differently from other beliefs. For example, Justice Thomas in his plurality opinion in *Mitchell v. Helms* stressed that religious schools should not be treated any differently from other schools. In many cases, the Court has said that a school should not treat religious groups any differently from non-religious ones.[10]

But this ignores that under the Constitution religion is different from other beliefs. Unlike all other views, the Constitution uniquely forbids that government from establishing religion. Indeed, the Court often has treated religion differently from other beliefs. For example, in *Sherbert v. Verner*, the Court held that the government cannot deny benefits to those who quit their jobs for religious reasons.[11] The Court followed this principle in many other cases.[12] But there never has been a case holding that a person must be given benefits if he or she quits a job because of secular beliefs.

There are many good reasons for treating religion differently from other beliefs. History shows the tremendous risk of intolerance, persecution, and divisiveness based on religion. There is thus a need to protect the ability of people to engage in the religion of their choice, but also a need to ensure that the government remains strictly secular. Religion is special because of the role it occupies in people's lives and it is because of this that religion is appropriately treated differently under the Constitution.

The Benefits of a Secular Government

There are many important values served by protecting a wall separating church and state. These benefits are particularly significant for minority religions, such as Judaism. First, the establishment clause protects freedom of conscience. I believe that freedom of conscience is the central and uniting goal of the various parts of the First Amendment. One way in which the separation of church and state protects freedom of conscience is by ensuring that people are not taxed to support religions other than their own. The famous statement of Thomas Jefferson concerning the need for a wall separating church and state and James Madison's Memorial and Remonstrance Against Religious Assessments were made in the context of opposing a state tax to aid the church.[13]

Jefferson spoke of the unconscionability of taxing people to support religions that they do not believe in. The Supreme Court has described Jefferson's belief that "compelling a man to furnish contributions of money for the propagation of opinions which he disbelieves is sinful and tyrannical; . . . even the forcing him to support this or that teacher of his own religious persuasion is depriving him of the comfortable liberty of giving his contributions to the particular pastor, whose morals he would make his pattern."[14] Madison said: "[T]he same authority which can force a citizen to contribute three pence only of his property for the support of any one establishment, may force him to conform to any other establishment."[15]

It is wrong to make me support a church that teaches that my religion or my beliefs are evil. It violates my freedom of conscience to force me to support religions that I do not accept. Justice Souter explained that "compelling an individual to support religion violates the fundamental principle of freedom of conscience. Madison's and Jefferson's now familiar words establish clearly that liberty of personal conviction requires freedom from coercion to support religion, and this means that the government can compel no aid to fund it."[16]

In a majority Christian nation, requiring support for religion inevitably would mean for Christian religions. The separation of church and state is thus key for minority religions in keeping them from being forced to support majority religions. In fact, more subtly, there is a benefit to the majority religions too. The separation of church and state prevents battles among Catholics and Christian sects for control of the government and resources from it.

Second, the establishment clause serves a fundamental purpose of inclusion in that it allows all in society, of every religion and of no religion, to feel that the government is theirs. When the government supports religion, inescapably those of different religions feel excluded. Equality does not solve this. In a society that is overwhelmingly Christian, those of minority faiths are meant to feel marginalized and unwelcome. If equality were the only constraint imposed by the establishment clause, a school could begin each day with a prayer so long as every religion got its due. Assuming a school reflecting America's religious diversity, the vast majority of days would begin with Christian prayers. Those with no religion would be made to feel that it was not their school, as would those of minority religions who routinely were subjected to prayers of Christian religions.

This goal of inclusion is central, not incidental, to the establishment clause. Justice O'Connor has explained: "Direct government action endorsing religion or a particular religion is invalid because it sends a message to non-adherents that they are outsiders, not full members of the political community, and an accompanying message to adherents that they are insiders, favored members of the political community."[17]

Consider the most blatant violation of the establishment clause: a city or state declares a particular religion, say Catholicism, to be the official religion. Assuming that the government took no actions to limit free exercise by those of other faiths, why is such a declaration unacceptable? The pronouncement that Catholicism is the official religion makes all of a different faith feel unwelcome. They are made to feel that they are tolerated guests, not equal members of the community. In Justice O'Connor's words, nonadherents unquestionably are made to feel outsiders and adherents are made to feel insiders.

I have been to banquets that begin with an overtly Christian prayer. I always feel uncomfortable: that it's a place where I do not belong. A school assembly emphasizing a re-creation of the Nativity scene causes Jewish children to have the same feeling. The establishment clause, by creating a secular government, prevents that; it is about ensuring that all in society, whatever their religion, feel it is their government.

In other words, the very core of the establishment clause prevents the government from taking actions that divide people in this way. The focus of the establishment clause is thus very much on the effect of the message on the audience. This helps to explain why Justice Scalia is simply wrong in his dissent in *Lee v. Weisman* where he expresses the need to protect the majority in the audience who want to hear a prayer. The establishment clause is about preventing the majority, through government power, from making those of other religions feel unwelcome. If the majority of the audience wants to hear prayers, of course it may do so; but not at an official government function, especially one where the audience is compelled to be present. The problem is much greater than it was when the First Amendment was adopted. The country is much more religiously diverse in the 1990s than it was in 1791.

Third, separating church and state protects religion from the government. If the government provides assistance, inescapably there are and should be conditions attached. For example, when the government gives money, it must make sure that the funds are used for their intended purpose. This necessarily involves the government placing conditions on the funds and monitoring how it is spent.

Such government entanglement is a threat to all religions, dominant and minority.

This concern is not new. Roger Williams, for example, expressed great concerns that "worldly corruptions might consume the churches if sturdy fences against the wilderness were not maintained."[18] Justice Souter also expressed this as a fundamental basis for the establishment clause: "[G]overnment aid corrupts religion. Madison argued that establishment of religion weakened the beliefs of adherents so favored, strengthened their opponents, and generated 'pride and indolence in the Clergy; ignorance and servility in the laity; [and] in both, superstition, bigotry and persecution.' In a variant of Madison's concern, we have repeatedly noted that a government's favor to a particular religion or sect threatens to taint it with 'corrosive secularism.'"[19]

The central point here is that viewing the establishment clause as creating a wall separating church and state has enormous social benefits, and particularly benefits for minority religions such as Jews.

The Emerging Threat to the Separation of Church and State

Political and Doctrinal Threats

The wall that separates church and state is under assault. The initial actions of the Bush administration show its indifference, or more accurately its hostility, to separation of church and state. At the inauguration of president George W. Bush, on January 20, 2001, the invocation and benediction were explicitly Christian prayers. In his first few days as president, Bush created an office of faith-based programs to channel federal funds to religious entities and proposed an education plan that included vouchers that could be used for parochial schools.

Increasingly, enforcing a wall that separates church and state is criticized as undue hostility to religion, rather than recognition of a constitutional mandate for a secular government. For example, in *Santa Fe Independent School District v. Doe,* in response to the majority's declaring unconstitutional student-delivered prayers at high school football games, Chief Justice Rehnquist, writing for the dissent, saw the majority's opinion as unjustified "hostility" to relig-ion.[20]

Most significantly, the Supreme Court seems much less commit-ted to enforcing a wall that separates church and state. For the last thirty years, the Court has followed a test in establishment clause cases that was announced in *Lemon v. Kurtzman*.[21] In *Lemon*, the Court declared: "First, the statute must have a secular legislative purpose; second, its principal or primary effect must be one that nei-ther advances nor inhibits religion; finally, the statute must not fos-ter an excessive government entanglement with religion."[22] A law is unconstitutional if it fails any prong of the *Lemon* test. Now, though, four justices have indicated that they want to overrule the *Lemon* test—Rehnquist, Scalia, Kennedy, and Thomas.[23] These four justices have expressed a desire for a new test that allows much more government aid to religion and much more of a religious pres-ence in government. They call for an "accommodationist" approach where the government would be deemed to violate the establishment clause only if it literally creates a church, or if it favors one religion over others, or if it coerces religious participation. Very little would violate the establishment clause under this approach, which would emphasize judicial deference to the government in its choices con-cerning religion.

President George W. Bush's nominations to the Supreme Court are likely to change dramatically the law of the establishment clause. Currently, as evidenced by the Court's decision in *Mitchell v. Helms* in June 2000,[24] there are four justices—Chief Justice Rehnquist and Justices Scalia, Kennedy, and Thomas—desiring a radical change in the law of the establishment clause. Thus, even one appointment to the Court, for example replacing Justice Sandra Day O'Connor, could bring about this shift.

There is every reason to believe that a Bush nominee to the high Court would be the needed fifth vote for a dramatic change in estab-lishment clause jurisprudence. While a candidate for president, Bush explicitly said that he wanted to appoint justices like Scalia and Thomas. Even more importantly, Bush obviously cares deeply about allowing more government aid to religion as evidenced by his proposals for charitable choice and vouchers. Through his appoint-ments to the Supreme Court, Bush can greatly increase the likeli-hood that his proposals will be approved.

The Flaws with Equality Analysis

Those who attack the wall separating church and state do so by invoking the rhetoric of equality; they argue that the central requirement of the establishment clause is that the government should treat
all religions equally. For example, Justice Thomas's plurality opinion in *Mitchell v. Helms* could not be clearer in its call for allowing
aid to parochial schools, so long as the government is evenhanded
among religions. Justice Thomas wrote: "In short, nothing in the
Establishment Clause requires the exclusion of pervasively sectarian
schools from otherwise permissible aid programs, and other doctrines of this Court bar it. This doctrine, born of bigotry, should be
buried now."[25]

The majority of the justices in *Mitchell* rejected this approach
and explicitly recognized that it would be a radical and unprecedented shift in the law of the establishment clause. Justice O'Connor, in an opinion concurring in the judgment, observed: "[W]e have
never held that a government-aid program passes constitutional
muster solely because of the neutral criteria it employs as a basis for
distributing aid."[26] Similarly, Justice Souter in dissent wrote: "The
insufficiency of evenhandedness neutrality as a stand-alone criterion
of constitutional intent or effect has been clear from the beginning
of our interpretative efforts."[27]

Never has a majority of the Supreme Court held, as Justice Thomas argued for in *Mitchell*, that neutrality is the sole test for government aid to religions. The fundamental change in the law proposed by Justice Thomas can be seen in many ways. First, the test
which the Supreme Court has followed for the last thirty years limits the government's ability to aid or foster religion, even if it is being neutral among religions.[28] The *Lemon* test, by its very terms,
does not emphasize equality among religions, but rather prohibits
government aid to religion, even if it is equal, if it is with the purpose or effect of advancing religion or would entail excessive
government entanglement with religion. Justice Thomas's approach
in *Mitchell v. Helms* obviously would mean overruling the *Lemon*
test that has been controlling for the past three decades.

Second, Justice Thomas's approach would profoundly change the
law because no longer would the establishment clause be a barrier to
government aid to religion or religious presence in government. For
at least a half century, the Court always has regarded the establishment clause as an affirmative limit on what the government may do,

even if it is acting neutrally among religions. Justice Thomas would reject that entirely.

For example, the Court has said that prayer, even voluntary prayer in public schools, is unconstitutional.[29] Justice Thomas's approach would make prayer permissible so long as all religions had an equal chance to present their prayers. Likewise, when the Court has approved government aid programs outside the area of parochial schools, it has stressed that pervasively sectarian organizations must be excluded. In *Bowen v. Kendrick*, the Court deemed constitutional the Adolescent Family Life Act, which provided for grants to organizations to provide counseling and care to pregnant adolescents and their parents, and also to provide counseling to prevent adolescent sexual activity.[30] The law specifically authorized receipt of grants by religious, as well as nonreligious, organizations. The law prohibited the use of any federal funds for family planning services, for abortion counseling, or for abortions.

Chief Justice Rehnquist wrote for the majority in the 5-4 decision and applied the *Lemon* test to uphold the law. Rehnquist said that the law "was motivated primarily, if not entirely, by a legitimate secular purpose—the elimination or reduction of social and economic problems caused by teenage sexuality, pregnancy, and parenthood."[31] The Court stressed that the law was constitutional because it excluded pervasively sectarian institutions and organizations from receiving money. The Court explained that cases holding aid unconstitutional had been where the assistance was to institutions that "were pervasively sectarian and had as a substantial purpose the inculcation of religious values."[32] The Court said that "[h]ere, by contrast, there is no reason to assume that the religious organizations which may receive grants are pervasively sectarian in the same sense as the Court has held parochial schools to be."[33]

Justice Thomas expressly declares that he wants the Court to disavow any limits on aid to pervasively sectarian institutions. Indeed, Justice Thomas's approach would allow massive aid to parochial schools, so long as all religions are treated equally. Justice Souter powerfully makes this point:

> Hence, if we looked no further than evenhandedness, and failed to ask what activities the aid might support, or in fact did support, religious schools could be blessed with government funding as massive as expenditures made for the benefit of their public school counterparts, and religious missions would thrive on public money. This is why the consideration of less than universal neutrality has never been recognized as dispositive and has always been teamed

with attention to other facts bearing on the substantive prohibition
of support for a school's religious objective.[34]

In other words, the Court always has seen the establishment
clause as a barrier of government aid directly to religion, even when
the government is being evenhanded. Justice Thomas would completely eliminate that constraint. As Justice Souter explains: "[O]ne
point [is] clear beyond peradventure: together with James Madison
we have consistently understood the Establishment Clause to impose a substantive prohibition against public aid to religion and,
hence, to the religious mission of sectarian schools."

Third, and perhaps most significantly, the implication of Justice
Thomas's approach is that the government must fund parochial
school education, at least to the extent that it provides any aid to
private secular schools. Justice Thomas's approach clearly implies
that excluding religion is not neutral and constitutes impermissible
discrimination under the establishment clause.

Justice Thomas argued that it is offensive for the government to
even look to whether an organization is religious in character.[35] But
if the government cannot consider religion in distributing money, it
will be required to subsidize religious schools on the same terms
that it funds nonreligious ones. Justice Thomas acknowledges and
endorses this: "The religious nature of a recipient should not matter
to the constitutional analysis, so long as the recipient adequately
furthers the government's secular purpose."[36]

Thus, Justice Thomas's equality approach would not simply allow massive government aid to religious institutions, it would mandate it. Never before has a justice suggested, let alone a plurality
endorsed, such a radical change in the law of the establishment
clause.

The shift to equality would be inconsistent with the values of the
establishment clause discussed above. First, freedom of conscience
would be offended because people would be forced to support and
subsidize religions that they don't believe in, even if all religions
are treated equally. Second, treating all religions equally does not
address the need to make all feel comfortable with their government. Those who disavow any religious belief are forced to support
all religions; indeed, they will be surrounded with parochial schools
supported by their tax dollars. Forcing them to hear prayers of every
religion inevitably makes them feel unwelcome in their own schools
and their own country. The establishment clause should be interpreted to forbid this. Third, nor does equality protect religions from

the intrusion of government involvement. Justice Thomas's equality theory would mean that the government would be enmeshed in almost every aspect of religious schools and religious institutions. The government, as a condition for funding, could—and should—set curricula and educational requirements. The government would need to monitor to see if these mandates were met. This is a threat to religion and it is no less so because all religions are threatened equally.

For all of these reasons, Justice Thomas's equality theory is undesirable as a way of interpreting the First Amendment. The establishment clause should be seen as a limit on government involvement with religion and religious involvement with government, not simply a requirement for evenhandedness.

What, then, is the rationale for a theory that never has been accepted in 210 years of establishment clause jurisprudence and that seems so at odds with what the provision is about? Two justifications seem strongest. First is the desirability of equality and the undesirability of discrimination. The rhetorical appeal of Justice Thomas's theory is that it calls for evenhandedness and nondiscrimination. His approach says that religion should be treated the same as secularism, no better and no worse.

But this rests on a basic misdefinition of equality. As Aristotle explained, equality is about treating likes alike and unalikes differently. Justice Thomas is assuming that religious and secular schools are alike in their relationship to the government. However, for all of the reasons explained above, they are not alike and the Constitution should be understood as commanding that religion be treated differently.

If Justice Thomas's theory were adopted by the Court's majority, a religious school could sue the government for funds claiming that the denial of money was impermissible discrimination in violation of the equal protection clause. But the government should prevail by explaining the compelling interest it has in treating religion differently for the reasons explained above. Equality only is a benefit if it is desirable to treat the recipients equally.[37]

Second, the equality theory has the virtue of simplicity. No longer will lines need to be drawn between types of permissible and impermissible assistance. The only requirement would be ensuring no discrimination among religions. This would eliminate the need for line drawing of the sort that has occurred for decades concerning what the government may give to parochial schools. For example, the Court has upheld the government providing buses to take children to and from parochial schools,[38] but not buses to take parochial school students on field trips.[39] The Court has allowed the government to provide parochial schools textbooks for secular subjects,[40] but not audiovisual equipment.[41] The Court has forbidden the government from paying teacher salaries in parochial schools, even for teachers of secular subjects;[42] but the Court allowed the government to provide a sign interpreter for hearing impaired students in parochial schools.[43] The Court has permitted the government to pay for administering standardized tests in parochial schools,[44] but not for essay exams assessing writing achievement.[45]

There are two major problems with this argument: it overstates the difficulties in line drawing and it overstates the benefits of clarity in this regard. As to the former, the reality is that for over a half century the Court had developed a workable set of standards concerning permissible government aid to religion. Although the distinctions described above often seem arbitrary, it is possible to identify several criteria that explain them. While not every case fits the pattern, in general, the Court is likely to uphold aid if three criteria are met. First, the aid must be available to all students enrolled in public and parochial schools; aid that is available only to parochial school students is sure to be invalidated. Second, the aid is more likely to be allowed if it is provided directly to the students than if it is provided to the schools. Third, the aid will be permitted if it is a type that likely cannot be used for religious instruction, but it will be invalidated if it can be easily used for religious education.

These criteria help explain the seemingly arbitrary distinctions described above. For example, buses to take children to and from school are provided to students at all schools and are not involved in education itself, but buses for field trips might be to see cathedrals or religious icons. The content of state prescribed standardized tests is secular, but teacher-written essay exams might be on religious subjects. Each of the three criteria is examined in turn.

Second, the value of simplicity is overstated by those who support equality theory. Line drawing is inherent to constitutional law. For the reasons described above, equality theory is so at odds with what the establishment clause should be seen as being about that it should not be deemed acceptable just because it is simpler.

The Issues to Be Faced in the Years Ahead

In the next few years, key issues will be litigated with regard to the establishment clause. Each of these is of crucial significance in preserving the wall separating church and state. Thus it is important that Jews play a key role in opposing the erosion or obliteration of this wall both in public rhetoric and in litigation.

Vouchers

One of the most important unresolved constitutional issues is whether school voucher programs that allow the aid to be used for parochial schools violate the establishment clause of the First Amendment. Although California voters on November 7, 2000, defeated an initiative to create a voucher system, such programs exist in many other parts of the country.

In *Zelman v. Simmons-Harris,* the Supreme Court upheld the constitutionality of voucher programs where vouchers can be spent in parochial schools.[46] The Sixth Circuit properly found that the Ohio program violates the First Amendment because it has the purpose and effect of advancing religion.

The case involved an Ohio law, the Ohio Pilot Project Scholarship Program that creates a voucher program for any school district in the state that was the subject of a federal court order "requiring supervision and operational management of the district by the Ohio superintendent."[47] The law was adopted after such a federal court order was issued for the Cleveland school district. The Ohio law provides scholarships for students in kindergarten through eighth grade in such school systems. The law says that preference in granting scholarships would be to children from low-income families, but other students may be given these vouchers. Under the law, the vouchers may be used only for private education, either at secular or sectarian schools. Schools directly receive funds from the government for students attending under this program.

In the 1999-2000 school year, 3,761 students enrolled in the program, with 60 percent of the families having income below the poverty line. Over 96 percent of all parents used their vouchers in parochial schools. Over 80 percent of the schools receiving funds were church affiliated. Schools receiving the voucher funds can use it for any purpose they choose.

The United States Court of Appeals for the Sixth Circuit appropriately declared this program unconstitutional. The Sixth Circuit said that under the test established in *Lemon v. Kurtzman*,[48] the program was unconstitutional because its purpose and effect were to advance religion. By excluding public schools from receiving voucher funds, the school had the goal of encouraging students to attend private schools, the vast majority of which are religious. The clear and obvious effect is to further religion, especially because there is no limit on how the money is spent.

The Sixth Circuit stated:

> We conclude . . . that the Ohio scholarship program is designed in a manner calculated to attract religious institutions and chooses the beneficiaries of aid by non-neutral criteria. The effect of the voucher program is in direct contravention to these Supreme Court cases which mandate that the state aid be neutrally available to all students who qualify, that the parents receiving the state aid have the opinion of applying the funds to secular organizations as well as to religious institutions, and that the state does not provide an incentive to choose a religious institution over a secular institution.

Voucher programs, like Ohio's, that allow the government's funds to be used for parochial school education are unconstitutional for several reasons. First, such programs violate the principle supported by a majority of the current justices that the government cannot give aid that is actually used for religious instruction. As recently as *Mitchell v. Helms*, Justice O'Connor said that the key rule is that government aid cannot actually be used for religious instruction. Yet, voucher systems do exactly this as government funds are subsidizing parochial schools where religion permeates virtually every aspect of the curriculum. The Ohio voucher program, like all voucher programs, provides funds that can be directly used for religious education.

As the Ohio Supreme Court noted, five justices certainly agree that it is unconstitutional for government funds to be used for religious instruction. Vouchers do exactly that as they provide government money which subsidizes every aspect of the religious institution.

Second, voucher programs, such as Ohio's, impermissibly favor religious over nonreligious education and this, too, violates the establishment clause. Earlier the Supreme Court had approved the receipt of very limited forms of aid by parochial schools. In *Mueller v. Allen*,[49] the Court approved a state law that provided a tax credit for books and locker fees for all students. In *Witters v. Washington Department of Services for the Blind*,[50] the Court upheld a blind student's use of state educational funds at a Christian college. But in both cases the Court emphasized that the student was free to use the money at any institution, public or private. In both, the money was provided to the student who chose where to spend it.

The Ohio voucher program prohibits the student from using the voucher at a public school. The Ohio Supreme Court noted that most private schools in Ohio are parochial and thus the exclusion of public education has the unmistakable purpose and effect of advancing religion. The Ohio program directly transferred the funds from the state treasury to the coffers of the religious institutions. The government was thus both symbolically and actually advancing religion in violation of the establishment clause.

Vouchers are a terrible idea for education. They will divert substantial funds from the public schools without ensuring adequate educational opportunities. The reality is that the more wealthy students will supplement the vouchers to attend expensive private schools, while poor children will be left with what, if anything, that's left. But worst of all, vouchers violate the establishment clause by subsidizing religious education.

Jewish day schools would benefit from vouchers and thus some Jewish groups favor them. But this is very shortsighted as vouchers would entail a major shift of funds from government coffers to churches. It would undermine any limits on government aid to religion. Unfortunately, the Supreme Court in a 5-4 decision reversed the Sixth Circuit and upheld the vouchers program.

Charitable Choice

A second major issue to be litigated are so-called "charitable choice" programs. These allow faith-based groups to receive government money to provide social services. As mentioned above, President Bush has proposed a major initiative in this regard and as of this writing it has passed the House of Representatives and is pending in the Senate.

Charitable choice is inconsistent with the values of the establishment clause discussed above. First, it is a threat to freedom of conscience because it would entail people having their tax dollars used to support religions that they don't believe in. Religious groups already can receive government funds to provide social services:

they simply must create secular arms to do so. Groups like Catholic Charities and Jewish Family and Social Services long have existed. What makes charitable choice different is that it allows the money to go directly to the religions.

Coercion is inevitable as people could be in situations where the only social service agency is a religious one. Imagine a person sentenced to prison, but allowed to avoid it only by going through a drug rehabilitation program. It happens every day in every city. But now the programs are secular. Under charitable choice it is easy to imagine a situation where the only remaining slots are in an overtly religious program that teaches that Christ is the way to stay off drugs. Even though the law says that there must be secular alternatives, there is no way to guarantee that a secular program or a secular slot will be there.

Charitable choice is a threat to religion, too, because inevitably government money comes with strings and government monitoring. Not surprisingly, some religious leaders, such as Jerry Falwell, have opposed it on exactly this basis. Also, charitable choice threatens to expand religious discrimination as the law would allow recipients of government money to discriminate in hiring those providing the social services.

Jews, as supporters of a wall separating church and state, have been in the lead in opposing charitable choice. They must continue to do so in the public arena and ultimately in courts. The reality is that charitable choice will be an unprecedented infusion of government money to churches.

Prayer in Schools

For almost forty years, the Supreme Court has said that prayer, even voluntary prayer in public schools, is unconstitutional.[51] Most recently, in June 2000, in *Santa Fe Independent School District v. Doe*, the Supreme Court declared unconstitutional student-delivered prayers at high school football games.[52] This case was decided by a 6-3 margin, with Rehnquist, Scalia, and Thomas dissenting.

However, and quite significantly, Justice Kennedy has been unwilling to join the three most conservative justices on the issue of school prayer. In addition to being in the majority in *Santa Fe Independent School District v. Doe*, Justice Kennedy wrote the opinion for the Court in *Lee v. Weisman*, which declared unconstitutional clergy-delivered prayers at public school graduations.[53] In *Lee*, Justice Kennedy emphasized the inherent coercion to such prayers. He did not join Justice Scalia's biting dissent that stressed accommodating those who desired to pray.[54]

Therefore, it likely will take replacing two justices from among Stevens, O'Connor, Kennedy, Souter, Breyer, and Ginsburg to overrule the many precedents limiting prayer in public schools. Certainly it is possible that two of these justices might retire in the next four years and there is no doubt that conservatives will push for replacements who would vote to overrule forty years of decisions prohibiting prayer in public schools.

I have heard from countless Jews, just a bit older than me, their stories of being in public schools with prayers. Inevitably, the stories are pained and describe feeling intensely uncomfortable in their classrooms as prayers were mandated. It cannot be assumed that the ban on prayers from the last forty years will continue in the future if there is a significant change in the composition of the Court with replacements picked by President Bush.

Conclusion

The main point of this chapter has been that the separation of church and state matters for Jews and that this basic constitutional concept is under great assault. Jews have played a crucial role in enforcing the establishment clause for decades. As a minority religion, Jews are acutely aware of the essential need for a wall separating church and state. The reality is that those in majority religions often just don't see the problem.

Jewish groups and Jewish individuals thus have played, and must continue to play, a key role in the fights to come. In political rhetoric, legislative activity, and litigation Jews must aggressively defend and fight for a continued separation of church and state. Simply put, the establishment clause is very important for Jews and Jews are very important for the enforcement of the establishment clause.

Notes

1. *Abington School Dist. v. Schempp*, 374 U.S. 203, 237 (1963).
2. *Wallace v. Jaffree*, 472 U.S. 38, 113 (Rehnquist, J., dissenting).
3. 115 S.Ct. 2510 (1995). James Madison issued his famous Remonstrance in arguing against a Virginia decision to renew a tax to support the

church. This is reviewed in detail in *Everson v. Board of Education*, 330 U.S. 1, 12 (1947); *id.* at 31-4 (Rutledge, J., dissenting).

4. Laurence H. Tribe, *American Constitutional Law*, 2nd ed. (Mineola, N.Y.: Foundation Press, 1988), 1158-60.

5. James Madison, "Federalist No. 51," *The Federalist Papers* (New York: New American Library, 1961), 322.

6. *Abington School Dist. v. Schempp*, 374 U.S. at 240 (Brennan, J., concurring).

7. *Id.* at 238.

8. Compare Phillip Hamburger, "A Constitutional Right of Religious Exemption: An Historical Perspective," 60, *Geo. Wash. L. Rev.*, 915 (1992); and Michael McConnell, "Accommodation of Religion," 1985 *Sup. Ct. Rev.* 1 (both considering the historical intent behind the establishment clause).

9. See Erwin Chemerinsky, *Interpreting the Constitution* (New York: Praeger, 1987).

10. See *Good News Club v. Milford School Dist.*, 121 S.Ct. (June 11, 2001); *Widmar v. Vincent*, 454 U.S. 263 (1981) (declaring unconstitutional a state university's policy of preventing student groups from using school facilities for religious worship or religious discussion).

11. 374 U.S. 398 (1963).

12. See *Thomas v. Review Board*, 450 U.S. 707 (1981) (holding that the government could not deny unemployment benefits to an individual who quit his job rather than accept a transfer to work in an armaments section of the factory); *Hobbie v. Unemployment Appeals Commission of Florida*, 480 U.S. 136 (1987) (the Court applied *Sherbert* and *Thomas* and held that the state was required to provide unemployment benefits to a woman who was fired when she refused to work on her Saturday sabbath); *Frazee v. Illinois Department of Income Security*, 489 U.S. 829 (1989) (holding that a state law that required unemployed individuals to be available for work seven days a week infringed free exercise when it was applied to deny benefits to an individual who refused to work on his Sunday sabbath).

13. Madison's Remonstrance is reprinted in *Everson v. Board of Education*, 330 U.S. 1, 63 (1947).

14. *Everson v. Board of Education*, 330 U.S. at 13.

15. *Id.* at 64-65 (reprinting Madison's Remonstrance).

16. 120 S.Ct. at 2574 (Souter, J., dissenting).

17. *Capitol Square Review Commission v. Pinette*, 115 S.Ct. at 2452 (O'Connor, J., concurring in the judgment), quoting *Wallace v. Jaffree*, 472 U.S. 38, 70 (1985) (O'Connor, J., concurring in the judgment).

18. Tribe, *American Constitutional Law*, 1158-60.

19. 120 S.Ct. at 2574 (Souter, J., dissenting).

20. 120 S.Ct. 2266, 2283 (2000) (Rehnquist, C.J., dissenting).

21. 403 U.S. 602 (1971).

22. 403 U.S. at 612.

23. See *Allegheny County v. Greater Pittsburgh ACLU*, 482 U.S. 573, 660-74 (Kennedy, J., concurring in the judgment in part and dissenting in part); *Lamb's Chapel v. Center Moriches Union Free School District*, 508 U.S. at 399 (Scalia, J., concurring in the judgment); *Lee v. Weisman*, 505 U.S. at 644 (Scalia, J., dissenting).

24. 120 S.Ct. 2530 (2000).

25. 120 S.Ct. at 2552.

26. 120 S.Ct. at 2557 (O'Connor, J., concurring in the judgment).

27. 120 S.Ct. at 2581 (Souter, J., dissenting).

28. *Lemon v. Kurtzman*, 403 U.S. 602 (1971).

29. See *Abbington School Dist. v. Schempp*, 374 U.S. 203 (1963); *Engle v. Vitale*, 370 U.S. 421 (1962).

30. 487 U.S. 589 (1988).

31. *Id.* at 602.

32. *Id.* at 616 (citations omitted).

33. *Id.* at 616.

34. 120 S.Ct. at 2581-82 (Souter, J., dissenting).

35. 120 S.Ct. at 2551.

36. *Id.*

37. See Peter Westen, "The Empty Idea of Equality," 95 *Harv. L. Rev.*, 537, 542 (1982). Professor Westen argues that equality is unnecessary as a concept because it always is necessary to develop standards to decide which inequalities are acceptable and which intolerable. Westen says that once these standards exist they can be the basis for decisions, making the concept of equality superfluous. In other words, in the context of the establishment clause, the issue is what aid should the government be providing to parochial schools. Once this is answered, then equality is not at issue.

38. *Everson v. Board of Education*, 330 U.S. 1 (1947).

39. *Wolman v. Walter*, 433 U.S. 229 (1977).

40. *Board of Education v. Allen*, 392 U.S. 236 (1968).

41. *Meek v. Pittenger*, 421 U.S. 349 (1975).

42. *Grand Rapids School Dist. v. Ball*, 473 U.S. 373 (1985); *Aguilar v. Felton*, 473 U.S. 402 (1985); *Lemon v. Kurtzman*, 403 U.S. 602 (1971).

43. *Zobrest v. Catalina Foothills School Dist.*, 509 U.S. 1 (1993).

44. *Committee for Public Education and Religious Liberty v. Regan*, 444 U.S. 646 (1980).

45. *Levitt v. Community for Public Education*, 413 U.S. 472 (1973).

46. 122 S.Ct. 2460 (2002).

47. Ohio Rev. Code §3313.975(A).

48. 403 U.S. 602 (1971).

49. 463 U.S. 388 (1983).

50. 474 U.S. 481 (1986).

51. See *Abbington School Dist. v. Schempp*, 374 U.S. 203 (1963); *Engle v. Vitale*, 370 U.S. 421 (1962).

52. 120 S.Ct. 2266 (2000).

53. 505 U.S. 577 (1992).
54. *Id.* at 645. Scalia's opinion was joined by Rehnquist, White, and Thomas.

6

American Jewry, Pre- and Post-9/11

Gertrude Himmelfarb

Solomon Schechter, a founder of Conservative Judaism in America, was approached in shul one Saturday by a friend who wanted to talk about some problem in the Jewish community. "Don't talk to me about Jews," Schechter told him, "it'll spoil my Shabbes."

Jews had been spoiling my Shabbes for some time. The recent election of President Bush, which I took to be a good omen for the country in general and for Jews in particular, had confirmed a quip coined by my brother, Milton Himmelfarb, many years ago: Jews live like Episcopalians and vote like Puerto Ricans. Four-fifths of Jews voted for Gore, compared with half of the electorate. After blacks, Jews were the strongest supporter of the Democrats in 2000. They even managed to be just ahead of Hispanics.

My brother wrote that just after the election of 1968. Much has happened in the intervening thirty-odd years. Yet one thing remained unchanged. American Jews still lived like Episcopalians and voted like Puerto Ricans. But perhaps they will no longer do so—or at least not in such large numbers. Like some liberals of an earlier generation, Jews have been mugged by reality (a quip coined by another member of my family). American Jews may not be converting to neoconservatism, but they have been awakened to some painful realities. The combined effect of terrorism at home and in Israel has been a powerful shock to our liberal, universalist sensibilities. Israeli doves are not nearly so dovish now; nor are American Jews. Nor are Jews, American or Israeli, quite so reflexively liberal. Liberal Europe, we have discovered, is far more anti-Israel, and anti-Semitic, than most of us suspected, and the UN, once the repository of liberal, universalist hopes for a peaceful world, has proved to be "the dangerous place" that the then ambassador Moynihan said it was many years ago.

At the same time, the Republican administration, and Republicans in Congress, and the American public in general (and especially those in the heartland of conservative America), have turned out to be far better disposed to Israel than many of us had expected. A poll taken by the Republican Jewish Coalition in November 2001 had Jews slightly favoring Bush over Gore had the election been held then. (Even then, however, only 17 percent identified themselves as Republican compared with 54 percent as Democrats.)[1]

Yet there is one area which has not succumbed to the reality principle, at least not to the same extent, although even here I detect some small signs of change. And this is the liberal creed that goes under the name of the separation of church and state—a misnomer, in my opinion, because what is at issue is not the separation of church and state but the separation of religion and society. That doctrine is deemed to be absolute and inviolable, prohibiting any exercise or expression of religion in the public square. Defenders of the doctrine profess to believe that it has been the established practice and persuasion of the country and that it has come under attack only recently by an aggressive religious movement determined to turn back the clock of history. In fact, the reverse is true. What is novel about the situation today is not the effort on the part of some people to bring religion into the public square, but the effort on the part of others to keep it out.

In the current debate on the subject we have been regaled with quotations from Washington, Madison, John Adams, and, of course, the eminently quotable Tocqueville, to the effect that religion is the prerequisite for republican virtue and (as Washington put it) "national morality." My favorite quotation is from Jefferson, not normally one of my heroes but on this occasion all the more quotable. He was going to church one Sunday—this was during his presidency—carrying his large red prayer book. "You going to church, Mr. Jefferson," remarked a friend who met him. "You do not believe a word in it." "Sir," replied Jefferson, "No nation has ever yet existed or been governed without religion. Nor can be. The Christian religion is the best religion that has been given to man and I as chief

Magistrate of this nation am bound to give it the sanction of my example. Good morning Sir."

American Jews once accepted the fact that we are living in a religious—and, indeed, Christian—nation and adapted to that fact with no great difficulty. Those of us of a certain age remember assembly days in public school when we listened to—or, more often, didn't listen to—a psalm or prayer recited by the teacher or principal. In Jewish neighborhoods the language was nondenominational; the word God was always invoked, the name Jesus rarely. But when it was, we Jewish children ignored it; it had nothing to do with us, any more than the Christmas trees that appeared once a year and as quickly disappeared. We had more important things to worry about: grades in school, our popularity ranking in class, and later, the economic depression and war, the relatively few universities open to us and the still fewer careers. We might become elementary or high school teachers, but surely not professors. What is remarkable is that now that discrimination against us is minimal—we are not only students and professors in the most prestigious universities, but provosts and presidents—we have become more suspicious than ever of any intimation of religion in the public square. Prayers, Christmas trees, the very word God, let alone Jesus, seem to threaten our security and well-being.

It is not, as I have said, the old doctrine of the separation of church and state that is at issue, but the relatively new doctrine of the separation of church and society. But in either version that doctrine is more passionately held by American Jews than by others. Almost four-fifths of Jews, compared with less than two-thirds of the country as a whole, think the separation of church and state is one of the most important principles of our government. More than three-quarters of Jews, but only half that number of Americans, think that school prayers violate the Constitution; 60 percent of Jews reject even a moment of silence, let alone of prayer.

The idea of the separation of church and society has as its corollary the separation of religion and morality. Here too Jews are distinctive. Most Americans, but far fewer Jews, believe that if people were to become more deeply religious, this would have a favorable effect upon American society. Half of Americans, but only one-fifth of Jews, think that politicians would be more honest; over four-fifths of Americans, but less than two-thirds of Jews, think that parents would do a better job of raising children; again, almost four-fifths of Americans, but only a little more than half of Jews, think that crime would decrease; over two-thirds of Americans, but well under half of Jews, think that there would be less greed and materialism. Indeed, many Jews believe that greater religiosity would have unfavorable consequences for society. Over half of Jews, but less than one-third of Americans, think it would not only lead to greater prejudice against religious minorities, but also that it would be perilous to our political system.

In all these instances, the polls show Jews agreeing with professed atheists far more than with Americans as a whole. This takes some explaining. It is one thing for atheists to be opposed to religion in the public square—quite another, one would think, for a religious group, even a minority group, to be so. Jewish sociologists have been pondering this paradox for a long time. The most familiar explanation is the historic connection between liberalism and Judaism. Liberal regimes, which have been most hospitable to Jews, have tended to be those without established churches or with only nominally established ones, whereas most authoritarian regimes, less tolerant of Jews, have had strongly established churches. That explanation, however, does not account for two of the most egregious outbreaks of anti-Semitism in recent times: Nazi Germany, where at worst it was acquiesced in, but neither initiated nor carried out, by the established churches; and the Soviet Union, where it had the imprimatur of the established religion—atheism.

Some time ago, I was interviewed by a British journalist commissioned to write a series of articles for a London paper about American Jews (an unlikely subject for an English paper, I would have thought, especially since he himself was not Jewish). He wanted me to explain what seemed to him to be an anomaly. He had just come from interviews with two couples, both young, well-educated, well-to-do professionals, who live similar comfortable, eminently agreeable, and civilized lives in different suburbs of Washington, both members of the local synagogue and of the local country club, and neither of whom has personally experienced any anti-Semitism. Yet their greatest fear, they told him, was that the country would become anti-Semitic. He asked me whether these families are at all typical, whether most American Jews share that fear. As it happened, I had just seen the results of a survey in which Jews were asked whether anti-Semitism or intermarriage is the greatest threat to American Jews. Almost two-thirds opted for anti-Semitism and only one-third for intermarriage[2]—this at a time when intermarriage has risen to unprecedented heights, when the Jewish population in the United States is dwindling, and when episodes and experiences of anti-Semitism are dramatically falling. (This was

well before the latest upsurge of fundamentalist Islam, which is ob-
sessively anti-Semitic, and before the anti-Israel sentiment in
Europe which is becoming indistinguishable from anti-Semitism.)

To account, at least partly, for this fear, I told him a story about
my mother, who was sitting one morning on the balcony of our New
York apartment overlooking Central Park watching the joggers run
in a circular path around the park. Unfamiliar with this peculiar
American pastime, my mother turned to me and asked: "What are
they running from?" An immigrant from Russia, she had all too
lively memories of Cossacks and pogroms, to say nothing of Nazis
and the Holocaust.

These young, affluent Washington Jews who had been interviewed—two generations removed from my mother, and far removed from her in every other respect (economically, socially, edu-
cationally)—evidently share her view of the world, a world in which
religion is not, as it was once thought to be, a haven, a source of
comfort and faith, but rather of anxiety and peril, a threat to well-
being and life itself. In this post-Holocaust world, they think it prudent to limit the scope of religion, of their own and of everyone
else's religion—limit it to the private sphere, the home and synagogue, where it would give solace to the faithful without impinging
on, or endangering, those of another faith—or of no faith.

Historic memories are compelling, for Jews even more than for
most people. After all, as we are reminded every Passover, our very
existence represents a triumph of faith and will over history—a
costly triumph in terms of human lives. And it is hard to eradicate,
even half a millennium later, the dramatic memory of the Inquisition, to say nothing of the recent memory of the Holocaust. Today,
of course, we have the all too evident reality of virulent anti-
Semitism in the Mideast and the less virulent but no longer latent
anti-Semitism in Europe. But neither is quite what American Jews
had in mind a year ago when they worried about American anti-
Semitism. I wonder what those two couples, so fearful of anti-
Semitism, thought the other week when they read about Vanderbilt
University deliberately seeking out Jewish applicants so as to raise
their academic ranking and SAT scores.[3]

Once again we have been mugged by reality. We did not expect
fundamentalist Islam to be quite so fundamentalist or so rapacious.
Our sociologists had assured us that modernization would bring
with it secularization, and both would lead to a diminution of religious passions. As for Europe, there the process of secularization
had gone so far that there was little left even of Christianity in its

most moderate form. We were therefore unprepared for the rabid and aggressive anti-Semitism of radical Islam on the one hand, or for the permissive and persistent anti-Semitism of irreligious Europe on the other.

Nor were we prepared for the near-philo-Semitism of Evangelicals at home. On the contrary, what had provoked the fears of American Jews was precisely the rise of the Evangelical movement as a political as well as a religious force. We had assumed that it was their fervent religiosity that would make them anti-Semitic, if only because they wanted America to be a more Christian society than it is. What we have discovered is that it is precisely the Evangelicals who are most pro-Israel and, as I say, very nearly philo-Semitic, regarding the Jews (as many Jews do not regard themselves) as the people of the Bible, the chosen people, the legitimate heirs of Israel. It is not the Jewish lobby that is the most effective power in favor of Israel. It is, we are now told, the "Christian Lobby," for theological, eschatological reasons that are central to their faith and that make the survival of Israel of paramount importance to them. And that Christian lobby is far more powerful, politically and socially, than the Jewish lobby.[4] Moreover, it is not only Evangelicals who are well disposed to Israel; it is Christian America in general—in dramatic contrast to Europe, where religion is very nearly dormant and anti-Semitism on the rise.

What we now have to wait for is the next stage in the mugging by reality, the translation of this new perception of reality into practice, which would result in a more realistic idea of the relationship between American society and religion—Judaeo-Christian religion, that is, as we know it in America. And Judaeo-Christian religion in multiculturalist and pluralist America, an America that has a larger Muslim population than it had before. It is not religious Evangelicals we have to fear but those secularists who provide no counterbalancing force to radical Islamists, who do not distinguish between fundamentalist Christianity and fundamentalist Islam, or, for that matter, between fundamentalist Judaism (Jewish Orthodoxy) and fundamentalist Islam.

Jewish Orthodoxy is interesting in this respect, because it is (paradoxically, one might think) more attuned to reality than Reformed Judaism—the reality of a predominantly religious and predominantly Christian America that is remarkably hospitable to Jews and Jewish interests. While American Jews as a whole have been especially resistant to any expression of religion in the public square, let alone state-funded religious institutions or activities, Orthodox Jews have been more pliant and accommodating. This is paradoxical because one would expect the Orthodox—doctrinally rigorous and inward directed, traditional and parochial—to be wary of change and suspicious of secular authorities. Yet it is they who have been most receptive to new attitudes and policies that further their religious interests: school vouchers, faith-based initiatives, government aid to religious schools, and other measures designed to counteract the prevailing counterculture (now the dominant culture). And it is they who find common cause with religious Christians (Evangelicals, most notably) in supporting these policies—and also with the political conservatives who have sponsored them.

One of the most interesting surveys of the recent election shows a remarkable correspondence between religious views and political behavior, the "more observant" in every religion voting for Bush, the "less observant" for Gore. But these electoral votes are only symptomatic of a larger social and cultural phenomenon. Within the Jewish "community," as it is mistakenly called (the plural, "communities," would be more accurate), there exists something very like the "dissident" culture (more traditional, moralistic, socially conservative than the prevailing culture) that exists in American society as a whole. And just as the American dissident culture is dominated by, although by no means confined to, the more religious denominations (Evangelicals, most notably), so it is among Jews. The Jewish dissident culture includes some mavericks in the other denominations, but far the larger number are Orthodox (Modern Orthodox as well as the Ultra Orthodox). (I myself happen not to be Orthodox; I once described myself as a nonobservant Orthodox—which, of course, as any Orthodox knows, is an oxymoron.)

The parallel with Christian Evangelicals is striking. In terms of belief as well as behavior, both groups—the Evangelicals and the Orthodox—are rigorous, demanding, focused on their own communities and practices. Yet these are precisely the groups that are today reaching out to society in ways that neither mainstream Christianity nor mainstream Judaism has done. This is a relatively recent development for both of them. It was clearly the counterculture of the sixties that prompted the Evangelicals to come out of their religious isolation and become an active political force. I suspect that something of the same motive operated in the case of the Orthodox, for it was about that time that young Jews, liberated from religion as from so much else, became prominent in the counterculture, radicalized, secularized, and intermarrying in larger numbers than ever before.

Where mainstream Judaism has responded to the counterculture with a policy of appeasement, accommodating itself to what it takes to be the irresistible force of modernity, Orthodoxy consciously and actively (even aggressively, in the case of the Chabad movement) has resisted it. In the course of doing this, it finds itself allied with those who are on the same side in the culture wars, who share a common enemy, a common ethos, and some common interests. In this situation, conservativism—political conservativism, that is—is no longer as alien, as forbidding, as it once was. Today almost half of the Orthodox, but less than one-quarter of other Jews, define themselves as politically conservative. We don't have a breakdown for the Jewish vote in the 2000 election, but we do for 1996, when over 40 percent of the more observant Jews voted for Dole, compared with only about 15 percent of the less observant. (The presence of Lieberman on the Democratic ticket in 2000 may have affected the Orthodox vote then.)

It is also interesting that while a quarter of other Jews believe the Religious Right to be anti-Semitic, only a little more than one-tenth of the Orthodox do. Perhaps it is because the Orthodox are confident of their own faith that they do not feel threatened by other faiths; they are too busy proselytizing among other Jews to worry about Christians proselytizing among them. Nor do they feel threatened by an encroaching government; they are not afraid that their own religious principles and practices will be compromised if they accept government money for their schools. Or perhaps it is simply that they are more pragmatic, more realistic, even more zealous in pursuing their own interests, so that they feel free to abandon old ideologies and causes when they no longer serve their purposes. For whatever reason, more than two-thirds of the Orthodox favor government aid to religious schools, while more than three-quarters of Jews oppose such aid.[5]

At this point, the parallel between the Evangelicals and the Orthodox no longer holds. Evangelicals constitute a substantial part of American Christians—one-third by some estimates, depending upon how Evangelicalism is defined. (In one poll of all Americans, almost half described themselves as "born again" or "evangelical" Christians.) When they entered the public arena, therefore, the Evangelicals became a considerable political force. The Orthodox, by contrast, represent only one-tenth of American Jews, compared with one-third each of the Conservative and Reform denominations, and another quarter identified in the polls as "just Jewish" (ethnically rather than religiously Jewish).

The Orthodox may loom large in the consciousness of other Jews; some Reform Jews make no secret of the fact that they regard marriage with an Orthodox as a form of intermarriage and would actually prefer their child to marry an Episcopalian who shares their values than an Orthodox who does not. But the Orthodox are so much a minority within American Jewry, let alone within America as a whole, that they hardly figure on the political and social land-scape.

Indeed, Jews as a whole figure less on the American scene than they once did. Fifty years ago we were 4 percent of the population; today we are 2 percent. It used to be said that in spite of our small numbers, we exercise a disproportionate political influence because we vote in larger proportions than the rest of the population. This is less true today, now that we are proportionately smaller than we once were—and even more so because we are at such variance with the country as a whole.

Yet post-9/11 finds American Jewry in a new situation. It used to be said that a Republican administration and Congress would be less solicitous of Jews and less mindful of Jewish interests (in Israel, most notably) because Jews are so consistently and, it seems, stub-bornly loyal to the Democratic Party. We now find a Republican president and Congress more pro-Israeli than we had any reason to suspect (or than we experienced with Democratic presidents and Congresses). We also find American Jews responding to this by be-coming more appreciative of Republicans in particular and conser-vatives in general. I have cited one poll suggesting that Jews would favor Bush over Gore (although only slightly) in a rerun of the elec-tion post-9/11. It is too soon to see whether this will be sustained, but there is already evidence of a significant change in the political climate. As one pollster has observed, "This is the first time in my lifetime that it's okay to be a Republican in the synagogue."[6]

Perhaps more interesting is what I perceive as a change in the cultural climate (which may also have political consequences). While American Jewry in general continues to be committed to its two principal articles of faith, the rigorous separation of church and state and the absolute right of abortion, there is evidence of a dissi-dent culture among Jews that has the vitality and self-confidence to challenge these dogmas. There are even signs that this dissident cul-ture is growing, if only because Orthodoxy itself is growing. In less than a decade the Orthodox have increased from 7 percent to 10 percent of American Jewry—an increase partially, but only par-tially, accounted for by the higher birthrate among the Orthodox.

My impression is (and I have no statistical evidence of this) that
there has been a small movement on the part of young people, especially couples with young children, from the Conservative (religious
Conservative, that is) to the Orthodox denomination. And I suspect
that this has as much to do with moral and cultural reasons as religious—the desire to have their children brought up in a more traditional atmosphere with more traditional values. For the same reason,
many non-Orthodox Jews send their children to Orthodox day
schools—and not only non-Orthodox Jews but, according to a recent
report, some non-Jews as well.[7]

More important is the spillover of Orthodox practices and rituals
into the other denominations. This is evident in the increased use of
Hebrew in Conservative synagogues, in the greater familiarity of the
congregation (especially the younger members of the congregation)
with the language and rituals of the services, and in the emergence
of something like a hybrid Orthodox/Conservatism—a religious
neo-Conservatism, so to speak. By the same token, Reform Judaism
is less distinctively Reform than it once was, less insistent, for example, upon not wearing a *kippa* in temple. And among all denominations there is a more serious attempt to educate children, not only
in the traditional Sunday morning schools but in Jewish day schools
which are flourishing as never before, among the non-Orthodox as
well as the Orthodox. With this religious movement to the right
comes a movement to the right politically and culturally—a movement more appropriate, I believe, to the present realities of American Jewry than the reflexive liberalism of old. Political neo-
Conservatism, in short, finds its equivalent in something like religious neoconservatism.

This dissident Jewish culture—still very much a minority—has
succeeded in affirming the religious and communal uniqueness, the
particularity and integrity of the Jewish faith, without isolating or
segregating itself from the country at large. And it has managed to
do so because it understands the social and moral as well as the
spiritual force of religion, a force that inevitably, and properly,
makes itself felt in the public square. These Jews appreciate, as
most of their coreligionists do not, the value and importance of religion as we experience it in America today—not in medieval Spain,
or Czarist Russia, or modern Islam. And not only of religion but of
fundamentalism—again, as we experience it in America today, in
the form of Evangelicalism, or old-fashioned Catholicism, or Jewish
Orthodoxy. There are those who would taint all fundamentalism (including Jewish Orthodoxy) by associating it with radical Islamic

fundamentalism—and who would then taint all religion by associating it with the fundamentalist sects that inevitably arise in all religions. That is a distortion of history and of contemporary reality. What has been dramatically demonstrated by recent events is that radical fundamentalist Islam is radically different from any other fundamentalism or religion in modern times. In its commitment to totalitarianism and terrorism, it recalls nothing so much as pagan Nazism and atheistic Stalinism.

This is the lesson that all of us, Jews and non-Jews, may learn from recent history: that religion is, by and large, a force for good, and that it does not become less good when it emerges from the home and temple and assumes its rightful place in society. Jews in particular have learned a great deal from the Bush administration and from the president himself. We are no longer so fearful of the rhetoric of religion, which comes naturally to a benign and tolerant president, or, for that matter, of the rhetoric of morality (the "axis of evil"), which was so appropriate a response to the events of 9/11. Nor are we so fearful of the conservatives, who have understood, as many liberals have not, the intimate relationship between America's War against Terrorism and Israel's. Nor are we so fearful of the Evangelicals who have been among Israel's staunchest defenders.

The nature of public discourse has changed, and it will inevitably affect our attitudes toward such issues as faith-based initiatives, or prayers in schools, or school vouchers. There are difficult administrative and constitutional problems to address in all of these cases. But however they are resolved, we are already, in a sense, ahead of the game. The Jewish religion is no longer bound by the liberal credo. More and more Jews have begun to recognize that the separation of church and state does not require a comparable separation of religion and society.[8] There may even come a time when Jewish women will no longer feel that the "right of choice" (that is, the unrestricted right of abortion) is their principal article of religious faith. 9/11 has called into question a good many of the old verities and taboos, not only about foreign policy but about domestic and cultural affairs as well.

In my more optimistic moments—and this is one of them—I permit myself to believe that American Jews will learn how to live like Jews, not Episcopalians, and even to vote like Americans, not Puerto Ricans. In any case, Jews no longer "spoil my Shabbes"—at least not on those occasions when I find myself in shul (Orthodox and Conservative, generally) celebrating the Bar Mitzvahs and Bat Mitzvahs of my family and friends.

Notes

1. Most of the statistics in this chapter relating to Jews are from the annual surveys conducted by the American Jewish Committee from 1997 to 2000, updated by David Singer, research director of the committee. Other statistics appear in my book, *One Nation, Two Cultures* (New York: Knopf, 1999), and in my article "Religion in the 2000 Election," *Public Interest,* Spring 2001. See also Fred Barnes, "Bush's New Best Friends," *Weekly Standard,* May 13, 2002, and National Survey of Jewish Americans, conducted by Lunzt Research Companies, Nov. 2001.

2. That survey was conducted in 1999. More recent figures, released since that interview, have 50 percent believing anti-Semitism to be the greater threat and 41 percent intermarriage.

3. Hillel Halkin, in "The Return of Anti-Semitism" (*Commentary,* February 2002, 36), makes the opposite argument. But all of his evidence for a return of anti-Semitism comes from Europe and the Mideast.

4. Tish Durkin, "Why Israel Matters, a Lot, to These Christians," *National Journal,* April 20, 2002, 1115-16.

5. *Bulletin of Institute for Jewish Policy Research* (London) and article by director of the institute, Barry Kosmin, in the *Forward,* October 5, 2001.

The fervent objection to government funding of religious schools is especially odd, because another great liberal democracy, Britain, does just that, and it has never been made an issue there, not by Jews or anyone else. In Britain this practice goes back to the early days of public education in the 1870s, and was reaffirmed in all subsequent education legislation. An act of 1944, for example, specified that children in state schools should be educated "in accordance with the wishes of their parents." Thus Jewish day schools are regarded as part of the public school system, the government assuming most of the costs of maintaining the schools, including the payment of the teachers, and leaving the governance of the schools, admission requirements, and religious teaching entirely in the hands of the board of directors of each school. The only restriction imposed by the government is that the school follows standardized curricula for nonreligious subjects. Any school that does not want to accept that qualification has the simple option of refusing government aid. The success of these schools, measured in purely educational terms (to say nothing of religious, communal, or other criteria), has been such that, while the Jewish population of the United Kingdom has declined by over 25 percent, the number of children in Jewish day schools has increased fivefold. It is astonishing to think that in a country which has not been notable for a vigorous Jewish community, nearly half of all Jewish pupils in Britain today attend state-supported Jewish schools. Tony Blair—a Labour, not Conservative, prime minister—whose own children attend Catholic schools, is so respectful of religious schools in general, and of Jewish ones in particular, that in the course of the last election campaign, he singled out the Jewish schools as "beacons of excellence in the state sector," promising that if demand warrants it, he would establish more "state-aided Jewish schools."

6. Barnes, "Bush's New Best Friends," 16.

7. *Wall Street Journal,* October 12, 2001, W1, 8.

8. See Murray Friedman and Alan Mittleman, "Jews and Compassionate Conservatism," *First Things* (January 2002): 17-20.

7

Traditional Judaism and American Citizenship

William A. Galston

From the destruction of the Second Temple to the onset of modernity, few Jewish communities held the status of full citizenship in the jurisdictions in which they dwelled. Many communities enjoyed a measure of administrative autonomy, but their relationship to the larger polity was fragile. Rights and powers extended to Jews were contingent on the good will and self-interest of the sovereign and were often reduced or revoked as circumstances changed. For the most part, Jewish politics consisted in a kind of diplomacy with authorities who were in effect external powers.

With the rise of the modern nation-state, two other possibilities emerged. Some nations offered Jews citizenship on the condition that they abandon Judaism, at least as traditionally understood and practiced. A smaller number—the United States among them—were prepared to accept Jews as citizens without such onerous conditions. Article VI of the U.S. Constitution declared that "no religious test shall ever be required as a qualification to any office or public trust under the United States." (By contrast, it was not until 1858 that Jews were permitted to occupy seats in the British House of Commons.[1]) Three years after the ratification of the Constitution, the adoption of the First

Amendment guaranteed the free exercise of religion for all faiths. From the earliest years of the Republic, Jews eagerly embraced this generous offer of equality with dignity.

Citizenship is not an unmixed blessing, however. It implies burdens as well as benefits, and it may impose requirements on citizens that challenge the requirements of their faith. U.S. citizenship poses some distinctive challenges for Jews. Consider the following: both Judaism and the United States rest on a fundamental and supremely authoritative text, made binding at a specific historical moment. Both see the text as constituting the core identity of their respective peoples. Both understand the authority of the text in covenantal terms. To apply that text to particular problems, both have developed elaborate traditions of interpretation, which have taken on a standing virtually equal to the text itself. And each text yields judgments and laws that are taken to be binding. On its face, this relationship would seem fraught with opportunities for conflict.

There are complications, however. The nature of the relationship between American Jews and the American polity depends crucially on how they understand their relationship to Judaism and to the United States. Some Orthodox Jews view their status in the United States as parallel to that of their ancestors in Poland: they are sojourners in a land not their own, prepared to take advantage of whatever opportunities may arise to widen the space for the unfettered practice of their faith. This may well involve the artful use of ballot-box strength as a negotiating tool, but the relationship of these Jews with the American polity is largely instrumental. A life obedient to Torah is the end; political arrangements are at best means in service of that end. A relationship between Judaism and America understood in this fashion produces some practical difficulties, but no deep issues of principle.

At the other end of the spectrum are those American Jews who view the Torah and *halakhic* law as matters of cultural and historical significance but not as sources of authority on a par with secular law. For them, the guarantee of religious free exercise confined to private life is sufficient. Indeed, they may well be most comfortable with an arrangement in which all faiths in the American polity agree to regard the private sphere as their appropriate realm. Here, as in the case of the Orthodox, some practical difficulties may arise, but not conflicts touching on fundamental principles.

The most interesting and complex problems arise in the case of Jews who simultaneously define themselves as "traditional"—that is, who understand Judaism in classically religious terms—and regard themselves as conscientious U.S. citizens rather than sojourners. Although I would not characterize myself as a traditional Jew, strictly speaking, the focus will be on this group as the basis for exploring some aspects of the relationship between Jews and the American polity. The heart of Jewish traditionalism is the commitment to certain texts as authoritative, to the interpretation of these texts as a necessary condition for prudent and moral action, and to the community and tradition of interpreters as the touchstone for reflection on practical issues here and now. Accordingly, this chapter will revolve around a handful of key biblical and talmudic texts that for millennia have served as touchstones in debates over the proper Jewish stance toward politics. Being a political theorist by training, I will deploy these texts to address some of the classic questions of political theory as well. While this procedure does not yield concrete answers to specific political problems, it can at least help us to orient ourselves.

It is of the essence of a tradition that develops in community over time that it contains within itself a range of defensible but competing interpretations. Both Judaism and U.S. constitutional jurisprudence manifest this internal plurality. There are interpretations of traditional Judaism that are more and less hospitable to the conscientious practice of U.S. citizenship, and likewise interpretations of American constitutionalism that are more and less hospitable to the practice of traditional Judaism. It is appropriate for traditionalist American Jews to seek out the legitimate possibilities of each tradition that will minimize the tension between them.

The Nature of Political Life

From the onset of modernity, many Jews have been attracted to romantic/optimist political creeds, at the heart of which is the assumption that human beings are fundamentally good (or at least perfectible) and that suffering and evil result from the oppressive and unjust ordering of institutions. Traditional Jews cannot accept this assumption. Immediately after God vows to Noah never again to unleash destruction on the human race as a whole, we read, "The impulse of man's heart is evil from his youth" (Genesis 8:21). Evil is permanent because it is rooted in our nature.

Jews do not take this fact to imply that our impulses are *only* evil, or that our sin is so deep-rooted, so "original" that we are powerless against it. Nor does it mean that human institutions are powerless in the face of our evil inclinations. But it does suggest that the structure of those institutions, and our understanding of them, must reflect the ineradicableness of evil. In one of the most familiar sections of the Talmud, *Pirkei Avot*, we find the following statement: "Were it not for fear of the political ruler men would swallow one another alive" (Mishnah Avot 3:2). Indeed, the first duty of public authorities is to prevent this from happening, by securing the peace and public order. Not only are these goods in themselves; they are the conditions for the effective pursuit of higher-order goods, public or communal; all the more for communities (such as American Jews) that constitute small minorities within the polity.

From this standpoint, it should not be difficult for traditional Jews to acknowledge the importance of the "domestic tranquility" cited in the Preamble to the Constitution as one of the core purposes of our institutions. Nor should they stumble at the threshold of Madisonian realism as the basis of those institutions; there is nothing in the strategy of counterposing interest to interest, passion to passion, ambition to ambition that contradicts the moral understanding of traditional Judaism. Impartial judges and public-spirited executives are always to be sought, and prized as treasures when we find them. But because we cannot count on individual goodness and virtue of citizens or leaders, we must arrange our institutions with an eye to avoiding the greatest evils, even when those who decide and act within them are less than wholly good.

Claims of Politics and Claims of Faith

One might imagine that traditional Judaism would tend toward theocracy. One can certainly find examples of theocracy in the Bible. During the founding of the modern State of Israel, there were many traditionalists who urged the supremacy of religious over political authorities and who were bitterly disappointed when this failed to develop. Isaac Halevi Herzog, a prominent rabbinic authority who welcomed the establishment of the state, writes that he "aspired to create a powerful movement among us whose purpose would be to influence the future legislative council to include in the constitution a basic clause stipulating that the law of the state will be Torah law."[2] For him, it was "inconceivable that the laws of the Torah should allow for two parallel authorities."[3]

If traditional Judaism were unequivocally theocratic, this would create a deep gulf between Judaism and American constitutional politics, which is emphatically antitheocratic. Fortunately for traditionalist

American Jews, there is a long line of biblical and talmudic interpretation that leads to at least a qualified endorsement of secular government.

The discussion takes as its point of departure the establishment of kingship. Gideon famously refused the people's demand that he become king over Israel: "I will not rule over you myself; nor shall my son rule over you; the Lord alone shall rule over you" (Judges 8:23). There was a problem, however—the Lord ruled, not directly, but through human intermediaries. What would happen when these theocratic authorities, the "judges," strayed from the true path? Samuel, the last of the judges, was a righteous man, but his sons were not: "they were bent on gain, they accepted bribes, and they subverted justice." The leaders of the people gathered to request that Samuel "appoint a king for us, to govern us like all the other nations." Samuel resisted their demands, to no avail. The elders insisted that the administration of justice and the conduct of war made kingship necessary: "We must have a king over us . . . [to] rule over us and go out at our head and fight our battles." In the end, the Lord said to Samuel, "Heed their demands and appoint a king for them" (1 Samuel 8).

Although the Lord also tells Samuel that the people's demand for a king means that "it is Me they have rejected as their king," the Bible does not characterize kingship as wrong in the same way that idolatry is wrong. Indeed, the period before kings is linked to stories of strife and disorder. Without a king, "everyone did as he pleased." It seems that the establishment of nontheocratic authority was needed to prevent the Jewish people from swallowing one another alive. Rightly understand, kings can perform limited but critical nontheological functions: ensuring public order, administering justice, and safeguarding the people against external danger.

As the discussion of this matter developed during the talmudic and medieval periods, kingship became a metaphor for secular government in general, not a particular form of political regime. Nissim Gerondi, a leader of the Barcelona Jewish community, argued explicitly for two "separate agencies," one to judge the people in accordance with Torah law, the other to uphold public order. The precedent for this, he insisted, was established during the biblical period: "at a time when Israel had both Sanhedrin and king, the Sanhedrin's role was to judge the people according to just [Torah] law only and not to order their affairs in any way beyond this, unless the king delegated his powers to them." Gerondi accepted that the secular authority would need to use coercion "to enhance political order and in accordance with the needs of the hour," even if the application of force is "undeserved according to truly just [Torah] law." He went so far as to acknowledge that "some of the laws and procedures of the [gentile] nations may be more effective in enhancing political order than some of the Torah's laws." No matter, the king would correct these deficiencies, acting in the name of political order. The secular authority, in short, has one sphere of authority, religious leaders another; and the former need not always give way to the latter in cases of conflict. The aims of Torah law may be more elevated, but the aims of secular law may be more urgent. Sometimes efforts to achieve a spiritually good life must yield to the necessity of preserving life itself.[4]

Once the legitimacy of two authorities, one secular, the other religious, was accepted, a question necessarily arose concerning the relation between them. This question assumed particular urgency after the fall of the Jewish commonwealth and the dispersion of the Jews among the nations of the earth. Shmuel, an authority of the early talmudic period, laid down a principle that became central to all subsequent discussion of this issue: "The law of the [secular] kingdom is law."

This might seem to give secular authority plenipotentiary power over the Jewish community subject to its jurisdiction. Over time, however, two important limitations emerged—one formal, the other substantive. In the Mishneh Torah, Maimonides articulated a version of the principle that we now call "equal protection," which he used to distinguish between genuine laws and arbitrary decrees:

> The general rule is: any law promulgated by the king to apply to everyone and not to one person alone is not deemed robbery. But whatever he takes from one particular person only, not in accordance with a law known to everyone but [rather] by doing violence to this person, is deemed robbery.[5]

To be valid, law must comply with the requirements of formal justice. When secular authority disregards these formal requirements, it exceeds its just powers and may be criticized, even resisted, if circumstances permit.

Alongside this formal restraint, there developed a substantive limitation on the content of secular law that Jews were required to obey. In the course of answering questions posed by Napoleon to the Jews of France, Ishmael of Modena observed that "All the [interpreters of Shmuel's principle] have written that as long as the laws of the kingdom do not contradict Torah law, we must abide by them."[6] But what does it mean to "contradict" the Torah? The maximalist interpretation would be that civil law contradicts the Torah if, and to the extent that it deviates from Torah law. To say this, however, would be to undermine virtually all civil law, contradicting the intention of the basic principle.

The most widely accepted interpretation, historically and down to the present, is that civil law is valid when it "does not contravene an explicit statement of the Torah."[7] Civil law loses its claim to be obeyed if it commands something that the Torah forbids, or forbids something that the Torah commands. It does not follow, however, that traditional Jews are always required to disobey civil law when such conflicts arise. A few civil demands (such as mandatory idolatry) must be resisted, to the death if need be. In most cases, however, it is permissible to take into account the severity of the consequences of disobedience.

The Politics of Traditional Judaism in a Liberal Democracy

In most contemporary liberal democracies, these sharp, explicit conflicts are relatively rare. In the United States, especially, the "free exercise" clause of the First Amendment offers substantial protections to those seeking to live in accordance with the dictates of their faith. Traditional Jews therefore join many other communities of faith in urging an expansive reading of this constitutional language. In 1990, the Supreme Court handed down a decision that reduced protections for free exercise by lowering the standard that government must meet to justify legal interference with religious practices.[8] Traditional Jews participated in a broad coalition to resist and reverse this decision by enacting the "Religious Freedom Restoration Act" (RFRA). This proposal, adopted by the Congress and signed into law by President Clinton in late 1993, required government to show that its interference was made necessary by a "compelling" interest and that the proposed intervention represented the least intrusive means of promoting that interest. (The Supreme Court subsequently invalidated RFRA as a violation of the separation of powers, and the struggle continues.) Liberal democracies can act in ways that either relax or exacerbate the conflict between civil and Torah law. A number of contemporary political philosophers resist the strategy of accommodation in favor of policies that emphasize the force of "civic" claims and that pursue aims thought to be broadly desirable, regardless of their impact on particular communities of faith. Brian Barry, a leading representative of this tendency, has recently published a book arguing that civil concerns nearly always take priority and that cultural and religious claims rarely constitute grounds for objection or accommodation. So, for example, the public demand to prevent (alleged) cruelty to animals suffices to warrant the legal suppression of current kosher slaughtering practices. This is not even a deprivation of religious liberty, Barry asserts, for the simple reason that "nobody is bound to eat meat. (Some Orthodox Jews are vegetarians.)"[9] Clearly, traditional Jews must oppose all arguments of this form and urge instead that liberal democracy rightly understood embodies a presumption in favor of wide religious liberty that is overridden only in the event of a severe clash between religious practices and fundamental human interests that the state must defend. The state may prevent human sacrifice, and it may require Jehovah's Witnesses to permit their children to receive life-saving blood transfusions. But in enacting a general prohibition against the consumption of alcohol or other drugs, it must not prevent their sacramental use.

While debates over conflicts between the demands of civil law and the requirements of faith are noisy, such conflicts are relatively rare. Much more usual is the opposite case, when civil law permits what Torah law forbids. Under these circumstances, traditional Jews face a dual challenge: They must do their best to insulate their own communities against the temptations of a permissive cultural environment, and they may do what seems prudently possible to foster changes in civil law that narrow the gap with (at least the spirit of) Torah law.

Earlier I remarked that living traditions contain multiple interpretive possibilities and that the challenge facing traditional Jews is to find defensible interpretations of both authoritative Jewish texts and the U.S. Constitution that to the greatest extent possible closes the gap between the demands of faith and the demands of citizenship. A strategy that addresses this challenge has now come into view. Following the Gerondian view, traditional American Jews must reject theocracy, instead acknowledging the legitimacy of autonomous secular political institutions that parallel and complement religious authority. At the same time, traditional Jews should embrace an interpretation of U.S. constitutionalism that is "liberal" rather than "civic republican"—that is, a stance that sees the legitimate scope of democratic political power as limited by individual rights, chief among them the right of free religious conscience and free exercise of practices commanded by faith.

Terms of Engagement

It remains to sketch the forms of political engagement that traditional American Jews may employ to implement the broad strategy of narrowing the gap between citizenship and religion. To begin with, some public issues raise concerns, common to all citizens, that can be addressed in purely secular terms. For example, it would have been inappropriate for traditional Jews to invoke principles drawn from Judaism as a basis for resolving *Bush v. Gore*. Whatever one ultimately concludes about that bitterly contested case, the argument should rest on U.S. law, the Constitution, and established practices of adjudication.

There are forms of civic engagement, however, that warrant a distinctively Jewish approach. For example, traditional Jews have an intense interest in sustaining a legal and regulatory environment conducive to *halakhic* practices. They will seek to prevent government actions that impede these practices (for example, burdensome restraints on ritual slaughter). From time to time, they may even seek to involve the government in protecting the integrity of *halakhic* practices—for example, by using truth in advertising statutes to thwart false representations about the kosher status of food products.

Most traditional Jews believe that they must, if possible, send their children to schools in which Jewish practices, interpretive traditions, and history are seriously and systematically taught alongside required secular subjects. For more than seventy-five years, the Constitution has been understood as protecting their right to do so. (The famous case of *Pierce v. Society of Sisters*, decided in 1925, declared it unconstitutional for the law of any state to prohibit parents from sending their children to private or parochial schools.) But it is one thing to have the right, quite another to be able to exercise it. Many families are hard-pressed to pay for a Jewish education, even with community support. Traditional Jews therefore have an interest in laws establishing school vouchers and in court decisions that vindicate their constitutionality.

Some may doubt that group self-interest is an adequate basis for public advocacy. One familiar interpretation of American constitutionalism—Madisonian pluralism—suggests that it is, so long as the group's pursuit of its agenda remains within legal bounds. From this standpoint, groups are not always obliged to adopt the "public interest"—the well-being of society as a whole—as their guiding star. For many (not all) purposes, the clash of interests among groups, coupled with the negotiations these conflicts make necessary—will produce satisfactory outcomes. In a context in which all groups are pursuing their self-interest, "Is it good for the Jews?" is an appropriate question. It is not the only question, however. As a practical matter, effective public advocacy requires groups to link their self-interest to wider societal interests and public purposes. As a matter of principle, Jews are famously reminded to ask themselves, "If I am only for myself, what am I?" I would suggest that this question applies to Jews, not only as individuals, but also as a collectivity. There are broader interests—of our fellow citizens, of humanity, of all Creation—that traditional Jews are required to regard with utmost seriousness.

How are these broader interests to be ascertained? In determining what purposes we share with our fellow citizens, the Preamble to the Constitution is an excellent guide. We are joined together "to form a more perfect Union, establish Justice, insure domestic Tranquility, provide for the common defense, promote the general Welfare, and secure the Blessings of liberty to ourselves and our Posterity." We may argue about *how* to pursue these goods, but not *whether* to do so.

This hallowed constitutional language takes us only so far. Not only do we disagree about the best means to these preambular ends (Which crime bill will best promote domestic tranquility? What level of military spending is needed to provide adequately for the common defense?), but also about the best understanding of the ends themselves. Terms such as justice, welfare, and liberty are far from self-interpreting.

To clarify them, we may have recourse to the tradition of interpretation that has developed since the American colonial period. We quickly discover that there is no single canonical tradition, but multiple and competing traditions, the relative strength of which varies over time. For example, "liberty" in the American tradition is often understood in individualistic and negative terms, as protection against external coercion. From time to time, however, liberty is understood more positively and collectively, as citizen participation in those activities that preserve our existence as a "free people." It was in that latter spirit that John F. Kennedy challenged his generation to "ask what you can do for your country."

Not only are there multiple interpretative traditions in American political thought; they appeal to different sources of authority. While some rest on secular Enlightenment philosophies, others draw unabashedly from religion. In particular, the influence of the Old Testament on the self-understanding and political thought of the Puritan colonists is a commonplace among historians, and the unfolding of the American Revolution only strengthened this outlook. "The finger of

God," said clergyman Phillip Payson in 1782, "has indeed been so conspicuous in every stage of our glorious struggle, that it seems as if the wonders and miracles performed for Israel of old were repeated over anew for the American Israel, in our day."[10] The influence of this potent analogy extended to an understanding of community as covenantal, of Americans as a chosen people, and of North America as a special land endowed with religious significance. These ideas were passed down through the generations, reappearing from time to time in the American public square, most recently in the speeches of Ronald Reagan.

In light of this history, it would seem arbitrary to rule out of bounds, as violations of norms of appropriate public discourse, all efforts by traditional Jews to bring their tradition to bear on the understanding of American public questions. Still, it matters how Jews do this. There is a difference between what may be called the defensive and offensive uses of religion. It is one thing to use the constitutional category of religious free exercise to defend the right of traditional Jews to engage in practices that others may find objectionable or incomprehensible; quite another to use propositions drawn from traditional Judaism as a basis for laws binding on all members of American society, Jews and non-Jews alike. The latter is clearly a more delicate matter calling for the utmost clarity and restraint.

While deliberating on possible laws for a diverse democratic society, interlocutors stand under an obligation to seek mutual intelligibility, so far as possible. This means that adherents of a particular tradition should do their best to state their claims in the broadly "constitutional" language common to all citizens. Nonconstitutional discourse should never be the first resort.

Still, some issues resist reduction to the concepts and categories of the Constitution. In such cases, the adherents of a particular tradition must do all they can to translate their understanding into terms that nonadherents can understand. They will not always be able to accomplish this, but they stand under the permanent obligation to try. When nonadherents ask why they should agree to a proposal, they are bound to be dissatisfied with an answer of the form, "Because the Lord our God has commanded *us* to do such-and-so." Nonadherents have every right to ask why they should consider themselves bound by rules seemingly binding only on members of a group to which they do not themselves belong.

There are three possible responses to this difficulty. One is to articulate what Jewish tradition calls the reasons for the commandments. For some Jewish thinkers—Maimonides chief among them—

underlying every particular commandment is a general reason that can
be articulated to others. If we are not able to explain a commandment,
it is because we have not yet studied it well enough to reach discern-
ment.[11] A more mainstream talmudic position distinguishes between
transparent ordinances (*mishpatim*) "which, had they not been laid
down, ought to have been laid down" and opaque edicts (*hukkim*)
which at least appear to be "senseless deeds," a product of Divine will
which traditional Jews have no permission to doubt.[12] Within the
framework of this distinction, we can say that traditional Jews may use
ordinances but not edicts as the basis of public arguments in a diverse
democratic society, because explanation of the ordinances rests on reasons in principle accessible to all.

A second response to the difficulty of employing tradition-based
claims as the basis of public discourse is to argue that certain principles found within a particular tradition are in fact binding on all human beings. David Novak has forcefully argued that there is in fact a
Jewish "natural law" teaching—the so-called "Noahide law." This
does not mean that all human beings are bound by exactly the same
practical norms. Indeed, he insists,

> One cannot say that Jewish natural law thinking in and of itself pro-
> duces any independent norms. It functions at the level of principles,
> not at the level of specific rules themselves. Actual law is always
> positive law at work with authority in a specific, concrete human
> community in history. What natural law does is to provide certain
> general criteria in the form of a *conditio sine qua non* for the formula-
> tion of this positive law so that it can have truth value in the world.
> Thus it is the limit of the law, not its content.[13]

If this is correct, traditional Jews can at least argue that certain positive laws are beyond the pale, and they can do so on the basis of principles binding on all and in principle rationally accessible to all.

A third response is to acknowledge that while mutual intelligibility
on the basis of shared universal principles is not always possible, there
are nonetheless some circumstances in which the resort to tradition-
based particularity is unavoidable. For example, the U.S. Constitution
speaks repeatedly of "persons," but—fatefully—it does not define per-
sonhood. Some of the bitterest struggles in American history have
been fought over the question, who is a person and therefore guaranteed the full and equal protection of the law? Because the Constitution
is incomplete—not fully self-explicating—it not only permits but actually requires propositions drawn from outside the perimeter of strictly
constitutional discourse to resolve some of the cases and controversies

to which it gives rise. There is no basis for excluding traditional Jews, or for that matter the adherents of any faith, from participating in the public process through which a binding specification of constitutional concepts ultimately emerges.

There is, finally, a form of Jewish public engagement that both affirms communal particularity and reaches out to others across communal boundaries. For some purposes, traditional Jews in the United States consciously separate themselves from their fellow citizens, but they do not withdraw from participation in the nation. These Jews interpret and honor their commandments in full view of non-Jewish citizens. In so doing, they send a message about how best to live. As others receive and react to this message, a kind of implicit civic dialogue develops. This dialogue cannot yield quick, clear results about specific public issues, but over time it can help shape a general civic consciousness.

Maimonides often quoted Deuteronomy 4:6 on this point: All who hear the statutes given to the Jews will say, "Surely this great community is a wise and understanding people." He interprets this to mean that "all the statutes will show to all the nations that they have been given with wisdom and understanding."[14] But how can this be unless they are not only given, but also accepted, with wisdom and understanding? Perhaps the highest form of Jewish civic engagement is to do our utmost, in speech and deed—with acts of justice and kindness and concern for all—to bear witness to the merits of what we have inherited.

Notes

1. Ian Machin, *Disraeli* (London: Longman, 1995), 90.

2. Michael Walzer et al., eds., *The Jewish Political Tradition, Volume One: Authority* (New Haven, Conn.: Yale University Press, 2000), 473.

3. Walzer, et al., *The Jewish Political Tradition*, 475.

4. For these quotations from Gerondi, see Walzer et al., 156-59. As an indication of Gerondi's enduring importance as the prime expositor of the "two authorities" view, note that Isaac Halevi Herzog argues for the rejection of British and Turkish law for the State of Israel through a critique of Gerondi's position.

5. Maimonides, *Mishneh Torah,* Laws of Robbery and Lost Property 5: 14.

6. Walzer et al., *The Jewish Political Tradition*, 451.

7. Ovadyah Haddayah, "Does *Dina de-Malkhuta Dina* Apply to the State of Israel?" excerpted in Walzer et al., *The Jewish Political Tradition*, 477.

8. *Employment Division v. Smith,* 110 S. Ct. 1595 (1990).

9. Brian Barry, *Culture and Equality* (Cambridge, Mass.: Harvard University Press, 2001), 40-45.

10. Quoted in Richard Vetterli and Gary Bryner, *In Search of the Republic: Public Virtue and the Roots of American Government* (Totowa, N.J.: Rowman & Littlefield, 1987), 49.

11. See especially *The Guide of the Perplexed,* 3:26-27, 31.

12. BT Yoma 67b.

13. David Novak, *Natural Law in Judaism* (Cambridge: Cambridge University Press, 1998), 164.

14. See, for example, Maimonides, *The Guide of the Perplexed,* 3:31.

8

A Jewish Policy on Church-State Relations

David Novak

Jews, Judaism, and Public Policy

Before proposing a Jewish public policy stand on any specific issue like church-state relations, one should have some clear understanding of why Jews as Jews should propose any public policy at all in a non-Jewish, secular society like the United States or Canada. By "public policy" is meant what a particular group, like the Jews, itself proposes for the larger secular society in which it is a full and active participant. "Secular society" means a society that does not look to any singular revelation of God in history to be its founding event, thus allowing members of any or no religious tradition to be equal participants in its founding. Without serious consideration of this question, a "Jewish" stand on any public policy issue is likely to be ineffective insofar as its justification has not been sufficiently put forth. Without such justification, the initial reaction of the society at large, to whom such a Jewish public stand on any specific issue, like church-state relations, is being addressed, is very likely to be: "Who are the Jews to be telling *us* what *they* think *we* should do?" Indeed, lack of such clear understanding has prevented some

Christian groups (who have far more experience than the Jews in taking such stands on public policy issues) from being as politically persuasive as they might have been. We Jews, who are relative newcomers to the business of proposing public policy issues in a secular society (other than our own self-interest in combating anti-Semitism and promoting the security of the State of Israel), should take appropriate heed. In other words, we Jews should do our philosophical homework on this general political question, and our ethical homework on it as a Jewish question, before we enter it into political discourse. (By "ethical" is meant the Jewish normative tradition.)

Before addressing the political question of church-state relations, however, we need to move beyond two opposite positions, held by many in the contemporary Jewish world outside of the State of Israel (where the question seems to be essentially different from our general political question in the diaspora), inasmuch as these two extremes essentially preclude the possibility of advocating policies that are both Jewish and public. The first such extreme might be termed "liberal"; the second "sectarian." The following is a quick explanation of the choice of these designations of two fundamentally different approaches taken by Jews on public policy in secular democracies.

The liberal stand has been one that the major secular Jewish organizations have long taken. Basing their arguments on the public duty to protect the private realm of individual citizens, these organizations, for the most part, have only taken public stands on issues where society seems to be infringing on the privacy rights of individual citizens by making religious demands on citizens. It is important to recognize that this stand assumes that the only authentically Jewish religious demands on society are inherently undemocratic, must be religious, but understanding the exercise of religion to be a privacy right which society has the duty to keep strictly private.[1]

Seeing the traditional American concern for the separation of church and state as being based on this classical liberal respect for individual privacy, these Jews have argued that there should be no religiously based advocacy of any issue of public policy inasmuch as religion, being a private matter, has no right to make any public claims at all. Its only legitimate claim is to let its adherents conduct their own religious affairs among themselves in protected privacy. (Due to considerable historical differences, church-state relations on a number of points, especially on questions of public education, have to be judged differently in Canada than in the United States.)

At most, the "Jewish" character of such advocacy has been based on the fact that even in democracies like the United States, it has been the experience of many Jews to find themselves in public situations where members of a Christian majority were exercising social pressure on Jews to participate in their publicly endorsed Christian religious practices (like prayers in schools), either actively or passively. Accordingly, on an issue like church-state relations, whose public advocacy is usually made in what seems to be religious terms, the liberal stand turns out to be quite consistent: religion is a strictly private affair, for both the Jews and everyone else.

The "Jewish" character of this type of advocacy turns out to be that Jews are taken to be the most visible victims of political or social pressures placed by a majority on a minority to have, in effect, their religious privacy invaded. But, surely, Jews are not the only such victims of the refusal of a majority to recognize the privacy rights of a religious minority. In fact, certainly in North America, other minority religious groups have suffered far more public persecution than the Jews have suffered here. (This point often makes comparisons between modern European Jewish history and modern North American Jewish history rather spurious. Such forms of public persecution as pogroms or forced conversions are not part of the Jewish experience in North America, whereas they have been part of the experience of such groups as Mormons, Quakers, and Roman Catholics.) Despite that historical fact, the liberal Jewish stance portrays Jews as if we were the most vulnerable religious minority in the history of our society in North America, which, in fact, we were not.

In a political context, or more specifically, in a legal context (the courts being the place where this type of Jewish advocacy has usually been conducted, and where it has won some significant legal victories), this liberal stance is seen as being "assimilationist" because it does not allow Jews to speak in the public square as Jews sui generis, but completely assimilates us into a larger class of anonymous private citizens.[2] In a social context, it is equally assimilationist because it assimilates us into a larger class of "victims of public persecution" (which usually turns out to be, at most, social rather than strictly political or legal pressure to conform). Since this approach to public policy has ruled out a truly distinct Jewish voice from speaking in public ab initio, it would regard "Jewish public policy" to be a political oxymoron. By its principles, what is "Jewish" must be kept private, and what is "public" must be kept "nonsectarian."

Furthermore, it is important to bear in mind that this type of liberal advocacy, which wants religious claims to be kept *out of* the public square, is essentially different from that type of advocacy which wants racial or ethnic barriers to participation *in* the public square to be abolished. Based on this difference, I applaud the efforts of some secular Jewish organizations to eliminate racial segregation, and the reverse racial segregation of affirmative action type quotas, to be removed from all spheres of public life. But it is too bad that these same organizations do not see the similarity between efforts to keep religions out of the public square and efforts to keep racial or ethnic minorities out of the public square. Such exclusionary efforts, whether based on prejudice against particular races or ethnic groups, are as unjustified as are the opposite attempts to privilege one religion or one racial/ethnic group in the public square. The true task of such political advocacy should be to promote the social inclusion of all and the social privilege of none, whether people define their prepolitical identity along ethnic or religious lines.[3]

The sectarian stand, conversely, is one that has characterized much of the public policy advocacy of the Orthodox Jewish communities in North America. Unlike the liberal, assimilationist stand, which basically claims for Jews the right to maximal participation in public life in a way totally separate from their private Jewish claims, the sectarian stand has been one that argues for maximal Jewish separation from public life and its claims. Whereas the liberals want a place in the public square for Jews who are unencumbered by their Judaism, the sectarians want an increasing number of exemptions for Jews from the public square altogether. Indeed, they want their exceptionalism to be the basis of their making claims on the public for maximal practice of their own, seemingly peculiar, privacy. It would seem they want religiously observant Jews to be tolerated in our society as we tolerate such arcane "sects" as the Mennonites or the Amish. Thus, whereas the liberals want Jews to be in the public square as much as possible in anonymous garb, the sectarians want to wear their distinctive garb (both literally and figuratively) as much as possible in their own, protected enclaves. And, whereas liberals usually invoke the language of universalism ("everyone ought to be enabled to do X"), sectarians usually invoke the language of the conscientious objector ("we, but not you, ought to be enabled to do Y").[4]

The best example of the difference between these two seemingly opposite Jewish stands on public policy questions per se is that of public funding for parochial schools. The liberals, whose greatest battles (and many victories) have been over issues of religious practices in the public schools, have been opposed to public funding for parochial schools (like current proposals for school vouchers) because it violates the strict separation of church and state (which they hold with a dogmatic literalism). No public support of any religious institution, no matter how pluralistic that support might be, can be tolerated without opening the door for the religious takeover of civil society by the most dominant religious community in that society—in their view. As such, only state-run schools can be truly neutral. The sectarians, conversely, argue in favor of public funding for parochial schools as not only a negative right (that is, a right not to have the state dictate to one where his or her children are to be educated, as long as the parochial school fulfills minimal, state mandated, educational criteria), but also as a positive entitlement. Thus in front of several Orthodox Jewish schools in Toronto, where I live, are signs saying, "Thank you Mr. Harris for your support." This refers to Mike Harris, the premier of the province of Ontario (of which Toronto is the provincial capital), who has actively supported a voucher system of tuition aid that can be accessed by parents who send their children to these parochial schools.

The theory behind this sectarian approach to the education of children is twofold. One, there is the economic argument, which appeals to the common good. It is argued that it is cheaper for the state to provide a voucher for parents to send their children to schools that are legally private (since only part of their funding comes from the state) than it is for the state to have to provide full education to all children for free. Two, and far more significantly, there is the real political argument. It is argued that the virtual monopoly of public schools in the area of the mandatory education of children has led to an undemocratic overextension of the power of the state in the social life of its citizens, especially in the area of moral education.

There is no doubt that the Orthodox approach to public policy questions is faithful to the normative Jewish tradition, yet it does not seem to be able to cogently advocate public policy for the secular society in which we are fully enfranchised citizens. In other words, it still seems to assume that we Jews are political outsiders who can only engage in special pleading. On the other hand, it seems that while the liberal or assimilationist approach ignores the specific strictures of the normative Jewish tradition, it does cogently recognize the full political enfranchisement of the Jews in our soci-

ety nonetheless. It does recognize quite well the fact that in this society we Jews are not the external objects of a foreign polity (as we
were in premodern times), but we are very much active subjects
within the political process of this society. That being the case, I
would like to suggest here what a Jewish public policy on the
church-state question might be. It is hoped that this suggestion will
incorporate Orthodox fidelity to the Torah and the Jewish normative
tradition (especially as defined by *halakhah*), and one that incorpo-
rates liberal Jewish interest in the larger public realm in which we
Jews are both necessarily and happily participate actively.

Criteria of Jewish Public Policy

The vast majority of the Jews in the world today would agree that
the best place for Jewish life to survive, let alone flourish, is in a
democracy.[5] That is why almost all Jews who can choose where they
want to live have chosen to live in democracies like the United
States and Canada. Even most of the increasing number of Jews who
have chosen to live in the State of Israel have chosen to live there
primarily because it is a democracy. And even those religious Jews
who have chosen to live in the Land of Israel because it has a
unique sanctity for Jews, even when they do not regard Israel's being a democracy to be a reason that would prevent them from living
there. And even those religious Jews who desire that the State of
Israel become a theocracy (that is, a state fully governed by *halakhah*) would only want that transition to come about through democratic means, namely, through the choice of the vast majority of
Jews in Israel (and probably in the whole diaspora as well). In other
words, very few religious Jews would want a theocracy to be instituted through an antidemocratic coup d'etat. (That is why the followers of the late, explicitly antidemocratic Rabbi Meir Kahane are
a fringe group even in Jewish religious circles, almost as much as
those *haredi* or ultra-Orthodox groups who refuse to recognize the
national sovereignty of the State of Israel de jure and sometimes
even de facto as well.) Therefore, it is quite certain that contemporary Jews want to be full participants in any democracy where we
live, be that in Israel or in the diaspora, and that we want to be more
than simply tolerated guests as we were in almost all premodern,
non-Jewish societies. That means we not only want to follow somebody else's public policy proposals, but that we want to propose
some of our own. Specifically, what can we propose to the secular,

democratic society at large concerning church-state relations that it is possible for them to accept with democratic integrity?

There should be three criteria to guide any Jewish public policy proposal: (1) the Torah and Jewish tradition; (2) the common good of the larger society in which we participate; (3) Jewish self-interest. Let us continue with our example of the issue of public funding of religious or parochial schools. What should a Jewish public policy position be on this issue? How should this position be argued to ourselves? How should this position be argued to others?

It is only when a Jewish public policy position is grounded in the Torah and Jewish tradition that it has any Jewish authenticity.[6] Happily, in Western democracies like the United States and Canada, the right of religious freedom is not simply an entitlement from the state. Rather, it is recognized as a right prior to the power of state, which the state is duty bound to respect, that is, to confirm not to initiate. This means one not only has the right to worship as one pleases (which usually means the right to affiliate with the worshiping community of one's choice), but also such humanly received rights as the right to base one's moral actions (that is, actions that pertain to interhuman affairs) on what his or her religious tradition accepts to be the will of God. Only a religious affiliation, as opposed to mere ethnic or racial identity, comes with its own morality built into it. For most people in North America (but probably not in Europe anymore), their religious outlook and their moral outlook are inextricably intertwined. Therefore, the right of the free exercise of our religion is prior to the state's duty to protect it. But, in order for us to properly exercise our religious morality in public, we must understand what it demands of us first, that is, what it requires us to do ("thou shalt") and what it requires us not to do ("thou shalt not").

The fact that a group of Jews, even a large group of Jews, can and do advocate policies that are contrary to the Torah and Jewish tradition, even if these claims are only made on fellow Jews, does not make these policies *Jewish* in a coherent way. Thus, for example, there is a publicly identifiable group of Jews who have adopted Christianity, yet who still regard themselves to be Jews, and who still believe their Christianity to be a form of Judaism. They usually designate themselves to be "messianic Jews." Yet, why has there been unanimous rejection of their "Jewish" claims by the entire Jewish community? It is not in any way a part of Judaism any longer, and that any Jew who practices Christianity has betrayed the Torah and Jewish tradition in a radical way—even though as individuals they are still regarded by religious Jews to be part of the

Jewish people because Jewish identity is irrevocable.[7] (And that is by religious, not racial, criteria.) This is the most extreme example, but the general principle behind it has wider application.

Another less extreme example of this point might bring it closer to the experience of more readers of this chapter. About eighteen years or so ago, several Jewish scholars, including myself, were invited by a major Jewish organization to write essays on four or five general social and political issues from "a Jewish point of view." After the papers were completed, we scholars were to meet with a committee charged with the task of editing and publishing our papers under the imprimatur of this prestigious organization. Of the papers written, only one provoked any real controversy. That was the paper one of the scholars wrote on the question of abortion, a topic on which he is an acknowledged expert. Even though this scholar recognized that the Jewish tradition permits, and sometimes even mandates, an abortion when the fetus presents a threat to the life or health of the host mother, he had to honestly admit that there is no right to abortion sanctioned by the normative tradition. As such, the debate among traditional legal authorities is not about whether there is a right to abortion or not; rather, there is only debate about the extent of the range of threats to the host mother that can justify an abortion. (The author of the paper himself recognized a wider range of such threats than do many—but not all—traditional *halakhic* authorities.[8]) That is why abortion has always been extremely rare among traditional Jews. In other words, no matter how many such threats one designates, the assumption is that abortion itself is prohibited, and that the burden of proof is on the mother and her advocates to show why there should be dispensation from this prohibition. It is a situation of where the burden of proof is on the accuser, that is, the mother who is accusing her fetus of being a direct threat to her life or her health.[9]

When this paper on abortion was presented to the committee for editing and final approval, the vigorous controversy began. One member of the committee, a professor of social work at a prominent American university, protested that the paper did not reflect her opinions or those of her Jewish colleagues and friends. This author reminded the objector that the papers were not to be sociological surveys of what various Jews think about the issues being researched. Rather, the papers were to be written about what the traditional Jewish sources say about these issues. Sometimes there is great debate within the sources themselves on the issue itself as, for example, on the issue of capital punishment: some being in favor of capital punishment; others being opposed to it (at least de facto). However, despite the "pro-choice" opinions of the objector and her colleagues and friends, there is no such debate about elective abortion in the Jewish tradition. It was suggested that she write a counter paper to the one she so opposed, and show what is truly *Jewish* about her opinion other than the obviously "Jewish" name of its author. To the author's knowledge no such counter paper was ever written. Perhaps the reason it was not written is that it could not have been written as "a Jewish point of view" with any real coherence. Accordingly, our primary attention should be paid to the question of what Judaism requires of Jews among ourselves.

The first question any Jew should ask himself or herself is not "what does the Jewish religion say about X?" but, rather, "what does *our* holy Torah require *us* to do in situation X?" In other words, "what does *my* God and the God of *my* Jewish ancestors demand of *me* here and now?"[10] The former question could be asked by anyone; the latter question, however, could only be asked by a Jew. There can be and there always have been disputes about just *what* is commanded in any specific situation, but there can be no dispute among traditional Jews *that* the Torah does require something to be done in any significant human situation; that is, no one in the tradition denied that God has indeed spoken to us forever in His commandments about everything. Without that sense of divine commandment (*mitzvah*), the author does not see how any public proposal can claim to be coherently—that is, traditionally—Jewish.

When it comes to what the Torah commands Jews, the mandate to educate our children in the Torah and Jewish tradition is clear. Originally, it is located in the commandment, "you shall teach them [the teachings of the Torah] to your sons" (Deuteronomy 11:19). That original commandment, however, only refers to a one-on-one father-son relationship, which we today would see as informal education or "home schooling" (which, by the way, some parents are demanding that the state recognize as their right).[11] Nevertheless, in most cases, formal education begins when a father delegates a teacher or teachers in a school to fulfill this pedagogical obligation for him.[12] It is understood that most fathers are unable to teach their sons on a regular basis due to either intellectual or emotional or financial impediments. Furthermore, the community is to provide schools for those whose fathers cannot pay for their education, or who have no fathers at all.[13] And, although the question of formal education required for girls has a long history of discussion in Jewish tradition, the overwhelming consensus today, even in the most

traditional circles, is that the obligation to provide primary and secondary education for Jewish girls is practically the same as that for
boys.[14] Finally, there is precedent for Jews receiving support for
Jewish welfare institutions like schools from non-Jewish sources.[15]
In our day, in fact, an even stronger case can be made for actively
accepting state aid for Jewish schools since the state is an institution
in which we participate as equals with the non-Jewish citizens. In
other words, it is possible for us to claim it as a justified entitlement
rather than as merely arbitrary charity. (This will be discussed later
in this chapter.)

With this question of what is required by the Torah and Jewish
tradition of ourselves settled in general, we should now move on to
the question of the moral requirement we envision for the gentiles.
Accordingly, we need to ask three questions: (1) Does Judaism advocate any universal moral norms? (2) If so, how are the gentiles to
know what are their moral responsibilities in general? (3) Are we
Jews obligated to advocate what Judaism considers universal moral
responsibilities and, if so, how?

Unfortunately, as we have already seen above, the liberals have
totally separated religious advocacy (making it private) and moral
advocacy (making it public). Thus, for them, these questions are
meaningless insofar as they presuppose a public presence for a religiously based political morality. So, we must turn to orthodox or
traditional Jews (whatever their official denominational affiliation)
for such answers. We must address our questions to those Jews who
follow in the traditional paths, who still look to the Bible and the
Talmud and the Codes for moral authority, that is, for governance
and not just arbitrarily accepted guidance—authority that has both a
voice and a veto. It is a very sad fact that we have lost a common
Jewish moral language with those Jews who have strayed from the
traditional paths, especially those who have done so with conscious
conviction. We can only speak to them on general moral issues as
we would speak to morally earnest gentiles. Only on political questions, where one can locate a factor of even secular Jewish self-
interest, can we sometimes still speak to them as Jews.

Many Orthodox Jews would answer that just as God commanded
a specific morality to the Jews, so God commanded a more general
morality to the gentiles. And, just as God's law to the Jews is written in the Torah and the rabbinic writings, so is God's law to the
gentiles written there. Therefore, in order for the gentiles to know
what are their moral obligations, they have to ask the Jews, which
means that they have to submit to the moral authority of Judaism.[16]

Now, in and of itself, this position is not morally offensive since it is not the type of imperialism that would make slaves out of outsiders, slavery being when a politically or even culturally dominant group makes more stringent rules for outsiders it controls than it does for the insiders who control them.[17] That is because Judaism has always taught that it is to make more stringent rules for the Jews than it can or should make for any non-Jews who come under its authority.

Nevertheless, this approach is irrational and undemocratic because it does not answer the obvious question: Why would non-Jews want to come under the moral authority of the Jews enforcing Jewish law? (Even in the State of Israel, non-Jews are only living under the *secular* political authority of the Jews, but in religious matters— including marital and most familial matters—they are under the authority of their own *religious* communities.) Why would non-Jews want to live under Jewish moral authority in a second-class status when they could just as easily fully convert to Judaism and thus attain first-class Jewish status? It would seem to require what could be well described as de facto conversion to a particular historical revelation—Judaism—by accepting the moral position being advocated de jure. Unfortunately, though, this is what is implied much of the time when Orthodox Jews advocate "the Jewish position" on any major issue of public morality. This has been especially so in the burgeoning field of biomedical ethics, where there seems to be keen interest in what Judaism and other religious traditions have to say about its fundamental moral questions (although where this general interest will ultimately or even eventually lead is still quite murky at present). Moreover, other questions of public morality are being addressed to Orthodox Jews, such as the church-state question, that do not necessarily or even very often involve medical practices. Most of the answers proposed so far, if the experience of Orthodox Jewish involvement in biomedical ethics is any guide, will turn out to be politically ineffective because of their philosophical inadequacy—that is, unless another type of moral argumentation is developed by Orthodox Jews.

Fortunately, there is a more rationally inclined strand of the normative Jewish tradition which, if properly explicated, enables Jews to teach morality to the world without, however, requiring conversion to Judaism either de jure (that is, literally requiring gentiles to become Jews for the sake of their moral integrity) or even de facto (that is, requiring gentiles to become the modern equivalents of the ancient "sojourners" or "resident aliens"—*gerei toshav*).[18] This cen-

ters on the key rabbinic category of the "Noahide laws," that is, the
seven basic normative categories that have been seen as pertaining
to all humankind in every time and place (all humankind being seen
as the descendants of Noah, that is, those descendants of Adam and
Eve who did not pervert human nature and who thus deserved to
survive the cataclysmic Flood). And in the rationalist strand of the
Jewish Tradition, it is assumed that these normative categories are
known through what Maimonides, the greatest rationalist theologian
in Judaism, called "rational inclination" (*mipnei hekhre ha-da'at*).[19]
In other words, these norms are known through rational reflection
on the ordinary, universal, moral experience of the justifiable claims
all humans need to make on each other and the recognition, therefore, of what are unjustifiable claims humans make on each other.

Of these seven norms, four are most pertinent to modern moral
discourse: (1) the prohibition of taking innocent human life (*shefik-
hut damim*); (2) the prohibition of sexual license (*gilui arayot*)—
specifically the prohibition of incestuous, adulterous, homoerotic,
and bestial acts; (3) the prohibition of robbery (*gezel*); (4) the prescription to any society to establish courts of law to enforce, as best
it can, the other six categories of Noahide law (*dinim*).

Of the remaining three norms, (5) the prohibition of eating a limb
torn from a living animal (*ever min he-hai*); (6) the prohibition of
blasphemy (*qilelat ha-shem*); and (7) the prohibition of idolatry
(*avodah zarah*) seem hard to justify in modern moral discourse. All
we can say is that perhaps the prohibition of eating a limb torn from
a living animal can be generalized into a rationally cogent prohibition of cruelty to sentient beings (what the rabbis called "the pain of
animals," *tsa'ar ba'alei hayyim*).[20] And, perhaps, the prohibition of
blasphemy can be generalized into a rationally cogent prohibition of
"hate speech" against anyone's religion/god. And, perhaps, the prohibition of idolatry can be generalized into a rationally cogent prohibition of the type of modern pagan ideologies like Nazism, which
advocate murder, robbery, and rape. Along these lines, it should be
noted that even though the Jewish tradition has always debated
whether non-Jewish religions like Christianity and Islam are idola-
trous or not, there has been a marked tendency in the tradition to
respect other religiously based cultures whose general moral commitments are close enough to the Noahide norms Judaism takes to
be universal.[21]

Even though a Noahide-like morality can be learned by ordinary
human reason, the historical fact is that it is usually learned through
religious tradition. Thus the great fourteenth century rabbi Mena-

hem ha-Meiri spoke respectfully of both Christianity and Islam as "nations bound by the ways of divine law" (*megudarot be-darkhei ha-datot*).[22] Moreover, the sense of absolute obligation, which is so necessary for morality to be more than what is relatively useful to its subjects, is best inculcated when morality is learned as that which is the direct will of God to human beings, and which is transmitted by religious traditions based on revelation. For this reason, then, it would seem to be in the interest of general morality that as many children in society receive the most explicitly moral education possible. Indeed, all education has a moral thrust. Thus, if education is about teaching truth, then it must be based on the moral norm to speak the truth and not lie. And, it would seem that a moral education which presents moral norms as divine commandments is more effective than a secular moral education that cannot speak about God at all because it cannot speak about moral absolutes.[23] But, such a morally relative education has become more and more prevalent in public schools because of the lessening cultural consensus about morality in our secular society.

This does not mean that I am suggesting that public education is not needed in our society. Religious liberty requires secular education be provided for those who do not want a religiously based education for their children. It is similar to the way religious liberty requires that civil marriage ceremonies be provided for those who do not want religious marriage ceremonies for themselves. Nevertheless, I am suggesting, based on the Jewish obligation to encourage the gentiles to follow universal moral norms, that Jews can encourage state support of religious primary and secondary schools as the best places to foster this type of moral education.[24]

The question now is: how do we Jews translate this moral argument about the benefit of a state-supported religious education into a politically effective argument? Clearly, the range of morality is greater than the range of politics since society can only effectively enforce a part of morality.

The Political Argument: The Social Contract

The best philosophical justification for a secular society like ours is the idea of "the social contract."[25] This idea underlies the constitutions of both the United States and Canada. It means that civil society and whatever state it founds are not imposed upon citizens from a separate sovereign but, rather, the citizens themselves are sovereigns who create a civil society and its state to protect and further their own rights or interested claims. The error, though, of much of contemporary, liberal social contract theory is that it assumes that the social contract is entered into by anonymous individuals, having no history behind them, and operating from behind what John Rawls, the most important liberal political theorist in the last half century, likes to call "the veil of ignorance."[26]

Nevertheless, since no one can really claim to have no history behind him or her, the current idea of social contract has to see it as a hypothetical construct. But since experience is a better foundation for practical reason than hypothesis, would it not be more rational to look upon the social contract—better, social contracts—as a real event in history, made between people who have histories and do not want to forget them (that is, to be ignorant of them and their claims for continuity into the future)?[27] One can look at the ratification of the United States Constitution in 1788 or the ratification of the Canadian Constitution in 1982 as such events of social contract. The parties to these social contracts are not lone (autonomous) individuals but, rather, they are fully communal, socialized, historically situated persons. Canadians, with their idea of "founding peoples," have a clearer conceptualization of historical social contracts than do most Americans, even though they are still unclear whether "founding people" is an essentially religious—as in "French Catholics" and "English Protestants"—or essentially a racial/ethnic term —as in "Quebecois" and "Anglos."

Unlike the morality with which they entered the social contract, the sovereignty of the people who enter the social contract is relative. That is, they confer on the state its legitimacy, but their own existential legitimacy is conferred upon them by a law whose sovereign they are not. When living according to their higher law in public, or when advocating some of its norms for the larger society by rational argument, religious citizens are exercising their religious liberty in the most politically significant way possible. The right to educate one's children, and the concomitant right of all others to educate their children, very much comes from that prior realm *from which* we all entered *into* the social contract.

What a historical idea of social contract does is to confirm that the establishment of the secular state as the governing structure of civil society inherits more than it creates. Thus the state creates such institutions as the national currency, the military, the official government institutions like the legislature, the judiciary, the administration, and the head of state. But what the state inherits from the overlapping histories of its contracting citizens is the fundamental law under which they live, and which enables them to enter into any contract, public (social) or private, with any real integrity. Thus, despite the fact that the United States formally severed its political ties to Britain, it still maintained its normative connection to English Common Law (which sees itself as rooted in the law of God). And, our current understanding of civil marriage is very much part of that legacy.[28] Accordingly, in a very significant way, one can say that the state comes into existence to promote what its citizens have *already* accepted as moral law, not that the moral law is the creation of the state or even the social contract that created the state. It is only revolutions like the French Revolution of 1789 and the Russian Revolution of 1917 that attempted to re-create the entire legal, social, and cultural order. And we all know all too well the horrendous political, legal, social, and cultural results of these "godlike" attempts by new states—in the persons of their totalitarian rulers—to create totally new societies, indeed, totally new human beings. (Fortunately, English and American notions of social contract are more beholden to biblically influenced philosophers like Spinoza and Locke than they are to atheistic philosophers like Hobbes and Rousseau, who formulated more radically innovative ideas of social contract.)

One could well say that one of the primary reasons for the willingness of citizens of the United States and Canada to enter (affirm) or remain loyal to (confirm) the social contract of their respective societies is because these societies have in effect promised to preserve and enhance the traditional institutions—like marriage and the family, and religion—that the citizens of the state have *brought with them* into the new polity. (Thus it is significant that the United States refers to itself as a *novo ordo*, yet does not regard its law to be unprecedented.)

Since Jews, even by the admission of many friends and many enemies, have as strong and as coherent a tradition as can be found anywhere—especially as it pertains to moral education—it would seem that Jews, who are unambivalently committed to that tradition, ought to recognize the benefit to society as a whole by having the state not only tolerate the religious education of those children whose parents are committed to it, but that society should partially support it as well. This can be represented as a political requirement for Jews in the larger secular society in which we live and where we are, happily, fully enfranchised with all the rest of our fellow citizens as political equals.

Jewish Self-Interest

It is an old Jewish question whether the Torah was given for the sake of the Jews or whether the Jews were chosen for the sake of the Torah.[29] However, there is actually a dialectic at work between these two positions. On the one hand, if the Torah was given for the sake of the Jews, then Jewish self-interest is itself Torah. If, on the other hand, the Jews were chosen for the Torah, then Jewish self-interest cannot identify itself with the Torah, but it must justify itself by the Torah that transcends it. This also implies that the Torah was truly given for all humankind, but the Jews are the only people so far to accept it fully.[30] I think one can correlate these two positions as follows: Since the Jews are the custodians of the Torah in this world, on any public policy question we should first ask ourselves: is this good or bad for the Jewish community? But since the Torah's intent begins but does not end with the Jews, we should ultimately ask ourselves: is this good or bad for humankind? The fact of our election should persuade us that nothing that is bad for the Jewish people can be good for humankind. The fact of our custodianship of the Torah should persuade us that nothing that is good for humankind can be bad for the Jews. So far, we have argued for the state support of religious education because it is good for society as a whole. It is clearly good for the Jewish people since there is clear evidence that Jewish children educated in Jewish day schools have a much higher rate of loyalty to the Jewish people and the Jewish tradition than do Jewish children who have only received a Jewish education that supplemented a secular education, or who have received no Jewish education at all.

Of course, all of this benefit has taken place within our *secular* society. Most Jews are happy to be living *within* secular society as first-class citizens rather than living in a society *under* Christian or Muslim rule as resident-aliens. Nevertheless, Jews should be wary of current *secularism*, which is the view that society requires no transcendent justification for its existence and its moral authority. Whereas religious people can make a religiously based commitment to a secular society, doctrinaire *secularists* cannot accept any such religiously based commitment as valid for anyone. And, although secularism is only one moral point of view among several in our society and culture, it often claims to be the only possible philosophical foundation for democracy, thus rejecting any view that bases itself on a transcendent justification to be hopelessly undemocratic, even antidemocratic.

Traditional Jews cannot, in good faith, make common cause with such secularists in our society, even though too many traditional Jews still do not understand that point very well. But we can make common cause with those traditional Christians (the chance of any common cause with Muslims at the present time is virtually nil because of the Arab-Israeli conflict) whose immediate and long-range public interests are threatened by the type of militant secularism that opposes any public support of religious education. (On this question of public funding of religious education, for significant historical reasons, the secularist threat is much more acute in the United States than it is in Canada.)

The success of such political alliances depends on these Christians being able to convince Jews that the promotion of our moral commonality—that is, the Judeo-Christian ethic—is not a ruse for proselytizing Jews, or for the reestablishment of an officially Christian society, that is, a return to "Christendom." There is, of course, such a risk in making these new alliances, but this author thinks the effort is worth it, barring sufficient evidence to the contrary.

In summary, then, public support for religious primary and secondary education is in the best interest of the world, in the best interest of the Torah, and in the best interest of the Jews. Advocating such support is very much a way Jews can exercise political responsibility in the secular order in which we now live. It is both an exercise of our religious right to continue our traditional way of life across generations, and it is our religious duty to support the common good of a society that truly facilitates our living that traditional Jewish way of life in its midst.

Notes

1. The most distinguished and successful proponent of the strict separationist argument was the constitutional lawyer Leo Pfeffer, for many years counsel for the American Jewish Congress. Pfeffer argued some of the most famous church-state cases before the U.S. Supreme Court. Aside from his legal briefs, Pfeffer's political views are found in his *Church, State, and Freedom* (Boston: Beacon Press, 1953), and his *God, Caesar, and the Constitution* (Boston: Beacon Press, 1975). For a more recent presentation of this argument, from a historian, see Naomi W. Cohen, *Jews in Christian America* (New York: Oxford University Press, 1992).

2. This type of political liberalism, which bases itself on the primary individualism of the right to privacy, has been the subject of much philosophical critique of late by a number of thinkers generally seen to be

"communitarian." See, for example, Alasdair MacIntyre, *After Virtue* (Notre Dame, Ind.: University of Notre Dame Press, 1984); Charles Taylor, "The Politics of Recognition," in *Philosophical Arguments* (Cambridge, Mass.: Harvard University Press, 1995), 225-56.

3. For a critique of the strict separationist view by a Christian social theorist, whose views have gained increasing influence on more socially conservative Jews, see Richard John Neuhaus, *The Naked Public Square* (Grand Rapids, Mich.: Eerdmans, 1984). For the most recent critique of the inability of liberal thinkers to recognize a true place for religiously based participation in a democracy, see J. Judd Owen, *Religion and the Demise of Liberal Rationalism* (Chicago: University of Chicago Press, 2001).

4. Some of the most important Orthodox arguments have been made by the constitutional lawyer Nathan Lewin. For some of his briefs and related materials, see Jonathan D. Sarna and David G. Dalin, *Religion and State in the American Jewish Experience* (Notre Dame, Ind.: University of Notre Dame Press, 1997), 271-81.

5. See D. Novak, *Covenantal Rights* (Princeton, N.J.: Princeton University Press, 2000), 29-31, 204-05.

6. The most famous enunciation of this principle was made by the ninth-century Jewish theologian Saadiah Gaon in his *The Book of Beliefs and Opinions*, 3.7, S. Rosenblatt, trans. (New Haven, Conn.: Yale University Press, 1948), 158: "Furthermore, our nation of the children of Israel is a nation only by virtue of its laws."

7. See D. Novak, *The Election of Israel* (Cambridge: Cambridge University Press, 1995), 189-99.

8. For the range of traditional Jewish opinions on abortion, all of which recognize specific cases where abortion is mandated, and none of which recognizes any general right to abortion, see David M. Feldman, *Birth Control in Jewish Law* (New York: New York University Press, 1968), 251-94.

9. The main rabbinic sources are *Mishnah*: Ohalot 7.6; *Babylonian Talmud* [hereafter "B."]: Sanhedrin 72b; Maimonides, *Mishneh Torah* [hereafter "MT"]: Laws of Murder, 1.9. Also, see D. Novak, *Law and Theology in Judaism*, 1 (New York: KTAV, 1974), 114-24; *Covenantal Rights*, 28-31. For the rabbinic principle of the burden of proof being on the accuser, see B. Baba Kama 46a-b.

10. This is best expressed in the talmudic principle, "it is greater to be commanded and practicing than not to be commanded and practicing" (B. Kiddushin 31a and parallels).

11. *Tosefta*: Kiddushin 1.8; B. Kiddushin 29b re Deut. 11:19.

12. Maimonides, MT: Laws of Torah Study, 1.3.

13. B. Baba Batra 21a.

14. See D. Novak, *Law and Theology in Judaism*, 2 (New York: KTAV, 1976), 54.

15. B. Baba Batra 8a and *Tosafot*, s.v. "yetiv"; Maimonides, MT: Laws of Kings, 10.10.

16. See Maimonides, MT: Laws of Kings, 10.11.

17. See B. Sanhedrin 59a and parallels; also, B. Yevamot 22a.

18. See Nahmanides, *Commentary on the Torah*: Gen. 34:13; also, D. Novak, *The Image of the Non-Jew in Judaism* (New York: Edwin Mellen Press, 1983), 53-6; *Jewish Social Ethics* (New York: Oxford University Press, 1992), 189-201.

19. MT: Laws of Kings, 8.11. See Novak, *The Image of the Non-Jew in Judaism*, 275-318.

20. See B. Baba Metsia 32a re Deut. 22:4; B. Shabbat 128b.

21. Thus, for example, Persian civil and criminal law could be accepted by the Rabbis as being valid for Jews who lived under Persian jurisdiction (B. Baba Batra 54b and parallels), even though the Persians themselves were certainly polytheists. Nevertheless, it was believed that their polytheism was more a matter of ancestral custom than theological conviction (B. Hullin 13a). This may have well been a rabbinic attempt to emphasize ethics more than theology when dealing with non-Jews.

22. See Novak, *The Image of the Non-Jew in Judaism*, 351-56.

23. See Joseph Albo, *The Book of Roots*, 1.8. Cf. Thomas Aquinas, *Summa Theologiae*, 2/1, q. 99, a. 2.

24. For Jewish support of gentile ethical/religious education, see Novak, *Jewish Social Ethics*, 230-32.

25. See D. Novak, "Law: Religious or Secular?" *Virginia Law Review* 86 (April 2000): 569-96.

26. See his *A Theory of Justice* (Cambridge, Mass.: Harvard University Press, 1971), 136-42.

27. See D. Novak, *Natural Law in Judaism* (Cambridge: Cambridge University Press, 1998), 12-26.

28. See John Witte, Jr., *From Sacrament to Contract* (Louisville, Ky.: Westminster John Knox Press, 1997).

29. See *Mishnah*: Makkot 3.16 re Isa. 42:21. Cf. B. Pesahim 68b re Jer. 32:25; also, D. Novak, *The Election of Israel* (Cambridge: Cambridge University Press, 1995), 241-48.

30. See *Sifre*: Devarim, no. 343; also, *Mekhilta*: de-ba-hodesh 1; Philo, *De Decalogo* 1.

9

Jewish Law and American Public Policy: A Principled Jewish Law View and Some Practical Jewish Observations

Michael J. Broyde

Mea Culpa

I am not a political scientist, and I am not active in American political life, such that my observations about what is good or bad for Jews in America are worthy of publication or even discussion. In the synagogue which I worship, we have a rule that the rabbi is not allowed to speak about naked political matters from the pulpit, even Israeli matters, and that has struck most of the congregants, and the rabbi himself, as a wise idea, since these are exceedingly divisive matters whose truth is hard to prove, other than with hindsight—and then it is too late!

Having said all of this, the reader might ask why I was asked to write a chapter on law and public policy—and why I agreed to do so.

The answer is that this chapter is primarily focused on what Jewish law *requires of Jews* in matters of public policy. This is a matter that my scholarly skill can address. At the end of the chapter, I cannot help but do that which I know I lack the credentials to undertake: I apply the principles that I develop to the public arena, as I perceive it. That final step is the one most vulnerable to criticism, and for that I apologize.

Monotheism and Fundamentals of Jewish Law

Jewish law[1] presupposes that there is just one God, and that such a Deity is the sole God in the heavens and the earth, unmatched and omniscient. Jewish Law expects that all people—Jews and gentiles—will accept this one God as THE GOD and worship God appropriately, Jews according to Jewish law, and everyone else according to Noahide law. (Noahide law is that area of Jewish law that discusses what Jewish law thinks gentiles should be doing, and is, in the eyes of Jewish law as binding as Jewish law itself).[2] To the extent that one can speak about a single Jewish contribution to religious civilization, it is this exact notion of monotheism; this single value permeates every single facet of rabbinic thought. Inversely, Judaism's distaste for polytheism or paganism, either by Jews or gentiles, is profound and pervasive.

A word on paganism—a word distasteful to the modern American mind—is needed. Jewish law is rigorously monotheistic and has a considerable amount of religious contempt for faiths that deny the unity of God. These faiths are referred to in this chapter as pagan or polytheistic.[3] Conversely, the Jewish tradition has a great deal of respect for the inherent validity of monotheistic faiths other than Judaism. The Jewish tradition does *not* maintain that all must acknowledge the "Jewish" God; rather, it recognizes that monotheism need not be accompanied by recognition of the special role of the Jewish people.[4] Maimonides' opening formulation of the Jewish view of messianic times is revealing. He writes:

> One should not think that in messianic times that the normal practices of the world will change or that the laws of nature will change. Rather the world will be, as it always is. The words of the prophet Isaiah "and the wolf will dwell with the lamb, and the leopard shall lie down with the goat" are metaphors meaning that the Jews will live peacefully among the gentile nations of the world.[5]

Even in messianic times, the Jewish tradition avers that there will and should be gentiles—people who are not members of the Jewish faith. The existence of those who are not Jewish is part of the Jewish ideal, which requires that all worship the single God, although not exclusively through the Jewish prism of worship. The Talmud insists that in messianic times conversion into Judaism will not be allowed; Jews and gentiles will peacefully coexist.[6] Jewish law is not the ideal legal code for all—only for Jews. For example, consider the remarks of Rabbi Judah Loewe of Prague concerning the Jewish law prohibition of crossbreeding in animals. He states:

> There are those who are aghast of the interbreeding of two species. Certainly, this is contrary to Jewish law which God gave the Jews, which prohibits inter-species mixing. Nonetheless, Adam (the first person) did this. Indeed, the world was created with many species that are prohibited to be eaten. Inter-species breeding was not prohibited because of prohibited sexuality or immorality. . . . Rather it is because Jews should not combine the various species together, as this is the way of Jewish law. As we already noted, the ways of the Jewish law, and the [proper] ways of the world are distinct. . . . Even those forms of creativity which Jewish law prohibits for Jews are not bad by definition. Some are simply prohibited to Jews.[7]

What flows most clearly from this is that there is nothing intrinsically wrong with crossbreeding, even if it violates Jewish law; indeed, Rabbi Loewe nearly states that such conduct by gentiles is good. Jewish law is not a general ethical category governing the conduct of all; its scope and application is limited to Jews, not merely jurisdictionally, but even theologically.

Jewish Law and Paganism

An interesting trend can be found in modern American culture; once freedom of religion was genuinely granted to all Americans (about fifty years ago),[8] pagan and polytheistic religions began to multiply—they asked to be a part of the public religious dialogue in American culture. It is almost as if the talmudic observation that the hunger for paganism was dead had been proven wrong in America.[9] No less a public religious figure than the Reverend Pat Robertson, founder of the Christian Coalition, recently decried this phenomenon, and has even indicated that he will oppose faith-

based government funding unless something can be done to eliminate the "deviant" religions from the right to receive government
funding. Robertson states:

> Our laws do not let government engage in content discrimination of
> speech. The same government grants given to Catholics, Protes-
> tants and Jews must also be given to the Hare Krishnas, the Church
> of Scientology or Sun Myung Moon's Unification Church—no mat-
> ter that some may use brainwashing techniques or that the founder
> of one claims to be the messiah and another that he was Buddha re-
> incarnated. Under the proposed faith-based initiative, all must re-
> ceive taxpayer funds if they provide "effective" service to the poor.
> In my mind, this creates an intolerable situation.[10]

Although Reverend Robertson does not explicitly tell us why
this is "an intolerable situation," what he means is that any religion
whose founder claims to be the messiah or Buddha reincarnated
ought not be allowed to be part of any government program. It is
better to have no government programs than to have a program that
supports any and all religions. These religions, Robertson feels,
ought to be suppressed and not supported.

This chapter will address whether the across-the-board support
for all religions—including pagan faiths—creates an intolerable
political situation for Jews who adhere to Jewish law. How should
we respond to attempts to deny pagans the right to worship freely?
We will explore how Jewish law and Orthodox Jewish society
should respond to requests for religious freedom by members of
secular society to the secular government, when we know that
many will use their newly minted freedom of religion to engage in
pagan rituals and practices that are categorically and absolutely
forbidden to all (Jew or gentile) according to Jewish law. It will
then address a related question: What should Jewish public policy
be when addressing matters that violate Jewish law or that encourage the violation of Jewish or Noahide law?

Consider for example, a stark case of conflicting values. In
1989, the city of Hialeah, Florida, passed an ordinance that suppresses the right to a group of pagans to engage in animal sacrifice,
a rite which is central to their religious belief and ritual conduct.
The members of the suppressed religious faith sued, alleging a violation of their First Amendment right to freedom of religion. This
case is more complex as a matter of American law than it might
appear, as the Supreme Court had recently ruled in *Employment
Division v. Smith*[11] that neutral governmental rules can be applied

against religious activity—thus, for example, a law that prohibits medically unnecessary surgical procedures for children could ban ritual circumcision.[12] Should a Jewish institute for public affairs support Hialeah's law because it does, in fact, suppress paganism (as Jewish law wants) or should it support the right of the pagans to worship freely, as freedom of worship is a valuable principle that we ought to defend even if the people who are now using this principle conduct their lives in violation of Jewish law (Noahide law) principles, since they are polytheists worshiping many gods?

The point I wish to make is that these decisions are, in the eyes of Jewish law, broadly speaking, political decisions, and not strictly Jewish law ones. They are not governed by a tight calculus that always requires that one seek from the secular government a policy that maximizes observance either of Jewish law or of Noahide law. If one can persuasively argue this approach with regard to paganism, then I believe that this argument extends mutatis mutandis, to every other violation of Jewish law, each of which is less serious than the utter rejection of monotheism.

Jewish Law Is Not Internally Religiously Pluralistic

Before one proceeds to analyze an exact response to polytheism in Jewish law, one must realize that the unvarnished Jewish law (stripped of any nuances and complexities) is neither very pluralistic in its core values nor deeply tolerant of rooted and structured dissent from its principles. This simple quotation from Maimonides directly lays out the pristine Jewish law as he understood it. Maimonides states:

> Heretics and apostates, those who worship idols yet are Jewish, or they sin in other ways to flaunt their sinfulness, even eating not kosher or wearing mixed wool and linen garments, are heretics. Heretics—which are those who deny torah and prophecy among the Jews—it is a good deed (*mitzvah*) to kill them. If one can kill them in public, with a sword, do that; otherwise, interact with them in stealth, until you can kill them. For example, if one sees one of them fall into a pit, and the ladder is in the pit, quickly grab the ladder from the pit and tell them "I am running to take my child down from the roof and then I will return it" [and then do not return it] or other such actions.[13]

One can find many medieval Jewish law commentators who argue with the details of this exposition of the Jewish law. One can note that most medieval commentators prohibit actually killing even an intentional first-generation heretic. However, merely permitting indirect murder or even merely noting that one should not save such people from death[14] is illustrative of the fact that there is very little substantive textual support in Jewish law for the "live and let live" classical religious pluralism adopted by American law.[15]

One is hard-pressed to find—internal to Jewish law—much that is positive about the value of letting people worship whichever gods they see fit. The structured response of one group of commentators is that such people ought to be killed in public as a display of what happens to those who rebel, and a "more liberal" view is that we should merely arrange for the indirect death of these people, without actually killing them! Yet a "more liberal" view posits that one should merely not save such people and let them die. None are very "pluralistic" in their orientation. Jewish law has the same theoretical view toward gentiles and central violations of Noahide law; violations are punished, by execution and sometimes by other means, and systemic rebellion is punished by death.[16]

Thus, those who seek to advocate tolerance and pluralism as a political agenda for the Jewish community will not find it in the classical rabbinic sources themselves when they deal with flagrant and open sinners. Where then does this approach come from? The answer, I suspect, is in the logic of practical calculus captured well by the rabbinic phrase *"yatza secharo behefsado"*[17]—the gain accrued through any given action can sometimes be lost through the price paid. Whenever the Jewish community sets out to advance a political or religious agenda, it should not only look at the gain from advance, but also the losses it must sustain to accomplish this advance, and whether—no matter how hard it tries—it will lose anyway, and thus ought not even try.

Elsewhere I have developed a model for reciprocal economic rights according to Jewish law, which is a more principled exposition of this notion. That article posits that:

[I]n the area of financial rights, duties and obligations, Jewish law frequently excluded gentiles from the full benefits of Jewish law because Jewish law did not consider them to be bound by the obligations of Jewish law. Thus, for example, Jewish law did not compel the return of the lost property of a gentile, since he was not legally obligated to return lost property belonging to others.

Exclusion was based on a failure of reciprocity—the privileges of Jewish law were given only to those who were fully obligated in and thus accepting of Jewish law, in this case, the laws of lost property.

Thus, one can now fully comprehend the importance that personal status and reciprocity play in the law of lost property. The unmodified talmudic rule for property of a person who does not consider himself bound by Jewish law is that one is under no obligation to return the lost property of such a person, since that person—honest as he might be—does not consider himself reciprocally legally obligated to return such property. Jewish law ruled that one may—but need not—return his property, just as he may—but need not —return your property.

On the other hand, in the case of a person who considers himself bound by Jewish law to return lost property, one is obligated to return the property of such a person precisely because the person feels legally obligated to do the same. Indeed, the same rule is true for the lost property of a person who is legally bound according to secular law to return lost property to others. Jewish law would require that his property be returned, as he would do the same to a Jew.[18]

In this approach, Jewish law codified reciprocity as the manner of measuring the gain and loss. Indeed, a case can be made that this type of balancing is substantively principled in that it extends Jewish law rights to people who grant Jews secular rights. However, it is clear that this calculus is not grounded in a moral theory of political rights such as Dworkin or Rawls would consider consistent with liberal conceptions of political justice. A case could be made that the principles demonstrated in that article can form a basis for political pluralism in the Jewish tradition grounded in more than the mere politics of survival.

If the proper Jewish response to a request for civil rights for pagan rites is to engage in a political calculus of reciprocity—rather than to automatically support restrictions that diminish paganism—the same political calculus is needed for every component of basic morality. The decision by the Jewish community to support the expansion or contraction of civil or political rights in secular law is not a Jewish law decision and it never has been. Why this is so is explained in the next section.

There Is No Obligation to Prevent Secular Society from Sinning

In an earlier article of mine, presented at an Orthodox Forum of Yeshiva University, entitled "Jewish Law and the Obligation to Enforce Secular Law,"[19] I review the relevant technical Jewish law and conclude that *classical Jewish law does not compel a Jew to persuade or entice a people generally to observe the law* and that Jewish law sees no technical obligation in most situations—even as it is morally laudatory—to insure that Noahides obey their laws.

Why is there no obligation to monitor secular law and values to insure that they are consistent with Jewish law? The answer (as explained in the above quoted article) is that most devisors of Jewish law rule that—other than in situations where one is the "but for" causation of a person sinning—Jews are not responsible, in a formal, technical, Jewish law sense, for the content of secular law or for its enforcement. (This is even more true for the general tone of secular society.)

Even though there is no technical Jewish obligation to inform uninterested gentiles of the Noahide law, and no obligation upon Jews to enforce Noahide law, there are no less than five reasons why the Jewish community might, nonetheless, choose to participate in the articulation of values and law in gentile community. They are:

A. Heightened Ethical Duties to All People Created in God's Image

Jewish law recognizes that it is morally laudatory to inspire people to observe Noahide law. Ethics of the Fathers (*Pirkai Avot*) states: "[Rabbi Akiva] used to say, Humanity is precious since people were created in God's image."[20]

Rabbi Lipman Heller comments: "Rabbi Akiva is speaking about the value of all people. . . . He wished to benefit all people including Noahides. . . . Rabbi Akiva seeks to elevate all inhabitants of the world."[21]

Rabbi Judah the Pious observes: "When one sees a Noahide sinning, if one can correct him, one should, since God sent Jonah to Nineveh to return them to his path."[22]

Thus, there are many theological reasons why it might be good to teach Noahide laws generally, and indeed, a claim can be made that Jewish law obligates a truthful response to an honest query from a person concerning his obligation under the Noahide code.[23]

B. Corruption in Society Affects Us All

Jews are part of the general society, and what ails a general society will come to ail Jews also.
Rabbi Moses Schick states:

> [I]t appears that any situation that involves judging violators, even if they are Noahides, is a Jewish person's concern, for others will learn from any wrong done in public and will follow suit and, in the least, the sight of evil is harmful to the soul. Thus, it is our concern. In any case, it is inconceivable that any person living among the residents of a given city be beyond the jurisdiction of the court.[24]

Rabbi J. David Bleich puts it a little differently. He states:

> Despite the absence of a specific *obligation* to influence non-Jews to abide by the provisions of the Noahide Code, the attempt to do so is entirely legitimate. Apart from our universal concern, fear lest "the world become corrupt," as Maimonides puts it, it is also very much a matter of Jewish concern and self-interest. Disintegration of the moral fabric of society affects everyone. Particularly in our age we cannot insulate ourselves against the pervasive cultural forces which mold human conduct. Jews have every interest in promoting a positive moral climate.[25]

Corruption of values affects all, and one needs to work to insure values in society—our society in which we fully participate.

C. Desecration of God's Name

By standing by silently when others sin, Jews sometimes appear to be supporting or condoning violations, which are a desecration of God's name. It is possible that there could be situations where public institutional silence by Jewish groups as to the propriety of a particular activity by government or other groups, particularly when other religious groups are protesting this activity as immoral, could lead to desecrations of God's name and thus a wrong. On the other hand, the more clearly known it is that governmental policy is nonreligious in nature and that Jewish law imposes no obligation on Jews to protest, the less serious an issue this becomes.[26]

D.   Fixing the World: *Tikun Olam*

The mandate of *tikun olam*, a Jewish obligation to make the world a better place, might provide some direction.[27] Volume VII of the Orthodox Forum series was directed toward this principle, and the many different essays shed some light on this concept.[28] However, fixing the world has never been treated as a mandatory Jewish law principle in the same way as any general *religious obligation*, or even as a rabbinic obligation. One can choose, in particular circumstances, not to fix the world now if the consequences of fixing are deleterious to one's long-term interest.

E. Being a Light unto the Nations: *Ohr Lagoyim*

There is the philosophical mandate to be a "light unto the nations of the world." As noted by medieval scholar Rabbi David Kimchi commenting on the words "light onto the nations" (Isaiah 42:6) "because of the influence of the Jews, the gentiles will observe the seven commandments and follow the right path." While an elaboration on this concept is beyond the scope of this chapter, and deserving one of its own, a brief review of the use of the term "light unto the nations" indicates that it is normally used to mean that the Jews should behave in an exemplary manner such that gentiles will wish to imitate Jews, and not as a mandate to proselytize observance of Noahide law.[29]

In Summation

There is a wealth of rabbinic sources that encourage one to be an active participant in the secular society in which one resides. However, this participation was never deemed, neither formally nor informally, to be a *mitzvah* and was never formulated as any sort of a Jewish religious imperative.

Concerns in the Opposite Direction

The absence of a general obligation upon Jews to increase observance of the Noahide code by gentiles, or to rebuke gentiles when they violate Noahide law, or to separate gentiles from sin, allows for a balancing of Jewish interests to occur; Jews need not participate in general society to the detriment of the Jewish community or individual Jews. This is even true given the presence of such concepts as the prohibition of generating hatred through rebuke,[30] which certainly allows one to be silent in the face of sin by both Jews and gentiles. So, too, the lack of obligation to rebuke an intentional sinner[31] diminishes the obligation mandating conduct to castigate sinners and remove sin.

Even more so, the license to facilitate sin when the sin will happen no matter what a Jew does (and the sinner is a knowing and willing participant in a deliberate violation of Jewish or Noahide law) even further reduces the force of the obligation.[32]

In sum, Jewish law does not mandate that Jews need to craft a policy toward secular law that always penalizes a violation of either Noahide or Jewish law. Jewish history supports this understanding of obligation. One sees very little overt response—in the sense of active involvement—by the Jewish law community to the conduct of the gentile community.

Of course, it would be ideal if we could always adopt a policy that increases fidelity to Noahide law by gentiles, Jewish law to Jews, and was also consistent with the Constitution of the United States. Sadly, we cannot, because these values are frequently mutually exclusive. Frequently, we are called upon to make hard choices about how to rank values that we want to put on the public agenda. The possibility that there might be circumstances where the unfettered teaching of the Noahide code in the United States (where distinctions based on religious affiliation, content, or practice cannot be governmentally defended) could be deleterious to the observance of Jewish law by Jews is not to be dismissed.[33] The possibility that a clearly Jewish attempt to seek enforcement of Noahide laws could result in vast antagonism and backlash toward Jews and Judaism from those groups whose conduct is categorically prohibited by Noahide law cannot be ignored. The consequences of endorsing and supporting a governmental policy that denies civil rights and encourages economic discrimination against people who engage in pagan conduct which violates Noahide law, but which harms no one other than other willing participants, might be very drastic and deleterious to the Jewish community, which has benefited mightily from ironclad rules against religious discrimination, both on a private and a public level.

This view of the mandates of Jewish law is supported by the Orthodox Jewish response to the *Church of Lukumi Babalu Aye*,[34] dealing with pagan animal sacrifice. This case, in fact, was litigated, and many different Orthodox Jewish organizations briefed in the Supreme Court in support of pagans' right to worship.[35] Not a single Orthodox group briefed in favor of the City of Hialeah and the suppression of paganism. Why? Certainly not because the conduct in this matter is permitted by Jewish law or Noahide law. One can claim that the conduct of this group is a central breach of everything the Jewish tradition stands for—monotheism. Nevertheless, the institutional advocacy groups within the Orthodox community realize that freedom to worship ought to be protected as a matter of secular law, even when the way worship occurs is a fundamental violation of our most basic Jewish rules and values. Were pagans to spread their religious values, one could readily see an anthropological change in how religion would be viewed, just as Judaism was viewed dramatically differently two thousand years ago when surrounded by polytheistic pagans. Nonetheless, the Orthodox Jewish community and its various institutions have all been diligent in supporting freedom of worship for all, because, in the totality of the picture, it is of benefit to Orthodox Judaism.[36]

Thus, the central question is simple to state when it comes to matters of civil rights: what policy will leave the Jewish community better off? Indeed, this is part of a very complicated general question about whether the Orthodox community ought to seek the expansion of civil rights generally and political pluralism specifically—so as to protect the economic and political interest of the Jewish community.

(My own view of what is needed is stated in the next section, but the answer I provide is centrally unimportant to this methodological discussion, because the details of my calculus may be wrong—I, of course, think not. However, precisely because there is no exact Jewish law mandate compelling one to support increased observance of Noahide law as a Jewish law obligation, one must weigh a political calculus of what to do.)

Legislative goals which do not necessarily seek to enforce Jewish law can be well supported from the positions taken by decisors of Jewish law on political questions. For example, in 1977 Rabbi Moses Feinstein—the dean of the Orthodox rabbinate in America—was asked what statutory changes Orthodoxy should seek from the New York State government on the issue of time of death. He replied that Orthodoxy should seek a legislative mandate that allows each person (or family) to determine the time of death in accordance with their own religious or personal beliefs. He did not suggest that the proper governmental policy to seek is that New York State should be urged to adopt Jewish law in this area. The public policy advocated by Rabbi Feinstein in the context of time of death—one of Orthodoxy seeking to allow Jews to follow Jewish tradition, without forcing our standards on nonbelievers—was the preferred one. This was so notwithstanding the certainty that some people, given this new freedom, will adopt a standard for time of death which violates Jewish law by withdrawing care before a time permitted by Jewish law and thus committing murder— the only violation on par with polytheism. Rabbi Feinstein did not feel compelled to seek the enforcement of Jewish law by the secular state.[37] As Rabbi Chaim David Zweibel of Agudath Israel of America puts it: "The principle of religious accommodation is one that has stood the American Orthodox Jewish community in good stead in a wide variety of secular legal contexts. . . . For what is really at issue here is . . . whether it is in the interest of the Torah observant community to combat secular laws that preclude individuals from following the guidance of their individual [Jewish law] decisors."[38]

Indeed, in the famous amicus brief filed by Agudath Israel of America in *Webster v. Reproductive Health Serv.*, 429 U.S. 490 (1989), Agudath Israel of America argued that secular abortion law ought never be allowed to become law if such a law precludes individuals from following the guidance of their individual religious leaders and have an abortion when mandated (as Jewish law sometimes does) by their own religious beliefs. This, one assumes, includes pagan religious leaders as well, and would include abortions that are murder in the eyes of Jewish law.

The portion of the chapter with which I feel fully comfortable is now over, and is worthy of summary. Jewish law imposes no religious obligation upon its adherents to seek to impose Jewish law as a personal religious value on individual members of society who do not wish to accept it. Thus, Jews who function according to

Jewish law are not obligated to adopt political strategies that maximize adherence to Jewish or Noahide law by others, and may instead adopt alternative strategies with alternative goals.

Practical Applications

What is the political calculus that one must weigh? What policy is in the long-term best interest of the Jewish community? To me, the answer is increasing religious, social and cultural freedom, even if it leads to violations of Jewish or Noahide law. Freedom is a better alternative for a Jewish society than one which suppresses people, as eventually we will be suppressed in such a society. Returning to our opening question in the Reverend Robertson's mind—that it is better to fund no faith than to fund one whose founder thinks he is the messiah—why should a religious faith that denies that the messiah has yet to come (Judaism) be treated any better, as a matter of principle, than one that thinks its founder is the messiah?

Thus, the decision by Jewish organizations to support, oppose, or remain neutral in a dispute where certain people desire to expand their civil rights or general legal rights is not determined solely by whether the group under discussion is one generally in compliance with Jewish law or morality or even whether this particular claim is grounded in Jewish law or ethics. It is in the best interests of Judaism to support the continued granting of basic civil rights to all, *while making clear our moral opposition to the underlying conduct of those who exercise their freedom in violation of basic ethical norms of Judaism.* We are providing no moral legitimization for an activity if we seek to prohibit firing a person from his or her job because of it, and we make no claim of general ethical application when we seek to legalize or even protect sinful conduct from suppression by the secular law.[39]

My political thesis can be summarized as follows: *Judaism is providing no moral legitimization to an underlying activity when it seeks to prohibit firing a person from his job, or eviction from his house, because of that (unethical) activity.* This ought to be the basic rule of civil rights. Like free speech, where we all understand that supporting the right of another to speak is not the same as agreeing with what the person says, supporting civil rights for people is not synonymous with morally approving of their actions. Thus, Judaism should support the right of all individuals to be free from harassment and discrimination in their jobs and homes and to insure everyone's physical safety. *Judaism should seek to prevent or prohibit people from being fired from their jobs or evicted from their homes for reasons unrelated to their suitability for the job or as a tenant.*[40] Certainly, traditional Judaism should oppose, for example, a law that seeks to give homosexuals a *preferred place* in the legal or social spectrum. Thus, school curricula that teach the moral equivalency of homosexuality, governmental attempts to redefine marriage to include homosexual relations, and governmental attempts to prohibit religious organizations from declining to hire overt homosexuals should be opposed.[41] However, merely because we favor the decriminalization of what we religious Jews insist is odious conduct and the granting of civil rights for those who engage in such conduct does not mean that, in the name of religious freedom, we need to support the placement of such conduct in a privileged position within society.[42] Indeed, it is a nearly risk-free[43] fulfillment of the Jewish people's mandate to be a moral "light unto the nations of the world" and demonstrate our moral and religious disagreement with such conduct.[44]

We must realize that the political freedoms granted to minority religious communities through laws which prohibit religious, racial, and sexual discrimination in commerce are quite vital to the economic survival of Judaism in America. These laws are not guaranteed by the Constitution, and are subject to simple repeal by Congress and the dictates of the majority. They have been passed through the support of a broad consensus of minority religious and political organizations. Should each of these groups conclude that they no longer support civil rights for the other groups due to philosophical or theological opposition to the underlying conduct, *all* of the groups risk losing the protection granted by law. In such a climate, one could easily imagine feminist groups supporting laws which discriminate against Judaism based on their understanding of our ritual practices.

There are those who will reply by asserting that I am understating the countervailing factor: the cultural influence secular society has on religious Judaism. The advocacy of governmental non-intervention in "private" matters will, these people claim, lead to a society so morally and socially disfavored by classical Judaism that our political freedoms will be of no value in such a society as we will not be able to function.

That is a danger; however, it seems to me that historical precedent runs counter to the belief that such a danger is the most serious. While one can cite numerous examples of Jewish societies within the last thousand years that have been destroyed by cultural and religious intolerance (the Crusades, the expulsion from Spain, the many pogroms, the Holocaust), one is hard-pressed to cite a Jewish culture destroyed by pluralism. Indeed, the Golden Age of Jewish life in Spain six hundred years ago and the incredible religious accomplishments of the Jews of Babylonia more than thirteen hundred years ago can be attributed to the religious freedom found in that time. Each magnificent era, however, ended as religious freedom was abolished in the area. In fact, the political, economic, and cultural resurgence of Orthodox Judaism in America since the 1960s can be directly attributed to precisely the pluralism in American society. The ability to work as a white-collar professional while keeping kosher, taking off for the Jewish holidays, and even wearing a yarmulke at work, is a result of tolerance by the secular society for cultural deviance. While Judaism does face certain challenges in a morally pluralistic society, these are challenges that we can (and will) overcome through heightened observance and additional outreach to the unaffiliated. Governmental persecution, massive societal anti-Semitism, or significant commercial discrimination against Jews are obstacles that pose much greater danger and are frequently beyond our ability to overcome.[45]

The tenuous basis of our religious freedoms is continuously demonstrated. In 1990 the United States Supreme Court, in *Employment Division v. Smith*[46] ruled that when a state passes a criminal law, it need not exempt from prosecution people who violate the law even if they harm no one and are motivated by a sincere religious belief. It was only through the efforts of a multi-denominational ecumenical coalition of very diverse religious groups that the detestable result the Supreme Court sought to make the law of the land was avoided through congressional legislation—*The Religious Freedom Restoration Act of 1993*, which was struck down as unconstitutional by the Supreme Court as it applies to the states in *Boerne v. Flores*.[47] The right to the free exercise of religion remains unclear in America, as legislation of general application (such as legislation that surgery may only be done by a licensed physician in an authorized hospital) can still be applied to destroy religious duties (such as the obligation to circumcise one's child)—and the right to free exercise of our Jewish faith is a right worth protecting.

Conclusion

This chapter sought to establish that no technical Jewish law obligation is present mandating that Jews seek to enforce Noahide law, and that even in cases where central values directly related to our Creator's revelation to us are at stake, we need advance an agenda focusing on what will be in the long-term best interest of the Jewish people. Jews need to look both ways before crossing the street, lest the society that we form to suppress "deviation" suppress us also.

Notes

1. Jewish law, or *halakhah*, is used herein to denote the entire subject matter of the Jewish legal system, including public, private, and ritual law. A brief historical review will familiarize the reader new to Jewish law with its history and development. The Pentateuch (the five books of Moses, the *Torah*) is the historical touchstone document of Jewish law and, according to Jewish legal theory, was revealed to Moses at Mount Sinai. The Prophets and Writings, the other two parts of the Hebrew Bible, were written over the next 700 years, and the Jewish canon was closed around the year 200 before the common era (B.C.E.). From the close of the canon until 250 of the common era (C.E.) is referred to as the era of the *Tannaim*, the redactors of Jewish law, whose period closed with the editing of the *Mishnah* by Rabbi Judah the Patriarch. The next five centuries was the epoch in which the two Talmuds (Babylonian and Jerusalem) were written and edited by scholars called *Amoraim* ("those who recount" Jewish law) and *Savoraim* ("those who ponder" Jewish law). The Babylonian Talmud is of greater legal significance than the Jerusalem Talmud and is a more complete work.

The post-Talmudic era is conventionally divided into three periods: (1) the era of the *Geonim*, scholars who lived in Babylonia until the mid-eleventh century; (2) the era of the *Rishonim* (the early authorities), who lived in North Africa, Spain, Franco-Germany, and Egypt until the end of the fourteenth century; and (3) the period of the *Aharonim* (the latter authorities), which encompasses all scholars of Jewish law from the fifteenth century up to this era. From the period of the mid-fourteenth century until the early seventeenth century, Jewish law underwent a period of codification, which lead to the acceptance of the law code format of Rabbi Joseph Karo, called the *Shulhan Arukh*, as the basis for modern Jewish law. The *Shulhan Arukh* (and the *Arba'ah Turim* of Rabbi Jacob ben Asher, which preceded it) divided Jewish law into four separate areas: *Orah Hayyim* is devoted to daily, Sabbath, and holiday laws; *Even*

Ha-Ezer addresses family law, including financial aspects; *Hoshen Mishpat* codifies financial law; and *Yoreh Deah* contains dietary laws as well as other miscellaneous legal matter. Many significant scholars—themselves as important as Rabbi Karo in status and authority—wrote annotations to his code which made the work and its surrounding comments the modern touchstone of Jewish law. The most recent complete edition of the *Shulhan Arukh* (Vilna, 1896) contains no less than 113 separate commentaries on the text of Rabbi Karo. In addition, hundreds of other volumes of commentary have been published as self-standing works, a process that continues to this very day. Besides the law codes and commentaries, for the last 1,200 years, Jewish law authorities have addressed specific questions of Jewish law in written *responsa* (in question and answer form). Collections of such *responsa* have been published, providing guidance not only to later authorities but to the community at large. Finally, since the establishment of the State of Israel in 1948, the rabbinical courts of Israel have published their written opinions deciding cases on a variety of matters.

2. The universalistic law code governing those who are not Jewish (called the Noahide code) requires the observance of many commandments that are basic to the moral existence of people. The Talmud (Sanhedrin 56a) recounts seven categories of prohibition: idol worship, taking God's name in vain, murder, prohibited sexual activity, theft, eating flesh from a living animal, and the obligation to have a justice system or enforce laws. These seven commandments are generalities which contain within them many specifications—thus, for example, the single categorical prohibition of sexual impropriety includes both adultery and the various forms of incest. As has been noted elsewhere, these Noahide laws appear to encompass nearly 60 of the 613 biblical commandments traditionally enumerated as incumbent on Jews from the Bible itself, which is nearly one-fourth of those biblical commandments generally applicable in post-temple times. See Aaron Lichtenstein, *The Seven Laws of Noah* (New York: Rabbi Jacob Joseph School Press, 1986), 90-91. The majority of the commandments found in Jewish law that are unrelated to ritual activity are also found in the Noahide code. The Noahide code was intended to be a practical legal code, and form a system that satisfied the social, legal, and religious needs of peoples outside the framework of Judaism. For more on this, see my "Jewish Law and the Obligation to Enforce Secular Law," in *The Orthodox Forum Proceedings VI: Jewish Responsibilities to Society*, D. Shatz and C. Waxman, eds. (1997), 103-43; and "Proselytizing and Jewish Law," in John Witte, Jr., and Richard C. Martin, eds., *Sharing the Book: Religious Perspectives on the Rights and Wrongs of Proselytism* (Maryknoll, N.Y.: Orbis, 1999), 45-60.

3. It is a complex matter of comparative theology to examine particular faiths and see where they fit. However, there is no doubt in this author's mind that many new age religions are polytheistic.

4. See, generally, Maimonides, Law of Kings, chapters 9 and 10. For a thorough discussion of these issues, see David Novak, *The Image of the Non-Jew in Judaism* (New York: E. Mellen Press, 1983).

5. Maimonides, Laws of Kings 12:1.

6. Yevamot 24b.

7. Judah Loewe of Prague (Maharal Me-Prague), *Ber Ha-Golah* (Jerusalem, 5731), 38-9.

8. Profound freedom of religion—by which I mean a person suffers no legal or economic consequences of his religious beliefs or conduct—did not really exist until after World War II. To explain why this happened in America when it did is beyond the scope of this chapter. For more on this, see John Witte, Jr., *Religion and the American Constitutional Experiment: Essential Rights and Liberties* (Boulder, Colo.: Westview, 2000), 117-49.

9. Sanhedrin 63a-b.

10. Pat Robertson, "Bush Faith-based Plan Requires an Overhaul," *USA Today* (5 March 2001), 15a.

11. 494 U.S. 872 (1990).

12. For exactly such an article, see Ross Povenmire, "Do Parents Have the Legal Authority to Consent to the Surgical Amputation of Normal, Healthy Tissue from Their Infant Children?: The Practice of Circumcision in the United States," 7, *Am. U.J. Gender Soc. Pol'y & L.,* 87 (1999). See also 139 Cong. Rec. H2356, H2363 (daily ed. 11 May 1993) (Rep. Maloney) ("The Jewish practices of kosher slaughter and circumcision, for example, might be threatened [by *Smith*]").

13. Maimonides, Laws of Murder, 4:10. This is not the place to address in detail the exact view of Maimonides, which also might prohibit direct murder. The first word of this section is, in the uncensored text of Maimonides, the Hebrew word *min*, which could be translated as "troublemakers" and thus this provision of Jewish law could be understood as limited to pagan troublemakers and not merely all pagans. With this tool, one can resolve the apparent tension between this section of Maimonides' code and his categorical statement in Laws of Murder 1:11 prohibiting all extrajudicial punishment, except in the case of a pursuer. This case, which permits extrajudicial killing, is thus limited to cases of people who are both sinful pagans and troublemakers. Mere sinful troublemakers are covered by the rules found in 1:11, and may not be killed. However, Maimonides in Laws of Murder 4:11 is quite clear that "gentiles with whom we have no dispute and Jewish thieves, one does not cause their death. But it is prohibited to rescue them if they are dying, such as when one sees such a person drowning in the sea one may not rescue him as it states "do not stand by while your neighbor's blood is shed" and "this is not your neighbor."

14. This is the view of the Rosh as cited in the Kesef Mishnah on Rotzeach 4:10.

15. Even the Rambam's formulation for wayward children (*tinokot shenishbu*) is not exculpatory in the classical sense of the word, as it is the possibility of repentance and change, combined with the status of these individuals as *annussim* that generates the leniencies. The conduct of these individuals is still "off the charts."

16. For excellent works surveying issues concerning Noahide law generally, see J. David Bleich, "Mishpat Mavet be-Dinei Benei No'ah," in *Sefer ha-Yovel Li-Khavod Morenu ha-Gaon Rav Yoseph Dov Soloveitchik*, S. Yisrachi, N. Lamm, and Y. Rafael, eds., vol. 1 (Jerusalem: 1984), 193-208; *idem.*, "Hasgarat Poshe'a Yehudi she-barah le-Erez Yisrael," *Or ha-Mizrah* 35 (5747): 247-69; Nahum Rakover, "Jewish Law and the Noahide Obligation to Preserve Social Order," *Cardozo Law Review*, 12 (1991): 1073-136; *idem.*, "Hamishpat ke-Erekh Universali: Dinim Bi-Bnei No'ah," 15-57 (Jerusalem, 5748); "Ben No'ah," *Enzyklopedyah Talmudit*, 3:348-62; Aaron Lichtenstein, *The Seven Laws of Noah* (New York: Rabbi Jacob Joseph School Press, 1986). While undoubtedly the view of Menachem ben Meir Ha-Meiri needs to be quantified, one is hard-pressed to accept that Meiri extends his view even to those who unquestionably violate central provisions of Noahide law. Rather, he is adopting a view of idol worship that excludes most Christians from that status. For more on this, see J. David Bleich, "Divine Unity in Maimonides, the Tosafists and Meiri," in *Neoplatonism and Jewish Thought*, Lenn E. Goodmann, ed. (Albany: State University of New York Press, 1992), 237-54.

17. Avot 5:11-12.

18. See "The Gentile and Returning Lost Property According to Jewish Law: A Theory of Reciprocity," *Jewish Law Annual*, 13 (2000): 31-45.

19. Shatz and Waxman, eds., *The Orthodox Forum Proceedings VI*, 103-43.

20. Ethics of the Fathers, 3:14.

21. Tosafot Yom Tov on *id.*

22. Sefer HaChasidim 1124.

23. Support for this proposition can be found in Seforno, commenting on Exodus 19:6 which clearly indicates that Jews must answer such questions from Noahides. See generally comments of Maimonides, Maseh Karbanot 19:16 and Meiri 59a.

24. Maharam Shick OC 144. An example of this can also be found in the letter of Moshe Feinstein sent to the New York State governor favoring the implementation of the death penalty for certain crimes; Iggrot Moshe, CM 2:68.

25. Rabbi J. David Bleich, "Teaching Torah to Non-Jews," *Contemporary Halakhic Problems*, 2, 339.

26. See Rabbi Yehuda Gershuni, *Kol Tzofech* (unnumbered pages in the back of the book, seven pages after numbering ends) (2nd ed. 5740) where he discusses the possibility of selective teaching of the Noahide laws.

27. See generally R. Nissim, Derashot haRan, Number Eleven, which uses the term *tikun siddur hamedini* to refer to Noahide activity. For a brief discussion of this issue, see Suzanne Last Stone, "Sinaitic and Noahide Law: Legal Pluralism in Jewish Law," *Cardozo L.R.*, 12 (1990): 1157. On the use of *tikun olam*, it is also important to examine the way that term is used by Maimonides, in Malachim 11:4 in the uncensored versions of his text (for example, see *Rambam Le'am*). This issue is quite crucial, as Maimonides' image of *tikun olam* seems to be directed at the reason for religions other than Judaism; see also Responsa Kol Mevasser 1:47 and Hechail Yitzchak OC 38.

28. Shatz and Waxman, eds., *The Orthodox Forum Proceedings VI.*

29. This is exemplified by the use of the phrase in Isaiah 60:3; for examples of that in rabbinic literature, see Bava Batra 75a; Midrash Rabbah Esther 7:11; Midrash Bereshit 59:7 and Midrash Tehilim (Buber) 36:6. For a sample of its use in the responsa literature, see Tzitz Eliezer 10:1(74); Yavetz 1:168 and particularly Chatam Sofer 6:84; see also Responsa of Rosh 4:40 which is also cited in Tur OC 59. None of these authorities use the citation in a legal context to direct Jewish participation in gentile activities—all of the citations are homoletical (Maharit EH 2:18 does appear to use it in a legal context concerning an inter-Jewish dispute; however upon further examination one sees that not to be so). This concept plays yet a more prominent role in kabbalistic literature; see Sefer Rasesai Layla, 57 *s.v. techlat* and *vezehu*. For a defense of this beaconlike (i.e., Jews behave properly and this illuminates the world) understanding of the verse as the proper understanding of the literal meaning of the Bible itself, see Harry Orlinsky, "A Light onto the Nations: A Problem in Biblical Theology," in Neuman and Zeitlin, *The Seventy-Fifth Anniversary Volume of the Jewish Quarterly Review* (1967), 409-28. For an indication as to why Radak might use both the phrase "observe the seven commandments" and the phrase "follow the right path," see Iggrot Moshe YD 2:130 who indicates that the two are separate concepts.

30. *Eva* in Hebrew.

31. R. Shabtai Meir HaCohen (*Shakh*), *Yoreh Deah* 151:6; and R. Ezekiel Landau, *Dagul me-Revavah*, commenting on *Yoreh Deah* 151.

32. Thus, a Jew may sell items whose purpose is sinful when others are selling these items also. See my *Pursuit of Justice: A Jewish Perspective on Practicing Law* (New York: Yeshiva University Press, 1996), where this issue is repeatedly addressed, and "Enabling a Jew to Sin: The Parameters," *Journal of Halacha and Contemporary Society* 19 (1990): 5-36.

33. For example, the promulgation of an abortion law in the United States consistent only with the Noahide code would cause situations to arise where *halakhah*'s mandates could not be fulfilled.

34. Supra text accompanying notes.

35. *Church of the Lukumi Babalu Aye, Inc. v. City of Hialeah*, 580 U.S 520 (1993).

36. See amicus curiae brief of COLPA in *Church of Lukumi Babalu Aye, Inc. v. City of Hialeah*, United States Supreme Court (No. 91-948) (which states in note 1 that both the Orthodox Union and the Rabbinical Council agree with the legal position taken in this brief). No Orthodox Jewish organization filed an amicus brief against the Church. Let me give another example. Recently there has been a great deal of discussion about government funding of religious schools, a concept that certainly is within the pale of both legal and social policy in the United States. However, such funding, were it to occur, would undoubtedly have to be blind to the substantive religious values these schools articulate. While a goodly number of the Jewish schools will remain (one hopes) true to authentic Jewish values, we can readily predict that many will advance visions of Judaism with which we do not agree. Among the parochial schools for gentiles, one hopes that most will be godly. Some of these schools will be centrally anti-Semitic even as they are godly; others will undoubtedly support and foster pagan worship—and some of these pagans will be sympathetic to Jewish causes and others will not. Nevertheless, the Orthodox Jewish community and its various institutes have all been diligent in supporting school vouchers, because, in the totality of the picture, it is of benefit to Judaism.

37. See Letter of Rabbi Feinstein dated 8 Shevat 5737 provided to me by Chaim Dovid Zweibel of Agudath Israel.

38. See Rabbi Chaim David Zweibel, "Determining the Time of Death: Legal Considerations," *Journal of Halacha and Contemporary Society* 17 (1989): 49.

39. I recognize however, that my answer to this question is based on my reading of American political history and a prediction of the future as I see it—and I could be wrong in either or both of these determinations. One makes the best political judgment that one can. That is all that is expected of us.

40. New York State has precisely such a law. The "legal activities law" essentially prevents a person from discriminating against employees or job applicants based on their participation in legally permissible activities unrelated to employment outside of times and places of employment; see "Employment Law Update," *New York Law Journal* (3 September 1992).

41. There historically have been statutory exemptions for religious organizations from antidiscrimination laws.

42. Thus, while homosexual activity should be legal, and economic discrimination against homosexuals should be prohibited, homosexual marriages should not be allowed. Not all conduct which is legally permissible is morally commendable or encouraged by government.

43. Thus, even in situations where the *realpolitik* factors indicate that advocacy of civil rights is in error (such as in a highly politicized environment where no matter which position one favors, there are significant consequences) institutional silence would be the preferred policy as it

minimizes the fallout resulting from actively supporting the denial of rights.

44. Now comes the difficulty: Do we, as religious Jews, seek to grant equal civil rights to all or should we join hands with those groups that seek to deny political rights to those engaging in a consensual, but immoral, activity. It requires nearly an act of prophecy to determine which position is in our best long-term interest. Frankly, I am inclined to answer that we should err on the side of more political freedom, rather than less. The fact is that many of the non-Jewish groups that seek to curtail the political rights of those who deviate from the "Judeo-Christian" ethic have historically been the profound enemy of the Jewish community.

Thus we are confronted by a set of difficult choices:

A. We can join politically with those who practice immoral acts to protect our own political future; or

B. We can associate with those who have oppressed (and murdered) us in the past (and who we fear will oppress us in the future) to make illegal an activity that we agree is immoral; or

C. We can decline to publicly involve ourselves in this dispute and adopt an institutional policy of silence while not actively opposing civil rights to all.

I would suggest that, as a matter of political expedience and survival, that the best path for religious Jews is to *generally favor (and certainly not oppose) granting civil rights and political freedom to all,* including those whose activity we find religiously repugnant, providing that the prohibited activity is one that is consensual and harms no one other than its voluntary participants; hand in hand with that, *we should seek to prohibit commercial discrimination against people based on factors unrelated to the commercial activity, such as religious affiliation, national origin, marital status, race, or sexual orientation.* This position is based not on the assertion that all such conduct or statuses are acceptable to Jewish law and tradition (they aren't); but on the assertion—borne out by history—that many of those that seek to curtail activity based on a "religious" sense of ethics quite plausibly will seek, when they are in control, to advance the cause of "Christian ethics" in a way that will be incompatible with the continued successful existence of Judaism in the United States. If we do not seek to protect the civil and political rights of those with whom we theologically disagree, we may find these groups will not seek to assist us when our rights are settled. At the very least, Jewish public policy should not publicly and institutionally oppose granting civil and political rights to all. The exact details of this approach are left to be spelled out later and it certainly does have some limitations. It is clear to this author that Jewish public policy need not favor the legalization of prostitution and pornography in the name of (religious) freedom; as a general matter, activity entered into purely for financial gain creates a different set of issues unrelated to this one. So too this approach should not be understood as preventing systemic governmental (financial) assistance to all religions in some of their charitable or educational acts. For example, governmentally sponsored tuition tax credits or payment vouchers to parochial day school—a governmental policy that would vastly increase Jewish education and thus continuity—is certainly proper under this rationale (and should be supported by all those concerned with the future of the Jewish community).

45. For example, in response to a number of European countries banning *shechita* (kosher slaughter) in the early part of this century, Judaism sought and Congress passed a law which states "No method of . . . slaughtering shall be deemed to comply with the public policy of the United States unless it is humane. Either of the following two methods of slaughtering and handling are hereby found to be humane: . . . or (b) by slaughtering in accordance with the ritual requirements of the Jewish faith"; see 7 U.S.C. 1902. If we adopt the principle of refusing to support legislation that explicitly violates any provision of Jewish law, can we really expect others to support our legislative needs that violate their ethical norms?

46. 494 U.S. 872 (1990).

47. RFRA is found at 42 U.S.C. 200bb-1. It was struck down in *Boerne v. Flores*, 117 S.Ct. 2157 (1997).

10

Religious Diversity and the Common Good

Alan Wolfe

Of all the societies in the world, the United States has been for the longest time—and, without doubt, to the strongest degree—committed to the principle of religious freedom. It was not only that our revolution, in rejecting the sovereignty of the British monarch, also by necessity rejected the establishment of the Anglican Church. It was also that we guaranteed the principle of religious liberty. Our society would not tolerate religious tests for office, oaths of fidelity, and the excommunication of nonbelievers. Here, unlike anywhere else in the world, people would have the liberty to worship God as they best saw fit.

Yet could a people who were given the gift of political freedom also become so completely separated from religion that faith played no significant role in their lives? Few if any of the Founders believed this to be the case. As George Washington expressed the point in his Farewell Address: "Of all the dispositions and habits which lead to political prosperity, religion and morality are indispensable supports. What ever may be conceded to the influence of refined education on minds of peculiar structure, reason and experience both forbid us to expect that national morality can prevail in exclusion of religious principle."[1]

It was not difficult to understand why people who believed in political freedom understood religion as central to the life of the Republic. It was because people were free in so many aspects of their lives that they required the wisdom, if not the omnipotence, of a Supreme Being. As he did in so many areas of American life, Alexis de Tocqueville understood this relationship perfectly: "For my own part, I doubt whether man can ever support at the same time complete religious independence and entire political freedom. And I am inclined to think that if faith be wanting in him, he must be subject; and if he be free, he must believe."[2] One of Tocqueville's great fears was that democracy and equality would lead to the naked clash of self-interest. Religion, is his view, contained a softening ingredient that would tame the clash and bring all sides involved in political warfare to recognize a higher interest.

Tocqueville's insight helps us understand one aspect of American life that has been puzzling to foreign observers ever since: America, the freest country in the world, is also one of the most religious. One sees the same fidelity to God's word in many societies as one sees here: Poland and Iran, to name just two. But those are not societies with a tradition of political freedom. On the other hand, one sees considerable political freedom in Great Britain or Holland, but they are countries that have all but lost a taste for organized religion. Only in America, to quote the distinguished philosopher Harry Golden, does one find freedom and faith so intermingled.[3]

There is one huge problem that has plagued the United States as it tries to reconcile what so many other countries render asunder. If one believes that religion is central to the proper and restrained exercise of freedom, which religion should it be? A religion so general that it loses all meaning can include people of many different beliefs, but it lacks the content that is capable of inspiring fierce devotion among its followers. A religion that speaks to a particular people—chosen or otherwise—can inspire such devotion, and indeed can lead people to martyrdom, but it of necessity excludes from the common morality all those who believe otherwise and is thus inappropriate for a society committed to respecting many different religions within its boundaries.

This dilemma divided the Founders right from the start. Some, such as Thomas Jefferson, were children of the Enlightenment. For them, religion tended toward sectarianism and dogmatism, which meant that the best hope for America lay in the advancement of reason and knowledge. For others, however, the Enlightenment solution was no solution at all, for it meant the eventual abandonment of faith. Their task, as they understood it, was to uncover a set of moral principles grounded in a specific religion, but general enough to apply to all. In pursuit of this goal, they had one great advantage: their own religion, the Protestant religion, emphasized the importance of each individual finding voluntarily their own way to God. In that sense Protestantism seemed fully compatible with a more general American commitment to political freedom.

Despite the fact that even at the Founding not all Americans were Protestant—one state, Maryland, was founded by Catholics, and Jews, if in small numbers, were here from the start—the common morality of America's first century and a half was Protestant morality. The ideas that guided our country until the period right after World War I—you can consider the Scopes trial of 1924 as the watershed event—were Protestant ideas. For more than half of its existence, in other words, the United States, whose constitution officially made impermissible the existence of an established religion, nonetheless informally established Protestantism for the purpose of guiding its affairs. Consider just a few examples:

1. As I have already suggested, the very principles by which church and state were separated in the United States were Protestant principles. John Locke, who did so much to shape our ideas of political liberty, also shaped our understanding of religious liberty. For Locke, a Catholic emphasis on hierarchy and obedience was subversive of religious tolerance and Jews, he wrote, had no commitment to the separation of religion and politics because God had given them their own state.[4]

2. Concepts of democracy, political participation, and equality all owed their particular character to the revivalist tradition of evangelical Protestantism. The tent meeting was the precursor of the modern media campaign and the modern election campaign. In America, religion would be synonymous with enthusiasm, not with theological debate.

3. America's educational institutions—from colleges and universities down to public schools—were shaped in the image of Protestantism. Massachusetts became the home of the public school because it was the state with a large Know-Nothing Party.[5] Without Catholic immigration, the American commitment to public education would have been in doubt. After they attended state-run Protestant

schools during the day, children were expected to populate
YMCAs in the afternoons and on weekends.

4. The single greatest challenge to America—the Civil War—
   was defined for Americans by the greatest political speech
   ever given in this country; Lincoln's Second Inaugural, a
   speech filled with Protestant understandings of sin and redemption.[6]

5. The winning of the West—Manifest Destiny, as it came to
   be called—like the expansion of American power around
   the World, were cast in specifically Protestant terms.

6. America's first great experiment with social reform—the
   Social Gospel—was drawn up by liberal Protestants at
   120th Street and Riverside Drive in New York City and
   taken out to the country by ministers committed to equality
   for all. Even when not tied to an explicit religious movement, the progressive tradition in American politics resonated with a Protestant understanding of human purpose.

Despite the importance of religious freedom in America, the Supreme Court managed to avoid handing down any decisions in this
arena until 1947, when cases involving the Jehovah's Witnesses began to draw the distinctions capable of balancing the importance of
common moral principles with respect for the freedom of individual
religious believers.[7] One of the reasons the Court entered this arena
so late was because the unofficial Protestant establishment lasted so
long. Non-Protestant religions either separated from the dominant
society to create their own institutions—Catholic schools are the
obvious example—or, as many Jews did, they confined their religious beliefs and practices to the private realm while not challenging Protestant domination in the public realm.

As the Protestant establishment crumbled, other methods of finding common religious principles that could unite a society divided
into diverse religions had to be found. One was particularly inge-
nious. America has always been an inventive land; many of the
world's most innovative technologies were first developed here.
Why not, in the same spirit, essentially invent a new religion? No
sooner was the need felt that the product came forward. It was
called the Judeo-Christian tradition. Despite the fact that Christians
had been killing each other for years in Europe, and the fact that a
large number of Christians were convinced that the Jews had killed
Christ, America's three great religious traditions—Protestant,

Catholic, and Jew—could be united around ideas held to be common to all three.[8]

If there was no actual religion called Judeo-Christianity, one quickly became a reality in America. Between the 1950s and the 1970s, each component religious tradition was going through changes that made ecumenism seem quite possible. Protestants were divided between liberals and conservative evangelicals, but the latter, at least until the election of Jimmy Carter, were withdrawn from American life, allowing groups like the National Council of Churches to include, as it actually did at one point, the Ethical Culture Society and the Hindu Vedanta Society in the *Yearbook of American Christianity* among the Protestant denominations. This same period witnessed the breakdown of ethnic Catholicism in the United States: Catholics, who tended to live in the cities, belong to unions, back conservative moral causes, and vote as a bloc increasingly resembled the rest of middle-class America in their suburbanization, cultural liberalization, and willingness to make up their own minds.[9] Finally American Jews in this same period increasingly intermarried, switched to Reform or Conservative synagogues, and found themselves at home in the decidedly nonreligious worlds of academia and Hollywood. There was a time in American life—not that long ago, actually—when serious people thought that Orthodox Judaism would disappear in the United States.

So long as each major religious tradition was losing its core identity, it was possible to celebrate—as many did—the emergence of a new, civil religion in America. Civil religion meant, as President Eisenhower once famously said, that it did not matter what you believed so long as you believed in something. While this formulation contained its own form of exclusion—atheists were outside the pale —it did express the truth that, although Americans were among the world's most religious people, they were also among its least theological. They say that God is in the details, but when it came to God, Americans did not want to argue over the details. In such an environment, the discovery of a Judeo-Christian tradition made perfect sense. True, it did not help Jews who did not want their kids to participate in Christian prayers in public schools. But even prayers, or so it was believed, could be written in a way capable of including both Christians and Jews.

Like the unofficial Protestant establishment that provided a common morality in America until the 1920s, the concept of a Judeo-Christian morality ultimately could not survive. There were two reasons.

The first reason that the idea of Judeo-Christianity collapsed is that there were discovered to be Americans who were neither. In 1998, the National Conference of Christians and Jews, first founded in 1927, changed its name; wanting to keep the same initials, it is now the National Conference for Community and Justice. Rumor has it—the kind of rumor one assumes to be true—that foundations found the former name too exclusionary; an organization once named to emphasize ecumenism had come to be perceived as hostile to Muslims and Hindus. We now live in a post-Judeo-Christian country; there are roughly 800,000 Hindus and 750,000 Buddhists (of whom about 100,000 are American converts) living here, compared to 5.5 million Jews and 3.5 million Muslims. The contest is on as to what this polyglot America will come to he called. The leading candidate is Abrahamic, since Christians, Jews, and Moslems all trace themselves back to Abraham.[10] The term may take hold, but it clearly will not do. For why adopt a name made already obsolete by the fact that not all of those who cannot conform to the Judeo-Christian label can also not conform to the Abrahamic label? The unprecedented immigration that has changed America since the reforms of 1965 have insured that never again will it be possible to include the religious believers who make this country their home by counting on one's fingers—because it will not take long before you will be out of fingers and there will be an awful lot of religious movements left.

The second reason the Judeo-Christian formulation broke down was because each of its components, contrary to all predictions made by sociologists, became more inward looking. The most rapidly growing Protestant denominations were among conservatives and evangelicals; not only were some of their leading voices wary of Jews, unless Jews played the role conservative Christians believed they were assigned by the Bible, but a number remained staunchly anti-Catholic. Anti-Catholicism, in fact, was the one thing that tended to link evangelical sects—otherwise radically different in their views of religious practice or biblical truth—together; as the Reverend Jerry Falwell said so well, he hoped to elevate the status of his Liberty University until it became the Christian Notre Dame. If Christians could not agree on who was a legitimate Christian, how were they ever to include Jews and everyone else?

At the same time, the rise of Orthodox Judaism undermined the Judeo-Christian formulation from the other side. The whole idea of a Judeo-Christian tradition seemed to legitimize intermarriage; after all, if it was a tradition, then a person from one part could marry a person from another part without the tradition being lost. Since Orthodox Jews—and many of the non-Orthodox as well—believed that intermarriage invariably diluted the tradition, then the tradition would have to be understood as a specifically Jewish one from which Christians—no harm intended, you understand—would have to be left out. Moreover, as Sam Friedman has shown so well, nothing prevented Jews from attacking each other with the same zeal that Christians engaged in internecine warfare.[11] If it became difficult to agree about who was Jewish, then agreement about who was Judeo-Christian became impossible.

We stand, therefore, facing the same problem described by George Washington—but without his, or any other, apparent solution. For Washington, a society had to have a common morality, and one, moreover, undergirded by a common religion, if it was to have political freedom. If he is right, then we cannot have political freedom—for we do not have, and will not have, enough commonality in our religion.

There are some voices in America certain that Washington was right. It follows, from their point of view, that the only way for the American experiment to succeed is for Americans to return to the Christian principles that Washington took for granted.

This is certainly the way organizations like the Christian Coalition diagnose the contemporary American situation. Look around, they say, and you can see immediately what happens when the bounds of morality are loosened: divorce and abortion rates shoot up, as do rates of crime; young people have no guidance; secular humanists dominate the schools and the media; and, in the worst example of all, a president engages in improper sex, lies about it, and is barely punished. Early Christians worried that some day Americans, unless they believed in God, would go to hell. Contemporary Christians such as Paul Weyrich—who gave the English language the term "moral majority"—believe it already has.

As they are increasingly discovering, conservative Christians will never be able to return America to the Christian country it once was. To remind them of this is not only to ask them to remember that they share their society with others who have just as much claim to citizenship as they do. It is also to teach them that there is no such thing as an uncontested Christian in the first place. Let us, for the sake of a thought experiment, imagine that somehow America were purged of most of its Jews and all its Muslims—even 95 percent of its Catholics. Then, presumably, we would be where we were at the time the Constitution was written. What conservative

Christians do not tell you is that back then, when we presumably were governed by Christian unity, we had more disunity than we do now. Protestant sect hated Protestant sect, often with a fervor completely missing from the more religiously civil America of today. The calls of men like George Washington for a common morality inspired by religion were issued because no such thing existed. The American tradition of religious freedom was created, at least in part, by dissenting and nonconforming sects, and what they do best is dissent—and refuse to conform. Today's conservative Southern Baptist was once a radical critic of the conventional morality associated with Puritans and Lutherans. If we were to go back to a Christian morality, it is far from clear to which we would return.

An alternative to the Christian coalition view of the world is to conclude that George Washington was half right: Americans, to protect their freedom, need a common morality derived from religion, but it can be derived from many religions, not just one. In the 2000 presidential campaign, Joe Lieberman was a prominent spokesman for this point of view. In September 2000, Lieberman expressed his views at the University of Notre Dame:

> We are still arguably the most religiously observant people on earth, and share a near universal belief in God. But you wouldn't know it from national public life today. The line between church and state is an important one and has always been hard for us to draw, but in recent years we have gone far beyond what the Framers ever imagined in separating the two. So much so that we have practically banished religious values and religious institutions from the public square and constructed a "discomfort zone" for even discussing our faith in public settings, ironically making religion one of the few remaining socially acceptable targets of intolerance.[12]

Now, no one could ever accuse Senator Lieberman of sharing the agenda of Pat Robertson: far from an evangelical, he adheres to a minority viewpoint within a minority religion. As I read his Notre Dame speech, I thought of the views of a man who teaches law at Lieberman's alma mater, Yale. His name is Stephen Carter. Unlike Lieberman, Carter is a Christian. But because, like Lieberman, he is a member of a minority group—in this case, African American—he too can call for greater respect for the religious sensibility without appearing to be one of those conservative evangelicals determined to return America to its eighteenth-century origins. When Carter— or for that matter, Lieberman, or, to include a Catholic, Father Richard John Neuhaus—discuss these issues, it becomes clear that the solution they have in mind is not a return to an emphasis on somewhat vapid principles of Judeo-Christianity; Lieberman is too Orthodox for that, Carter's conception of Protestantism too prophetic, and Neuhaus's Catholicism too conservative. Indeed, Carter rejects most forms of accommodation between religion and the state in favor of a Christianity that speaks truth to power.

Although neither Carter nor Lieberman would entertain any effort to re-Christianize the United States, their solutions are far from completely satisfactory. Senator Lieberman at one point during the campaign came close to endorsing the eighteenth-century idea that religion was the sole source of morality, even if he subsequently backed off. One cannot help wondering what the long-term effect of Senator Lieberman's repeated calls to God will be. One likely scenario is that his efforts will encourage evangelical Christians in future elections to talk about God and, when criticized for so doing, to respond by saying that Lieberman's remarks constitute a precedent. After all, they will add, to suggest that it is appropriate for a Jew to invoke God in politics but not for a Christian to do so is to create a double standard that makes Christians victims. As odd as it might sound, this notion that Christians are a persecuted minority because secular humanists run the country is widespread in conservative Christian circles; it even attracts writers as intelligent as Stephen Carter.

Once introduced into the public square, there is no way for religion to enter quietly. It is in the nature of a certain kind of religious belief to proclaim, loudly and with gusto, one's faith. For many American Christians, and for some American Jews, a religion without a public presence is no religion at all. But the moment religion is made public, the never-resolved questions involving the rights of nonbelievers or of those who believe differently are once again raised.

It does not help, or at least it does not help me, that many of those calling for a greater role for religion in American public life do so in an apocalyptic language that would be dangerous if exported from the religious sphere to the political. The most extreme statement of this position was contained in Father Neuhaus's magazine *First Things*, in which a group of writers questioned the legitimacy of what they called "the American regime" in ways that moved friends of the magazine, such as Gertrude Himmelfarb, to protest.[13] Senator Lieberman's comment that religion has been banished from the public square is far less incendiary, but I find it unsatisfactory in explaining most aspects of public life in America,

including, I might add, the very positive reception Americans gave
to the Lieberman candidacy. And Stephen Carter, who is a political
moderate, becomes as extreme as Father Neuhaus when he talks
about America's lack of respect for people of faith. "I love this nation, with all its weaknesses and occasional horrors, and I cannot
imagine living in another one," he says in a recent book. "But my
mind is not so clouded with the vapors of patriotism that I place my
country before my God. If the country were to force me to a choice
—and, increasingly, this nation tends to do that to many religious
people—I would unhesitatingly, if not without some sadness for my
country, choose my God."[14] Carter's choice of words could not be
better designed to illustrate why there may be reasons to keep our
public square neutral where religion is concerned. When people feel
that passionately about a way of life, it is best to keep the whole
matter away from the arena of politics, where compromise and bar-
gaining—not absolutist positions—make the whole process work.

We are therefore thrown back on a third way to think about the
relationship between religion and a common morality. This is the
idea of erecting a sharp wall of separation between church and state.
Government should, in this view, not only be neutral between one
religion and another, it ought also to be neutral between religion and
nonreligion. Short of murder, polygamy, and a few other vices, people should be left alone to practice their religion however they see
fit, but when we come together in public, our government, our symbols, our official speech ought to be stripped of religious content.

Critics of the sharp separation idea, including Stephen Carter, are
quick to point out that while professing neutrality between religion
and nonreligion, such an approach is anything but neutral. In insisting that the public be cleansed of faith, it clearly sides with those
who do not believe and relegates those who do to second class
status. If I am atheist, I can look at a state that never uses religious
language and symbolism and identity with it, but if I am a believer,
especially one who believes in religion's public side, that same state
will clearly be one that has sided with my opponents.

Although there are many sincere religious believers who strongly
support the separation of church and state, there are also others who
give credence to Carter's criticism. They are clearly hostile to religion, and they want very much to use the courts to uphold their
view of the world, which, they believe, is a better view—more ma-
ture, more cosmopolitan—than that of religious believers. If we pursue a solution of strict separation along those lines, we cannot find a
way to live with different religious views in one society, for we do

confine all religious views to the seats in the balcony, reserving the orchestra for the "enlightened" few.

But there is, I believe, another way to approach the issue. George Washington, as we know, believed that a society requires common religious convictions to sustain political freedom. It is time to flat out acknowledge that he was wrong. We are a far freer society now than we were in the early nineteenth century—just ask the descendents of former slaves, let alone women, recent immigrants, and nonbelievers—yet we have become more free in the absence of either an unofficial Protestant establishment or the persistence of the Judeo-Christian tradition. So obvious is this fact that those who argue for a greater public presence for religion in American do not really argue against it. Instead they claim that we are, if anything, too free, that our individualism has led us to ignore ties of all kinds, not only those of faith, but also those of family and community.

The reason political and religious freedom can exist together is because a people who insist on one will also insist on the other. The single most striking fact of religious life in America is the emergence of choice.[15] Survey after survey, and book after book, concludes that Americans remain as religious as ever, but that they want to play a role in the practices and beliefs of religious persuasions freely chosen by themselves. Our most conservative religious believers, born-again Christians, announce that, in being reborn, they leave religions in which they were raised in favor of stricter forms of faith that correspond to their own needs. Other Americans like to pick and choose their beliefs, admiring, for example, the rituals associated with Catholicism, while not accepting its teachings on sexuality; over 80 percent of American Catholics believe that one can be divorced, or have had an abortion, and still be a good Catholic. Still others reject all forms of organized religion in favor of new age spirituality. Yet another group finds a different degree of faith appropriate for different stages in their lives; we all know secular Jews who rediscover their faith when they marry and have children, only to lose some of it again when their children grow up. As the sociologist Wade Clark Roof describes the situation: "Looking to the future, religious communities are likely to become understood and appreciated as depositories of symbols, practices, teachings, and moral codes for assembling and reassembling strategies of faith and action. That is to say, they will function less as a unified normative body prescribing a singular religious or spiritual style and will better institutionalize internal pluralism and the acceptance of diversity; individuals and small groups will turn to

traditions as resources yet exercise freedom in making religious
choices and in modes of spiritual cultivation."[16]

Defenders of the faith—whatever the particular faith happens to
be generally find themselves puzzled by the widespread phenomenon of religious choice. The notion that religion should so resemble
the marketplace of commodities detracts from historic ideas of
obedience, transcendence, and discipline. Religion ought to be, in
their view, more noble, more sacred, than it often is. The key word
here is "ought," for in the discussion of religion and public life so
widespread among American intellectuals, religion as it is actually
practiced gets short shrift compared to religion as it ought to be.
Hence Stephen Carter likes religion to be prophetic and pure, while
most Americans like their religion practical and purposeful. But
who is Carter—indeed, who am I or who is Joe Lieberman or
Richard John Neuhaus—to tell people how they ought to believe in
God. People will find their own way to God. Indeed in a modern
society devoted to political freedom, the best way to insure that
faith survives and flourishes may well be to appreciate, rather than
condemn, one area of life that Americans care deeply enough about
to put their personal signature on the way it is practiced.

The emergence of religious choice makes it possible to imagine
arguments on behalf of separation of church and state that do not tilt
the balance so heavily in favor of the state. The idea of creating a
wall between church and state developed at a time when Supreme
Court judges, and liberals of many persuasions, were convinced that
one religion, Christianity, was so dominant that its official recognition inevitably harmed those of other religious persuasions. But we
have become so religiously diverse a society, and our way of practicing religion has come to accept such a wide role for choice, that
we no longer need fear a takeover of our public institutions by one
religious tradition. If we are to continue to support the separation of
church and state—and I believe we should—it ought to be so that
many religions can flourish and can flourish in ways they, and their
adherents, think best for themselves. There are arguments to be
made on behalf of religious freedom not unlike the arguments made
on behalf of economic freedom; a society that relies on enterprise
and initiative will be more innovative and respectful of diversity
than one that tries to regulate the unregulatable.

The American tradition of religious liberty is strong enough to
survive any challenge. It is already clear that efforts by conservative
Christians to impose their view of faith on the country have failed.
America will easily survive recurrent attempts in political cam-

paigns to invoke God for one side or the other. Creationism has not in fact defeated evolution in nearly all parts of the United States, even in the South. We therefore find ourselves in something of a new situation. We need not sit around and wonder how we can retain our freedom even as we have become so religiously diverse. We can instead marvel at the fact that our diversity has strengthened our freedom. Americans are usually at their best when they are at their most practical. We ought to pay more attention to what Americans do than to what some disgruntled critics say.

Notes

1. "Washington's Farewell Address to the People of the United States (1796)." A version is available online at http://www.yale.edu/lawweb/avalon/washing.htm.

2. Alexis De Tocqueville, *Democracy in America*, translated by Henry Reeve (New York: Bantam Classic: 2000), vol. II, ch. v, 532.

3. Harry Golden, *Only in America* (Cleveland, Ohio: World Publishing Company, 1958); Harry Golden and Martin Rywel, *Jews in American History, Their Contribution to the United States of America* (Charlotte, N.C.: H.L. Martin, 1950).

4. John Locke, *A Letter Concerning Toleration in Focus*, John Horton and Susan Mendus, eds. (New York: Routledge, 1991).

5. Charles Glenn, *The Myth of the Common School* (Amherst: University of Massachusetts Press, 1988).

6. Gary Wills, *Lincoln at Gettysburg: The Words that Remade America* (New York: Simon & Schuster, 1992).

7. See, for instance, *Everson v. Board of Education* (330 U.S. 1 [1947]) where the court found that the First Amendment means at the least that neither a state nor the federal government can set up a church. Neither can pass laws which aid one religion, aid all religions, or prefer one religion over another. Neither can force nor influence a person to go or to remain away from church against his will or force him to profess a belief of disbelief in any religion.

8. Will Herberg, *Protestant, Catholic, Jew: An Essay in American Religious Sociology* (Chicago: University of Chicago Press, 1983).

9. Charles R. Morris, *American Catholic: The Saints and Sinners Who Built America's Most Powerful Church* (New York: Vintage, 1998).

10. Francis Peters, *The Children of Abraham* (Princeton, N.J.: Princeton University Press, 1984).

11. Samuel G. Freedman, *Jew v. Jews. The Struggle for the Soul of American Jewry* (New York: Simon & Schuster, 2000).

12. Senator Joe Lieberman, "Vision for America: A Place for Faith," delivered at Notre Dame, October 24, 2000. The full text is available at http://pewforum.org/issues/lieberman2000.htm.

13. See *The End of Democracy? The Celebrated First Things Debate, with Arguments Pro and Con*, Mitchell S. Muncy, ed., and Richard John Neuhaus, *The Anatomy of a Controversy* (Dallas: Spence, 1997).

14. Stephen Carter, *God's Name in Vain: The Wrongs and Rights of Religion in Politics* (New York: Basic Books, 2000).

15. Alan Wolfe, *Moral Freedom: The Search for Virtue in a World of Choice* (New York: W. W. Norton, 2001).

16. Wade Clark Roof, *Spiritual Marketplace: Baby Boomers and the Remaking of American Religion* (Princeton, N.J.: Princeton University Press, 1999).

11

Religion and the Public Good

Michael Gottsegen

Many have argued that religion is a public good.[1] But how is this to be understood? Some would emphasize religion's status as a public good as distinct from its status as a private good. But the significance of this distinction is itself open to interpretation. From one perspective, the import of this distinction is to differentiate between goods that individuals can acquire for themselves individually and goods that must be bestowed upon all—upon the public as a whole, as it were—if they are to be enjoyed by anyone. Clean air or safe streets are typically cited as examples of public goods, of goods that must be provided to all the members of a given community if they are to be enjoyed by any of the members at all.[2] Now some would argue that religion is a public good of this kind and that the government must support religion generally if any citizens are to enjoy it individually.[3]

But there is another way of construing what is meant by calling religion a public good, which turns on an understanding of the public sphere as the space that is common to us all, as the space where we gather together to engage in those collective activities that unite us as a single people sharing a common life.[4] The public in this sense includes our public spaces—the marketplace, the theater, and the forum or public meeting place where citizens assemble to deliberate in common about the public or political business of the day.[5]

To claim then that religion is a public good might be to claim that religion is more than a private good that might be regarded with indifference or neutrality by the commonwealth, and that it bestows a benefit upon the polity and is thus a public good in the strong sense. It is to claim that the public (or polity) fares better for the widespread "consumption" of this private good than it would if this private good were "consumed" by a smaller percentage of the citizenry. The claim, in other words, is that religion contributes to the commonweal by directly and indirectly enhancing our *public* life through its effects upon our political ethos and upon the quality of our civic deliberations. According to this stronger claim, we will be better and more capable citizens, both individually and collectively (and not just better persons, individually, in a moral sense), to the extent that we are a religious people.[6] Of course, such a claim calls into question the taken-for-granted assumptions of the guardians of the secular city who champion that aspect of modernity that is synonymous with secularization, that is, with the relegation of religion to the private sphere and with religion's banishment from the public square. To suggest that this process has gone too far, that our public life has been harmed by the attempt to exclude religion from political life and that our collective well-being may depend upon the return of religion to the public square, is heresy to such ears.

But one hardly needs to be a member of the liberal intelligentsia or a militant secularist to have serious doubts about the prudence of lowering the wall of separation between church and state. In the premodern period, the devout of many faiths felt the sharp sting of intolerance and persecution whenever they chanced to find themselves living as members of a religious minority in a land in which the political authorities believed it was their religious duty to employ their coercive power in defense of the majority faith and true religion.[7] That this medieval conception of the right relation between church and state was bad not only for religious minorities, but bad for the religious majority as well was made apparent to many by the collapse of social order and the magnitude of the devastation brought about by the seventeenth century's wars of religion.[8] It should come as no surprise, then, that the process of privatizing religion and of secularizing citizenship begins in earnest with the end of the bloody wars of religion. For the princes, secularization was a matter of political prudence; for the newly ascendant mercantile interests, it was a matter of securing a stable business climate; for religious minorities it was a question of religious freedom; and for the champions of

Enlightenment, it was a matter of freeing society as a whole from the oppressive trammels of religious authority and superstition.[9]

For American Jews and the members of other religious minorities who have benefited so much from the secularization of public life, the suggestion that public life could benefit from a closer relation between religion and politics is highly suspect.[10] Knowing that secularization and the privatization of religion were the preconditions of the modern freedoms of thought and conscience, of speech and association, and knowing that secularization and the privatization of religion were also the basis for their social and political integration, those with a memory of persecution by the religious majority rightly insist that the burden of argument falls upon those who would advocate any departure from the secular status quo.

To make the case for realigning the relationship of religion and politics, it is helpful to begin by recalling how the dynamic of modernization worked to transform the social and normative orders in the transition from the medieval to the modern era.[11] For the argument on behalf of a new and closer relation between religion and politics builds upon the belief that, in the modern period, politics suffers from a normative disorder that was produced, and continues to be abetted, by the privatization and depoliticization of religion that came about in the transition from the Middle Ages to Modernity.

The story of religion's privatization and depoliticization belongs, of course, to a broader and more extensive process of secularization and rationalization that is widely regarded as synonymous with the development of modernity.[12] Driving this process were the forces that brought the medieval era to a close: the Protestant Reformation, urbanization, the development of the modern state, the growth of capitalism, and the early stages of the scientific revolution.[13] In this process—a process in which a largely rural, mostly agricultural, and thoroughly traditional society was transformed into an increasingly urban, industrial, and secular society—life, which was once widely regarded as forming a seamless whole, was fractured into a mosaic of disparate spheres and autonomous realms.[14] The various dimensions of existence were separated and divided according to a logic of functional differentiation and specialization. Along the way, the sense that the whole constituted an ordered cosmos in which everyone and everything had its rightful place was undermined.[15]

The result is that ever since we have lived in a world of thoroughgoing compartmentalization. Social life's many spheres have been separated from one another: home from work, economics from politics, science from religion, and public from private. It is not only that these spheres have been separated, but that they are also understood to operate according to different rules—according to rules that are unique to each sphere and without application to any other.[16]

The separation of social life into different spheres is itself not new. Since remote antiquity, social life has been differentiated into different sectors. What is new to modernity, however, is the general acceptance of the notion that each sphere is intrinsically autono- mous, that there is no master science or discipline that applies across the board, that no sphere has the authority to direct all the rest.[17] Thus, for example, moderns typically assume that religion and science are entirely distinct and that the values of the former ought not to be applied to the latter. (We assume, in other words, that the Catholic Church was way out of line when it censured Gali- leo and forced him to recant.) In an earlier era, such an assertion would have been blasphemous. The categories of good and evil, of vice and virtue, of pious and impious were regarded as coextensive with the whole of life.

In the Middle Ages, the Catholic Church took the view that every sector of life—from philosophy to politics, from science to art, from economics to law—fell within its orbit of concern.[18] This same ex- pansive conception of the extent of religion's proper reach is found in the Talmud. The rabbis' legislative concern encompasses not only the synagogue and the social relations of the household, but extends to the marketplace, the judge's chambers, and the councils of gov- ernment. To argue that religion had no business speaking to such issues would have seemed ridiculous. Does God's concern with the goodness of human action know any borders or limitations? Of course not! Nor then should the moral authority of the church or synagogue. The furor that greeted the publication of Machiavelli's *The Prince* in 1513—which asserted that political life should be governed by its own autonomous nature and not by Christian moral- ity—gives clear evidence of just how entrenched these assumptions were at the time.[19]

As the name Machiavelli symbolizes the idea of the autonomy of politics, the name Adam Smith symbolizes the idea of the autonomy of the market and of capitalism more generally, and in the course of the transition to modernity, these ideas came to hold sway and the world changed accordingly. Where once the church (and the rabbis within the relatively autonomous Jewish communal sphere of the *kehillah*) had sought to regulate commodity prices, working conditions, and the market itself in order to more closely approximate the Christian (or Jewish) vision of the good society, as modernity advanced society's religious leaders lost the authority that had enabled them to exert such influence on behalf of their understandings of justice, equity, and the common good.[20]

Modernity, then, brought into being the autonomy of life's various orders, thus freeing science, art, law, politics, and the economy from subordination to religious imperatives. By so doing, it shrank the sacred canopy that religion had once cast over the whole of life. No longer permitted to shape the social order as a whole in the image of the City of God, religion more and more came to be identified with the hearth and the home, and with the sphere of family life. There alone would religion and religiously grounded moral norms have their place.[21] The separation of church and state, the relegation of religion to the private sphere, and the transformation of citizenship into a wholly secular concept constituted the full realization of this tendency.[22]

In many ways, this compartmentalization has been a boon to our collective life. Science, technology, and free markets, unshackled by external restraints of religion and ethics, have become powerhouses creating economic abundance and material well-being. At the same time, our unsanctified polity and secular society have been spared the noxious effects of religious intolerance and have enjoyed the benefits that flow from the personal freedoms of thought, association, and expression that many religions have typically been unwilling to allow. The profusion of religious sects gives evidence, moreover, that dethroning religion from its supervisory role over the whole has been a boon to religion as well.

In theory, the differentiation of spheres does not bear upon the relative importance of the various spheres. In theory, the separation of spheres and even the fact that they operate according to their own logics and according to their own sphere-specific hierarchy of values do not mandate that one sphere be regarded as more important than the others. In theory, the separation of the realms of science, art, economics, politics, family life, and religion from one another says nothing about the relative importance of the spheres vis-à-vis one another or of the values realized in each. In theory, politics could tend to the common good while economic life secures the production and consumption of a steadily increasing level of goods and services, and the family sphere could promote the values of love, intimacy, and mutual aid while the religious sphere teaches basic morality and ritually sanctifies the life cycle moments between birth and death.

In practice, however, the real meaning of separation is only grasped when it is understood that though the spheres were now separate, they were surely not equal. Modernity did not only diminish the church's standing by freeing the secular realm from the church's supervision. Rather, it enabled the secular realm to expand in size and significance relative to the religious sphere and eventually to displace it as the hegemonic locus of social and intellectual authority.[23] But the religious realm's standing (its authority and the validity of its teachings) was undercut as well by the direct and indirect critiques of religion that emanated from the new science and new philosophy that increasingly came to set the intellectual standards in a new age.[24] Thus it was that the religious conception of truth as grounded in revelation, as demonstrated by scholastic reasoning and as vouchsafed by the authority of tradition were called into question, and eventually superceded, by the conception of truth that was promulgated by the new empirical science with its emphasis upon scientific method, and by the new philosophy with its emphasis upon systematic doubt and freedom from all (traditional) presuppositions. The new conception of nature as a uniform mechanism undercut the belief in miracles that was at the heart of traditional faith. The conception of truth as universal and as rationally available to all undercut the belief in the plausibility of special revelation, that is, the belief in the plausibility of a truth revealed to just one people, and undercut the belief in the religious efficacy of ritual and of adherence to a system of divine law that had been accepted hitherto as God's revealed will for humanity. The development of the secular disciplines of history and literary criticism in the early modern period undercut the standing of religion from yet another angle as it undermined belief in the historical accuracy of the Bible and in the historical claims of religious tradition. While these critiques only gradually eroded popular belief and practice, their corrosive effect upon the religious beliefs of the educated class was much more rapid and thoroughgoing.[25]

If the net effect of the rise of science and the critique of religion was to diminish religion's intellectual authority, its moral and social authority was undercut more directly by the development of industrial capitalism and by the emergence of the modern secular state.[26] Ultimately and inexorably, capitalism, and the growth of the cities which it made possible, transformed the material and social conditions of life in ways that made the moral teachings and otherworldliness of the church—moral teachings and an otherworldliness that were well suited to a world of low social mobility and economic scarcity—increasingly irrelevant to increasingly large segments of the population.[27]

The rise of the modern state, especially in the period after the seventeenth century's wars of religion, also served to diminish religion's role as a moral and social arbiter. The wars of religion (between Catholics and Protestants) were ruinous to commerce and social peace, and were born of a religious intolerance that enlightened opinion came to regard as retrograde and incompatible with the new doctrine of freedom of conscience. To inoculate the state and society against such internal discord, the new political theories and increasingly the states as well espoused the privatization of religion, liberating the state from the burden of defending the faith and further marginalizing the relevance of religion as a political force.[28]

With the church and religion, more generally, relegated to the sidelines, a new understanding of the state and of political life emerged. In the medieval period the church (and the rabbis within their own sphere of influence) had defined the purpose of government in terms of the pursuit of the common good that was understood as including worldly and religious aspects. To this end, the government had been tasked with supervising economic and social life, in order to preserve social harmony, and with assisting the church in its supervision of morals.[29]

With the privatization of religion, however, and with the emergence of a new understanding of government as the guardian of property and protector of individual liberty (cf. Locke), the state eventually ceases to be seen as a supervisor of morals. As the common good comes to be redefined as the protection of property and persons and the fostering of economic growth, the government's role is circumscribed to consist of the protection of property and of individual liberty (and economic liberty in particular) from enemies foreign or domestic and the promotion of economic growth by creating and maintaining the infrastructure of commerce.[30] Beyond this, the state's own interest in increasing its power relative to other states gave it an interest in promoting the growth of the economy, which is the ultimate basis of its own power.[31] In the context of this overriding concern for the protection of property, democratic forms and constitutional checks and balances are espoused by Locke, for example, not so much as intrinsic goods but as the best means for insuring that the government does not exceed its proper bounds and become a danger to property or persons.[32] That democratic reforms were implemented as a means to this end and not because democracy was thought to be a good in itself can be seen if one recalls the rather high property qualification that stood in the way of the extension of the franchise beyond rather narrow bounds until well into the nineteenth century. In short, the state's role as the protector of capital and of capitalism was not to be placed in jeopardy by some foolhardy extension of the suffrage.[33] It is interesting to note that by the time universal suffrage did prevail, the capitalist system was so well entrenched that electoral majorities were not disposed to overthrow it.[34]

With the extrusion of religion from politics in the modern period, a process was set in motion that culminated in the loss of an approach to politics that, since antiquity, had placed the question of the good life and the good society at its center. This way of thinking about politics asked the question of the common good, but did not define it in exclusively economic terms. Indeed, common to this sort of discourse was an understanding that unlimited accumulation of goods, or a life dedicated to such accumulation, was a stunted life, a life that did not come near to realizing the truly human good, a good that could only be achieved by one who transcended this self-centered and materialist concern. This way of thinking about politics and the life of the community also took for granted the principle of social solidarity and understood the common good as consisting more of what was shared in common than of what was enjoyed individually by each person in his or her private domain.

From this perspective, the best government could never have been defined as that government which was most conducive to the increase of private wealth and its private enjoyment, as if—as Locke asserted—that were the primary reason why men instituted society and government. But in the modern period, Locke's assumptions, which would have been most controversial a hundred years before he wrote, have come to be regarded as self-evident, and political discourse has shifted accordingly. In contemporary politics, as has been the case by and large for most of the modern period, the economic question remains foremost. Political life itself is roundly understood as the continuation of economics by other means. Other issues certainly arise as well, but the economy is the main thing and the government's ability to insure economic health is typically the primary criterion by which its fitness is assessed. In the era of globalization, the primacy of the economic factor continues, now forcing states to outsource and downsize in order to create a more favorable business climate for the transnational corporations that hold the fate of nations in their hands.

Today, the hegemony of an economistic (or rational choice) orientation over all other understandings of political, social, and even familial and religious life is manifest. It is taken for granted that the largest corporations will be the most significant political players and that they will seek to bend legislation to serve their own particular interests. That politicians are marketed like deodorant or sneakers, with focus groups and slick advertising campaigns, hardly surprises anyone anymore. Even the leaders of religious denominations assess their performance in the idiom of market share analysis and hire business and advertising consultants to help them to expand this share.

As indicative of the economy's present day hegemony are the contours of our own personal experience. Should we happen to meet a stranger at a social gathering, it is most natural to ask what he or she does (or did) for a living. We ask that question first because we are socialized to understand our identities first and foremost in terms of our jobs or professions—in terms of our economic status, in other words. Should the conversation proceed further, it is natural to speak of one's investments, of what one owns, of where one has recently been on vacation, etc.—in short, of so many indicators of how one is faring or has fared in the economic sphere. Most of us will speak of our job and of our leisure time activities of consumption and not of our religious life or our political concerns. Women may speak of relationships and men of sports or cars, but such pastimes are understood as pastimes, not as activities that are ranked among our most serious concerns.

A further sign of the market's hegemony is the increasing tendency to think about the familial and social spheres of our lives in terms of metaphors drawn from economic life. In the marketplace, we have learned that human relations are about competition, about relations of exchange, about utility maximization and advancing one's self-interest. If one is a good businessman, one will manage to profit from every encounter. Exchanging equal value for equal value does not make one rich. One can succeed only if one manages to buy cheap and sell dear, only if one manages to get more than one gives in every trade or exchange. In business, one strives to close the deal, to make the sale. But just take a look at the books that are to be found in the ever expanding self-help section of any Barnes & Noble, and you will see that this mentality now extends to dating, making friends, organizing one's time, and living a fulfilling life.

Fulfillment itself is increasingly defined in terms of economic success and in terms of the social status that comes with economic success. This is not to say that most people do not also want meaningful relationships, to be good citizens, and to be moral. But as
measured by the amounts of time and effort that are dedicated to
achieving these ends, it is fair to say that for most of us these other
ends are very much subordinated to the end of achieving economic
success. How far this de facto hierarchy of ends departs from the
hierarchy espoused by classical Christianity or Judaism is self-
evident.

Ours, then, is a world in which the culture and politics of possessive individualism reigns supreme. The question before us in this
chapter thus becomes whether politics can possibly achieve its
proper end of securing the common good: once most citizens regard
politics as an extension of economics by other means, once they
have been socialized to treat politics as just another venue for the
legitimate pursuit of self-interest, and once they believe that the
form of instrumental rationality that guides the behavior of firms in
the marketplace should also determine how citizens pursue their
economic or social interests in the political sphere. Plainly, the answer to this question is negative. Where these suppositions about
the relation between politics and economics prevail, the common
good can be neither pursued nor attained. To put the point somewhat
differently, we would observe that in the course of modernity's development, the distinction between *homo politicus* and *homo
economicus* was vitiated and that in its place there prevails an assumption that the two are essentially the same, an equation of rough
identity that in practical terms has proven quite detrimental to our
political life. In this context, the interest of political and social theorists in religion hinges upon the practical hope that religion might
become a means of undoing this false identity that modernity has
forged and that religion might thereby contribute to the freeing of
politics from its improper subordination to economic forces and that
this will foster a renewed politics that is dedicated to its proper task
of securing the common good.

Robert Bellah made an interesting argument along these lines in
several important articles and books.[35] Bellah argued for the existence of what he called the "American civil religion" and argued
that it has played, and continues to play, an important and salutary
role in American political life.[36] Bellah's conception of American
civil religion, insofar as it concerns the present era, purports to be
descriptive of what has been and remains the case, but his concep-

tion seems to me to be more descriptive of what he would like the case to be. While my argument differs from his, we share enough in common that his work forms a useful point of departure.

First, by way of clarification, when Bellah speaks of American civil religion he has in view what he describes as the unofficial national religion of the American people that is distinct from their particular creeds and denominational affiliations, but is a religion nonetheless with its own patriarchs and prophets, sacred events and sacred places, solemn rituals, symbols, and martyrs.[37] This religion that is built around the sacred narrative of the American errand "is concerned that America be a society as perfectly in accord with the will of God as men can make it and a light to all the nations," wrote Bellah in a 1967 essay.[38] Not only did America have such a religion, he argued, but also America was the better society for it.

In a 1978 article, Bellah went further and endeavored to provide a theoretical account of the functional role and importance of American civil religion.[39] In the spirit of the theoretical concerns that animated the American founders, Bellah recalls the republican theorists from Machiavelli to Montesquieu who argued that popular regimes could only remain healthy so long as individual citizens placed the good of the *res publica* ahead of their own.[40] For these republican theorists, the citizen who placed his own well-being ahead of the public good, or preferred private gain to public service, was a danger of the first magnitude to the very life of the republic and personified the corruption that brings republics to their grave.[41] Lest this fate overtake a republic, Machiavelli advised those who would found durable republics to take steps to insure that the citizenry remained relatively poor compared to the state, and that private wealth was equally distributed.[42]

The American founders, however, despite their close attention to classical republican theory, were determined to build a republic that departed from the classic republican ideal in two central ways.[43] They would create a large, and potentially continental, republic. More significantly, they would create a commercial or liberal republic, a republic that according to the canons of classical republican theory could not last, a republic that would combine all the benefits of popular government with the free and unrestrained pursuit and accumulation of wealth.[44]

In Bellah's telling of the tale of the American founding, civil religion enters—or should enter—at just this point as the medium that transforms the individual who pursues his self-interest in the marketplace into the citizen who transcends narrow self-interest to pursue the common interest as is required of citizens in a healthy republic.[45] In Bellah's rather idealized narrative, it is the American civil religion that saves the republic from the fate that would otherwise await it if the mercantile spirit were to reign unchecked.

According to Bellah, the American civil religion differs in an important way from the civil religions of antiquity that posited a relation of identity between the city and its gods.[46] Making an argument that is quite similar to that which H. Richard Niebuhr made in his *Radical Monotheism and Western Culture*, Bellah observes that in pagan antiquity the city itself was identified with the Absolute.[47] Serving one's city and serving God was the same thing. But in the American civil religion this is not the case. The God of the American civil religion transcends the polity. The God of American civil religion is the God of Abraham, Isaac, Jacob, and Jesus. He is a transcendent God whose justice and mercy transcend the blessing He may or may not choose to bestow upon America. He is a God of judgment who sits in judgment upon America, and he demands of America that it be true to a standard of justice that is distinct from the vox populi. Ultimately, loyalty to this God, which is distinct from loyalty to any country, protects America against the dangers of self-deification or fascism. That the fear of divine judgment can operate to good effect has been demonstrated time and again in American political life, from Lincoln's second inaugural address to the civil rights movement of the 1960s. This inherent gap between loyalty to God and loyalty to country made Christianity the object of derision among republican theorists from Machiavelli to Montesquieu and Rousseau, and led them to condemn Christianity as the most antipolitical of religions. But in Bellah's view, this gap redounds to the benefit of the polity.[48]

The role of the American civil religion then—at least according to Bellah—is twofold. (1) It is a force that counters the individual's self-seeking spirit, calling Americans to a higher patriotic duty of selfless service to their country and the common good, and (2) it is a force that counters national self-love by reminding Americans that they owe ultimate allegiance to a divine sovereign who is ranked above the political sovereign and to moral norms that transcend the transient political determinations of the American democratic system.

To summarize, American civil religion calls Americans to a higher way of life and opposes the twin idolatries to which America would otherwise be susceptible: the idolatry of self and the idolatry of nation. Furthermore, we can surely agree with Bellah that any religion that served these ends would surely serve the public good and, indeed, it would itself be a public good.[49]

In a general way, I am prepared to accept Bellah's case for the potential political significance of religion in American life as a force that *could* act to counter other tendencies in American life that would make politics an extension of the marketplace or lead Americans to turn away from politics altogether. Where I disagree with Bellah, however, is with his insistence that there exists a distinct entity, which he calls the American civil religion that exists by itself and actually accomplishes all these good things. Rather, what Bellah catalogues under the rubric of American civil religion and its effects seems to me to be the fruit not of civil religion per se, but of the religious monotheisms that place neighbor ahead of self and allegiance to God above all else. The American civil religion by itself is neither thick enough, nor sinks roots that run deep enough, to motivate a critical mass of American citizens to become devoted champions of the public good.[50] The symbols, the rites, the narratives, and the special days and places, of which Bellah speaks, live by a borrowed power if they live at all and this borrowed power is lent—or not, as the case may be—by the American denominations of the monotheistic faiths which ultimately understand themselves not in terms of the American errand, but in terms of a loftier system of truly transcendental coordinates.

Of course, there is no guarantee that any particular religion or faith community will choose to identify with the American errand and play the public part that Bellah has allotted to them. There will always be communities of faith that are indifferent or hostile to the American project and situate themselves politically accordingly. There will also be communities of faith that in the passage of time will variously associate or disassociate themselves from active participation in the American experiment according to their own needs and internal evolution. The shifting relationship between American evangelicals and American politics is a case in point.

We can speak then—at least potentially—of religion as a public good, and of the good that religion *might* bring to the public square. But the very concrete question of whether religion is or is not, *at this very moment*, a public good is not usefully answered in the abstract. Indeed, the answer to this question will vary from one era to the next, from one religion to the next, from one denomination to the next and, indeed, from one congregation to the next, according to whether or not it is contributing at that moment to the proper primacy of the ideals of the common good and of social solidarity in

American political life. A good measure of how our religions are doing in this regard today can be gleaned by assessing the current standing of concern for the common good and of social solidarity as animating principles of our political life.

Even a cursory glance at American political life provides evidence of just how little thought is given to the common good, of how weak the principle of social solidarity has become. One could cite many issues to substantiate this claim—from the problem of poverty and substandard housing, to the continuing increase in the cost of health care and the growing ranks of the uninsured, to the growing economic gap between the northern and southern hemispheres.

As evidence of how little traction the concepts of the common good and of social solidarity possess today, consider the ongoing stalemate over social security reform.[51] For nearly a decade, there has been a consensus among experts that the system is in trouble, and that the ratio between the number of retirees drawing social security checks and the number of wage earners paying into the social security trust fund will shift an increasing burden to the latter as the Baby Boomers begin to retire en masse after 2015.

The politics of social security reform has pitted one generation against another, today's elderly against tomorrow's elderly, the World War II generation against the Baby Boomers, and the Baby Boomers against Generation X. Each cohort presses for its own advantage. Today's elderly want to insure that their benefits are undiminished, and Generation X worries about the burden that will fall upon it when the Boomers retire. Politicians meanwhile pander to today's elderly, knowing that they vote in the largest numbers and fearing punishment by AARP if they dare to suggest that benefits be cut or that recipients whose net income is above a certain level be taxed. Raising payroll taxes to pay for the increasing aggregate benefit levels is equally dangerous politically. Fearing they will be penalized whichever way they turn, politicians properly regard social security as the third rail of American politics and refuse to touch it, praying for the appointment of yet another bipartisan commission that will spare them from having to choose. Consequently the issue remains unresolved year after year.

America's continuing failure to deal with the social security issue gives evidence of just how far we are from a politics that really aims at securing the common good. It also gives evidence of the fact that, at present, we as a people lack the prepolitical social and cultural prerequisites that are most conducive to the politics of the common good taking root. Americans, it seems, lack the deeply felt bonds of fellow-feeling that are needed to weave a diverse civic association into a single body in which each member feels the good of the whole to be her own good, and any injury to any part of the whole to be an injury to herself. Such fellow-feeling would unite Americans in bonds of sympathy and identification—in bonds of strongly felt peoplehood, as it were—that would cut across the socioeconomic and generational fault lines that divide America today. Were the American body politic united in this way, the contours of American political debate would presumably shift from a zero-sum competition between different self-interested groups over the relative distribution of burdens and benefits to a collective search for a common good that all segments of society regard as their own good. Were the American body politic woven together by such bonds of solidarity and shared identity, the politics of social security would be quite different from what they are today, as would the politics of environmental protection, health care, and global trade. (Were the peoples of the world similarly woven together, one can also imagine that the politics of North-South relations, human rights, and global environmental challenges would be analogously transformed.)

Admittedly, most people do not come to an awareness of, or a concern for, the common good naturally or automatically. Both human instinct and our socialization for life in a competitive market economy tell us that it is natural to place our own interests and the interests of our family and of our little tribe ahead of the interests of other families and other tribes with whom we are less closely identified. It is natural—in our society, at least—to regard the others as competitors, and as lying beyond the circle of one's own proper concern. One may come to terms with them for prudential reasons, or may make common cause with them to establish fair rules of the game to regulate the competition for scarce social goods, but this is not really to include them within the circle of one's self-concern.

In our society, it is easy to suppose that egoism is natural and that humans are capable of expanding their circle of self-concern to only a very limited degree. Yet, we also know from our own individual experience that the circle of self-concern can be expanded, that the good of others can become almost as important to us as our own individual good, that their good can even come to be understood by us as an element of our own good. Another way to think about this is in terms of the concept of solidarity. The circle of solidarity can be narrowly drawn, but it can also be wide open and broadly inclusive. Let us define the common good, then, as a good that is common to all who are encompassed within the circle of our solidarity. Indeed, the proof of our solidarity is that we pursue their good as well as our own.

As Rousseau observed, we all are servants of one common good or another, but we differ in how wide a circle we draw, in how many persons and in how diverse a range of persons we include within our circle of concern.[52] In this same vein, Augustine observed that even a gang of thieves pursues a common good.[53] But, of course, the good that is common to the robber gang is contrary to the common good of those who fall prey to the gang. In the good society, however, citizens will define the circle of their political concern as all encompassing. No fellow citizen will be defined as other or outside this circle.[54] In a good world order, individual states will define the circle of their own concern in an analogously broad manner, regarding no countries or peoples as falling outside of this circle of human concern.

If religion were really serving the public good today (and hence itself a public good), the churches, synagogues, and mosques would be fully engaged in an effort to transform the general understanding of political life and to elevate its standing as a calling relative to the other aspects of human existence. If the churches, synagogues, and mosques were effective in this regard, they would engender a radical transformation in the American spirit that might make this country at long last that shining city on a hill, that New Jerusalem that inspired the Puritans who first settled this land.

Can the religions in today's America play this role? Have they any chance of having this impact? As we know from experience, a dogmatic (or rhetorical, or theoretical) commitment to the common good, or a dogmatic affirmation of the unity of mankind as children of the one God—which all the great monotheistic religions assert— need not necessarily translate into a genuine passion for, and active commitment to, the practical endeavor that follows from these concepts.[55] The question comes down then to whether within the synagogues, churches, and mosques forms of religious life might be cultivated that can turn pious phrases into deep and powerful and action-animating sentiments. Tocqueville spoke of the New England town meetings as schoolhouses of democratic life where Americans learned the arts and habits of self-government.[56] For us the question is whether, at the dawn of the twenty-first century, the synagogues, churches, and mosques can serve as schoolhouses for the cultivation of the love of, and dedication to, the common good.

Certainly the churches and synagogues have played that role at crucial moments in the nation's past.[57] The abolitionist movement, for example, was a religious movement that unfolded in the political domain and challenged the economic definition of black men and women as property.[58] The suffrage movement was also largely religious in its inspiration, as were the movements for prohibition and civil rights.[59] In each case, the autonomy of the political and economic realms was called into question by a religious movement that insisted on the rightful supremacy of the ethical dimension and upon an expansive conception of the common good.

But can the religions play this role today? The challenges in the way of the churches, synagogues, and mosques becoming catalysts of a fundamental shift in the tenor of American politics are significant. Except on the evangelical (or orthodox) right and the (liberation theology influenced) far left, contemporary (middle and upper middle class) religion largely accepts the compartmentalized status quo and practically accedes to the separation of religion and politics.[60]

The focus of most middle and upper-middle-class congregations seems to be more inward than outward, and increasingly so, if Robert Wuthnow, the dean of American sociologists of religion, is correct.[61] The social suffering that matters most to the members of the congregation is that of their fellow congregants.[62] The norm that matters most is to provide mutual aid and support to members who are in need.[63] Thus we see the proliferation of self-help and support groups for all manner of social ills in addition to the more familiar support that congregations provide to the ill and the grieving and to the victims of fire and flood.[64] The free loan societies that exist within many synagogues, the *bikkur holim* ("visitors to the sick") group and the *chevra kadisha* ("guardians of the dead") are all examples of the typical way in which religious congregations respond to social needs and social suffering. It is there, where macro forces make themselves felt on the micro and individual levels as afflictions that befall members of the congregation, that the response to the larger social forces comes.

It would be a mistake, however, to suggest that most congregations show no interest in the fate of those who are not counted among their members or among the members of their brother or sister congregations. Indeed, many congregations do see themselves as having an obligation to the wider human community and, with this in view, act to establish or to staff soup kitchens, homeless shelters, communal clothes closets, and food pantries to meet the needs of those who are down on their luck. Of course, these programs are typically small and hardly make a dent in the larger problems, even as they make a real difference in the lives of those lucky few that are the recipients of their generosity. Vis-à-vis the larger social and economic issues that make for poverty and homelessness, these programs are in effect agnostic. They are concerned not with attacking the causes, but with humanly responding to consequences. The response to the underlying problems that these soup kitchens and shelters represent is intimate, local, and personal. It is also apolitical. The members of the congregations who are moved by the plight of their neighbors and want to do something, and to feel like they are doing something are given a hands-on opportunity to make a concrete difference in the life of an individual or family that is in need. At the same time, it needs to be underscored that the minister or rabbi who summons his congregants to create and staff a homeless shelter or a food pantry is not summoning them to engage in political action to address the systemic social and economic causes that have produced the misery to which the congregants are ministering. The question is whether we can imagine the ministers, rabbis, and imams of America calling their congregants not to small-scale social service delivery, but to political engagement on behalf of that extensive segment of the population that is demographically similar to that pitifully small handful of souls who are served by their soup kitchens and shelters.

If you talk to ministers or rabbis about the need to take this political step, they will acknowledge that their own programs are no more than a band-aid, but they will also tell you that, while they agree in principle, it is not realistic to expect that their congregants could be enlisted to become soldiers in a political campaign. It is not that their congregants are unmoved by social solidarity, but that they do not have the time for such things. They are too busy with their own lives, their careers and their families. A night in the shelter or an occasional Sunday manning the food pantry they can manage, but to imagine they can give any more is wishful thinking. Besides, their congregants are not interested in politics but in doing something concrete. They work in the soup kitchen because they want to make a difference.

Both of these sentiments—that congregants do not have enough time and that they want to do something concrete and personally meaningful—need to be countered from the pulpits if the congregations of America are to become a real basis of national renewal.

From the pulpit it must be stressed that the desire to do something concrete, to bind up a wound and help a neighbor in dire need, is meritorious. It is an expression of basic human solidarity in a stratified society in which life chances and opportunities are unfairly distributed. At the feeling level, it expresses the intuition that this distribution of life chances is unfair and that the human face in abject distress commands our response, commands us to open our hands and our hearts in response.

To not act to alleviate the distress that claims us through the face of the other and demands our response is to incur guilt. To open our hand is to alleviate this guilt. This action may even give us a "feel good" moment. But though our distress may be momentarily alleviated, we also know that the underlying social and economic reality that afflicts so many others who are in the same situation as the one person whom we have chanced to help remains unchanged. We also know that, if it can be changed, it can only be changed through political effort. Our rabbis, pastors, and priests need to bring home this fact to their congregants.

In emphasizing that the appropriate response to human suffering is often (at least in part) political, it is important to acknowledge that not all suffering is socially produced or socially remediable. But much suffering is entirely man-made. Much suffering is produced as the intended or unintended consequence of human action, a fact that we obfuscate when we speak of suffering as the product of economic or social forces—as if these were forces of nature, like volcanoes or floods. When the causes of social suffering are systemic, the response too must be systemic, and the proper lever of systemic change in a democratic society is political action.

It also needs to be pointed out to those who prefer the face-to-face way of compassionate personal response, and invoke the authority of their religious traditions on behalf of this approach, that the traditions' codifications of the ways of mercy were arrived at centuries before political rights were extended to the masses. They were also defined centuries before we came to understand that our social and economic systems are neither natural nor eternal, but are the contingent and changeable inventions of human beings.

Understanding that the systems that define our social existence are modifiable, and possessing the political right to act in concert with our fellow citizens to modify these systems, our situation is fundamentally different from that of our ancestors whose wherewithal to respond to human tragedy and suffering was extraordinarily limited. For them, sharing their meager bread with the hungry was the apt, and indeed the only possible, way of rendering their compassion practical. We, however, who are blessed with much greater power of action, can render our compassion practical in ways that our ancestors could not have imagined.

Moral logic tells us that we cannot be commanded to do that which is not within our power. But as our power is much greater than that of our ancestors, so too is our obligation to do all that is within our power. Thus it is incumbent upon us to transform our immediate compassion into political advocacy on behalf of the common good. Having the power to act and the duty to use our power for good, we are of course culpable if we fail to use the power that we possess. Homeless shelters and soup kitchens in our churches and synagogues? By all means! But, in good conscience, we cannot stop there.

Oh, the weight of the burden that this would place upon religious Americans! Who has the time or the energy?

We return then to the rabbi who said to us, "You've got to be kidding. You want me to ask my congregants to do even more than they're doing already? They can barely manage to staff the soup kitchen and the shelter as it is. . . . They're too busy to make time for that and you want me to ask for more? They'll think I've completely lost touch with reality."

Our rabbi makes a good point. What then is the answer?

Most congregants are too busy with their lives, careers, and families. But this source of resistance must be attacked directly. Our religious leaders must have the courage of their convictions and dare to become countercultural if religion is to truly serve the public good. They must be willing to call their congregants' priorities into question. If their congregants are too busy for serious and sustained political engagement on behalf of the common good, if they are too busy getting and spending and trying to build a private (gated) heaven for themselves and their families, if they are too busy with their golf and tennis and vacations—if they are too busy, in sum, doing what they regard as being really important—then it is the rabbi's (or the priest's) responsibility to critique his congregants' scale of values, not to accommodate it. From the pulpit, the rabbis and priests must put the critical existential question to their congregants: What kind of person do you want to be? What really matters? What do you want to do with your life?

The answer of Judaism (or Christianity or Islam, for that matter) to such questions is quite clear. Each of these traditions has harsh words for the man or woman who strives only on his or her own behalf or only on behalf of his or her family. Each tradition understands human realization as coming about when we transcend our self-love and each espouses an ethic of compassionate service to the neighbor that serves as the vehicle of this self-overcoming or self-transcendence. For each of the three monotheistic traditions, the neighbor who is the proper object of my concern includes the nearest neighbor and the farthest, the one who is so like me as to be flesh of my flesh and the one who is a stranger to me, a foreigner, an alien. While the religions have all failed (and continue to fail) to varying degrees at various times and places to practice what they preach in this regard, ultimately each espouses an ideal of righteousness before God according to which the most perfect human being is the one whose circle of concern and active care encompasses the whole of humanity, for every person has been created in the image of God and endowed with supreme dignity.

If the churches, synagogues, and mosques are to become nuclei of political renewal, preaching and religious education will need to change accordingly. Their aim must be to cultivate a sensibility that feels the suffering of others as one's own suffering and feels the common good to be one's own good as well. A religious education or homiletics that is too text centered or therapeutic in its orientation often colludes in supporting the status quo in values and politics and must be resisted. A religious education or homiletics that focuses exclusively upon the fate of one's coreligionists is unlikely to lead congregants to a sufficiently inclusive sense of the common good, and so it too must be resisted.

Can sermons or educational programs that press congregants to reevaluate the contours of how they have chosen to live their lives really make a difference? Can congregants be persuaded to break with the authoritative consensus that places work and family ahead of everything? Only if the effort is made from the pulpit can we find out. The fate of our republic may hang in the balance. If citizens are not inspired to act on behalf of the common good, who will do it for us? There is no one else but us.

Yet, for all this talk of the good that religion might bring to our public life, even those who are somewhat receptive to the idea that religion could prove to be an important means for cultivating love of the common good, and a source of political renewal, may be bothered by the relative inattention in the argument so far to the potential danger that may arise from too close a connection between religion and politics. That religion has exerted a positive influence upon political life from time to time is not to be denied. Nor, however, can it be denied that Western history provides us with ample evidence of the poison that can emanate from this nexus. Witness the bloody politics of intolerance that prevailed in the premodern and early modern periods. Given this record, is it not naïve and dangerous to espouse a closer relation between religion and politics, knowing that the consequences of such proximity in the past were so awful that the separation of church and state, and the privatization and depoliticization of religion, came to be accepted throughout the West as the unequivocal counsels of prudence?

The doubters are certainly right to be concerned about what is being espoused here. Ultimately, the question becomes one of whether religion and politics can be brought into proximity on a "new basis" that will be unlikely to be productive of the odious religious politics of yesteryear. The burden of argument here is properly placed upon those who urge a departure from the status quo.[65]

In thinking about what this "new basis" might be that would serve to inoculate the polity against the dangers that religious forces have engendered in the past, some might argue that we need not fear any social harm from any religious party that seeks the public good with all sincerity. On this view, the evils wrought by politicized religion in the past owed to the fact that the partisans of one religious vision or another placed their own good ahead of the common good, and that priestly protestations of benevolence and philanthropy were a cover for an all too human and rather worldly will to power. But this view of the matter fails to grasp that the danger to the polity has been greater still when the religiously inspired were driven by the purest and most selfless love of common good and neighbor.

In the premodern period, the greatest threat to social peace arose when those who were in possession of what they regarded as the absolute truth, and were animated by the most sincere love of neighbor and by the deepest commitment to the common good, felt themselves to be morally obligated to impose this truth upon all who were in error and to do so by means of the sword if necessary (albeit from the purest of motives). To avoid the social chaos and social suffering born of such a loving embrace, religion was privatized in the modern period and the separation of church and state was instituted to protect the commons from true believers. That the danger to the polity came not so much from religion per se as from a certain readiness to impose one's beliefs upon others (albeit for their own good) might be inferred from the bloody history of the twentieth century in which true believers of the political left and right violently imposed their conceptions of the common good upon all who disagreed with them.

Thus it becomes clear that the impact of religion upon political life depends entirely upon *how* people of faith orient themselves in political life. It depends not so much upon the *fact* that they inject religion into politics, but upon the *tenor* of their political culture, and upon how it fits with the wider political culture of the time. This will determine how persons of faith articulate their religious convictions, values, and arguments in a political arena in which persuasive speech rules, in which issues of the day are debated and decisions on matters of public significance are taken.

It was Hannah Arendt's profound insight that the currency of politics is not truth but opinion, and that the political process is not about securing the truth but about producing a consensus of opinion.[66] In a strange kind of alchemy, she observed, that which counts as truth outside of politics becomes just one more opinion as soon as it gets enunciated in the political realm.[67] Building on her insight, I would argue that upon being articulated in the political realm, the truth claims of particular religious traditions undergo an important change that is the sine qua non of political life in general and, more especially, of political life in our pluralist and open society.

Thus it comes about that religiously grounded claims that are existentially authoritative for an individual, claims that an individual regards as true because they are believed to be revealed, communally sanctioned, and/or time tested, are stripped of this authority when they are offered to the wider political community as pertinent to one or another challenge of our common political existence. In this movement, what was absolutely true for the individual becomes just one political opinion among many and it can only achieve a wider political validity if the individual succeeds in persuading his fellow citizens of its cogency and adequacy.

The question then becomes: what is the proper character of persuasive speech in a pluralist society, especially as concerns claims originating from religious traditions and commitments? It seems that as a matter of civic respect for one's fellow citizens, it becomes incumbent upon the individual citizen to translate his religiously based claims, arguments, or assertions into the idiom of secular reason and to forgo parochial appeals to his coreligionists—whether they constitute a religious majority or minority—even as he proudly acknowledges the particular religious provenance of the claims he is espousing. Expediency alone dictates that members of religious minorities should translate their positions into the secular lingua franca of the public square if they want the majority to embrace a given position, but, in the political culture being envisioned here, even citizens who belong to the majority religion would translate their positions into the idiom of secular civic discourse out of a principled commitment to a civic culture in which religious differences do not function as sources of political advantage. A commitment to the translation of religiously derived claims or arguments into the most widely accessible language expresses a commitment to a broadly inclusive political life that is nourished but not ruined by the wellsprings of religious wisdom.

By this act of translation, the good citizen will ideally manifest a laudable dual loyalty to both his own particular religious tradition and to the wider human community to which he belongs as a citizen. Love of neighbor demands that one offer to the wider community whatever wisdom one possesses that may be of assistance, but it also demands that the offering be conveyed in a manner, and in a language, that can be generally understood and can find acceptance, at least potentially. In public life, this means that when what one has to offer is an idea or an opinion as to why x should be done and not y, one must set forth good reasons, and good reasons are reasons that have been translated into a secular language of the widest possible accessibility and appeal.

Whoever accepts this orientation toward political life as a matter of principle (or even on pragmatic grounds), and is willing to accept that in political life the common good can only be defined through a process of mutual exchange of opinion that culminates in a consensus as to wherein the common good lies, need not be feared as a danger to our political life. We, in the modern West, are living in an era in which more religious people than ever before accept this norm and are willing to abide by it. That is why I do not fear and, indeed, strongly support the return of religious energy and enthusiasm to our public life, and also trust in the bulwark of the constitutional separation of church and state as providing enough security to permit the passionate union of religion and politics.

Having benefited politically, socially, and economically from an era in which religion was politically marginal, most American Jews are understandably wary of countenancing the renewed commingling of religion and politics. It is hard for us to imagine how invoking our Jewish faith, history, or values in the public square will not "other" us, will not become politically self-defeating and lead us to forfeit everything we have gained since the Emancipation. In reality, however, the wall of separation between religion and politics has become increasingly permeable and the return of religion to public life is ongoing. Just where this process will lead is still an open question. But insofar as we want to influence this process, we should support the emergence of a relationship between religion and politics that will minimize the potential for injury and maximize the potential benefit to our public life.

In closing, we might say that politics is all about walls and bridges—about erecting walls and building bridges. At the beginning of the twenty-first century, we must ask ourselves whether the political manifestation of religious difference, in general, and of Jewishness, in particular, is a wall or a bridge. After millennia in the West in which we experienced our Jewishness as a wall of separation—and after fifty years in America in which muting our public Jewishness proved to be the recipe for social and political inclusion—it is hard to imagine that it could now be a bridge. But for religion to play this role, citizens must not be asked to leave their religious identities outside the statehouse door.

To return, in conclusion, to the question with which we began: Is religion a public good? Not necessarily. Indeed, it has often been a public scourge. But it can be a great good if the way to the public square is cleared and if the pastors, priests, and rabbis set about the hard work of inculcating the proper political ethos of civic participation and love of the common good.

Notes

1. Among recent books making this case, see Martin E. Marty, *Politics, Religion and the Common Good* (San Francisco: Jossey Bass, 2000); and Stephen L. Carter, *God's Name in Vain* (New York: Basic Books, 2000).

2. On the modern theory of public goods, see Paul A. Samuelson, *Foundations of Economic Analysis* (Cambridge, Mass.: Harvard University Press, 1955); and R. A. Musgrave, "Public Goods," in E. C. Brown and R. M. Solow, eds., *Paul Samuelson and Modern Economic Theory* (New York: McGraw-Hill, 1983). See also Raymond Geuss, *Public Goods, Private Goods* (Princeton, N.J.: Princeton University Press, 2001).

3. In effect this is the argument of some on the Christian right when it is argued that the secular state's support for irreligion creates an environment that is hostile to all religions.

4. Hannah Arendt develops this conception of the public sphere in *The Human Condition* and argues that this was the meaning of the public sphere in Greek (Athenian) antiquity. See Hannah Arendt, *The Human Condition* (Chicago: University of Chicago Press, 1958), 22-78.

5. For Arendt, the essential quality of the public sphere is associated with the forum or town meeting which is home to political action, to action in which the common interest is foremost. Thus the marketplace, while public insofar as it is a "space of appearance," is a problematic instance insofar as the "action" of the marketplace is primarily focused on the acquisition of private goods. The theater is also a mixed form, but comes closer than the marketplace, in Arendt's opinion, to realizing the essential form of the public space.

6. In the parlance of public goods theory, one could argue that the religions directly provide a shared good to a limited circle of adherents (making religion more of a "club good" than a public good in the strong sense), but that this "club good" in turn generates "positive externalities" that are a great good for the members of the wider society insofar as society as a whole benefits from the elevated civic ethos and superior commitment to the commonweal that are manifested by religious citizens.

7. See R. R. Palmer and Joel Colton, *A History of the Modern World* (New York: A. A. Knopf, 1964), 89-131.

8. Palmer and Colton, *History of the Modern World.*

9. This process, which begins with the circle of philosophers of the radical Enlightenment, proceeds at variable speeds in different countries and does not receive widespread legal expression until the revolutions of the late eighteenth and early nineteenth centuries. On the intellectual developments that played an important part in this process, see Jonathan L. Israel, *The Radical Enlightenment* (New York: Oxford University Press, 2001).

10. Of course, not only members of religious minorities regard secularization as a gain. Arguably, the religious majority has gained even more in being freed from the oppressive weight of religious, moral, social, and intellectual conformity.

11. On the dynamics of social modernization and secularization and the changes in status and role of religion attendant upon this process, with particular attention to the changing relation between religion and politics that emerges in this process, see Max Weber, *The Protestant Ethic and the Spirit of Capitalism* (New York: Scribners, 1958); Jurgen Habermas, *The Theory of Communicative Action*, v. 1, *Reason and the Rationalization of Society* (Boston: Beacon Press, 1984), 143-272; v. 2, *Lifeworld and System* (Boston: Beacon Press, 1987), 43-112; Jurgen Habermas, *The Philosophical Discourse of Modernity* (Boston: MIT Press, 1990), 336-67; and Jose Casanova, "Secularization," in Neil Smelser and Paul Baltes, eds., *International Encyclopedia of the Social and Behavioral Sciences* (Oxford: Elsevier, 2001).

12. Weber, *The Protestant Ethic;* Habermas, *Reason and the Rationalization of Society,* 143-272; Habermas, *Lifeworld and System,* 43-112; Habermas, *The Philosophical Discourse of Modernity,* 336-67; Casanova, "Secularization."

13. For a good synopsis of this process, see Jose Casanova, "Secularization," in *International Encyclopedia of the Social and Behavioral Sciences* (New York: Pergamon Press, 2001).

14. Habermas's refinement of Weber's argument regarding the processes of societal rationalization provides the theoretically richest articulation of this process. See Habermas, *Reason and the Rationalization of Society*, 143-272; and *Lifeworld and System*, 43-112.

15. Habermas, *Reason and the Rationalization of Society*, 143-272; Habermas, *Lifeworld and System*, 43-112.

16. Habermas, *Reason and the Rationalization of Society*, 143-272; Habermas, *Lifeworld and System*, 43-112.

17. See Habermas, *Philosophical Discourse of Modernity*, 336-67, where he defends this relative autonomy of modernity's multiple realms against the postmodern critics who would bring a single value to bear as a master criterion of validity.

18. See works cited in note 11 above.

19. See J. G. A. Pocock, *The Machiavellian Moment* (Princeton, N.J.: Princeton University Press, 1975).

20. Regarding religiously directed or inspired regulation of economic life in the medieval period, see Diana Wood, *Medieval Economic Thought* (Cambridge: Cambridge University Press, 2002), generally; and Henri Pirenne, *Economic and Social History of Medieval Europe* (New York: Harcourt Brace & World, 1937), 1-14, 27-28, 68-69, 138-39, 168. See also Jacob Katz, *Tradition and Crisis: Jewish Society at the End of the Middle Ages* (New York: New York University Press, 1993), 38-87.

21. This story of secularization is more ideal-typical (in the Weberian sense) than real, and in practice unfolded in some parts of the West more completely than others, and in Western Europe more than in the United States. A growing awareness of the historical and sociological inadequacies of the strong version of the secularization thesis has led in recent decades to a recoil against the long unquestioned hegemony of the secularization thesis. In my opinion, while the strong version of the thesis does not meet the test of historical evidence, a weaker and more qualified version of the secularization thesis seems to be largely correct and is borne out by the historical evidence. For more on this debate, see Jose Casanova, "Secularization," in Smelser and Baltes, *International Encyclopedia*.

22. It is generally understood that when the Jews gained entry to society in the nineteenth century, they were required to give up their public religion and to create instead a religion that centered on the home and hearth, and that spoke no more to the concerns of the public square and the marketplace. Furthermore, while this is true, it is important to understand that this rather narrow circumscribing of the religious domain was imposed upon Christianity as well in the passage to modernity.

23. See Weber, *The Protestant Ethic*; Habermas, *Reason and the Rationalization of Society*, 143-272; Habermas, *Lifeworld and System*, 43-112; Habermas, *Philosophical Discourse of Modernity*, 336-67.

24. Weber, *The Protestant Ethic*; Habermas, *Reason and the Rationalization of Society*, 143-272; Habermas, *Lifeworld and System*, 43-112; Habermas, *Philosophical Discourse of Modernity*, 336-67.

25. On the impact of these developments in science and philosophy on the religious belief of the educated elites, see Jonathan L. Israel, *The Radical Enlightenment* (New York: Oxford University Press, 2001); Peter Gay, *The Enlightenment*, vol. 1, *The Rise of Modern Paganism* (New York: W.W. Norton, 1966); Owen Chadwick, *The Secularization of the European Mind in the Nineteenth Century* (Cambridge: Cambridge University Press, 1975); and Claude Welch's two-volume study, *Protestant Thought in the Nineteenth Century*, (New Haven, Conn.: Yale University Press, vol. 1, 1972, vol. 2, 1979, 1985). Welch's work provides a comprehensive treatment of these issues as they work themselves out in late- and post-Enlightenment religious thought and sensibility.

26. On the American dimension of this story, see Henry F. May, *Protestant Churches and Industrial America* (New York: Harper & Row, 1949). For the European dimension, see Chadwick, *The Secularization;* and Claude Welch, *Protestant Thought in the Nineteenth Century*, especially vol. 2, 212-55.

27. May, *Protestant Churches and Industrial America;* Chadwick, *The Secularization;* Welch, *Protestant Thought*, vol. 2, 212-55.

28. On the emergence of modern political thought in this context, see Julian Franklin, *Constitutionalism and Resistance in the Sixteenth Century* (New York: Pegasus Books, 1969); Richard Tuck, *Natural Rights Theories: Their Origin and Development* (Cambridge: Cambridge University Press, 1979); Peter Gay, *The Enlightenment*, vol. 2, *The Science of Freedom* (New York: W. W. Norton, 1969); and Jonathan L. Israel, *The Radical Enlightenment* (New York: Oxford University Press, 2001).

29. Franklin, *Constitutionalism and Resistance;* Tuck, *Natural Rights Theories;* Gay, *The Science of Freedom;* Israel, *The Radical Enlightenment.*

30. See C. B. Macpherson, *The Political Theory of Possessive Individualism: Hobbes to Locke* (Oxford: Oxford University Press, 1962).

31. See Julian Franklin, *Jean Bodin and the Rise of Absolutist Theory* (Cambridge: Cambridge University Press, 1973).

32. See Macpherson, *Political Theory of Possessive Individualism.*

33. Macpherson, *Political Theory of Possessive Individualism.*

34. One might recall in this context Marx's demand for universal manhood suffrage in *The Communist Manifesto*. On the one hand Marx thought that the bourgeoisie would never grant the demand lest they dig their own graves thereby; on the other hand he assumed that the day this demand was met would be the day that the proletariat would be able to prevail via the ballot box. The irony, of course, is that by the time this right was granted, the workers were no longer disposed to put it to revolutionary use.

35. See Bellah's 1978 article, "Religion and the Legitimation of the American Republic," in Robert Bellah, *The Broken Covenant: American*

Civil Religion in Time of Trial, 2nd ed. (Chicago: University of Chicago Press, 1992).

36. Bellah first called attention to the American civic religion in his 1967 article, "Civil Religion in America," that appeared in *Daedalus* (Winter 1967) and has been reprinted in Robert Bellah, *Beyond Belief; Essays on Religion in a Post-Traditionalist World* (Berkeley: University of California Press, 1970).

37. Bellah, "Civil Religion in America," 171-86.

38. Bellah, "Civil Religion in America," 186.

39. Bellah, "Religion and the Legitimation of the American Republic," 164-88.

40. Bellah, "Religion."

41. On the republican theory tradition, see Pocock, *Machiavellian Moment*.

42. See Machiavelli's "Discourses on the First Ten Books of Titus Livius," a commentary on Livy's History of the Roman Republic, which occasions the fullest expression of Machiavelli's theory of republican governance.

43. See Bellah, "Religion and the Legitimation of the American Republic," 170-72.

44. For more on how the American founders and framers mastered the constitutional, sociological, and political challenges that arose in the endeavor to constitute a liberal republic, see Gordon S. Wood, *The Creation of the American Republic 1776-1787* (New York: W. W. Norton, 1978).

45. See Bellah, "Religion and the Legitimation of the American Republic," 176, 180-82.

46. See Bellah, "Civil Religion in America," 171-72, 185. See also Bellah, "Religion and the Legitimation of the American Republic," 173-75.

47. Bellah, "Civil Religion in America," 171-72, 185; Bellah, "Religion," 173-75. See also H. Richard Niebuhr, *Radical Monotheism and Western Culture* (New York: Harper & Row, 1960), on henotheism and politics, 24-37, 64-77.

48. Bellah, "Civil Religion in America," 171-72, 185; Bellah, "Religion," 173-75.

49. On a historical note, it is striking that Bellah's delineation of the American republican problem and of its solution represents an Antifederalist interpretation of the problem and a conception of civil religion as a solution that is very much in the Antifederalist spirit. At the same time, it is rather curious that Bellah makes no mention of the Federalists' own preferred approach to resolving the problem of insuring the stability of large and commercial republics, that is, Madison's solution as articulated in Federalist 10 and as enshrined in the U.S. Constitution's system of checks and balances, a device that—in theory at least—would rescue the American republic from the fate that has historically awaited republics when the well of self-transcending civic virtue has run dry.

50. In the Afterword to "Religion and the Legitimation of the American Republic," Bellah does acknowledge that the substance of the American civil religion is rather thin (in this essay he describes it as "formal and marginal") and that the real source of its motive power emanates from "the religious community entirely outside any formal political structures," from "what Talcott Parsons calls the 'societal community,'" or what might be called "the nation as opposed to the state" (176) that was initially formed through the Great Awakening that swept the colonies in the 1740s. The mention of the Great Awakening in this context is a step in the right direction of acknowledging that the viability of the American civil religion depends upon pre- or extrapolitical foundations of monotheistic religious faith and commitment.

51. See R. Douglas Arnold, Michael Graetz, and Alicia Munnell, eds., *Framing the Social Security Debate: Values, Politics, and Economics* (Washington, D.C.: Brookings Press, 1998).

52. See J. J. Rousseau, "Discourse on Political Economy," in J. J. Rousseau, J. R. Masters (trans.), *On the Social Contract with Geneva Manuscript and Political Economy* (New York: St. Martin's, 1978), 212-13.

53. See Augustine, *City of God*, Bk. 4.4 (London: Penguin, 1984), 139.

54. See Rousseau, *On the Social Contract* (Bk. 2.3), 61-62; and "Discourse on Political Economy," 212-13.

55. As Dewey pointed out in *A Common Faith* (New Haven, Conn.: Yale University Press, 1934), humans only act to realize an end if they have a vivid conception of the end and experience a strong attraction that impels them to make the realization of this end their business. Without this vivid conception of the object and strong attraction to it, we may pay lip service to the object but nothing of serious magnitude should be expected from our efforts on its behalf.

56. See A. de Tocqueville, *Democracy in America,* vol. 1 (New York: Knopf, 1945), 66-86, 89-102, 250-53.

57. An excellent general history of religion in America that attends, inter alia, to the social and political role of religion in America is Sydney F. Ahlstrom's *A Religious History of the American People* (New Haven, Conn.: Yale University Press, 1972). For an excellent account of religion's role as a driving force in the history of America's "progressive" social movements, see Stephen L. Carter, *God's Name in Vain* (New York: Basic Books, 2000).

58. See Ahlstrom, *Religious History,* 648-69, and Carter, *God's Name in Vain,* 83-99.

59. Regarding the role of religion in the movement for women's suffrage, see Ahlstrom, *Religious History,* 642-44; regarding the role of religion in driving the temperance movement, see Ahlstrom, *Religious History,* 867-72, 902-4; and regarding the role of religion in the civil rights movement, see Ahlstrom, *Religious History,* 1072-81.

60. Lip service may be paid from the pulpit to national and local political issues, but the tone is usually homiletic and the reference to political issues oftentimes serves no purpose beyond letting the congregants know that the rabbi or pastor is well-read and on top of the news. Moreover, given the equation that most Americans make between religion and personal morals, when current events are spoken of from the pulpit, it is typically those events that bring a question of personal morality to the fore (such as Clinton's lying and infidelity or Bush's drinking and lying about his DUI conviction) and not general questions of public policy (such as NAFTA) that receive attention.

61. See Robert Wuthnow, *Sharing the Journey: Support Groups and America's New Quest for Community* (New York: Free Press, 1994), 317-40.

62. Wuthnow, *Sharing the Journey.*

63. Wuthnow, *Sharing the Journey.*

64. Wuthnow, *Sharing the Journey.*

65. The attacks upon New York and Washington on September 11, 2001, reminded us all of just how lethal the combination of religion and politics can be. Since that awful day, the burden upon those who would lower the wall of separation between religion and politics is all the greater, as is the need to build such an argument upon a case for Western exceptionalism. The violence in the Balkans, Sudan, Nigeria, India, and the Caucuses may not be religious in provenance but only in manifestation, but there is no denying that the increasing disorder in many parts of the world that seems to take the form of religious conflict has made many in the West who might have been receptive to a closer relationship between religion and politics before 9/11 increasingly wary since.

66. See Hannah Arendt, "Truth and Politics," in Hannah Arendt, *Between Past and Future* (New York: Penguin Books, 1968), 227-65.

67. Arendt, "Truth and Politics," 246-47.

12

Judaism Influencing American Public Philosophy

Elliot N. Dorff

Encounters with Religion in the Public Sphere

In recent years, I have been increasingly involved in government. During March and April 1993, I served on the Ethics Committee of Hillary Rodham Clinton's Health Care Task Force. About the same time, I was appointed the Jewish consultant to review and revise the graded series of social studies books for California public schools that for the first time presented religion as part of the curriculum. In 1997 and 1999, I represented the Jewish tradition before the President's National Bio-ethics Advisory Commission on the issues of cloning and stem cell research. Then I was part of the Executive Committee of the Surgeon General's task force to create a Call to Action for Responsible Sexual Behavior, and now I serve as a member of the National Human Resources Protections Advisory Committee of the Department of Health and Human Services whose mandate is to review and revise the federal guidelines for research on human subjects. While I have a Ph.D. in philosophy with a dissertation in ethics, I am keenly aware that in all of these cases I am being asked to serve also—and maybe even primarily—as a rabbi.

This has raised an important issue for me with immediate consequences in practice: as a Jew who has been trained since childhood to
value and defend a strong wall of separation between religion and
government, should I accept appointments to governmental posts when
I know that it is my identity as a rabbi that suggests my appointment?
If I do accept such assignments, how should I integrate my American
and Jewish identities in helping to shape national policy? More
broadly, what ought to be the role that Judaism plays in national affairs?

Note that the question is not what role *Jews* should play in government. As long as they fulfill the minimal duties of citizenship like paying taxes and abiding by the law, American Jews, like American citizens of all other faiths, have the right to be as active or inactive in
government as they choose to be. The harder question, the one to
which this chapter is addressed, is this: should Jews consciously invoke their Jewish heritage in the process of serving their government,
and, if so, how?

The same issue of the relationship between religion and state has
become part of my life in a very different way. For sixteen years, I
have served on the Board of Directors of Jewish Family Service of Los
Angeles, where I am now a vice-president. Until the 1970s, almost all
of the agency's budget came from Jewish sources, with a little from
United Way. Now 86 percent of the budget comes from various levels
of government, and President George W. Bush wants to expand the
role of religion in "faith-based initiatives" of exactly this sort. Because
accepting government money entails that our services and our staff be
open to anyone, regardless of religion, the Jewish identity of the
agency has come into serious question. In fact, I now chair a standing
committee of the board, the "J in JFS Committee," to explore the ways
in which we still can and should be a distinctly Jewish agency. As we
struggle with this, ancient rabbinic comments take on new meaning:
"Love work, hate lordship, and seek no intimacy with the ruling
power," one of the rabbis said, and another warned "Be on your guard
against the ruling power, for they who exercise it draw no person near
to them except for their own interests; appearing as friends when it is
to their own advantage, they do not stand by a person in his hour of
need."[1] As Jefferson and Madison knew so well, religion's entanglement with government comes at a great cost for both.

The Role of Religion in Conceiving
of Public Issues

One might reasonably ask why one should bother considering the views of a religion like Judaism on any public policy issue at all. After all, one might argue that appropriate health care, for example, is and should be a medical decision.

Not so long ago, many physicians thought just that way. In America particularly, medicine was seen mechanistically, such that the task of the doctor was to fix the machine called the body.[2] In accomplishing that task, so conceived, the only significant issue is what works and what does not.

We have learned a great deal in the past several decades, however, about the intricate context in which medicine takes place. Many factors, beyond the strictly physical, influence the success of a particular therapy—or the possibility of using it in the first place. Doctors' diagnoses and prescriptions are useless without patient cooperation, but that invokes each patient's views about the body, medicine, the patient-physician relationship, medical personnel, the purpose of life, and, in critical cases, the nature of death and the hope for life after death. Decisions as to proper treatment are *not*, in other words, exclusively a matter of means, but also of goals, and those, in turn, are rooted in each person's moral views and overarching philosophy of life. The same is true for what one thinks about related public policy issues such as what research and treatments the government should fund, and how health should be weighed against other social needs. In such matters, people's priorities and their view of the proper role for government come immediately to the fore.

It is precisely here that religion plays an important role. The word "religion" comes from the same Latin word from which we get the word "ligament," connective tissue. Religions describe how we are and should be connected to each other in families and communities and how we should act in relationship to the environment and to the transcendent (imaged in Western religions as God). Religions articulate a philosophy of life, a view of all the pieces of our experience and of the relationships among them.

Religions, though, go beyond this: they teach their specific philosophy and its implications through story, ritual, prayer, custom, and law within the context of a living community. As a result, they are often more powerful influences on humanity than worldviews are by themselves. Religions share with philosophies, however, the task of depicting who we are and ought to be, and it is such a broad view of the larger scheme of things that ultimately grounds our specific moral judgments.

The religions and secular philosophies of the world, though, have very different pictures of what is and ought to be; they differ in their concepts and values. Who are we as individuals, and what should we strive to be? What are the significance and proper roles of the community? How should we conceive of, and relate to, the environment? How should we respond to that which lies beyond our ability to understand or control—or, for that matter, to that which we can understand and control? What role, if any, does God have in all of this? Contrasting the views on these questions of Judaism, Christianity, and Buddhism, for example, will reveal some overlapping features but also some major differences. Since I live in Los Angeles, I am keenly aware that significant numbers of Americans now espouse Asian religions. These varying worldviews, with their attendant values and practices, play a critical role in determining what individuals think about what kinds of health care, for example, should be prohibited, permissible, desirable, or required, and what role government should play in health care generally.

The American Context for Jewish Involvement

How, then, can we Americans rise above our varying views of life to come to some kind of social policy on concrete issues that face us all? And how shall we think about the extent and nature of our national involvement from the perspective of Jewish sources?

In two previous articles,[3] I have examined these theoretical issues in detail. Here I will only summarize my own understanding of these matters and move on to the substance of what I want to consider—namely, some ways in which Judaism can and should be a force in national affairs, and some ways in which it should not be, illustrated by a number of concrete examples taken from my own experience in government.

In some societies, of course, social decisions are made by decree of a tyrant or tribal leader, and that is the end of the matter. In others, a high degree of ethnic homogeneity enables a nation to use its heritage to make moral decisions with little, if any, regard for alternative views—although the current struggle within Iran indicates that even in largely monolithic societies political and social decisions may not be obvious or easy to come by. Other countries, like the Philippines, find themselves embroiled in civil wars as people of two religions fight for dominance.

The United States since its beginning has been an overwhelmingly Christian country. Nevertheless, the religious persecution that brought many of the colonists to these shores combined with Enlightenment notions of religion as a private affair to create the unique American separation of church and state. In our day, though, as citizens of virtually every world religion and view find their home here, the American experiment in freedom of religion and pluralism is being tested as it never was before.

How, then, can the United States engender social discourse and decision making in a thoroughly multicultural format? Frankly, only if people are willing to discuss issues in a multicultural setting where one's own view of things will be challenged and not necessarily adopted; only if people have sufficient flexibility to see and seize areas of agreement; only if people have respect for both varying points of view and for those who hold them; and only if people are resolved to live together not only peacefully, but cooperatively, despite their differing views and practices. The cocky assuredness that some might have had when living in isolated conclaves of people who think and act like themselves must give way to greater openness and respect. This is not moral laxity or indifference; one might—and hopefully would—still argue forcefully for one's own convictions. One must, however, come to recognize that one's own way of seeing and doing things is not the only possible way that a person of intelligence and moral character could adopt.

The remarkable thing is that, despite different premises, sometimes a remarkable degree of agreement occurs. For example, Daniel Wikler, in describing the essays produced during and for the President's Commission on Health Care in the early 1980s, noted that the widely different premises held by the members of the commission did not preclude agreement on a number of conclusions:

> It is true that each essay provides a different account of equity in access to health care and insists that rival accounts are mistaken. Yet there is one policy recommendation supported by each of these essays: Every person ought to be assured of access to some decent minimum of health care services. This conclusion cannot be said to have been "proved" by this collection of arguments, but the fact that a recommendation of universal access to (at least some) health care follows from such disparate sets of premises suggests that the recommendation is "insensitive" to choice of moral theory. Even if we do not know which moral theory is correct, then, and thus cannot provide

a ground-level-up proof that all should have access to a minimum of
health care, such a belief has been rendered reasonable and perhaps
,even compelling. In this sense, this diverse and inconsistent collection
of theories of justice in health care delivery supports the consensus
reached by members of the President's Commission concerning the
moral obligation of our society to ensure access to health care for all
its people.[4]

Often, though, differences in perspective lead to conflicting policy
recommendations. That is true for religious perspectives: consider, for
example, the varying religious views on abortion and the consequently
varying policies recommended by Roman Catholics, on the one hand,
and Reform Jews, on the other. Religions are not unique in this: secular viewpoints also produce differing proposals for social action. Consider, for example, the ongoing differences in both the perspectives
and programs of Democrats and Republicans on such issues as the environment and gun control. One, in fact, would *expect* differing outcomes from the various views embedded in our religious and secular
theories of who we are and ought to be.

How, then, can we live together as a nation? Philosophically, as I
develop more thoroughly in the other articles to which I alluded, we
need to shun what Van Harvey[5] has called "hard perspectivism," where
one can see life only through one set of lenses, and also "non-
perspectivism," in which one pretends that people can see the world
without lenses altogether. Instead, we must adopt "soft perspectivism,"
where we generally see the world through our own eyeglasses—those
provided by our own religion and culture and by our own experiences
—but we can try on the lenses of other people as well.

Politically, Thomas Jefferson understood the matter this way: "The
practice of morality [is] necessary for the well-being of society. . . .
The interests of society require observation of those moral principles
only in which all religions agree."[6] So, for example, since America's
religions differ on abortion and stem cell research, the government
should not legislate, permitting people of all religions to act on their
own views. Even within these bounds, hard questions remain. For example, should government not only permit abortion or stem cell research, but support them financially? Those issues are clearly matters
of debate in American theory and practice in our own time.

What emerges from these philosophical and political considerations
is that in all matters of public policy religious arguments should not be
denied simply because they come from a religious source and use religious language and reasoning, but neither should they be privileged
over secular arguments simply because they are religious. Stephen

Carter, in *The Culture of Disbelief,* has made the former point elo-
quently with regard to court cases,[7] and I would like to extend it to
public policy discussions as well. Indeed, as a matter of American
principle, all of America's religions should see it not only as a right,
but as a duty to articulate their views and advance the arguments for
those views in the public forum. Only then can America benefit by
forming its public policy based on the insights of the variety of religious and ethnic groups that constitute America. This effectively imposes an *American* duty on Americans to learn more about their own
religions' views so that they can participate in an informed, intelligent,
and distinctly religious way in shaping American public policy.

Jewish Theological Justifications for Pluralism

How, though, should we understand government service in a free, democratic country from a *Jewish* point of view? I believe that a contemporary Jewish philosophy of government service must rest on one's
view of the relationships that Jews *should* cultivate with non-Jews and
that that ultimately depends not only on a judgment of what is appropriate in changing historical circumstances but also on deep theological convictions about revelation and about appropriate relationships
with other Jews and with non-Jews.

Historically, many Jews, subjected to discrimination and persecution, sympathized with the rabbi's prayer in *Fiddler on the Roof:* "May
God keep the Czar—far away from us!" In a free and democratic country like the United States, however, where Jews have both the right
and, as I have argued, the patriotic duty to enter into the process of
forming national policy, the question becomes this: can one develop a
theology of Judaism that would encourage Jews to interact with non-
Jews in the shaping of national policy not only from the pragmatic motives of protecting Jewish interests, but also from a genuine appreciation of plural avenues of truth and wisdom while still retaining one's
claim to Jewish notions of what is true, right, and good?

In several previous articles,[8] I have pointed out that while some Orthodox rabbis reject pluralism completely, even within the Jewish
community, historical, philosophical, and theological considerations
should prompt Jews to take a pluralistic attitude in their relations with
fellow Jews. Such an attitude definitely does not preclude standing up
for what one believes; one just has to recognize, I have argued, that
the most philosophically warranted epistemological and moral position
is neither absolutism nor relativism, but relativity. Moreover, I discuss

there some classical sources about God and revelation that would argue on theological grounds as well for a clearly pluralistic position
among Jews.

Classical Jewish sources are considerably less positive about most
non-Jews. In light of the idolatry practiced by many nations of the ancient world and the degradation, if not outright hostility, to which
Jews were historically subjected by many groups of non-Jews, such
negative reactions are to be expected. Still, rabbinic sources maintain
that non-Jews do all that God wants of them if they just abide by the
seven laws given, according to rabbinic tradition, to all descendants of
Noah,[9] and so Jews have not actively tried to convert non-Jews. Moreover, some sources within classical Judaism and some medieval and
modern Jewish thinkers have argued for more positive relations with
non-Jews on a variety of grounds. Thus, according to the Torah, we
are not to abhor an Egyptian in gratitude for providing a home for us,
even though they enslaved us; according to the rabbis, we must care
for the non-Jewish poor and sick "for the sake of peace"; Franz
Rosenzweig would have us abhor Islam but appreciate Christianity for
bringing the Jewish message to the world; and Jewish universalists,
especially in the late nineteenth and early twentieth centuries, often
appealed to the biblical principle that all human beings are created in
the image of God together with Amos's declaration, "'To Me, O Israelites, you are just like the Ethiopians,' declares the Lord."[10] Clearly,
none of these sources urges acceptance of other faiths to the point of
advocating conversion from Judaism to another faith or assimilation
into some form of syncretism or secular religion, but they do argue for
positive relations with those of other faiths on theological, and not just
practical, grounds.

In our own day, when many Jews in the United States enjoy economic prosperity and are increasingly accepted as equals in the United
States not only in theory, but in practice, Jews have taken a major role
in public affairs. Most importantly, American Jews do this not only to
protect specifically Jewish interests, but to live out their strongly held,
genuine love of their country. In several other articles,[11] I have tried to
create—again, on historical, philosophical, and theological grounds—a
more positive Jewish theology of Jewish relations with non-Jews to
provide the theoretical grounding for the respectful and productive
interfaith relations that form the basis for active Jewish involvement in
government.

Ways in Which Judaism Should Not Be Invoked in the Political Realm

In light of the conceptual grounding in both American and Jewish thought that I have briefly described above, I would now like to turn to a consideration of some of the concrete ways in which Judaism should or should not be invoked in social policy. I will begin with the negative so that, in good Jewish fashion, I can end with the positive.

The foundation for all such discussions is the First Amendment, which, among other things, prohibits the *establishment* of any religion while guaranteeing individuals the free exercise of any religion. That amendment has been the focus of numerous Supreme Court decisions, which I will not rehearse here. Suffice it to say, though, that by its terms, neither Catholics nor Jews, for example, may determine national policy on abortion or stem cell research as a matter of prerogative.

On the other hand, at the other end of the spectrum, the First Amendment guarantees Americans the *free exercise* of their faith. As a result, people may choose *not* to avail themselves of liberties provided in American law out of religious conviction. For that matter, Americans routinely choose not to use some of their liberties for many reasons other than religion. Even though American law permits me to eat a half gallon of ice cream every night of the week, for example, I reluctantly choose not to do so for reasons of health. Similarly, even though the Supreme Court has affirmed the American right to abortion, Catholics and Jews, to use my two examples, may and should choose to avoid abortion out of loyalty to their faith (except, for Jews, when the mother's life or health is at stake or when the fetus suffers from a lethal genetic disease or is seriously malformed). Moreover, religious institutions have the right of refusing government aid for reasons of faith. Catholic Charities, for example, simply does not apply for those government programs that require the distribution of condoms to prevent the spread of AIDS.

While those are the broad parameters of the two clauses on religion in the First Amendment, American law and practice have blurred the lines.[12] Thus, despite the Establishment Clause, Christmas counts as a national holiday; states may require businesses to be closed on Sundays with no allowance for the Sabbath of any other religion; the postal service may suspend service on Sundays; and government funds may be used to pay for nonreligious instruction in parochial schools and for a chaplain to the houses of Congress itself. And despite the

Free Exercise Clause, Mormons may not practice polygamy; Jehovah's Witnesses may not deny medically necessary blood transfusions to their children; Christian Scientists may not refuse life-preserving medical care for their children; and Indians may not use peyote in their rituals.[13] Until Congress acted to reverse the Supreme Court's decision, the Free Exercise Clause did not guarantee Jews the right to wear a *kippah* in the military.

Still, for all the ambiguity in their interpretation, the Establishment and Free Exercise Clauses of the First Amendment together establish the end points of the line that defines permissible and impermissible forms of governmental involvement in religion and the reverse. It is the area in between these two extremes that is murky. Still, I think that some guidelines can be set for religious involvement in government, the side of the issue addressed by this chapter.

First, Judaism, and, for that matter, any other religion should *not* present its own stance as the only intelligent or moral one. The essence of living in a genuinely pluralistic society like the United States requires respect for people who hold differing moral views together with the willingness to speak and work with them on an even plane. This is, in a sense, an implication of the Establishment Clause, although applied not to Congress but to all Americans: so that America may function as a society, we all must listen and cooperate with each other, including especially those with whom we differ, in a context of interest and respect. Thus American Catholics who follow the pope's lead in denouncing embryonic stem cell research as "evil" when we Jews and many others consider it evil *not* to pursue that promising form of medical inquiry are acting contrary to the welfare of America and to the principles of pluralism on which it is based. One may surely oppose suggested or established policies, but one must not demonize those who disagree. Furthermore, one must provide *reasons* for one's opposition and respond respectfully to the reasons provided by others for their views. As Stephen Carter has argued, we should respect and even cherish "epistemic diversity," in which religious people are not required to translate their concerns into a secular language but can rather assert religious foundations of knowledge and express their reasons in religious terms.[14] But respect for religious reasons must be accompanied by respect on the part of religious people for views of other religions and for secularists. The abortion and stem cell debates, where the "pro-life" camp suggests that only they care about life and that all who oppose them are morally obtuse, are both good examples of illegitimate forms of religious intercession in government.

Second, religions should not proselytize in public areas like schools. The whole point of establishing public education is to provide a forum for education in which one's religion is not a factor. That applies to admissions standards for students, hiring standards for faculty, and curriculum. Thus the Supreme Court was right in 1963 when it banned prayer in public schools, and it was even right in subsequent decisions in banning attempts to create a neutral prayer, for the First Amendment must protect not only people of all religions but also people who affirm no religion. I thus find it problematic that the Supreme Court upheld the right of municipalities to display a creche at Christmas time; even though they may do so, according to the court's opinion, only if they permit displays of other religions as well, the public square should be free of any affirmation of any religion. Thus Chabad is wrong in trying to erect Hanukkah *menorot* on public property, particularly since they then light the candles according to Jewish law during the holiday and with the standard blessings. They thereby indicate that the *hanukkiah* is not simply a cultural symbol of the holiday season—which it could be if, for example, all eight lights were lit throughout December, much as Christmas trees in public areas are—but a flagrantly religious symbol.

If American law does or should forbid such moves toward establishment of religion, Jewish considerations should also dissuade us from taking steps to invade the religiously neutral public square. On pragmatic grounds, of course, any permitted act to affirm religion will most likely favor the majority religion, Christianity. Even when Christmas songs in school are accompanied by a Hanukkah song or two, the latter will pale by comparison in both quantity and quality. Furthermore, Jewish religious acts in schools may well be done improperly and may be explained incorrectly, especially since the teachers are predominantly not knowledgeable Jews. Moreover, from the standpoint of Jewish law, Judaism has shunned proselytization for over two thousand years, and so to the extent that religious activities in public schools or public displays of religious symbols induce people to consider conversion, classical Jewish law would object to them.

Ways in Which Judaism Should Be Invoked in the Political Realm

On the other hand, the public square need not be "naked," to use the phrase coined by Richard John Neuhaus.[15] On the contrary, proponents of religions like Judaism *should* have a role in government in at least several ways.

First, even though this is not the topic of this chapter, it is worth repeating that American citizens of any religion have a right to argue for their stance on a given issue. The fact that for some Americans their stance is rooted in religious concerns does not preclude them from making their case in the public marketplace of ideas. On the contrary, even if the reality seriously fails to reach the ideal, as Stephen Carter has argued,[16] the effectiveness and wisdom of American policies depend critically on people of all religions and none taking an active role in public debate.[17]

Second, religious neutrality should not mean that religion is ignored in public forums. So, for example, the effort in which I was involved to describe religions and their history in the social studies textbooks used in public schools is not only appropriate, but necessary, for, after all, any history that pretends that religions have historically not influenced culture and politics would be grossly inaccurate. For that matter, discussions of current events should also take account of the role of religions in shaping public opinion and policy. *Describing* religions and their positions is one thing; *advocating* a particular religion and its views is another. Sometimes, of course, the line between description and advocacy can become all too thin, and one must always worry about how much teachers will impose their own views in class discussion. Still, whatever the difficulties in defining this line and making it real, the line is crucial if the United States is to maintain both freedom of religion and intellectual honesty.

Similarly, Jewish sources would support such a line. After all, God's seal is truth, according to the tradition,[18] and so Jews have a theological mandate to seek the truth as part of the way they know and imitate God. That includes an honest understanding and appraisal of the history, beliefs, and current actions of other religions. Moreover, on sheer practical grounds, Jews cannot afford to hide from or ignore the immense impact on public life in the past and present of other religions; to do so would make Jews live in a fantasy, ghettoized world, with immediate negative consequences for their welfare. At the same time, Jews must fight diligently to ensure that no religion is affirmed by public officials in the public arena, for if that is allowed to happen, Jews will inevitably be subjected to proselytization by religions like Christianity. This is especially a concern for students in elementary and high schools, where impressionable and gullible youngsters may be swayed by such missionizing without the intellectual tools to analyze it properly and combat it, but adults in public colleges should also be shielded from such conversionary efforts by public officials.

Third, public discussions and documents may and should recognize religious motivations for religious Americans in advocating or opposing a particular policy, even when other rationales lead nonreligious Americans or Americans of other religions to the same conclusion. So, for example, I was involved in crafting the preamble to the proposed legislation of the Clinton Health Care Task Force. We indicated that in an age of effective but expensive health care, the primary motive for the federal government to organize health insurance and be the insurer of the last resort was the Constitution's mandate for the government to "provide for the general welfare." Still, for religious Americans, another motivation applies—namely, our religious duty to be good stewards of our God-given bodies. When that draft was considered by the entire committee, some secularists on the committee objected vociferously that such language would violate the separation of church and state. I argued just as strongly that that was not true, that the primary motive for the legislation was religiously neutral and that it did not hurt to mention that religious Americans might also have religious motivations to support the legislation. As a result, the committee sent two forms of the preamble to the president, one with the additional religious motivation and one without it. Similarly, while the Surgeon General's Call to Action for Responsible Sexual Behavior was primarily based on the public health concerns to stop the spread of family violence and sexually transmitted diseases, I maintained that it would not hurt to mention in that document that widely varying religions demand responsible sexual behavior for religious reasons as well, even as they define "responsible sexual behavior" quite differently, ranging from abstinence only to birth control education. Acknowledging religious beliefs and the role they play in Americans' lives does not amount to establishing religion.

Finally, it is both permissible and desirable for religions to participate in defining values to be taught in schools. In part because homes and religious institutions have failed to inculcate basic moral values in many children, some school districts have adopted programs to fill the gap. That immediately raises the question about what values should be taught and whether the many components of America's crosscultural and interfaith society can agree on any list and on the programs to teach them. Truthfully, when I first read about this effort, I myself was skeptical that a culture-neutral curriculum of values education could be created. I must admit that I have been pleasantly surprised by the most important of such efforts. Specifically, the Character Counts!

Coalition, whose advisory council includes individuals from a variety
of religious backgrounds and whose member organizations include
sixty-one institutions, including such national educational groups as
the American Association of School Administrators, the American
Federation of Teachers, and the National Education Association, formulated the Aspen Declaration:

1. The next generation will be the stewards of our communities, nation, and planet in extraordinarily critical times.
2. The present and future well being of our society requires an involved, caring citizenry with good moral character.
3. People do not automatically develop good moral character; therefore, conscientious efforts must be made to help young people develop the values and abilities necessary for moral decision making
and conduct.
4. Effective character education is based on core ethical values which
form the foundation of democratic society—in particular, respect, responsibility, trustworthiness, caring, justice and fairness, and civic
virtue and citizenship.
5. These core ethical values transcend cultural, religious, and socioeconomic differences.
6. Character education is, first and foremost, an obligation of families; it is also an important obligation of faith communities, schools,
youth and other human service organizations.
7. These obligations to develop character are best achieved when
these groups work in concert.
8. The character and conduct of our youth reflect the character and
conduct of society; therefore, every adult has the responsibility to
teach and model the core ethical values, and every social institution
has the responsibility to promote the development of good character.

Along with this declaration, the Josephson Institute, which coordi-
nated the effort to formulate the Aspen Declaration and to have it approved by a wide variety of national bodies, has produced a series of
educational materials for children and adults to explain these values in
greater detail and to apply them to issues in daily living.[19] It is hard to
argue with the six values in plank 4 of the Resolution; they do indeed
seem to be impervious to cultural variance—although I suspect that the
interpretation of them as applied to specific situations will vary. Still,
this project has proven that religions may and should have a role in
creating such a curriculum for teaching moral values in public arenas
like schools. Certainly, Jewish sources would have us inculcate respect, responsibility, trustworthiness, caring, justice and fairness, and

civic virtue and citizenship, and Jewish sources may be proposed as part of that curriculum.

Bringing Religion and Nation Closer Together

Jefferson and Madison had good reason to fear the entanglement of religion in national matters. The European experience had demonstrated beyond all reasonable doubt that that is not good either for religion or for the state. At the same time, we do ourselves, religion, and the nation a disservice if we think that religion should have no role in shaping national policy. No religion should determine national policy as a matter of right, but each religion must enter the fray of public debate if that discussion is to reflect the nation as a whole and if it is to attain the richness that only multiple parties with differing views can give it. Americans should surely be ever on their guard to prevent undue entanglement of church and state, but a healthy relationship between the two, as defined by both American and Jewish sources, demands open religious contributions to discussions of matters of public policy.

Notes

In the following notes, M. = Mishnah (c. 200 C.E.); T. = Tosefta (c. 200 C.E.); J. = Jerusalem Talmud (c. 400 C.E.) ; B. = Babylonian Talmud (c. 500 C.E.); M.T. = Moses Maimonides' *Mishneh Torah* (1177); S.A. = Joseph Karo's *Shulhan Arukh* (1565).

1. M. Avot 1:10; 2:3.

2. This is not by any means the only way to conceive of medicine, and medical practices in other countries reflect very different conceptions of the body and of the role of medicine. See Lynn Payer, *Medicine and Culture* (New York: Henry Holt, 1988).

3. "Jewish Tradition and National Policy," in *Commandment and Community: New Essays in Jewish Legal and Political Philosophy*, Daniel H. Frank, ed. (Albany: State University of New York Press, 1995), 85-109; and "The King's Torah: The Role of Judaism in Shaping Jews' Input in National Policy," in *A Nation under God? Essays on the Fate of Religion in American Public Life*, R. Bruce Douglass and Joshua Mitchell, eds. (Lanham, Md.: Rowman & Littlefield, 2000), 203-22. These have been combined and reprinted in revised form in *To Do the Right and the Good: A Jewish Approach to Modern Social Ethics* (Philadelphia: Jewish Publication Society, 2002), ch. 4, 96-113.

4. Daniel Wikler, "Philosophical Perspectives on Access to Health Care: An Introduction," in his *Securing Access to Health Care* (Washington, D.C.: U.S. Government Printing Office, 1983), vol. 2, 48.

5. Van A. Harvey, *The Historian and the Believer* (New York: Macmillan, 1966), 205-30. See note 3 above.

6. Cited by E. Rabb, untitled essay, in *American Jews and the Separationist Faith*, David G. Dalin, ed. (Washington, D.C.: Ethics and Public Policy Center, 1993), 110-11.

7. Stephen L. Carter, *The Culture of Disbelief: How American Law and Politics Trivialize Religious Devotion* (New York: Basic Books, 1993). On p. 21, he says specifically, "I speak here not simply of arguments for or against the adoption of any *government* policy, although that will, of necessity, be part of my subject. My concern, more broadly, is with the question of what religiously devout people should do when they confront state policies that require them to act counter to what they believe is the will of God, or to acquiesce in conduct by others that they believe God forbids." This chapter, in contrast, concentrates on the former issue—that is, the shaping of government policy in the first place. In his subsequent book, *God's Name in Vain: The Wrongs and the Rights of Religion in Politics* (New York: Basic Books, 2001), Carter takes his basic point about the need for respect for religion on its own terms much further, taking umbrage at even thoughtful critiques of religion's intercessions in government, and he advocates that religion stay out of government—"a place of depravity"—altogether. As reviewer Brent Staples has said, Carter has become much too shrill in this latter book, ignoring Americans' rejection of those who would criticize other people's religion and relegating religion to a prophetic role outside of government with little ability to affect it. See Brent Staples, "If You're Devout, Get Out!" *New York Times Book Review*, November 26, 2000, 13-14.

8. Elliot N. Dorff, "Pluralism," in *Frontiers of Jewish Thought*, Steven T. Katz, ed. (Washington, D.C.: B'nai B'rith Books, 1992), 213-34; reprinted in a somewhat different form in "Pluralism: Models for the Conservative Movement," *Conservative Judaism* 48, 1 (Fall 1995): 21-35.

9. The doctrine of the seven Noahide laws appears in T. *Avodah Zarah* 8:4 and B. *Sanhedrin* 56a-b; it is thoroughly discussed in David Novak, *The Image of the Non-Jew in Judaism: A Historical and Constructive Study of the Noahide Laws* (New York: Edwin Mellen Press, 1983). The doctrine that righteous non-Jews inherit a place in the world to come appears in the *Sifra* on Leviticus 19:18.

10. The Egyptians: Deuteronomy 23:8. Non-Jewish poor: B. Gittin 61a; M.T. *Laws of Gifts to the Poor* 7:7. According to B. Gittin 59b, obligations that, like these, are for the sake of peace have Pentateuchal authority. Franz Rosenzweig, *The Star of Redemption*, William W. Hallo, trans. (New York: Holt, Reinhart & Winston, 1971): on Christianity, Part III, Books I and II; on Islam: 166, 172-73; 181, 215-17; cf. also 116-18, 122-24, 225-27. Martin Buber, *Israel and the World* (New York: Schocken, 1948), 28-40. For an analysis of both of their approaches, see my article, "The Covenant: How

Jews Understand Themselves and Others," *Anglican Theological Review* 64, 4 (October 1982): 481-501. Amos 9:7.

11. I first developed these themes with regard to Jewish relations to non-Jews in my article "The Covenant: How Jews Understand Themselves and Others," *Anglican Theological Review* 64, 4 (1982): 481-501. There I used Rosenzweig and Buber as examples of modern Jewish nationalism (Rosenzweig) versus modern Jewish universalism (Buber). Another consideration of these themes based on different Jewish theologians (Mordecai M. Kaplan for philosophical objectivism and Hermann Cohen for existentialism) appeared in my article "The Covenant as the Key: A Jewish Theology of Jewish-Christian Relations," in *Toward a Theological Encounter: Jewish Understandings of Christianity*, Leon Klenicki, ed. (New York: Paulist Press, 1991), 43-66. I expanded this discussion to formulate a Jewish approach to Asian religions in my article "A Jewish Theology of Jewish Relations to Other People," in *People of God, Peoples of God: A Jewish-Christian Conversation in Asia*, Hans Ucko, ed. (Geneva: World Council of Churches, 1996), 46-66, reprinted in Elliot N. Dorff and Louis E. Newman, *Contemporary Jewish Thought* (New York: Oxford University Press, 1999), 263-77, and in *To Do the Right and the Good* (see n. 3 above), ch. 3, 61-95.

12. A nice collection of relevant Supreme Court cases on these issues is Robert T. Miller and Ronald B. Flowers, *Toward Benevolent Neutrality: Church, State, and the Supreme Court*, 5th ed. (Waco, Texas: Markham Press Fund of Baylor University Press, 1996).

13. An appellate court just recently affirmed the constitutionality of a California law requiring employers that afford drug coverage to their employees to offer contraceptives to workers in secular jobs, such as hospitals and universities, even when the employer is the Roman Catholic Church that sees artificial means of birth control as "intrinsically evil and a great sin." The lawyer for the Church said that "this substantially burdens the religious freedom rights of the Catholic Church in California," but the court ruled that "Requiring the policies to cover prescription contraceptive methods—so as not to discriminate against women—cannot be said to inhibit religion, even if its parent entity is a religious organization that believes the use of contraceptives is a sin." According to the decision, prescription contraceptives are not included in 49 percent of health plans nationwide, and as a result women pay up to 68 percent higher out-of-pocket health care costs than men. See Jean Cuccione, "Catholics Lose Case on Contraception," *Los Angeles Times*, July 3, 2001, B-1, B-10.

14. Carter, *The Culture of Disbelief*, 230-32.

15. Richard John Neuhaus, *The Naked Public Square: Religion and Democracy in America* (Grand Rapids, Mich.: William B. Eerdmans, 1984).

16. See generally his book, *The Culture of Disbelief*.

17. See n. 3 above for the articles in which I have argued for this thesis.

18. B. Shabbat 55a; B. Yoma 69b; B. Sanhedrin 64a; Genesis Rabbah 81:2; Deuteronomy Rabbah 1:10; Song of Songs Rabbah 1:46.

19. The Aspen Declaration was formulated in the Summer 1992 Aspen Summit Conference on Character Education. The Josephson character education program has spread to more than 2,500 schools nationwide since it was launched in 1993, and if Congress approves President Bush's education budget, $25 million of federal money will be devoted to character education—three times the current amount. (See Mary Lord, "Morality Goes to School," *U.S. News and World Report*, June 4, 2001, 50-51.) The Josephson Institute has also conducted ethics seminars for government groups and the staffs of a number of corporations as well as training the personnel of these schools to educate their students in the six values delineated in the Aspen Declaration. Books on character education include Thomas Likona, *Educating for Character*, and Michael Josephson, *Teaching Ethics in the 90s*. I would like to thank Dr. Michael Zeldin, professor of education at Hebrew Union College in Los Angeles, for introducing me to these materials.

13

9/11 and the Aftershocks: Rethinking American Secularism and Religious Pluralism

Carl A. Raschke

The calamitous attacks of September 11, 2001, did far more than shatter America's sense of national invulnerability and supply the occasion for a ringing declaration of a global war on terrorism. They also threw into question many of the irenic assumptions about religion in America that have pervaded academic discourse for at least two generations now.

Since the early 1960s, at least, the reigning supposition has been that religious belief and conduct must be comprehended in the context of a sprawling secularism and an ever more intricate texture of cultural and religious pluralism. Religion has also been increasingly regarded as a personal affair—a "habit of the heart" in Robert Bellah's memorable phrase—that configures individual identity and moral behavior, yet remains outside the prefecture of public discourse. The sphere of public conversation is, and should be, overshadowed by the "political." It concerns not only the electoral, but the ethico-cultural dimensions of personal desire and choice. Unlike traditional or "totalitarian" societies, American liberal democracy is founded on a rational economy of singular interests, reckonings, and strategies. The religious is of necessity subordinated to the volitional. Indeed, it is inscribed within the very same anthropic calculus that the classical political economists from John Locke to J. S. Mill viewed as essentially naturalistic and worldly. The ideal of religious pluralism, along with the companion values of tolerance and mutual respect, belong within this idiom. It has its origins during the late seventeenth century with the final breakdown of medieval authority and the growing power of dissenter conventicles, who asserted their own "inalienable" rights to freedom of doctrine and worship.

The American experiment, intended initially as an outlet for religious dissent in the same way that the American frontier later became, in Jackson Turner's expression, a "safety valve" for economic unrest, gradually evolved into the multicultural conglomerate with which we are familiar today. Under the multireligious big top the passions of particularity are ultimately subordinated to a republican faith. Jean-Jacques Rousseau first described this phenomenon in the eighteenth century as a "civil religion," which sociologist Robert Bellah in his landmark essay of the late 1960s appropriated and made current. "What we have . . . from the earliest years of the republic," Bellah wrote, "is a collection of beliefs, symbols, and rituals with respect to sacred things and institutionalized in a collectivity. This religion—there seems to be no other word for it—while not antithetical to and indeed sharing much in common with Christianity, was neither sectarian nor in any specific sense Christian."[1]

The dissenter paradigm per se gained new momentum during and following the Vietnam era when radical political activism took a spiritual turn. The prominent critic Paul Goodman had already named the cultural upheavals of the 1960s as a "new Reformation,"[2] and the efflorescence of exotic spiritual groups and devotions that author Charles Reich termed "the greening of America" began to resemble in the theoretical imagination the English Revolution of the 1640s. The analogy even seemed to stick with the practitioners, as one hippie commune from the Haight-Ashbury in San Francisco called itself the Diggers after the dissenters who in 1649 sought to abolish private property and cultivate common lands. The process is described vividly by Wade Clark Roof. Those who grew up "in the late 1950s and early 1960s were a generation well on their way to a normal respect for the political process. . . . But within a span of ten years—from 1963 to 1973—they abandoned their once hopeful outlook for a new course of political independence and institutional separation . . . greater separation from institutions and a corresponding increase in emphasis on individual choice."[3] Twenty years later the dissenter paradigm had morphed into what came to be known as the New Age Movement with its wild eclecticism, embracing everything from Tibetan Buddhism to Celtic witchcraft, and assertions of unqualified spiritual autonomy, epitomized in such popular slogans as "I am God, you are God." By the 1990s, the notion has largely gone mainstream, enshrined in the concept that it is "politically incorrect" to make value distinctions among the myriad facets of the new cultural and religious pluralism.

The underlying premise of this new "postmodernist" republicanism was that religious diversity could no longer be conceptualized, as it was during the Enlightenment, as a collage of disparate communitarian beliefs and practices, but must now be understood as a broth of countless spiritual preferences, longings, and modes of entrepreneurship. The libertarian ethos of unbounded autonomy in the political sphere had now passed over into the religious arena, and the "civil" character of religion had for the most part dissolved. In its stead emerged what might be best described as a vast, devotional cosmopolitanism constrained in no way by the symbologies and conventions of Western social democracy. The emergence of this new cosmopolitanism, which had its roots in nineteenth and twentieth-century religious esotericism, particularly theosophy, was a crucial ideological mechanism for spreading the dogma of "multiculturalism." It was a huge departure from eighteenth-century notions of religious liberty, as well as earlier Lockean conceptions of disestablishment and tolerance. But there remained a definite continuity of development over the last three centuries.[4]

The postmodernist version of religious republicanism, however, could not be articulated along a broad political arc without the neutralization of all critical methods of religious valuation and assessment. One of the oldest, and most obvious, of such a critical method is the "theological" enterprise, which we construe in the most general sense of the word and as a modality of reflection that can be found in all religious traditions. Theology lends the force of faith and conviction to religious ideology. The marginalization of theological reflection within the American academy during the past generation, and its replacement by the generalized and nonsectarian concept of the "study of religion," was quite conducive to the sentiment that spiritual matters are neither accountable nor negotiable, that they neither weigh in heavily for good or for ill, and that in some curious fashion they are all commensurate with each other. Such a romanticized cosmopolitanism went a long way toward undermining the tacit historical understanding of a distinctive American religiosity, or religious Americanism. New Age privatism, which aptly describes the phenomenon we are considering, became the general theme for an age that actively sought to be "nonjudgmental." In the long run this trend amounted to a denial of the significance of religious faith as a whole.

The breach was, of course, filled not only by familiar secularist theories of democratic political economy, but also by new communitarian formulations of ethnic, gender, or class identity that came to be termed "cultural Marxism." This strange mélange of spiritual libertarianism and socialist polemic served to discredit older doctrines of civil religiosity, although the process of delegitimation can be said to have begun during the late 1960s and reached a crisis magnitude by the mid-1970s when Robert Bellah began to speak of a "broken covenant" between America and the God of the founders.[5] As the century waned, it even became fashionable to restyle what had once been dubbed civil religion as religious privatism itself. Harold Bloom's much-discussed book on "gnosticism" as "the American religion" actually took this kind of tack.[6]

The tragedy of September 2001, on the other hand, cast a sudden and lowering shadow over what seemed to have become the received academic wisdom. The New Age idyll of a benign eclecticism was dramatically confounded by a snarling and media-savvy style of Islamic fundamentalism that vowed destruction of all Jews and American "crusaders." Meanwhile, the devastation of "9/11" roused a kind of primal fury in America that had unmistakable religious dimensions and had not been witnessed since the early days of the Cold War, if not the Second World War. The flurry of flag displays and collective recitation of "God Bless America" evoked what nineteenth-century sociologist Emile Durkheim viewed as the experience of collective solidarity expressed in totemic religiosity and reincarnated in the modern allegiance to the nation-state.[7] Such a patriotic and sacrificial piety was, according to the received wisdom, a thing of the past. But it had been ignited in response to the rhetoric of a fierce, anti-Western, and tribalistic form of "Islamism" that seemed more akin to the barbarous Bedouin blood lust that predated the teachings of Mohammed than the medieval orthodoxy, to which it was frequently compared. Indeed, the antipluralistic and increasingly totalitarian fervor of "revolutionary" Islam represents a distinct style of political countermodernism. It is this countermodernism, which may or may not be indigenous to Islam, which suddenly and brutally confronted the traditions of Western liberal democracy.[8]

If New Age pluralism and privatism had its roots in the English Revolution of the seventeenth century, countermodernism arose out of the chaos of the Napoleonic wars and their aftermath across Europe. Countermodernism, which in its initial stages parlayed into Romanticism as a philosophical trend and nationalism as a political force, became the silage for mass movements and social violence that manifested itself in Communism, populism, syndicalism, fascism, and Nazism. Countermodernism, as these instances suggest, was always driven not simply as a protest against "bourgeois liberalism," but as a deep, collective, virtually religious rage against the anomie of commercial civilization and the confusion of authority and legitimacy that attended the collapse of feudal society. This religious furor, however, sought not the kind of pietistic separatism that had been common in the early modern era, but an all-encompassing political solution that would erase the ambiguities of status, belief, and personal identity that permeated democratic civilization.

Countermodernism has routinely engendered totalitarian regimes and mystical cults of personality because it always ended up as what Peter Vierick in his famous study of fascism called "metapolitics"—a cosmopolitanism that was far more cosmos than polis, a social metaphysics that demanded absolute unity in the face of proliferating difference.[9] New Age pluralism, even though it frequently profiled itself as an antimodernistic stance, was always a hypertrophied form of the Enlightenment ideal. New Age pluralism had always presupposed the sovereignty of the individual and, to a large extent, the rationality of self-interest, even though the rhetoric of classical utilitarianism was not expressed in terms of spiritual attitudes and preferences.

As the latest variant of countermodernism, Islamism is nevertheless significantly different to the degree that it calls into profound question the universalistic presumption of Western, democratic, and pluralistic values. What Samuel Huntington has called "the clash of civilizations" is the operative concept here. According to Huntington, writing in 1996, "the dangerous clashes of the future are likely to arise from the interaction of Western arrogance, Islamic intolerance, and Sinic assertiveness. . . . As the relative power of other civilizations increases, the appeal of Western culture fades and non-Western peoples have increasing confidence in and commitment to their indigenous cultures."[10] Huntington goes on to argue that the conflict is not ultimately between democracy and totalitarianism, as has been the Manichean dividing line for liberalism over the past two centuries, but between "the West and the rest." The struggle is between irreconcilable religious visions, which define one civilization in relationship to another. "The West, and especially the United States, which has always been a missionary nation, believes that the non-Western peoples should commit themselves to the Western values of democracy, free markets, limited government, human rights, individualism, the rule of law, and should embody these values in their institutions. Minorities in other civilizations embrace and promote these values, but the dominant attitudes toward them in non-Western cultures range from widespread skepticism to intense opposition. What is universalism to the West is imperialism to the rest."[11] Huntington goes on to quote a "prominent Indian Muslim" that "the West's 'next confrontation is definitely going to come from the Muslim world. It is in the sweep of the Islamic nations from Maghreb to Pakistan the struggle for a new world order will begin.'"[12]

Huntington's views, in retrospect, must now be taken as prophetic. They clash sharply, for example, with the vision of the "new secularists," such as Richard Fenn, who argue that the ideal of civil religion must be expanded to a global magnitude. The new secularists, in comparison with New Age pluralists, see the diffusion and privatization of spiritual commitments as the end of a historical process in which the social order per se is desanctified. This desanctification is the inevitable outcome of the increasing differentiation of religious meanings and options. The emergent global civilization makes this process seemingly irreversible. Globalization redirects the scepter of legitimacy away from traditions and institutions that allege some kind of all-enveloping, or transcendent, sovereignty while religiously enfranchising the personal seeker. Secularization and modernization go hand in hand, because they are tantamount to the transformation of the sacral into the political. The political, in turn, adds up to the grand sum of personal idiosyncrasies, the dissenter paradigm in secularized attire. Dissent becomes the foundation of political right itself. Religious freedom, so to speak, becomes the essence of religion, and this unique religion of modernity leads to the undoing of religion itself.[13] The emancipation of religion from the political serves also to free the political from religion. Such a departure unleashes a sequence of historical moments whereby religion effaces itself, and the secular state emerges. "It is the claim by the political community to have its own sources of legitimacy apart from those owned and controlled by the established religions of Judaism and Christianity that presents the greatest threat."[14]

The events of 9/11 throw into doubt, however, these very assumptions of "secularization." If the catastrophe of World War I sent crashing to earth once and for all the eighteenth and nineteenth-century idea of progress, the cultural shocks of 2001—and their aftermath—will most likely leave in disarray the utopian expectation of planetary democracy and pluralism. The historical sources of this disenchantment are eerily similar. In many ways the social and intellectual convulsions now under way in the West are symptomatic of the trauma of 1914 when confidence in European civilization was shattered by recognition of the primitive savagery that underlay European nationalism and colonialism.

Today the scenario is different, but only slightly. The end of the Cold War in 1989 in many ways only capped the conflicts that began at Sarajevo. The defeat of Communism seemed to give currency once again to the late Victorian optimism about the universality and eventual triumph of democratic capitalism, which in turn was predicated on the premise of an eventual harmony of cultural interests in the global marketplace. The coup de main came this time, however, from those "extra-territorial" forces which the West under the economic and military leadership of the United States had sought to press into this paradigm and in a certain sense had tried to conquer through recolonization. The Enlightenment project of tolerance, which had its antecedents in Roman imperial paganism and later in the Renaissance of Moorish Spain, always presupposed the pacification, and ultimately the neutralization, of religious drives by mercantile or statist aims. Ironically, the same countermodernist passions that have engulfed Islam in the late twentieth and early twenty-first centuries and precipitated an epochal clash with the West are for the most part identical with the same "fundamentalist" tendencies that took hold on the Iberian peninsula in the late Middle Ages, stirred up Catholic fanaticism, and led to the Reconquista in 1492, from which the age of European expansion and the opening of America ensued.

The argument here, of course, is not against democratic pluralism per se. Nor does it entail assent to the countermodernist argument itself, which creeps into a spectrum of contemporary political rants from "antiglobalism" to "deep ecology." Our concern is the weakness of the secularist paradigm. We can of necessity contrast the American secularist paradigm with, say, the French one, which has its roots in the Revolution of 1789. French secularism has always been built on anticlericism, which seeks the elimination of conventional religious practice and belief. American secularism, in contrast, has evolved in the measure that its aspiration to democratic inclusivity, initially regarded simply as a franchise for White Anglo-Saxon Protestants, has progressed from its earlier Eurocentric frame of reference to the "multiculturalist" and "globalist" standpoint. The logic of American secularism has continually proceeded from two largely unproven theses: 1. that religious diversity is an innate social good, but must be tempered by certain "checks and balances" of constraining institutions, including political ceremonies that are self-consciously nonsectarian and public schools designed to foster and inculcate the values of a common culture; 2. that the centrifugal tensions of a multi-faith and polycultural environment can be offset by the encouragement of a singular allegiance to certain material and diffusely moral ends.

The piety of Americanism, or "the American way of life," for almost two centuries encompassed this half secular, half religious sentimentality.[15] And the September "attack on America" has almost reflexively kindled an old-time religious ferocity that lay coiled in this sentimentality. The belief in democratic pluralism and religious separationism would have remained implausible throughout the nation's history without an accompanying commitment to the unifying mandate of economic progress and social amelioration.

But this twofold mandate is now under assault at both the international and domestic levels. The rage of Al-Qaida is not only against representative democracy and religious pluralism as understood by the West, but against the tacit secular materialism that has been the viscera of the American dream ever since Coronado wandered the desert southwest in search of the seven cities of gold and the Dutch landed on Manhattan with the objective of outflanking the other seafaring nations in the rush for riches. Significantly, the same violence has been manifest in the more radical wings of the American left since the 1960s, and not too long before the downing of the twin towers manifested itself in the street riots by black-masked protesters at Seattle and Milan.

Both Al-Qaida and the antiglobalism movement are the outworking of countermodernist tendencies that have deeply entrenched themselves in world civilization and have prompted a backlash against Westernization and secularization. These tendencies have reared their hydra heads over the centuries. Romanticism in Europe with its disdain for analytical reason, its celebration of heroism and the spiritual sublime, and its attraction to ultraconservative and revolutionary politics was the first major worldwide wave of countermodernism. Romantic ideology also whetted some of the darkest impulses of early American nationalism, including Manifest Destiny and the nativism that persecuted Catholic immigrants in the 1840s and 1850s. Within the next hundred years it had ignited pan-Germanism and what the Jewish poet Heine called the furor Teutonicus that exploded as National Socialism in the 1920s and 1930s. Countermodernism in its most profound aspects was an affirmation of religious zeal and ecstasy, contrasting with the relative inconsequence of civil religion, where political stability takes precedence over private feeling and motivation.

More recently, countermodernism can be discerned in the New Age subculture that developed in the late 1970s and 1980s, which in turn crystallized from the social and intellectual extremism of the prior decade. The antiglobalist alliance of radical activist groups that have staged the demonstrations against world trade and development in the past few years constitutes a muddle of causes that in a previous generation were known simply as "countercultural." Counterculturalism, as the homegrown variety of countermodernism, has basically the same historical endgame as the militant Islamism that is nowadays, albeit wrongly, termed "Islamic fundamentalism." Both counterculturalism and Islamism are vehemently antimodernist and anticapitalist. Both counterculturalism and Islamism revere some sort of return to the primal and mythic wellspring of culture. Islamism characterizes this return through an invocation of the medieval rule of the caliphate, which was both temporal and spiritual. Counterculturalism distinguishes itself by a proliferation of pseudo-collective, or "multiculturalist," identities which express a pre-Christian, and to a certain extent pre-Western, mosaic of "pagan" polities. Both counterculturalism and Islamism reject the values of material advancement, not to mention the Enlightenment concept of the "citizen" who tempers his or her feelings and religious convictions for the sake of a secular system of obligations and loyalties.

The paradox of this postsecular age into which we are rapidly heading is that the very pluralistic tenets which modern secular democracy invented in order to forestall "wars of religion" have generated a new, and more deadly, kind of culture war. In this new global culture war, which the rhetoric of the current "war on terrorism" is apt to conceal, religion is not pitted against religion so much as religion against civil society. The Western constructs of civil society remained viable so long as two conditions persisted: 1. the processes of cultural differentiation were coextensive with the patterns and proclivities of European history, or the two-thousand-year struggle between Roman centralization and "barbarian" autonomy; 2. religion itself was not allowed to achieve the kind of totalizing dynamic that much anthropological research has routinely attributed to the phenomenon. If religion is, as the German theologian Paul Tillich opined, the sphere of "ultimate concern," then the intensity of that concern must lead to spectacular rows between religious cultures. That eventuality is what is truly implied in Huntington's dicta. And it is a truth that an increasingly secularized and policy-obsessed America has suppressed with what is now disclosed as a dangerous insouciance.

The attraction of Al-Qaida's rendering of jihad among the dispossessed Moslem masses does not testify to some curious aberration within the cosmopolitan consensus about the meaning and end of religion. It bespeaks a grim reckoning with the fiery ordeal of religiosity as it has suffused human institutions since the cockcrow of awareness. It also vouchsafes how the secularist paradigm is itself an historically contingent, and unsteady, innovation. The thrust of religion throughout human history has always been double bladed. Religion has simultaneously inspired the worst aggression and the most dogged resistance, the highest instincts to civilization and letters and the most debased forms of obscurantism, the most noble gestures of self-sacrifice and martyrdom along with the most cringing examples of petty-mindedness and conventionality.

The greatest mistake nevertheless has been to seek to domesticate religion, at least to the extent that it has lost its aura ultimacy and has become one more "functional" component in the computations of the social scientist. So far as the politics of secularization has either trivialized, or factored out the religious factor in the cultural equation, it has also fomented a separate milieu for the growth of apocalyptic cults and fanatical enthusiasms. On the international scene the economic and military might of the West has not spawned an admiration for democracy and pluralism, but a deep-reaching contempt. This state of affairs is painfully obvious now, but it continues to be misconstrued to the degree that anti-American critics tend to focus on our alleged imperial transgressions without acknowledging that the very Moslem concept of the *dar-al-islam*, or "realm of submission" to the will of Allah, demands conflict with the infidel, the *dar-al-harb*. Even the much-touted medieval Muslim touchstone of tolerance for other religions is constrained by the

Koranic injunction that personal conversion is in no way merely an option.

One of the lasting ironies of the terrorist attacks is the reinvigoration of a sense of "Judeo-Christianity" as the core of American civil religion, even though such a hyphenated sense of the Western heritage has been dismissed, especially by many contemporary Jews in recent years. Before 9/11 Judaism in America was seen as much more problematic from both a Jewish and non-Jewish vantage point. But the radical Islamic assault, justified largely in the terrorists' mind by America's ongoing support for the Jewish state, has overnight nurtured an unprecedented feeling of solidarity, if mainly within the general population itself, between the United States and Israeli causes. Bin Laden's chilling declaration that his declared "holy war" is against Jews and "Crusaders"—read Americans—was probably more effective in forging this mood of solidarity than the deaths of victims at the World Trade Center, because it targeted Americans as equivalent to their designated victims. This development in many ways is unprecedented. The notion of Judaism as part of the consensus of civil religion in American is something relatively new, and it contrasts with an earlier history and deep-seated Christian anti-Semitism. At the same time, ever since the founding of the Jewish state and its ongoing wars with Arab neighbors, this strain of anti-Semitism has eroded, and in the past generation Christian evangelicals have made a special case of pro-Israel policies, much of which is based on a distinct reading of eschatological sources in the New Testament. The prestige and moral character of presidential candidate Joe Lieberman has also had an impact.

But the forging of a new "Judeo-Christian" cultural idealism in opposition to the terrorist worldview is more deeply rooted than many might believe, or would care to admit. Although Judaism during the early years of the republic was for the most part an alien faith, it retained a certain measure of sympathy among the nonsectarian political leadership, many of whom were influenced by Masonic teachings which did not draw the line between "old covenant" and "new covenant" in the way that the reigning Calvinist theology of the age did. It may be argued also that the very principle of "freedom of religion," as opposed to disestablishment, which had a distinctly Christian meaning, could be seen as a covert way of accommodating Judaism. There is no sole common thread of thought among the Founding Fathers concerning the nature and scope of religious freedom and diversity. Such thinking compassed certain Protestant sectarians who still yearned for a national church, as in

England, to those who wanted to support Christianity in general as a
national religion. James Madison, however, along with Jefferson,
had the final say. Madison viewed "freedom of religion" almost in
contemporary fashion and was not simply a "moderate pluralist,"
recognizing only an opportunity for unlimited dissent among established Christian denominations.

> Because we hold it for a fundamental and undeniable truth, "that
> Religion or the duty which we owe to our Creator and the manner of
> discharging it, can be directed only by reason and conviction, not by
> force or violence." The Religion then of every man must be left to
> the conviction and conscience of every man; and it is the right of
> every man to exercise it as these may dictate. This right is in its na-
> ture an unalienable right. It is unalienable, because the opinions of
> men, depending only on the evidence contemplate by their own
> minds cannot follow the dictates of other men: It is unalienable
> also, because what is here a right towards men, is a duty towards the
> Creator. . . . This duty is precedent, both in order of time and in de-
> gree of obligation, to the claims of Civil Society.[16]

The movement toward disestablishment, urged upon the country
even before the outbreak of the War of Independence, effectively
treated Judaism as just another persecuted sect and hence as a curious kind of "denomination." The Jews' long experience as what
might be described as proto-dissenters in Western Christendom,
with no lingering pretensions of victory in its political struggle or
the establishment of any kind of hegemony, also made them immediately receptive to finding a place in civil society. This accommodation happened long before it was the general case in Europe. Jews
quickly acceded to disestablishmentarian doctrine. They already understood the ground rules for theological heterogeneity in accordance with which the new civil religion was chartered, mainly because they already possessed a "voluntary religious association,
readily affirmed religious voluntarism, religious liberty, and religious pluralism."[17] When Will Herberg in the 1950s fatefully defined the nascent parameters of the new civil religion as one of
Protestant, Catholic, and Jew, it was not as much of an innovation
as contemporary generations of scholars are wont to presume.[18]

If Judaism in the earlier phase of the Republic served as a leaven
for the development of the true pluralism envisioned by Madison, it
may ironically in these days following 9/11 also work as an impetus
to recast the American civil religion as a unique "Western" faith, as
opposed to the sort of globalist microcosm it was enroute to becom-

ing. The "postcolonial" cosmopolitanism that flourished at the end of the Cold War and called itself simply "multiculturalism" was predicated on the historically naïve, and empirically unsustainable, premise that all faiths, no matter how differentiated and exotic, are somehow equivalent and capable of reciprocal respect and tolerance. As we have seen, the assumption of a peaceful planetary polyreligiosity may be far more historically contingent, episodic, and chimerical than we are willing to admit. It is a strange sort of mirage, perhaps even odder than the Wilsonian attempt in the 1920s to make the world "safe for democracy." Though the assumption devolved from the bedrock Anglo-American idea of a vital dissenter culture, it has become something misshapen, neither resonating with authentic traditions of democracy nor with the real global polity now emerging. We are paying a stiff price for having put on this peculiar Halloween mask of social thought. Huntington observes acidly that "some Americans have promoted multiculturalism at home; some have promoted universalism abroad; and some have done both. Multiculturalism at home threatens the United States and the West; universalism abroad threatens the West and the world."[19]

The seemingly intractable political and religious situation in the Middle East is a compelling case in point. Since the creation of the State of Israel, the region has been buffeted by incommensurable eschatologies spun from different, and very ancient, readings of the Abrahamic promise. These eschatologies can never be reconciled by some sort of benign New Age concordat. Now that Al-Qaida has asserted its own fearful eschatology under the guise of a violent and totalitarian rendition of the *dar-al-islam*, the American ideal of civil religion is suddenly, and fatefully, tied to a defense of the Isaacian type of "sacred history." Radical Islam comprehends the West in this manner, even if the West still refuses to understand itself accordingly.[20] In the age of global terror important and courageous distinctions must be made. Pluralism can no longer be defended simply as a congeries of infinitely distinguished "religious" beliefs and behaviors that somehow melt into the abstract concept of a secular culture. As James Davison Hunter has noted in his analysis of the "culture wars" of the last two decades, our public culture has been a tousle between "biblical theism," which served for most of our history as "a cultural cement in American public life," and an amalgam of libertarianism and secularism that denies any mode of transcendent authority for moral and political affairs.[21] Until the fall of 2001 it appeared for the most part that the latter had triumphed. But now American society, facing perhaps the gravest threat to its existence in two centuries, may be heading rapidly in the opposite direction. We do not know where the momentum may be carrying us. But the one surety we have gained is that nothing is sure any more.

Notes

1. Robert N. Bellah, *Beyond Belief: Essays on Religion in a Post-Traditional World* (New York: Harper & Row, 1970), 175.

2. See Paul Goodman, *The New Reformation: Notes of a Neolithic Conservative* (New York: Random House, 1970).

3. Wade Clark Roof, *A Generation of Seekers: The Spiritual Journeys of the Baby Boom Generation* (San Francisco: HarperSanFrancisco, 1993), 57. Ronald Thiemann calls the late 1960s a period of the "third diseestablishment." "The divisions that emerged during the 1960s and early 1970s shattered any illusion of political and religious unity within the American populace. . . . Political opponents no longer assumed that they shared a common set of values or principles by which to adjudicate their differences." Ronald F. Thiemann, *Religion in Public Life: A Dilemma for Democracy* (Washington, D.C.: Georgetown University Press, 1996), 36.

4. The continuity is explored by Charles H. Lippy in *Pluralism Comes of Age: American Religious Culture in the Twentieth Century* (Armonk, N.Y.: M. E. Sharpe, 2000). Lippy writes: "Looking back, it becomes increasingly clear that the pluralism that came of age in the twentieth century was a natural development emerging from forces that had long shaped American religious life. The Europeans who embarked on colonial settlement brought diverse understandings of Protestant Christianity with them, laying the groundwork for the development of the denomination as a form of religious organization and the multiplicity of denominations that long constituted most approaches to pluralism. . . . The history of openness to immigration from diverse sources, prevalent throughout most of American history . . . paved the way for other forms of pluralism to come to life. . . . As American society became increasingly industrialized and ever more complex during the century, yet other features of an expanding pluralism came to light, particularly in the area of personal spirituality." Lippy goes on to celebrate American pluralism as a model for globalism. "On balance, it may well be that the greatest contribution made by the United States to global religious life is its demonstrating that, however vast the pluralism, a vital religious culture can flourish" (p. 162). For a discussion of how New Age pluralism has evolved, see John H. Berthrong, *The Divine Deli: Religious Identity in the North American Cultural Mosaic* (Maryknoll, N.Y.: Orbis Books, 1999). For a historical look at the process, see Ferenc Morton Szasz, *Religion in the Modern American West* (Tucson: University of Arizona Press, 2000); also Sandra Sizer Frankiel, *California's Spiritual*

Frontiers: Religious Alternatives in Anglo-Protestantism (Berkeley: University of California Press, 1988).

5. Interestingly, Bellah himself contributed to the delegitimation of the very notion of "civil religion" which he earlier helped clarify and articulate. In his book written in the mid-1970s, Bellah echoed in a less polemic way the attack of the cultural Marxists, who faulted the lack of inclusion of racial and ethnic minorities in the regnant civil faith. "The struggle of oppressed racial groups to improve their position in America is a major aspect of our third time of trial. That struggle has called into question all the existing beliefs about America as a successful multicultural nation. We will have to consider both the idea and the reality of cultural pluralism to see whether it has any substance or is merely screen for the dominance of the Anglo-Saxon minority." Robert Bellah, *The Broken Covenant: American Civil Religion in a Time of Trial* (New York: Seabury Press, 1975), 88.

6. See Harold Bloom, *The American Religion: The Emergence of the Post-Christian Nation* (New York: Simon & Schuster, 1992).

7. See Durkheim's discussion of the flag as a totemic object that marshals spiritual forces that "determine man's conduct with the same necessity as physical forces." See Emile Durkheim, *The Elementary Forms of Religious Life*, trans. Karen E. Fields (New York: Free Press, 1995), 228-29.

8. The question of whether the violence of *jihad* is essentially Koranic continues to be debated by scholars. Abdulaziz Sachedina writes that the political notion of *jihad* is a result of Islamic expansion in the eighth century when "Muslims began to expand the mission of Islam to create a worldwide society under their political domination." See A. Sachedina, *The Islamic Roots of Democratic Pluralism* (New York: Oxford University Press, 2001). Islam, according to Sachedina, "was conceived as a political ideology that would first rule over and then supersede other communities" (p. 138). Sachedina talks about a "tradition of Koranic pluralism" which he contrasts with later "exclusionary" notions. "The foundation of a civil society in Islam is based on the equality in creation in which the privilege of citizenry attaches equally to Muslim and non-Muslim, entailing inclusive political, civil, and social membership in the community" (p. 137). Mark Juergensmeyer, in his groundbreaking study of Osama bin Laden and Muslim terrorism, points out that while the Koran itself is "ambiguous about violence," the contemporary writer Abd al-Salam Faraj invigorated the ideal of *jihad* as Islam's "neglected duty" in a booklet published in the early 1980s. "What is significant about this document is that it grounded in the activities of modern Islamic terrorists firmly in Islamic tradition, specifically the sacred text of the Qur'an and the biographical accounts of the prophet in the Hadith." Mark Juergensmeyer, *Terror in the Mind of God: The Global Rise of Religious Violence* (Berkeley: University of California Press, 2000), 81.

9. Vierick defines "metapolitics" as a "semi-political ideology" that blends romantic struggle, ethnocentricity, a "vague economic socialism" that assails "capitalist materialism," and a supernaturalism. See Peter Vierick, *Metapolitics: The Roots of the Nazi Mind* (New York: Capricorn Books, 1965). With a few qualifications, Vierick's analysis applies aptly to Islamic radicalism, and may be considered as an ascendant form of this most dangerous phenomenon, in short, as a lethal kind of non-Western fascism.

10. Samuel P. Huntington, *The Clash of Civilization and the Remaking of World Order* (New York: Simon & Schuster, 1996), 183.

11. Huntington, *Clash,* 183-84.

12. Huntington, *Clash,* 213.

13. The dilemma was summed up by Reinhold Niebuhr in 1943: "In so far as modern tolerance has been achieved by disavowing religion it may rest merely on indifference toward the ultimate problems of life and history, with which religion is concerned. Since religious questions have been a particularly fecund source of fanaticism and conflict, the gain in provisional toleration has therefore been great. But the weakness in the modern position is also quite apparent. Either it achieves toleration by taking an irresponsible attitude toward ultimate issues; or it insinuates new and false ultimates into views of life which are ostensibly merely provisional and pragmatic." Reinhold Niebuhr, *The Nature and Destiny of Man* (New York: Charles Scribner's Sons, 1963), vol. 2, 227. Niebuhr's approach is discussed in Robert McKim, *Religious Ambiguity and Religious Diversity* (New York: Oxford University Press, 2001), 142-43.

14. Richard K. Fenn, *Beyond Idols: The Shape of a Secular Society* (Oxford: Oxford University Press, 2001), 141. According to Leonard Levy, the secularization principle was already inherent in the Establishment Clause of the Constitution. The Establishment Clause segregates political authority from religious faith "so that we can maintain civility between believers and unbelievers as well as among the several hundred denominations, sects, and cults that thrive in our nation." See Leonard Levy, *The Establishment Clause* (New York: Macmillan, 1986), ix. Another view of the "new secularists" is that of Mary C. Segers and Ted G. Jelen, who argue that religion is "dysfunctional" for democracy and requires "political containment." The authors write that "if the American constitutional order is ultimately based on the value of self-governance, it follows that individual citizens must be granted a certain level of personal autonomy and self-determination." Religion, according to the authors, militates against autonomy and personal choice. See *A Wall of Separation: Debating the Public Role of Religion* (Lanham, Md.: Rowman & Littlefield, 1998), 31.

15. Robert Wuthnow, a well-known sociologist of religion, discusses this situation at length. He terms this version of civil religion a "secular legitimating ideology" where freedom is "not in itself enough." In this ideology the affirmation of American virtue is inextricably bound up with

"American success." The secular legitimating ideology is contrary to Richard Nixon's statement that "America is great because America is good." According to Wuthnow, "the pragmatic myth turns this slogan around: America is good because America is great. It has been argued that this myth grew into prominence during the nineteenth century. As the nation became richer, pragmatic justifications apparently became more compelling, besides being more compatible with the prevailing worldview accompanying commerce and industry. . . . Whether this myth was in fact a nineteenth century development or not, the further rise of the United States to world prominence in the twentieth century seems to have given added plausibility to the greatness-is-goodness thesis." Robert Wuthnow, *The Restructuring of American Religion: Society and Faith since World War II* (Princeton, N.J.: Princeton University Press, 1988), 264-65. Richard Wentz weighs in on the other side of this discussion by noting that the "civic" ideal of civil religion, derived in most respects from eighteenth-century thinking, is not the entire story either. There is also a mythical and mystical sense of national identity that determines various forms of religious consciousness. "Critics of the notion of civil religion are often confused by the false assumption that religion must always assume the voluntary, individualistic, institutional form adopted by American denominations. A religion, they assume, must be an entity that an individual can voluntarily join or decide not to join. They have little understanding of religion as organic, communal, and spatially related—the customs of a people in relation to a special, sacred place." Richard E. Wentz, *The Culture of Religious Pluralism* (Boulder, Colo.: Westview Press, 1998), 51.

16. "James Madison's Memorial and Remonstrance, 1785," in Edwin S. Gaustad, ed., *A Documentary History of Religion in America to the Civil War* (Grand Rapids, Mich.: Eerdmans, 1982), 262. For a discussion of Madison's position, see John G. West, Jr., *The Politics of Revelation and Reason: Religion and Civic Life in the New Nation* (Lawrence: University Press of Kansas, 1996), 124-26.

17. W. Widlick Schroder, Victor Obenhaus, Larry A. Jones, and Thomas Sweetser, S.J., *Suburban Religion: Churches and Synagogues in the American Experience* (Chicago: Center for the Scientific Study of Religion, 1974), 19. Jonathan Sarna goes even further in noting that "voluntaryism" and interfaith rivalry, which mirrors America's competitive economic marketplace, has strengthened Judaism as a religion in itself and made it a kind of standard-bearer for the pluralistic ideal. See Jonathan D. Sarna, "Jewish-Christian Hostility in the United States: Perceptions from a Jewish Point of View," in Robert N. Bellah and Frederick E. Greenspahn, eds., *Uncivil Religion: Interreligious Hostility in America* (New York: Crossroad, 1987), 17.

18. See Will Herberg, *Protestant, Catholic, Jew: An Essay in American Religious Sociology* (Garden City, N.Y.: Anchor Books, 1960).

19. Huntington, *Clash,* 318.

20. As recently as August of 2001, Mahmoud Abd Al-Mun'im wrote in the government-sponsored daily *Al Akhbar*: "The age of the American collapse has begun. If the U.S. thinks that with its policy, it is actualizing American interests within and without the U.S., it will quickly discover that the price of this bias is extremely high. The U.S., including the American people and the Israeli people, has rightly become Enemy No. 1 of the nations." Quoted in "Islamic Articles and Calendars Discussed Destruction in Lower Manhattan Weeks before the Attack—Coincidence?" *The Jewish Voice and Opinion* 15 (October 2001): 60.

21. See James Davison Hunter, *Culture Wars: The Struggle to Define America* (New York: Basic Books, 1991), 73ff.

14

The Jew in the American Public Square

Mickey Edwards

Do Jews Have a Place in the Public Square?

Shortly after Democratic presidential nominee Al Gore chose a Jewish U.S. senator to be his party's candidate for vice president, I was invited to speak at a private Jewish high school in the Boston suburbs. Mr. Gore's willingness to embrace Mr. Lieberman as his running mate was more than just another, and very visible, indication of social acceptance, another welcome sign that we had moved well past the time when public notices advised that "No Jews Need Apply" for a room, a job, or a membership. This was something more: the opening of a new kind of opportunity on the public stage, Jews not merely as advisors but as decision makers themselves, and not just among the half a thousand members of the United States Congress, but right up there at the very top, a heartbeat, as the saying goes, from the presidency itself.

Mr. Lieberman's nomination was a great step forward for America, too, which moved that much closer to fulfilling its own inchoate promise (fudged over in the Constitution, but clearly stated in the Declaration of Independence) of political equality.

Some of the older members of the audience saw something very different, however. To the inevitable question, "Is it good for the

Jews?"—and who can blame us for asking it—their answer seemed to be, "No; this is a disaster." How could we Jews safely keep our heads down—in modern terms, how could we fly under the radar screen—when one of our own was allowing himself to be so *visible*. Was he not, by virtue of the prominence he had attained, sticking *all* of our heads into the field of fire?

Thus, the dilemma of the Jew on the public stage. America, after all, is not entirely immune from the anti-Semitism that has burrowed so deeply into the communal mind-set of other societies around the world. True, the signals and warnings are subtler here. Unlike the shtetls and ghettos of Eastern Europe, in which Jews were on occasion slaughtered by their neighbors, anti-Semitism in the United States has generally been rhetorical or exclusionary, the sort of thing that draws no blood while it may nonetheless send a clear message, a warning of underlying attitudes and assumptions that could be seized upon by those who seek power. Many years ago, Sinclair Lewis wrote a book called *It Can't Happen Here*, the clear message of which was, "Oh, yes it can": The extremist evils that so often surface elsewhere can surface here as well.[1]

In his book *The Common Good: Its Politics, Policies, and Philosophy*, Marcus Raskin describes a theory of governance that purports to distinguish between "citizens," who are entitled to full participation in a society's decisions, and "associates," who have no real claim to a role in the society's governance. In Raskin's description, the wall between the two is formed by the associate's landlessness, state of dependence, *or* identity. He mentions two such identity distinctions, color and gender, but one could well imagine a religious-based exclusion as well.[2]

Jews today do not, for the most part, attract the same kind of hostility sometimes shown to African Americans, or to Asians, or to Hispanics, who may be seen as an economic threat and thus become targets of those who have risen to the second lowest rung of the ladder and are determined to kick at the hands of those climbing up behind them. While there are those whose anti-Semitism has a distinctly religious flavor (Jews as "Christ killers"), much of the anti-Semitism in America is a reaction to what is seen by some as disproportionate influence on the public stage—in the media, in publishing, in Hollywood, in government, in business. It is often the participation of Jews *in the public square* that draws the attention, and incurs the wrath, of the bigots in American society. To those older Jews who remember not only what happened in Russia and Poland and Germany, but who remember the anti-Semites of this country as well, what Joe Lieberman was doing was a distinct threat to everybody who wore a yarmulke or had a name like, well, Lieberman.

More than a quarter century ago, when Charles Liebman wrote his book *The Ambivalent American Jew*, the ambivalence he referred to was the tension between a desire for integration into the larger American community and a strong desire to keep Judaism alive, that is, not to integrate to the point of extinction as a separate entity.[3] What we saw in the last election, at least among some Jews, was another kind of ambivalence: the desire to affect public policy and yet not to stir the latent pot of anti-Semitism which one fears is out there somewhere, lurking just beneath the surface. It would be a mistake to simply dismiss those who shrink from the prospect of seeing a Jew at the center of division and controversy. Just as surely as Colin Powell became not just the secretary of state but the black secretary of state, Joseph Lieberman would have been the Jewish vice president.

The choice is not whether to ignore the concern, but whether to confront it or give in to it. Joe Lieberman not only proclaimed *his* faith openly; more important to some people, he proclaimed *faith* openly. Mr. Lieberman poses a great dilemma on both counts—his openness about *faith* and his openness about his own *non-Christian* faith.

On the day I was first sworn in as a member of the United States Congress, I was merely one of 435 men and women simultaneously taking the oath of office. I was certainly one of the more obscure people on the House floor that day. Nonetheless, it seemed to me and to my family a singularly momentous occasion. I can still hear the words of my mother's question as that event unfolded—my mother whose parents, like my father's parents, had come to America from the Jewish settlements of Eastern Europe. "Who are *we*," she asked, "to have a congressman in our family?"

That is perhaps, in a sense, the question that was on the minds of those older people in the audience at that Jewish high school so many years later: not a sense that Jews were not entitled, or not capable, but a sense of Jews as the perennial outsiders. In their daily bantering (is this, I wonder, a way in which we Jews keep the seriousness at bay?), my father would call my mother a Litvak and she would call him a Polack, and as a small child I assumed that I was, in fact, Jewish *and* Lithuanian *and* Polish, a confusion to which I still, on occasion, fall victim. But my father's family wasn't Polish, or at least the Poles didn't think so. And when Jews tried to be

Germans in Germany or Spaniards in Spain, had we not in the end been reminded that we were not Germans, we were not Spaniards, and that what passed for citizenship was not the result of birthright but of forbearance?

America is a land, and this is a time, of a rare acceptance and one of the periods of great assimilation of Jews into a larger culture. But as George Santayana famously said, "Those who do not learn from history are doomed to repeat it," and there are those among us who are conscious every day of the bitter lessons of Jewish history. For a woman whose time was not far removed from the pogroms of Eastern Europe, there may have been this fairly obvious question: Did we really belong here? Did our common citizenship apply even to the public square—the public *discourse* square—or was *that* somebody else's private property? Was I, in other words, forgetting my place?

Does Religion Have a Place
in the Public Square?

Before we can address the question of the Jew in the public square we must also come to grips with an underlying question, and that is whether religion itself is a *public*, as opposed to merely a private, good. It is likely that most Americans would agree that religion is certainly a private good; that is, that one benefits, personally, in a variety of ways from the addition of a spiritual dimension to one's life, and that one may be further enriched by an immersion in the comforts of specific religious beliefs and by the ability to commune with fellow believers. And while it may or may not be true that all moral behavior can be seen as a derivative of religious teaching, properly understood and integrated into one's life, religious belief is almost surely a positive force, helping not only the individual believer, but also enhancing that believer's contributions to the larger community.

That does not, however, automatically translate into an equal certainty that religion is a positive force in the public, or communal, parts of our lives. Indeed there is sound reason why many Jews are insistent on keeping religion *out* of public life. While the First Amendment's separation of church and state consists solely of a proscription against the creation of an official national religion, thereby protecting the freedom of all American citizens to engage fully and openly in the observance and practice of whichever religion they choose, including Judaism, many Americans have felt more comfortable—more secure—in redefining the "establishment clause" so that it now means to many not a protection *of* religion but a protection *against* religion. This rewriting of the Constitution is motivated by the awareness that one does not undertake a religious belief merely in the same sense that one subscribes to the maxims of Marcus Aurelius. There is inherent in religious belief a conviction that one has found the right way; some, having found this way, and having found that it gives them comfort, or hope, or joy, are eager—bursting at the seams, in fact—to share this good news with others. In some faiths, furthermore, there is the belief that one is obligated, required, to bring others to this awareness and insight and understanding. Considerable discipline is required to keep a true believer from crossing the line between "my way is the right way" and "your way is the wrong way," and even more discipline to then let others continue to pursue, and to preach, "the wrong way." Religion is susceptible to abuse, and religious belief contains within it the danger that it may breed both zeal and intolerance. In human hands, religion may be used for considerable good, but it may also be used for not so good.

The question, then, is what happens when private religious belief is carried over into the public square. Religion, of course, may be a force for considerable good when it is a church or mosque or synagogue through which benevolence is exercised. Professor Meredith Ramsay, of the University of Massachusetts, Boston, writes that "religion brings people together in mutual solidarity around matters that concern their most exalted hopes and deeply held values."[4] Indeed, followers of many faiths—the men and women whom President George W. Bush and Senator Lieberman, among others, believe to be a great and insufficiently tapped national resource—have already undertaken much of the community building and caregiving. Former president Jimmy Carter has notably immersed himself in humanitarian undertakings in accord to what he believes to be the obligation imposed by his religious faith. Professor Ramsay, in fact, suggests that "forces of modernity have so emptied the public sphere of its normative and transcendent dimensions that the church alone is left with enough moral standing" to spearhead a return to a more directly participatory form of democracy.

President Bush's desire to increase the involvement of the religious community in providing social services puts the question of "religion as a *public* good" squarely on the public agenda. But, in a

different way, so did the September 11 attacks on the World Trade
Center and the Pentagon. Mr. Bush, and many who share his view,
proceed from two mutually reinforcing premises: the first is that
religious belief nurtures the human proclivity for compassion and
infuses the believer with a will to do good; the second is that religious institutions have at their disposal substantial resources that
might be drawn upon to simultaneously (a) improve the efficiency
with which society cares for its less fortunate members and (b) alleviate the burden that providing such services would otherwise place
upon the public treasury, thereby freeing resources for everything
from national security to the improvement of public education and
medical research. Supporters of this view will find it tempting to
conclude that those who resist Mr. Bush's initiative have as their
primary concern a political preference for government as provider-
in-chief.

Unfortunately, the infusion of religion into the political realm
raises concerns that are not easily dismissed, whether in terms of
civil liberties or religious practice. There is, of course, general
agreement that any religious organization that undertakes to provide
social services with funds provided in part from the public treasury
must not use its interaction with service recipients as an opportunity
to preach or proselytize. In each such interaction, the individual
beneficiary will be engaged with representatives of a single religious institution, and there is little, if any, disagreement with the
general notion that the federal government may not use its authority
or its resources to press a religious belief on any of its citizens, directly or indirectly.

What's more, churches, mosques, and synagogues themselves
must be cautious: one cannot merely stick one's toe into the secular
world as though one were standing on the beach, testing the waters.
In is in, and "in" means adherence to all the laws that govern recipients of federal grants, including prohibitions against discrimination
based on, say, sexual orientation. Participating institutions may find
themselves engaged in activities which fly in the face of the religious teachings that seem to them fundamental and inviolate. In
such a case, one might rightly wonder whether the service provider,
infused with certitude, will choose to obey the public law or the revealed Truth. Some worry that a mixing of religion and government
will have disastrous consequences for those whose primary concern
is the practice of government: the danger is equally great for those
whose interest is the practice of religion. Religious institutions have
always enjoyed a considerable independence in America; one should

tread carefully when undertaking any activity that might compromise that independence.

The attacks of September 11 suggest a different way in which one might assess the effect of religion in public life. While few would argue that the violence unleashed by Osama bin Laden, or the tyranny of the Taliban who sheltered him, reflect Muslim values (indeed in the wake of the attacks many Muslim clerics were eager to emphasize the religion's emphasis on peace, and to condemn Mr. bin Laden's distortion of the faith), the religious rhetoric in which the terrorists cloaked themselves underlined once more the ease with which the certitude of faith may support extreme and deadly acts. Whether it is the horror of nearly 3,000 innocents murdered in a single moment, the prolonged tortures of the Inquisition, or the slaying of young women at an abortion clinic, religion at times steps onto the public stage in frightful manifestation.

The question must be divided. Religion, as a private good, the addition of a spiritual and moral dimension to an individual life, may be quite beneficial in its effect on those adherents to religious faith who choose to participate in public affairs. Certainly in the wake of the Enron scandal—a tale of document shredding, nondisclosure, and insider cashing in—one might long for the benefits of a moral compass as a guide to the decision-making process. But the line between a "moral compass" and religious certitude is a fuzzy one. There are, in fact, many ways in which religion is injected into our secular public life. What happens, for example, when a holder of public office, acting not through a religious institution but as part of a distinctly and purposely secular government, allows his or her religious beliefs—his or her belief in what is right and what is wrong—to affect his or her decisions in regard to public policy. Many modern politicians have developed a habit of professing faith routinely and at almost any public occasion. Does a profession of faith require the posting of the Ten Commandments or the recitation of prayer in the schoolroom, as some would propose? In a secular society, should policies—about abortion, about marriage, about contracts, about public relief—be derived from the policy maker's personal religious experience and beliefs, even if they are not universal and extra-constitutional? Here the injection of religion into the public square is less clearly a positive. Patrick Buchanan, a former high-level presidential assistant and later a presidential candidate himself, and a self-proclaimed religious man, states publicly that the United States is a Christian nation; what, a Jew—or Muslim or Buddhist or atheist—might wonder, would guide a Buchananite public agenda?

We all take our beliefs, all of our beliefs, with us wherever we go. Our sense of values determines how we manage our businesses, how we behave in a classroom, how we undertake our research, how we practice our professions. When one enters public life, holding an elected or appointed position in government, he or she is unlikely to proceed as though his or her decisions were value-neutral. Some might argue that such a value-neutral approach would be an ideal form of government for a large, diverse, multiracial, multiethnic, multireligious wholly secular society. It is not, however, a form of public participation we are likely to see.

What is called for is a sense of restraint among our public officials: a sense that large-scale generic values—care for one's neighbors, a preference for peace to war, a belief in constrained government (or a belief in government activism)—are valuable tools to bring to the public debate, but that specifics indigenous to one's own faith ought to be parked at the door. Massachusetts elected a new congressman in 2001 to succeed Joe Moakley, who had died in the middle of his term of office. One of the candidates in that race explained his switch from a pro-life position to a pro-choice position by saying that he was personally opposed to abortion but did not believe it was the role of a government official to impose his personal views on other people. Needless to say, there were many, including his opponents, who thought he had seen the polls rather than the light, but all in all it was a good formulation. It is not, however, a formulation that is often followed in practice. The rules of the House of Representatives require members to excuse themselves from voting on any issue on which they might have a conflict of interest. It is a rule that is rarely observed, and never on an issue in which the conflict came as a result of a member's commitment to the teachings of a particular faith. Seldom, of course, is religion—or at least a particular set of religious beliefs—cited as argument for a bill or an amendment (on abortion, say), or in opposition to a bill or an amendment, but it is quite clear in the various Bible study and prayer groups in which members of Congress meet regularly that there is a significant confluence between one's religious views and one's political actions.

There is a problem here for Jews. Many Jews are fearful, for example, that so-called non-denominational prayer in schools—advocated by politicians who believe daily prayer to be essential to a good society—would eventually become more and more sectarian, with one of two effects: either Jewish children will be subjected to a daily dose of Christian prayer *or* a Jewish parent will succeed in getting such prayer activity stopped, again raising the profile of Jewish "otherness" and antagonizing the Christian community.

While it is certainly true, as Tocqueville and many scholars since have pointed out, that there is a strong religious underpinning to much of American life, it seems likely that omnipresent religiosity is much more common in geographic regions where the Jewish presence is relatively small, and that the Jewish sense of religion as a more or less private matter is reinforced by the fact that the larger Jewish populations are in the large—and largely secular—urban areas of the two coasts. Both in preference and in the context of the social norms of the communities in which they live, Jews and secularism seem to go together and this in a society in which it seems that non-Jews are much more comfortable with the mixing of religion and public life.

So is religion a public, as opposed to merely a private, good? Perhaps the best answer is that religion has attributes that ought to contribute wonderfully to the public life, but that religion's tendency to unleash passions and certitude—a dangerous combination—make the mixing of the two something to be approached with great care in a society which purports to value individual choice.

The Jewish Role in the Public Square

Bringing one's religious certainties into the public square poses a potential danger to those who do not subscribe to the prevalent views in the community. And this sense of differentness can only be heightened by the considerable divergence between Jews and non-Jews in terms of political preferences. Republicans (for the most part, conservatives) won six of the nine presidential elections from 1968 through 2000. As of the beginning of 2002, Republicans have held the White House for twenty-one of the previous thirty-three years; Republicans in January of 2002 held most of the nation's governorships and for most of the 1990s held both houses of the U.S. Congress. At the same time, Jews, in overwhelming majorities, voted for the candidates who lost. Jews were, in fact, among the most loyal supporters of the candidates most soundly rejected by voters nationally—Dukakis, Mondale, McGovern: all of them soundly trounced by non-Jews and roundly endorsed by Jews. Edward Shapiro in his article, "Liberal Politics and American Jewish

Identity," says that "At times, the contrast between the voting behavior of Jews and Gentile Americans has been bizarre": only 30
percent of white non-Jews voted for George McGovern; 65 percent
of Jews voted for him; 71 percent of Jews voted for Walter Mondale.[5] By the time the last election was over, Americans had memo-
rized those maps that seemed to show two different Americas—rural
versus urban, the coasts and the heartland: imagine what it would
have shown if the maps had shown the votes of Jews and non-Jews:
not two different Americas but two different planets.

It should be noted, however, that both the typical Jew and the
typical non-Jew are guilty of oversimplifying their characterization
of the Jewish community's political leanings. Certainly there are a
great many Jews who have played leading roles in the American
progressive movements over the past century. Not only do Jews vote
overwhelmingly for liberals, but Jewish names are prominent on the
rosters of civil rights activists, liberal scholars, and contributors to
left-wing causes. Overlooked, however, both by Jews and by non-
Jews is the role Jews have played in the development of modern
conservatism as well. The right, too, has its share of Jewish writers
and activists, and while they are decidedly a tiny minority in the
Jewish community, they are important beyond their numbers in the
conservative intellectual community.

So one wonders, is there something in the teachings of Judaism
that has so populated the political world with Jews beyond their
proportions in the population? Is there a describable Jewish public
persona? Clearly, many Jews—most, in fact—simply live as non-
Jews do: they run shops, they play baseball, they build houses, with
little, if any, participation in the public square. Yet it is also true
that Jews are found in substantial numbers, in greater percentages
than the Jewish population might explain, in almost all public activities. Often this participation is in service to what would generally be called progressive or liberal causes. But just as there are
conservative blacks, conservative Harvard professors, and conservative women, Jews, too, have their own minorities within the minority. Edward Shapiro writes that "From the perspective of [Ellen]
Willis and *Tikkun* (magazine), a conservative Jew is a contradiction
in terms."[6] Perhaps, but they do, in fact, exist.

Nonetheless, because we're talking not about a Jewish persona
but a Jewish *public* persona, we have to acknowledge that in the
public square Jews are, for the *most* part, quite different from
Southern Baptists in Oklahoma or Protestant farmers in Nebraska.
Shapiro, referring to Willis, writes that "for radicals" like her, "vic-

timization is central to their understanding of themselves as Jews. Even for those Jews who don't share Willis's radical politics, the sense of being a victim, this emphasis on the 'oy vays' rather than the joys of Jewishness, has been important in shaping their politics."[7]

The persona of the Jew in the public square is, by both teaching and history, that of a fighter for the underdog, and fighters for the underdog, regardless of how they believe they can best wage that fight, simply cannot stand on the sidelines when the fate of the community is being decided. There is a need to be at the table or at the barricades that is as ingrained as one's own DNA, and to ask whether a Jew should participate in the public square is much like asking whether the sun should rise in the morning.

There are Jews who run for and are elected to public office. There are Jewish campaign consultants and Jewish contributors to political campaigns. But the public square is a big place, a place where dialogue takes place about both formal and informal policy making. Much of the public square is rhetorical: the place where debate takes place over issues of social and political concern. This is an arena in which the Jewish presence is certainly real and hard to ignore. The public square is also the arena of activist organizations, non-profits, a place of both providers and advocates. Here, too, Jewish names abound. However one defines the American public square, Jews are there, often overrepresented, and often influential.

There are things that dissuade Jews from participation in the public dialogue, including fear built on the remembrance of things past, an acute awareness that whenever one thinks that "it can't happen here," one is invariably proven wrong. And yet America does seem different: nowhere have Jews lived so comfortably for so long in such harmony with their neighbors, and here those who raise their voices in hate, and those who act out their hatred, are subject to both derision and punishment. We Jews are skittish about things that raise the specter of intolerance—things like school prayer and the ascendance of politicians openly proclaiming their faith as central to their public decision making, and we find ourselves drawn into the public debate.

That which impels Jews to participate in public dialogue is an overriding imperative: a sense of obligation to the community as a whole and to the unfortunate in particular. Jews learn in childhood that their people had been slaves, too; they observe still the remembrance of Jews slaughtered—in Germany, in Russia, in Poland—simply because they were Jews; they know that Jews mastered certain professions because they were prohibited from participation in others; they learn early that "if I am for myself alone, what am I?" They may disagree among themselves as to what this understanding requires, and thus where they may choose to stand on various public issues; they may consider that the Jewish narrative proves the need for a strong central government to protect the weak from the strong, or they may consider that that same history proves the dangers of centralized authority. They may disagree over whether to provide the poor with a fish or a fishing pole. But *wherever* they stand, the question of *whether* to stand seems clearly answered in the affirmative. Even Jews who have had little in the way of religious training and whose observance is sporadic, at best, seem impelled to take the imperatives of social conscience into the public debates. Shut out of the public square in so many lands, over so much time, Jews in America seem to say, on this, too, that in this, too, things will be different.

The Jewish Voice in the Public Square

It has been common in the Jewish community to consider that the participation in liberal or "progressive" politics is the means by which the traditional and religious values of the Jewish people are best translated into public action. Certainly there are issues of public policy to which Jews bring a common concern, including the most obvious: the protection of religious minorities and maintaining the secular nature of the nation-state. Further, the traditional Jewish concern for the less fortunate, the oppressed, and the disenfranchised—a concern born of the Jew's own history—seems an inseparable part of the Jewish impulse to help shape public policy. The difficulty comes with the attempting to prescribe specific policies to address those concerns; I will argue that the religious imperative extends to the concern and not to the prescription.

Jewish concern for the oppressed or the disadvantaged (two different things) may impel one to decide, on purely secular political grounds, to endorse one position or another, but Judaism itself is agnostic on such questions as whether taxes ought to be higher or lower, whether recipients of state welfare ought to be required to work, and even the extent to which states ought to provide a public support to the disadvantaged. There is, in fact, no "Jewish position" on virtually any public policy issue, and to suggest that a Jewish conservative presents a contradiction in terms is a sad attempt to appropriate religion to serve one's political agenda.

There are certainly Jewish teachings and traditions to take into account. Charity, for example, is a Jewish imperative. Jewish children, as part of their religious training, are encouraged to dig into their pockets or backpacks and to fish out some of their coins, perhaps a crumpled dollar or two, and to put the money into a container from which the funds will be distributed to help those who are less fortunate. This is the obligation of *tzedekah*, and the relative affluence of the giver (or of the giver's parents) is without relevance: the Jewish child of a poor home, no less than the child of the wealthy, is taught this important fundamental of Jewish life: one is to share what one has with those who have less. Charity begins at home is a distinctly non-Jewish concept. Jews are raised to think of themselves as part of a community, a collective, and they are to contribute to the well-being of all. The world is the Jew's congregation.

One may choose to translate that mandate—or that tradition, if one is less theologically inclined—into support for a state-imposed system of redistribution. In such a case, the funds to support the needy are coercively obtained, through the imposition of taxes, but in a democracy, unless one is disenfranchised he or she may be said to have given his or her consent to such a policy. This is a perfectly legitimate position, but it is not a theological position and not a "Jewish" position; it is a secular point of view, though it may be informed by, and perhaps encouraged by, a specific concern for the hungry and the homeless that flows from Jewish teaching. It is not charity and it is not *tzedekah*. To be charitable is to give willingly from one's own resources to aid another. One may choose to do so directly or indirectly. But it is not charity, but merely a political policy preference, to take money from somebody else to fulfill the same purpose.

One who attempts to use Jewish concepts of *tzedekah* to justify support—as a Jew—for government programs runs into another difficulty. *Tzedekah* rests on an underlying concept of community. Indeed the idea of community resonates throughout a variety of political traditions. In his book *Conservatism in America*, Clinton Rossiter emphasizes the transcendent importance of community in conservative thought.[8] But community and the state are not necessarily the same. That is, one may fully embrace traditional Jewish teaching about both charity and community—one may be a "good Jew" politically—without ceding to the federal government the responsibility or the authority to become the chief provider of public relief. It is thus acceptable, in Jewish terms and according to Jewish tradition, to support devolutions of welfare authority to state and local governments, to support a lowering of the federal income taxes, to oppose national health insurance. One may support high levels of taxation, large-scale government programs, and substantial redistribution policies and to claim that such preferences spring from the impulses gained when one stuffed one's leftover coins into the synagogue's *tzedekah* box, but one cannot claim such preferences to be the Jewish way: they are merely secular political choices; they are the policy preferences not of Jews, but of liberals. Conversely, therefore, one who believes that welfare may best be managed by local authorities or private charities, or one who believes, with Maimonides, that giving alms is lower on the *mitzvot* scale than teaching one to earn one's own subsistence, may just as properly lay claim to a public policy in keeping with the mandates of the faith.

Those who argue for a strong centralized government as the means to address traditional Jewish concerns do so for at least two reasons which are unarguably supportable as a political point of view. The first is related to the concept of *tzedekah*. If one believes oneself to be furthering the obligation to be charitable by advocating redistribution policies or a variety of social assistance programs, one may logically determine that such programs can best be implemented by a large and powerful central government. Further, many Jews, concentrated in large urban areas with liberal political traditions, may fear that state legislators in distant, poorer, or more conservative states will not be willing to pass the programs embraced in places like Boston, Albany, or Sacramento. Because they may tend to think globally (or, in this case, nationally), rather than locally, and may be unwilling to take a chance that some in Mississippi or Alabama may not receive the benefit of public help, they may turn to the national government to intervene.

A second reason why many support a strong central government, unrelated to the first, is the belief that the primary threats to one's survival, economic or physical, are posed by powerful individuals or groups capable of inflicting hardship on those who are less powerful. Government may seem the only force powerful enough to protect the weaker segments of society (those who are less numerous, perhaps, or those with fewer resources) from a variety of predators. This is a view fully consistent with the perception—often valid—of the exploitative wealthy. Thus, it is argued, one can be protected against sweatshop labor, low wages, arbitrary dismissals, inferior or dangerous housing, the dumping of toxic pollutants into the air and water, only by summoning the protection of somebody even bigger than those who would take advantage of a society unequipped to fight back on anything like equal terms. Thus, even labor unions, the collective effort to fight the power of capital, may need the protective cloak of government.

There is considerable historical justification for such fears. This is, again, not a position mandated by one's Jewish faith, but Jews, having long been oppressed in countless societies, and a particularly small minority even in America, are sensitive to oppression. Some have thus focused on the potential, and sometimes real, examples of unchecked capitalism and to buy into a view of capitalism itself as inherently evil, and a powerful state as being the only means to keep such predatory predispositions in check.

Finally, Jews being invariably a minority in each country of settlement (except Israel, where Jews are surrounded by adversaries who are far more numerous), there is a natural fear—a fear justified by history—of persecutions inspired by, perhaps implemented by, other, more numerous, religious communities. Again one is inclined to turn to a force large enough to protect against such treats: a strong central government.

But history teaches other lessons as well, and if Jewish history teaches anything at all (that is, history of Jews as Jews, as identifiably and collectively a Jewish community in a non-Jewish world) it is that the single greatest threat to the survival of the Jewish people has been the concentration of great power in the hands of a central authority. Where rape and slaughter have come in a broad sweep, across many communities, they have come at the hands of an unchecked government, from the enslavement by Egypt's pharaohs to the pogroms of Czarist Russia to the holocaust of Hitler's Germany. Even when persecution has been instigated by forces other than government (one thinks here of the Spanish Inquisition) it has been facilitated by the presence and support of complicit, compliant, co-opted, and powerful central government.

Theoretically, government may be the protector of the weak against the strong, and certainly in terms of economic exploitation, where the oppressor is individual or corporate, government has frequently been called upon to redress legitimate grievances. But there are other, greater, dangers. Historically, it has been Jews who have been the weak and the governments under which they have lived that have been the strong; the persecution of Jews throughout the ages has been the result of those who hate the Jews having sufficient

armed power and legal authority to impose their will. It is legitimate, therefore, for Jews, as Jews, to consider that the greater danger lies in the concentration of state power.

It can be argued that America is a nation immune to the dark impulse that has led so many Jews to slaughter, that American democracy is itself a bulwark against the sorts of oppression with which
the Jewish people have become so familiar. Yet it is in the very nature of a representative democracy that the people—the masses—
have the ultimate potential to turn government to the service of the
public impulse. In this light it is disturbing to note how often
Americans, including some in government and many in the public
arena, have shown impatience with many of the civil liberties protections afforded by the Constitution. After the terrorist attacks on
Washington and New York in September of 2001, one began to hear
the first faint rumblings of those who would, at least partially, lay
the blame for the attacks, and the resulting deaths, on America's
long-standing support for Israel. When Palestinian suicide bombers
escalated their attacks on Israel, killing innocent civilians on buses,
in shopping malls, and in restaurants, still louder voices began to be
heard rationalizing the murders and decrying the Israeli "occupa-
tion." When the Israeli government launched a military offensive to
try to destroy the terrorist network responsible for the killings, the
voices of condemnation grew louder and American Jews increasingly found themselves on the defensive.

It is one thing to note that historically America has been a nation
open to Jews, and one in which a Jew just two years ago was nomi-
nated by a major political party to serve as the vice president of the
United States; but as September 11, the Palestinian suicide bomb-
ings, and the outcry against the Israeli retaliation should remind us,
anti-Semitism has also been part of the American landscape and
many otherwise "good" American citizens may sometimes see Jewish claims and concerns as bothersome or worse. Knowing that
American government is susceptible to being "controlled" by the
people is not a sufficient reason to set aside all of one's worries
about the potential of concentrated economic and police powers.

None of this, of course, is to suggest that support for a strong
central government is necessarily un-Jewish, nor even to suggest
that it is invalid for Jews to draw upon their faith and traditions to
support liberal political policies; it is rather to stipulate that there
are other positions that may be validly argued as consistent with
Jewish teaching (private charity) and Jewish history. When one argues that "a conservative Jew is a contradiction in terms," one sim-

ply trivializes, and misunderstands, both teaching and history. There are, indeed, reasons why Jews become conservatives, and why a number of the leading thinkers in American conservative politics are Jewish. While Jews will undoubtedly continue to be active on the public stage, and centrally involved in the great policy debates of the day, there will continue to be great difficulty in attempting to claim one set of views as "the Jewish way." There will be Jews in the public square, and conservative Jews will be among them.

Conclusion

When Woody Guthrie sang that "This Land is Your Land," he was speaking to all Americans. It is in the public square, in the debates, the political campaigns, the town hall meetings, the political process, that Americans decide their national course. Both because Jews, like all Americans, will be affected by the nation's general policies—tax rates, import quotas, environmental regulations—and because Jews have traditionally had to be alert to the dangers that threaten those who are "different," Jews will, and must, be active in that public square.

But it is one thing to advocate participation in the public square and another to advocate participation in the specific garb of religiosity. Religion is almost undoubtedly a private good: it offers believers solace, hope, pleasure, and a prescribed moral code. Religion is also susceptible to the dangers of excessive certitude, of extremism, of the conviction that one must "save" or "convert" or "overcome" those who do not subscribe to the "true" faith. Thus the religious may, and should, participate politically, but must do so conscious that different rules, and different considerations, apply in a secular state.

The traditional concerns of the Jewish people will undoubtedly draw many into the public dialogue, and into public life. Many will be led to the support of "liberal" or "progressive" policy positions which seem to them consistent with the teachings and traditions of Judaism. But both Torah and Jewish history may just as easily lead a concerned Jew to adopt policy positions that favor limits on the scope and power of central authority. A conservative Jew is not, as some suggest, a "contradiction in terms" but a serious response to the lessons of Jewish life.

What positions Jews take in the public square, and how boldly or fearfully Jews enter that arena, will vary greatly, but one thing is clear: Jews do have a right, and perhaps an obligation, to fully participate. To my mother's question, "Who are *we* to have a congressman in our family," the best answer may simply be we are Jews, and we are Americans, and this land *is* our land.

Notes

1. Sinclair Lewis, *It Can't Happen Here* (New York: Doubleday, Doran and Company, 1935).

2. Marcus G. Raskin, *The Common Good: Its Politics, Policies, and Philosophy* (New York: Routledge & Kegan Paul, 1986).

3. Charles Liebman, *The Ambivalent American Jew: Politics, Religion and Family in American Jewish Life* (Philadelphia: Jewish Publication Society of America, 1973).

4. Meredith Ramsay, "Redeeming the City: Exploring the Relationship between Church and Metropolis," *Urban Affairs Review*, vol. 33, 5 (May 1998), 595-626.

5. Edward S. Shapiro, "Liberal Politics and American Jewish Identity," *Judaism*, issue 188, vol. 47, no. 4 (Fall 1998), 430.

6. Shapiro, "Liberal Politics," 430.

7. Shapiro, "Liberal Politics," 430.

8. Clinton Rossiter, *Conservatism in America* (New York: Knopf, 1962).

15

From China to Jersey City: Religious Pluralism, Religious Liberty, and Human Rights

Kevin J. Hasson

What does pluralism have to do with religious liberty? You might call this the new China question. China? A ruthless dictatorship that represses Buddhists and Yoga enthusiasts with equal fervor may seem a strange place to begin a discussion of pluralism and religious liberty. But exploring our reaction to religious repression in China is helpful, precisely because it exposes the shallowness and inadequacy of the way many Americans understand our own religious freedom and our own experience of pluralism.

When China imprisons Tibetan Buddhists simply for possessing pictures of the Dalai Lama, and we Americans say, "This is an outrage against religious liberty," China inevitably responds: "You're interfering in our internal affairs." Are they right?

Similarly, when the Sudan enslaves Christian and Animist children simply for being Christians and Animists, and Americans say this is an outrage against religious liberty, the Khartoum government replies: "You are interfering in our internal affairs." Are they right? When Iran persecutes the Bahai simply for being the Bahai and we protest, they say: "You are interfering in our internal affairs." Are they right?

Most Americans are naturally confident that this kind of repression is wrong. We use our common cultural assumptions as an excuse to ignore the question these repressive governments raise. But the question these governments raise is terribly important for religious liberty, not only in China, Sudan, and Iran, but in America—because it's a restatement of the question "Where does religious liberty come from?"

What do Americans have to say about that? This chapter discusses four common defenses of American religious freedom that in my judgment fail. The first is the positive law approach: Americans enjoy religious liberty because it's in the Constitution, stupid. The second defense grounds religious liberty in the desirability of avoiding arguments. Religious liberty, on this view, is more or less synonymous with privatization of religion. The third is what I call minoritarianism: religious liberty is supported by religious minorities as a practical alternative to religious oppression by the majority. The fourth is the marketplace-of-ideas defense: we support each other's right to religious freedom because it guarantees that our own traditions can speak and have a chance to be heard.

Notice something very important all these arguments have in common: they are ultimately based on a utilitarian (or else a positivist) calculus: *Religious freedom is good only because it is useful or because the government says so.* In this worldview, freedom is an instrumental good, not a necessary response to the truth about the human person. It is not a good in and of itself, much less a public one. This mistaken premise leads to a dangerously deficient view of religious pluralism. If religious search and expression is not a public good, what of religious pluralism in public? At best, it is a nuisance to be tolerated, a necessary evil we must carefully circumscribe. That view not only makes late December a "fighting season" in the United States, but it also makes it impossible to argue for a respectful pluralism abroad. It leaves us having to admit to the Chinese—and the Sudanese and Iranians—that, yes, indeed we are interfering in their internal affairs.

This chapter will suggest an alternative: because religious liberty is the quintessentially human right to search for and embrace truth, religious expression from all traditions is a public good. First, though, let us review the four most common mistakes.

It's the Constitution, Stupid

Too often, Americans seek to avoid the question of where rights come from. We have the First Amendment, how wonderful, isn't that enough? Do we really need to haggle over *why*? Anything more strikes the practical American mind as overly metaphysical and ethereal.

But it cannot be avoided. If American supporters of religious liberty want to respond to the Chinese government, they have to figure out *why* they support religious liberty. They cannot talk to China about the Constitution because the Chinese constitution is very different. Article 48 of the Chinese constitution is nice—and it would be even nicer if they would enforce it—but it is still no First Amendment. In short, Americans cannot talk to China about American positive law because China does not have American positive law. If religious liberty is merely a political right derived from the Constitution, then the answer to the accusation China hurls at us, "You are interfering in our internal affairs!" is *yes*, you are right. Any attempt to impose American positive law on other countries would, in fact, be meddling in other nations' internal affairs. Too bad for the Buddhists. Next case. Sudan and Iran likewise have nothing comparable to the First Amendment. Next case.

And the next case, if that is our theory of religious freedom, may turn out to be America. The positive-law view is equally troubling for this country because if religious freedom is not a fundamental human right, then it's repealable. The same government that gave it can take it away. Positive law alone is inadequate to ground a right of religious freedom, here or elsewhere.

Secondhand Smoke

Many Americans try to defend guarantees of religious liberty on the basis of practicality. Governments and societies simply work better when public life excludes religion altogether. Proponents of this theory end up defending not religious liberty per se but the privatization of religion. The primary function of a right to "religious liberty" is to remove religion from government and from the political landscape.

This has justly been called the secondhand smoke model. It says, in effect: "Religion is so dangerous that we have to relegate it to

purely private life. You can imbibe religion like you can cigarette
smoke, in private, consensually. It's very impolite to do it in public
and it's the government's job to protect you from it in courthouses
and train stations."

The appeal of the secondhand smoke model is obvious. Controversies with religious implications are emotionally charged. Americans don't want to replay the Wars of Religion. On a much less
grandiose scale, everyone finds his or her neighbor's religious beliefs strange and sometimes inconvenient. When one is awakened on
a Saturday morning by door-to-door proselytizers, or when one
hears one's own religious tradition used by politicians to justify
policies with which one radically disagrees, it is easy to slip into the
belief that religion is best when it is kept off the sidewalks and out
of public view.

But religion, of one flavor or another, is important to us not only
individually, but culturally. Claiming to have a pluralistic public
culture while ruthlessly rejecting the religious elements of different
communities' celebrations is simply dishonest. If the government
were just the night watchman of libertarian fame and merely provided for the common defense and ran police departments, then it
might be natural for it to say little or nothing about religion. But in
America there is a broad area of overlap between government and
civil society, in which government attempts to acknowledge and appreciate civil life without encroaching on civil prerogatives. Thus
government celebrates all kinds of things, everything from National
Catfish Day to National Jukebox Week—and, as Dave Barry might
say, "I am not making that up." We have a comprehensive public
culture. We have a comprehensive public education. And if our
government comprehensively says absolutely nothing about the human thirst for transcendence its silence is deafening. (And silly—
does anyone really want to pretend that in late December the shops
put out holiday decorations and the homes are strung with lights because it's "Sparkle Season"? Does anyone really want to treat the
fasts of Ramadan as if they are some sort of new-wave diet?) When
government entities recognize all aspects of human culture except
this deepest layer, the layer of human transcendence, the layer on
which most of the rest of culture is built, the government says that
this fundamental human thirst is at best an optional hobby. That lies
to us about who we really are. It is also a false pluralism—
homogenization in disguise.

But in addition to its other limitations, defining religious liberty
as privatization does not help when dealing with countries as di-

verse as China, Sudan, or Iran. The governments of those countries have very different ideas about how to privatize divisive ideas. Why dillydally when you can maintain public harmony and order even more efficiently by simply locking up religious dissidents? Grounding religious liberty on its supposed practical benefits may lead us to interesting discussions of culturally relative notions of prudent strategy; it cannot give us a ground on which to protest, much less intervene, when governments jail, harass, punish, and intimidate people for their religious beliefs.

What's in It for Me?

A third attempt to answer the question "Why religious liberty?" might be called the minoritarian approach. In this model, minorities promote religious liberty—again understood as a hygienic seal separating religion and public life—in order to avoid oppression or a sense of alienation. Religious liberty is a defensive weapon. We wield it if, when, and to the extent that it is in our self-interest.

This response does not even attempt to ground pluralism. But it also fails when put to the "Is China right?" test. Sticking up for the religious liberties of Tibetan Buddhists, Sudanese Christians and Animists, and Iranian Bahai may well produce exactly zero benefits for American minority groups. True, in some cases, minoritarians might be well advised to press religious liberty claims for other countries' minorities, but only because of the way such claims might become symbolic tools within American politics—for example, an American minority might stick up for Sudanese Christians solely in order to make the point that Christians too can be oppressed, and thereby to win sympathy and support from Christians in this country. But in many other cases, minorities elsewhere will be at best irrelevant to minorities here.

Moreover, to the extent minorities here are also minorities there, it may be downright counterproductive. For China, Tibetan Buddhists are the worst kind of dissidents there are, because they are separatists. In a land where "One China" is a maxim, they want to free Tibet. In the Sudan, the Christians and the Animists in the South are likewise rebels. And, of course, in Iran, the Bahai are heretics. People who defend these various sorts of dissidents do themselves no favors. If religious liberty is just an exercise in realpolitik, why defend minorities overseas? Why should Jews or Christians stick their necks out for, say, the Iranian Bahai when that could get Iranian Jews or Christians in trouble?

It's a Hunting License

The final mistaken attempt to ground religious liberty is a cousin to minoritarianism; it is based on the belief that religious liberty makes it possible for the truth to be spoken in public. This is an approach that *almost* successfully grounds religious liberty. At least it holds that religious liberty is some sort of public good that has something to do with truth. At bottom, though, it is still a utilitarian argument. One might seek First Amendment liberties for all because without them his or her voice might be silenced. "We need religious freedom so we can proclaim the Gospel," a Christian might say. Or an atheist might look to the future and propose a tit for tat: "Let's compromise—the Christians can argue for their beliefs but they have to let me argue for mine." This worldview is akin to minoritarianism because it bases a defense of religious liberty on membership in a particular subgroup of the human race: religious liberty is good because it is good for Christians, or religious liberty is good because it is good for atheists, full stop. There is still no sense that religious liberty is good because it is good for *people*, people outside one's own group, people viewed not solely as potential converts.

This sort of utilitarian defense of religious liberty is deeply dangerous because, of course, there will be times when the practical benefits of religious liberty for all are not obvious. There will be times and places when Christians can repress other groups while still proclaiming the Gospel; there will be times and places when atheists can make their own voices heard while still shouting down believers. In short, there will be times and places when the horse-trading supports not religious freedom but religious repression.

And what if one has no hope for converting China? Or belongs to a tradition that simply does not want to? Then one would have to admit that whether or not China persecutes Buddhists is nobody's business but its own.

No, It's a Human Right

But we cannot admit that. We know better. China's persecution of religious minorities truly is an outrage against human rights. Why? Because it is an offense against the dignity of the human person. If religious liberty is truly a human right, its origins will be found not in the contours of American positive law or in some utilitarian calculus. It will be found in the contours of the human mind and heart.

We humans naturally thirst for transcendence, both vertical and horizontal, and therein lies our dignity. We are born with both intelligence and free will. We view our lives as projects, and we quest for ultimate purpose. We naturally seek both truth and goodness. In fact, we are downright restless about it. We continually hunger for ever more profound truths, ever better goods, ever more exquisite beauties. Through it all, we yearn for vertical transcendence—to embrace an ultimate truth, to taste a surpassing good and contemplate a sublime beauty that lies far beyond the horizons of ourselves. It is only necessary to look at human history and culture to see that humans are art-making and truth-seeking beings. And it is when we are engaged in this search for vertical transcendence that we are at our best.

Humans also seek a horizontal transcendence. We seek to reach out and embrace not just an ultimate truth, but other people around us. We are social creatures; we yearn for community. It's not that we *can't* live alone—we can. But we don't enjoy it. "Solitary" is one of our harshest punishments. We are community builders just as we are art makers and truth seekers. We bring the community into the most intimate and important moments of our lives; we seek witnesses and friends. We don't smuggle babies home from the hospital in secret; we have brises, we have baptisms. We don't come of age in secret; we have bar mitzvahs, bat mitzvahs, confirmations. We don't (typically) elope in secret; we have egregiously expensive, outlandishly elaborate celebrations. And we don't, unless we have murdered somebody, sneak off in the dead of night to bury the body in a landfill. We gather to weep together. We don't do all these things alone because we don't live alone.

And because we don't live alone, we don't believe alone. Because humans are social beings that seek rich connections with one another, personal belief necessarily seeks public expression. That is why people spent generations building medieval cathedrals in the midst of otherwise modest villages. And it is why groups today gather in perfectly well-illuminated buildings to light candles. These behaviors would be merely absurd if they did not respond to one of the deepest and most tenacious longings of the human heart and mind. We naturally want to celebrate our traditions in public. We naturally want to bring our vertical transcendence together with our horizontal transcendence, to celebrate the truth we have found just as we celebrate a marriage or a birth. Some might argue that religion is a public good because it is good for the public. But in truth, it goes deeper than that. Religion is a public good because religion is a *human* good, and humans are public people.

This account of religious liberty makes it the freedom to seek and to publicly embrace truth. It grounds that freedom not in some positivist provision, or utilitarian calculus, but in a truth claim about the human person—that we are truth-seeking, social beings.

Notice that this grounding of religious freedom relies simply on observation of human nature, not on the revelation of any particular tradition. Religious discourse in public life is often denigrated because religious arguments are unintelligible to those who do not accept the particular revelation on which those claims are based. But it is possible to see that religion does have a place in public life precisely because of something that everyone can investigate and understand: the nature of the human person.

And this account of the basis of religious liberty leads to a strikingly different conclusion from that of the varied attempts to ground religious liberty described above. Not only can this claim about human nature be universally applied to oppressed groups in China, Sudan, and Iran; it also has major practical consequences for religious pluralism in the United States.

America's religious life is strikingly different today from what it was when the Constitution was signed. Today a throng of competing and sometimes clashing worldviews can be found on every street corner. Some find American religious variety exhilarating; some find it exhausting (how many parades can one city have in a year?); some find it an invigorating challenge to be heard over the din. But if Americans wish to preserve their liberties, pluralism must be acknowledged as the inevitable result of a human good—religious freedom.

How would America's pluralistic public square look under this understanding of religious freedom? Like Jersey City under former mayor Bret Schundler. Jersey City is one of the most ethnically and culturally diverse cities in America. There are scores of different ethnicities represented in the city's population. And under Mayor Schundler there were nearly constant celebrations of one cultural tradition or another: flag raisings, parades, festivals, and displays—including a menorah for Hanukkah, a nativity scene for Christmas, a proclamation of Ramadan, and a parade in honor of the Hindu Festival of Lights.

A time-lapse photographer would catch it all, and anybody who saw that time-lapse photograph would realize that the government was not pushing Hinduism or Islam, Judaism or Christianity, any more than it was pushing the alleged superiority of one or another ethnicity. It was simply recognizing the cultures of the society it served. Here, religion and culture were not separated; they were treated as intertwined, complementary expressions of human desires, much like ethnicity in culture. This is exactly how government ought to treat religion in culture. Constitutionally, religion and ethnicity hold similar places. The establishment clause bars preferential treatment of religions just as the equal protection clause bars preferential treatment of ethnicities. But Anglophiles do not bring lawsuits objecting to St. Patrick's Day parades; the courts are not clogged every February with brouhahas over whether Black History Month is an unconstitutional affront to white Americans. And the reason for this civil peace is simple: no one in his right mind thinks the St. Patrick's Day parade is an Irish supremacist plot, or Black History Month a racial power grab. Everybody knows they are cultural celebrations with ethnic elements. The same should be true of holiday displays with religious elements.

That is the model that logically follows from who human beings really are. True pluralism can only follow from authentic religious liberty. And authentic religious liberty must be based on an accurate understanding of the human person.

The Jersey City model is the most threatening one for the regimes that seek to repress religion, because it proclaims that repression is profoundly opposed to human nature. But this model is also the most threatening one for those who seek to use the power of the state to impose their own religious or antireligious visions, for the very same reason; and it is threatening to all those who seek to make religion something you do in private, almost in secret. So it has a lot of opponents. But it proclaims the truth about the human hunger for transcendence—both vertical and horizontal—from China to Jersey City.

Afterword

Looking Forward:
From Jewish Interest to
Judaic Principle

Jonathan Sacks

Readers of these collected essays will come away, as have I, impressed by their depth, vigor, and erudition. They will have learned about American Jewish voting patterns (they "earn like Episcopalians but vote like Puerto Ricans"). They will have discovered something, too, about ingrained Jewish distrust of governments, born of long and bitter experience especially in Eastern Europe ("God keep the Czar—a long way from me"). They will have learned that Jews believe in the Jeffersonian separation of religion and state. They will have discovered (from Michael Broyde) that Jewish law imposes no obligation of Jews to ensure that non-Jews observe the Noahide laws and that therefore they are mandated, (a) to disengage from politics and (b) when forced to give an opinion should prefer a minimalist state with maximalist individual freedoms. They will, in short, have gained insight into the shifting ways in which American Jews have seen their interests served, first by left-wing politics of a Roosevelt kind, now perhaps by a more conservative dispensation conducive to the maintenance of group identity and certain shared moral standards. All these things are interesting and I for one have gained from them.

There is, however, a distinction worth making. There are Jews, and there is Judaism. We know, through many of the essays in this book, how Jews behave when they come to vote and express political opinions. Others, notably Alan Mittleman, David Novak, Elliot Dorff, and William Galston, address themselves to a quite different question: What of Judaism? Does it have something to say about our present political predicaments or the proper direction of our social endeavors? To be sure, there may be Judaisms rather than a single essentialist entity, "Judaism." Alasdair MacIntrye reminds us that "Traditions, which vital, embody continuities of conflict"[1]—a characterization particularly apt in the case of Judaism, many of whose key texts are in fact anthologies of arguments. But Jews, if they are to have something distinctive to say in the public square, must be more than an ethnic group with a history of suffering, whose political stances reflect that experience. If they are no more than Episcopalians who were once Puerto Ricans, we should not expect anything especially noteworthy in their political involvements.

But that is clearly not all they are. Whether or not they embrace it, Jews are carriers of one of the oldest and most distinctive religious traditions of all: the world's first monotheism, which in turn gave rise to Christianity and Islam, representing today the faith of more than half of the six billion people on the face of the earth. Judaism has a family resemblance to its two daughter religions, but it also differs from them in salient ways, not least in its view of politics, society, and the nature of mankind. There is more to a Judaic politics than the political behavior of American Jews.

Is there a Judaic view (or set of views, a debate, a faith that has something to say about the *polis* or is it rather about salvation and the private communion of the soul with democracies of the contemporary West or the radical individualism of its postmodern culture? Are they a consummation devoutly to be wished, or a sad falling away from an older and more morally vigorous tradition? There is, in other words, a story to be told, not about the shifting orientation of Jewish interests but rather about the politics of Judaic principle—of Judaism considered as a religious faith.

This is all the more compelling given the luminous fact that Judaism is from the beginning a deeply political faith and a revolutionary one. Its foundational moments are inherently political. There is the exodus which, as Michael Walzer has shown,[2] has been the inspiration of many, if not most, of the revolutionary movements of modern times. There is the giving of the Torah at Sinai when the Israelites, hitherto a group of escaping slaves, became a body politic through the making of a covenant which constituted them as a nation under the sovereignty of God, whose written constitution was the Torah and whose interpretation throughout the ages was one of the primary religious acts. In this concluding chapter, therefore, I reflect on the core Judaic project, namely the construction of a society based on retributive and distributive justice—*mishpat* and *tzedakah* respectively—under whose spacious canopy human beings might enjoy freedom and dignity, life, liberty, and pursuit of holiness.

The historical significance of this story in an American context lies in the fact that the new nation's founding fathers consciously built their hopes on the Hebrew Bible. They were familiar with its words. They constructed their earliest compacts on the model of the biblical covenant.[3] They believed that in escaping from England they were like the Israelites on their journey through the wilderness in search of a promised land. As Herman put it in *White-Jacket* (1849):

> We American are the peculiar, chosen people—the Israel of our time; we bear the ark of the liberties of the world God has predestined, mankind expects great things from our race; and great things we feel in our souls. We are pioneers of the world; the advance guard, sent on through the wilderness of untried things, to break a new path in the New World that is ours.[4]

As late as 1965, President Lyndon B. Johnson could echo this idea in his inaugural address: "They came here—the exile and the stranger, brave but frightened—to find a place where a man could be his own man. They made a covenant with this land. Conceived in justice, written in liberty, bound in union, it was meant one day to inspire the hopes of all mankind; and it binds us still."[5] The French and Russian revolutions were based on philosophical systems; the American enterprise was driven by the narrative of the Hebrew Bible, encountered and interpreted by the Puritans.

The founders of America understood, more than many Jews today, that Judaism in its canonical expressions does not mean being liberal, pro-abortion, voting Democrat, supporting the ACLU, privatizing virtue, or giving primacy, in John Rawls's phrase, to the right over the good. They knew that biblical Judaism was one of the most remarkable attempts to establish a free society worthy of becoming a home to the Divine presence, an arena of societal beatitude. When non-Jews sense more accurately than many Jews "what the Lord our God requires of us" we are in the presence of a phenomenon that needs explanation.

The Tragedy of Jewish Modernity

The explanation is not far to find. Jews were not merely "latecomers" to modernity. They were also its primary victims. Having suffered for centuries under Christian and Islamic rule, with neither civil rights nor political enfranchisement, they believed that with the coming of the secular nation state—alongside European enlightenment and emancipation—they would at last be free and equal. Understandably they felt that they were witnessing the millennial fulfillment of a prophetic dream. The 1885 Pittsburgh Platform of the American Reform movement said so explicitly: "We recognize, in the modern era of universal culture of heart and intellect, the approaching of the realization of Israel's great messianic hope." This was an American statement, but its equivalent could be heard in virtually every other center of Jewish life, especially in Germany. To be sure, Jews knew there would be a price for this freedom. The Count of Clermont-Tonnerre spelled it out in the debate on the eligibility of Jews for citizenship in the French National Assembly in 1789: "The Jews should be denied everything as a nation, but granted everything as individuals." He went on to add, ominously, that "if they do not want this, they must inform us and we shall then be compelled to expel them."[6]

The disappointment of these hopes is one of the most tragic chapters of modern history. Enlightenment did not cure anti-Semitism. It would be more accurate to say that it created it (the word "anti-Semitism" itself was coined in Germany in 1879). The centuries-old Christian hostility to Jews and Judaism mutated into a new and devastating secular counterpart. Whereas in the past Jews had been hated for what they believed and did, now they were hated for what they were. Race did duty for what had once been the work of religion. The result was an anti-Jewish prejudice that was truly protean. Jews were hated because they were capitalists and communists; because they were rich and because they were poor; because they were uneducated and over-educated; because they kept to themselves and because they were everywhere; because they clung to an ancient faith and because they were "rootless cosmopolitans." Already in 1895 the Viennese journalist Theodor Herzl, in Paris covering the Dreyfus trial, had seen the specter of rampant anti-Semitism (the crowd crying "*Mort aux Juifs*") in the very home of the revolution, France itself. Within a year he had come to the conclusion that there was no future for the Jews in Europe. If the new nation-state had no room for Jews, Jews would have to have a nation-state of their own. Thus was Zionism born out of the failure of European emancipation.

The course of modern Jewish politics is inseparable from this night-mare, whose denouement in the Holocaust exceeded even Herzl's worst fears. From then on, two scenarios dominated the Jewish world. One lay in the construction of a Jewish state in the ancestral homeland of the Jewish people. The other was the reconstitution of Jewish life in the United States where, if Jews were immigrants, so too was everyone else. The great hope of America was that it had no history of state-endorsed religious persecution for the simple reason that it was con-structed by men and women who traveled to the shore to escape reli-gious persecution. Jews sensed, not wrongly, that there was a deep kinship between their own experience and that of the many other groups who had come to shape a new society in the new world. The overriding Jewish question in the late nineteenth and early twentieth centuries was not, where can we live as Jews, but where can we live. It was a time not for the articulation of a Jewish political philosophy, but for sheer survival.

Today, however, that period is behind us. Anti-Semitism has not ceased. Instead it has undergone a metamorphosis into anti-Zionism, as like and unlike its predecessor as racial anti-Semitism itself was to ear-lier religious anti-Judaism. Yet the political situation of Jews has changed out of all recognition, and this for two reasons. The first is that, however besieged and isolated, there is today a thriving Jewish state in the Land of Israel. This affects not only the Jews who live there, but all Jews everywhere. They have, and know they have, a home in the Robert Frost sense, as the place where "when you have to go there, they have to let you in." Jewish politics worldwide has been liberated from the fear that there may be nowhere else to go.

The second difference lies in the demographic and cultural compo-sition of the West's liberal democracies themselves. Jews are no longer the most conspicuous minority. In a non-Jewish school in South London, which I visited while writing this chapter, there were no Jew-ish students. There were, however, children from almost every other faith community, speaking thirty-eight different first languages. What was significant about the encounter was that its theme was the Holo-caust. Two of the pupils, one African, the other an Asian Muslim, spoke movingly about their visit to Auschwitz and how deeply they identified with the Jewish experience. The school, precisely because of its racial and religious mix, had internalized the lessons of the Holo-caust and was using it to teach tolerance, respect for diversity, and the obligation to resist evil. The occasion reconfirmed what I long ago discovered: that there is a difference between a Judaic voice and a

Jewish vote. A Jewish vote is exercised by Jews. A Judaic voice is often sought and heeded by non-Jews as well.

Jews therefore face two political situations for which there is no obvious precedent, at any rate in the past two thousand years. The first, which exists in the State of Israel, is the opportunity to construct a macro-society on Jewish lines. The second exists in the diaspora, made possible by the demise of two earlier conceptions of society. One—the assimilationist or melting-pot model—envisaged the eventual integration of all minorities into a single dominant cultural (if not religious) pattern. The second—the libertarian model of the sovereign self[7]—saw substantive identities as lying outside the political arena. They are simply the lifestyle choices of individuals in the private domain.[8] In neither of these was a Jewish voice salient in the public square, either because it represented the not-yet assimilated identity of first- and second-generation immigrants, or because religion had no public case to make. It was simply something you did at home or in church or synagogue and left behind when you spoke to your fellow citizens on matters of common concern. Often, Jews clung to these models, even though they threatened Jewish identity and continuity, because they promised anonymity at a time when any Jewish visibility seemed fraught with danger. As the philosopher Sidney Morgenbesser once put it: Jewish identity in the modern world could be summed up in the words *incognito ergo sum*.

But that age has passed. Today's liberal democracies are multi-ethnic, multi-faith, and consciously pluralist. There has been much debated as to what political discourse should be like and how policies should be framed in the presence of such diversity. To enter this argument go beyond the confines of this volume, but this much can and should be said: Despite Rawlsian demurrers,[9] no politics can be purely procedural. Each nation, state, and polity embodies a vision, collectively arrived at, of the moral universe of which it is a part and to whose values it aspires. That vision is less product than process, the results of an ongoing conversation between the members of society on how best to conceptualize and realize the common good. In a plural society, this conversation is scored for many voices, each with its own distinctive accent to bring, and its unique contribution to make, to the public square.

The very nature of the democratic conversation in complex societies imposes limitations and restraints. Each of us knows that we cannot hope, nor should we try, to impose our own vision of the good on others. Jews, Christians, and Muslims may not attempt to turn the United States, for example, into a Jewish or Christian or Muslim state, for that would exclude others and breach the very terms of the social contract. Nor, when we speak in the public domain, may we do so in narrowly confessional terms, using terms or proof-texts inaccessible to those of other faiths. We must use something like what Rawls calls "the language of public reason."[10] We must aim, in other words, to be intelligible to people who are not members of our community of faith. Neither of these things should prove difficult for Jews or, for that matter, for other religious believers. The question before us is therefore: What can a Judaic voice bring to the shared conversation of liberal democratic societies in late modernity?

Interests and Principles

To answer this adequately we must be mindful of three distinctions. The first has already been alluded to, namely the difference between Jewish interests and Judaic principle. In British Jewry these have different institutional embodiments. The Board of Deputies, established in 1760, defends Jewish interests. The Chief Rabbinate, which dates back to 1691, articulates Judaic principle. The former speaks on behalf of Jews, the latter on behalf of Judaism. The two often converge, but not always. In the early 1990s, for example, the British government was considering deregulating Sunday trading. The proposal was that shops, hitherto closed on the Christian Sabbath, should be allowed to open. The legislation was clearly favorable to Jewish interests. It made observance of Shabbat easier. Jews could now shop, and in some cases work, on a day not holy to them. Considered from the vantage point of Jewish values, however, the case was less clear. The Sabbath was an institution taken over by Christianity from Judaism, though it is observed on a different day. Enshrined in the law of the land, it made an important statement about the limits of wealth and power as the basis of citizenship.[11] My late predecessor, Lord Jakobovits, who by that time sat in the House of Lords, and I took the view that we should support our Christian colleagues in defense of their holy day. The result—paradoxical but not unreasonable—is that the Jewish community was both in favor and against the proposed legislation, because it considered it from two different perspectives. That is what political debate is like on complex issues and it would be reductivist to wish it otherwise. The distinction, however, is fundamental. Interest is one thing, principle, another, and they generate different kinds of politics.

The second is the truism that not every free society is the United States. There is a widespread assumption, certainly among American

Jews, that religious freedom and dignity depend on the constitutional separation of church and state. They therefore find it difficult to understand that a country like England, which has an established Church, might nevertheless be a tolerant and benign environment for Jews. Yet that has been the English experience. In some respects English Jews have been more prominent in politics than their American counterparts. There was a time, for example, under Prime Minister Margaret Thatcher, when Jews held a fifth of Cabinet positions (prompting the Waspish comment of the late Harold Macmillan that the government contained "more old Estonians than old Etonians"). Under her successor, John Major, two Jews were simultaneously Home and Foreign Secretary. Two of the past three Lord Chief Justices have been Jews. Jewish day schools, as Gertrude Himmelfarb notes, receive financial support from the government. There is an official Jewish presence at state events, and so on. The point is simply that different nations find their own way to create space for a multiplicity of religious groups to feel that they belong, are valued, and are heard. The First Amendment is the American way, but not the only way.

Finally, we should not expect ancient religious traditions to provide precise and unequivocal guidance on contemporary political dilemmas. That is not what they are about nor should we seek it from them. Politics lives in the present, religion in eternity. Politics makes a virtue of compromise, religion of absolutes. What a great faith can bring to the democratic conversation is a set of values and a vision, narratives of memory and hope, and a sense of responsibility to the past and future. It can remind us of the moral limits of power, the sanctity of human life, the nonnegotiable dignity of the human person, and the humane and humanizing institutions—among them the family and the community—without which our commitment to the common good may atrophy and fail. Religion takes its place, alongside the ballot box and the marketplace, as one of the matrices of our common life. It is a culture-shaping force rather than a set of policy prescriptions and should be valued for what it is, not sidelined for what it is not and could not aspire to be.

When Thomas Jefferson and his coauthors sat down in 1776 to frame the American Declaration of Independence they wrote a memorable sentence: "We hold these truths to be self-evident, that all men are created equal, that they are endowed by their Creator with certain unalienable Rights, that among these are Life, Liberty and the pursuit of Happiness." What is striking is that these truths are anything but self-evident. They have been denied by most societies for much of human history. They would have been incomprehensible to Plato, who believed that people were not created equal (they belong to three classes: common people, soldiers, and guardians), and equally to Aristotle who held that while some were born to be free, others were born to be slaves. Whatever the provenance of the Declaration of Independence in seventeenth- and eighteenth-century Enlightenment thought, its ultimate origin lies in the Hebrew Bible, the most influential political text in Western civilization, and the most neglected.

It has been the fate of the Bible to be seen as a "religious" text for several centuries during which, for the West, religious has meant: pertaining to the inner life of the soul and the private domain of family and community. The Reformation, in the political thought of Luther and Calvin, added impetus to the long, slow separation of religion and state whose supreme expression is the First Amendment. Whatever religion is or should be in the West, it is not political. That at any rate has been the orthodoxy of the past several centuries and there is much to be said for it. It is one thing to construct a community of fellow believers on the basis of shared ideals, quite another to build a society of many faiths and cultures, each leaving space for the other. This has tended to privatize religion and cast politics as an inherently secular pursuit.[12] Thus conceived, politics has its origins in the Greek city-states of the fifth and fourth centuries BCE, the Athens of Plato and Aristotle in particular.

There is, however, a different story to be told. That is what I want to do here: in summary form to chart the main features of the biblical tradition in politics, not merely as an antiquarian exercise but as a source for contemporary thought. As Quentin Skinner reminds us: "The intellectual historian can help us to appreciate how far the values embedded in our present way of life, and our present ways of thinking about those values, reflect a series of choices made at different times between different possible worlds." Historical reflection gives us, in his phrase, a "a broader sense of possibility."[13] That is certainly true of the biblical heritage, a quite different, less systematic but no less profound set of reflections than those of ancient Greece as to what we seek when we join together to create the collaborative project called society.

Revelation and Revolution

Any systematic political philosophy begins with an anthropology, a theory of mankind, the human person and our place in the universe. In the case of Judaism it begins with a phrase, perhaps the most consequential in the history of the West: the declaration, in the first chapter of Genesis, that the human person was created "in the image and likeness" of God. What are the political implications of this phrase?

The first is a radical egalitarianism. The idea that human beings might be in the image of God was not new to the ancient world. Kings, rulers, tyrants, emperors, and pharaohs were often believed to be gods, or the children of gods, or the gods' representative on earth. What is utterly new in Genesis is the belief that this is true not of one person but of all. It is hard to overstate the significance of this idea. Here, if anywhere, are the first intimations in history of a free society, of human dignity and the sanctity of life and perhaps even democracy itself, not as one way among others of structuring society but as an ethical ideal. Here certainly is the provenance of the phrase in the Declaration "that all men are created equal, [and] that they are endowed by their Creator with certain unalienable Rights."

Equally significant is the decisive break with a certain kind of politics, sometimes termed organic or cosmological. The earliest societies were formed with the birth of agriculture, which in turn gave rise to settled populations, the division of labor, and the growth of trade. For the first time individuals were able to accumulate substantial surpluses, and economic inequality made its first appearance on the human stage. The city-states and empires of the ancient world were hierarchical, under the supreme governance of a ruler, a court, and an administrative class. The stability of this order was based on more than power alone. It was believed to lie in the very structure of the universe. Just as there was a hierarchy among the heavenly bodies and the elemental forces which held sway over nature, so there was among human beings on earth. Sociology was the mirror of cosmology. The shape of human society—its rulers and ruled, leaders and led—was written into the architecture of reality. Hierarchy was no mere human artifice. It was a law of nature. Shakespeare has left us an immortal description of such politics:

The heavens themselves, the planets, and this centre,
Observe degree, priority, and place,
Insisture, course, proportion, season, form.
Office, and custom, in all line of order . . .
Take but degree away, untune that string,
And, hark, what discord follows![14]

In organic societies rank, status, and privilege—the division of mankind into masters and slaves, patricians and plebeians, feudal lords and serfs—are givens of birth, part of the natural order or divinely ordained destiny. Thus Calvin argues that "each individual has his own kind of living assigned to him by the Lord."[15] In a similar vein the sixteenth-century Puritan William Perkins says that "persons are distinguished by order, whereby God hath appointed, that in every society one person should be above or under another; not making all equal, as though the body should be all head and nothing else."[16] Even in the late nineteenth century F. H. Bradley could speak of "my station and its duties." The idea that hierarchy is embedded in the metaphysics of the social world is one of the most tenacious in civilization.

What is revolutionary in the Hebrew Bible is the idea that God is not within nature and subject to its laws but beyond nature, and the creator of its laws. Thus is born the concept of the will and its associated ideas: choice, agency, and moral responsibility. By making mankind in His image, God endows the human person with these same attributes, exercised, to be sure, in the context of finitude and mortality, but real nevertheless. There is nothing given, fated, or inexorable about the societies human beings create. We are not merely the products of our environment; we are also its creators. We are called on to become, in the rabbinic phrase, God's "partners in the work of creation." The result is to strip all political dispensations of their supposed grounding in a hierarchical universe. There is nothing inevitable or preordained about social status: "He raises the poor from the dust and lifts the needy from the ash-heap; he seats them with princes and has them inherit a throne of honour."[17] Divine transcendence revitalizes all social structures. They are not given but made, and can be unmade.

This is the significance of ancient Israel's foundational experience, the exodus from Egypt and liberation from slavery. The drama of the encounter between God and pharaoh is precisely that between human freedom and dignity and the power structures of the ancient world. The Egypt of Ramses II, identified by some scholars as the pharaoh of the exodus, was the most powerful and long-lived of its time. That God might intervene as an actor in history, that He might not endorse but overthrow a social structure, above all that He identified not with power but the powerless, not with a ruler but with a group of slaves; these were astonishing ideas and have endured across the centuries as the West's single most influential meta-narrative of liberty.

The ongoing political project of the Hebrew Bible—subject to countless setbacks and false turns but never lost as an ideal—is the construction of a society that honors the equal dignity of human beings in the image, and under the sovereignty, of God. As Norman Gottwald puts it, the God worshipped by Israel was:

The historically concretized, primordial power to establish and sustain social equality in the face of counter-oppression from without and against provincial and non-egalitarian tendencies from within the society. Israel thought it was different because it was different: it constituted an egalitarian social system in the midst of stratified societies.[18]

Or as the prophet Micah envisioned his utopia, in the eighth century BCE:

Every man will sit under his own vine
And under his own fig-tree,
And no-one will make them afraid,
For the Lord almighty has spoken.[19]

Independence and Interdependence

What then of the human person? The opening chapters of Genesis present two portraits of humanity, the conflict between which frames the political dilemma. In Genesis 1, the human individual per se is described as a being in the image of God. In Genesis 2, we hear the proposition that "It is not good for man to be alone." The tension is articulated at the outset, therefore, between human independence and interdependence. On the one hand, the individual is endowed with metaphysical dignity. On the other, he or she is existentially incomplete. At the core of the human situation is the question of relationship. How do two or more persons relate in such a way as to honor the freedom of the other while generating the mutual trust on which collaborative activity depends?

The problem is resolved in its most rudimentary form with the creation of the "other" in Genesis 2, in this case woman. The man (*ha-adam*) wakes to find that he is no longer alone and utters a poem of recognition:

This is now bone of my bone and flesh of my flesh:
She shall be called "woman: [*ishah*] for she was taken
from man [*me-ish*].[20]

The Hebrew text contains a nuance at this point—lost in translation—whose significance is immense. Until now, man has been described as *adam* (that which is taken from the soil, *adamah*). This verse is the first time man is called *ish* (person, personality, human subject). The man must first pronounce the name of woman before he can pronounce his own name. He must be able to say "Thou" before he can say "I." We are, in John MacMurray's phrase, "persons in relation."[21] The encounter with otherness is chronologically and ontologically prior to the discovery of self.

Already implicit at the start of the biblical narrative is a vision of the human situation fundamentally at odds with two of the dominant political traditions of the West. The first is the view that the state is prior to the person, the collectivity to the individual. Against this, Judaism consistently maintains that the state exists to serve mankind, not mankind the state. It is a rejection of totalitarian social orders. The second, essential to the liberal tradition from Hobbes and Locke to John Rawls, is that the individual is an atomic self, prior to his or her roles and relationships. Against this, Judaism sees the individual as embedded in a network of constitutive attachments. In Michael Sandel's justly celebrated formulation, we enter the political domain as "members of this family or community or nation or people, as bearers of this history, as sons and daughters of that revolution, as citizens of this republic." We are not "unsituated selves":

> To imagine a person incapable of constitutive attachments such as these is not to conceive an ideally free and rational agent, but to imagine a person wholly without character, without moral depth. For to have character is to know that I move in a history I neither summon nor command, which carries consequences none the less for my choices and conduct.[22]

This view, that the "Thou" precedes the "I," that the self is born out of the dialogue with others and that the primary human domain is neither objective nor subjective but inter-subjective, chimes with and anticipates the sociology of G. H. Mead and the Wittgenstein of the *Philosophical Investigations*, with its attack on the concept of a private language and its emphasis (in contradistinction to John Locke) on the essentially shared world of meanings.

The Matrices of Sociality

The Book of Genesis does not begin with a state, nation, or people. After its account of the archetypal figures of humanity as such (Adam and Eve, Cain and Abel, Noah and the Flood) it narrows its attention to the story of a single family (Abraham and Sarah) and their descendants, a family which becomes a tribe and then a collection of tribes.

Genesis is the prehistory of Israel as a nation, and the existence of this prehistory has political implications.

The family is the primary social unit in Judaism. It is there that the Israelites perform their first religious ritual—the Passover—before leaving Egypt. It is there that education—the conversation between the generations—takes place: "You shall teach these things diligently to your children, speaking about them when you sit at home or walk on the way, when you lie down and when you rise up."[23] The covenant between God and Abraham, the moral bond that frames the identity of a people, is construed in familiar terms: "For I have chosen him," says God, "so that he will direct his children and his household after him to keep the way of the Lord by doing what is right and just."[24] The family is, for the Hebrew Bible, where we learn the grammar of reciprocity, the syntax and semantics of concern for the other. It is where we acquire the lineaments of continuity, of fidelity to the past and responsibility for the future; where we discover where we came from and of which narrative we are a part. Society itself, with its obligations of care for the needy and compassion for the suffering, is envisaged by the Bible as an extended family: "when your brother [i.e., your fellow citizen] becomes poor."[25]

Equally, the community plays a significant part in Jewish life. Ancient Israel is portrayed, from the book of Exodus to the age of kings, not as a primordial entity but as a group of tribes, each of which, with the exception of the Levites, has its own territory and autonomy. During the period of the judges Israel was an amphictyony, or loose tribal federation, an arrangement briefly superseded by the institution of monarch until, after three kings, the nation divided into two along tribal lines.

During the Second Temple period, as the legitimacy of the Hasmonean kings began to be questioned, and especially after the destruction of the Temple itself, Judaism developed strong communal institutions—the synagogue, the school, and the house of study—which allowed it to survive and sustain its identity during the long centuries of exile. The most important conceptual leap was the idea of community (*edah, tsibbur*) itself: that wherever ten adult males assembled, the Jewish nation was reconstituted in microcosm. Its prayers substituted for the sacrifices once offered in Jerusalem. Its house of worship (*bet knesset*, literally, "home of the congregation") was a minor temple. Jewry became a global nation, constituted not by territory but by laws. Its political structure was unique: a community of communities, dispersed across the globe, linked by a covenant of mutual responsibility (*kol Yisrael arevin zeh bazeh*, "all Jews are sureties for one an-other").[26]

The political theorist who comes closest to the Judaic understand-ing of society is Althusius, a transitional thinker between Bodin and Hobbes, and more broadly between the biblical heritage and the mod-ern state. In his *Politica* (1603) he argued that the polity or common-wealth is a compound political association formed by the coming to-gether of other primary associations, among them families, guilds, and voluntary groups, and larger complexes such as cities and provinces. The state, in other words, is not an entity imposed by a ruler or an elite. It is established by consent, on the basis of preexisting political institutions smaller and more local than the state.[27]

Recently, thinkers have paid renewed attention to the role of fami-lies, communities, and voluntary associations as significant elements in the political landscape. Together, they represent a "third sector" mediating between the individual and the state. Communitarian think-ers on the one hand, "civil society" theorists on the other have recalled Burke's "little platoons," Alexis de Tocqueville's "habits of associa-tion," and Peter Berger's "mediating structures" as converging insights into the importance of small, face-to-face institutions in generating relationships of trust, reciprocal altruism, and "social capital." Fami-lies and communities are the primary agents of socialization, the "seedbeds of virtue,"[28] and without them individuals are left vulner-able and exposed to the impersonal workings of the state and the mar-ket. This new politics, with roots both in the conservative right and the liberal left, has a profound kinship with both biblical narrative and the post-biblical experience of diaspora Jewry.

Social Contract

At this point, we must leap forward in time to the first fully articulated system of national government in biblical Israel, the creation of mon-archy. Throughout, the Hebrew Bible is ambivalent about monarchy, and the medieval Bible commentators and jurists were divided as to its place in the framework of Jewish values. Maimonides saw it as an ob-ligation, Ibn Ezra as a permission, Abraham as a concession. When the people come to the prophet and priest Samuel and ask him to appoint a king, God tells him this is a rejection of Divine sovereignty ("It is not you they have rejected as their king, but Me"), but that he must do what they ask. First, though, he must warn them of the consequences of their choice. Samuel does so.

"This is what the king who will reign over you will do: He will take your sons and make them serve with his chariots and horses, and they will run in front of his chariots. He will take your daughters to be perfumers and cooks and bakers. He will take the best of your fields and vineyards and olive groves, and give them to his attendants. . . . When that day comes, you cry out for relief from the king you have chosen, and the Lord will not answer you in that day."[29]

The people nonetheless insist that they wish for a king, and Samuel duly anoints Saul.

Biblical scholars, struck by the ambivalence of the biblical account, resolve it by attributing it to two or more different authors, one sympathetic to, the other critical of, monarchy. This, however, is to misunderstand the nature of the political process involved. As the nineteenth-century scholar Rabbi Zvi Hirsch Chajes, correctly points out, the creation of a king in the Book of Samuel is the enactment of a Hobbesian social contract.[30] The people cede certain of their rights of property and person to a central power so that he may conduct battles on their behalf. Evidently, as in the Hobbesian scenario, they believed it in their interests to do so. Without a national army or government— "In those days Israel had no king; everyone did as he saw fit"[31]—life for the Israelites may well have been "nasty, brutish and short"—not because Israel in the days of the judges was in a "state of nature" but because, surrounded by external enemies, it was subject to the continuous risk and reality of attack.

What the biblical account registers is the real—if necessary—cost of government in terms of freedom of person and property. Ideally, suggests the Bible, Israel should live without the Leviathan of a coercive state under the sacred canopy of its trust in God. From time to time, as need arose, an individual would emerge to fight its battles, as happened in the days of the judges. The people, placing their faith "neither in might nor in power but in My spirit,"[32] would triumph over superior forces. They would attribute their victories to God and their defeats to moral, not military, failings. They would live in as close as possible to a society of equals in which none had political power over others.

The Hebrew Bible is unintelligible without a sense of the depth of its conviction that empires and city-states, with their division into rich and poor, rulers and ruled, are a profound offense against the human condition and the equal dignity of all. All power, therefore, is to be governed by consent and kept to a minimum. To be a servant of God is to be free of servitude to man. The state, therefore, is not the supreme expression of collective human existence but a necessary compromise of personal liberty for the sake of survival. It carries with it constant risks of the corruption of power and the oppression of the powerless. That is the burden of the prophets, the world's first divinely ordained social critics.[33] The state is brought into being by social contract, and its authority is limited to pursuit of the common good.

Social Covenant

The Book of Samuel has historical interest as the first recorded instance of a social contract bringing into being a mode of national governance. What is truly original in the biblical narrative, however, is that this is only the second act in the drama by which Israel becomes a nation. It is the first act which constitutes the Bible's enduring contribution to the concept of a free society. This was the revelation at Mount Sinai, by which Israel became a body politic under the sovereignty of God. Sinai was not a social contract but a social *covenant*.

The broad outlines of the story are well-known. God had rescued a people from slavery. Now, in the wilderness, He proposes a form of ongoing relationship. He tells Moses to say the following to the assembled people:

> You yourselves have seen what I did to Egypt, and how I carried you on eagle's wings and brought you to Myself. Now if you obey Me fully and keep My covenant, then out of all nations you will be My treasured possession. Although the whole world is Mine, you will be for Me a kingdom of priests and a holy nation.[34]

The Israelites assent and God then speaks the Ten Commandments, followed by detailed prescriptions conveyed to Moses. The people then reaffirm the terms of the relationships.

The concept of covenant (*brit*) is one of Judaism's greatest contributions to political thought. Historians have pointed out that it owes its origin, and some of its formulaic features, to the international treaties common in the ancient Near East, usually between stronger (suzerain) and weaker (vassal) states, by which the latter pledge their loyalty to the former in return for protection. In the Bible, however, it is transformed into something grander and more visionary.

In the first instance, one of the parties to the agreement is God Himself. It would have been unthinkable by any ancient or even later theologies that the supreme power might bind Himself to a quasi-contractual relationship with human beings. Not only does He do so at

Sinai, but (in contradistinction to earlier covenants with Noah and Abraham, for example) He invites their active consent. Not until the people have signaled their agreement does He proceed. The implication is radical: there can be no legitimate government without (in the phrase used in the American Declaration of Independence) the consent of the governed, *even when the governor is creator of heaven and earth.* God Himself cannot rule a people without their agreement. The reason lies deep in the foundations of biblical theology. A free God desires the free worship of free human beings. There is no alternative if persons are to achieve their full stature as responsible moral agents. As with contract so with covenant: what is essential is respect for the integrity of the will, freely exercised, of both parties. A politics of freedom must be grounded, not in hierarchies of power, wealth, or birth, but in uncoerced consent. No more dramatic example exists than the moment in which God, having led His people to freedom, exercises self-limitation so that the people are free to accept or reject His rule.

No less radical is that the second party to the covenant is not, as it was in other ancient treaties, a king or leader but the entire people. The Bible repeatedly emphasizes that it was "all the people" who were addressed and gave their consent.[35] Significantly, when the ten commandments were given, Moses was not on the mountain alone, but among the people at its base. Later, when the Bible prescribes a seven-yearly covenant reaffirmation ceremony, it specifies that everyone ("men, women and children and the stranger within the gate")[36] should be present. This is not democracy—rule of the people by the people— but it points toward something no less profound, namely, that all the members of a society have a share in its constitution. Each has inalienable dignity as a citizen under the sovereignty of God. This is an idea unknown to Athenian democracy and its successors until recently, all of which restricted the full exercise of citizenship to certain (essentially property owning) classes. For the Bible citizenship is not conferred on the basis of what one owns but what one is, a being in the image of God and thus capable of self-governance.

Perhaps the most significant feature of the covenant, however, is that it transcends particular modes of governance. Immediately prior to the revelation at Mount Sinai we read of Israel's first system of government, suggested by the non-Israelite Jethro, namely of "rulers of thousands, hundreds, fifties and tens" exercising power delegated by Moses. Israel, and later Jewry, were to experience many and varied forms of government, by elders, prophets, judges, kings, patriarchs, exilarchs, and two councils. Above them all, however, was the covenant itself, specifying Israel's terms of reference as a nation constituted by its relationship with God and bound by His laws. Political structures are temporary, but the covenant is eternal. At different times in history and varying circumstances in the life of a nation, different modes of governance may be appropriate, but one thing does not change: the fundamental definition of its vocation, the moral-spiritual project that accompanied its birth as a body politic.

It was Alexis de Tocqueville who coined the phrase, later quoted to great effect by John Stuart Mill, "the tyranny of the majority." Democracy, the rule of the majority, does not in and of itself guarantee the rights of the minority. Nor does it contain the most significant defense of freedom, namely, a coherent theory of the *moral limits of power*. That is what is achieved by the Sinai covenant with its nonnegotiable Thou shalt's and Thou shall not's. All power, delegated by the people to a central authority, is bounded by the fundamental commandments of the covenant. Any breach of these rules is necessarily ultra vires. Covenant is prior to contract. It sets boundaries, essentially those respecting life, liberty, property, the family, and the rule of justice. Within these, the people may choose how and by whom they wish to be governed. Beyond them, there is no legitimate authority, however elected. Thus was born yet another phrase of the American Declaration of Independence, the concept of *unalienable rights*.

Covenant is one of the great, and neglected, political ideas. In the words of one of its contemporary exponents, Philip Selznick:

> Faith based on covenant might be called a constitutional faith. In so-called federal theology, the foundation of religious belief and commitment is a giving and receiving of promises. The parties are not equal. They both act, however, as responsible agents whose word is their bond. Covenant creates expectations that the divine sovereign will act reasonably and without injustice. Bound by His word, God is no despot. For their part, the covenanted people accept subordination with dignity, as free persons entering a sacred compact; they are not debased, degraded or enslaved.[37]

The clearest example of a covenant in modern times is the American Declaration of Independence (1776), preceding the Constitution by some thirteen years. Unlike the Constitution, it did not spell out the details of the government by which the citizens of America were to be ruled. Rather, it established their moral parameters as a nation. That is one of the differences between covenants and contracts. Contracts are usually limited to terms made explicit in the agreement. Covenants are more open-ended. They define—and by defining—create a moral bond that brings an association into being. They are couched in broader and

more moral terms than a contract. They are less to do with the pursuit
of self-interest, more to do with a vision of the common good, the
good that exists in virtue of being shared with others. Selznick quotes
John Schaar's summation of Lincoln's view of America's self-
definition:

> We are a nation formed by a covenant, by dedication to a set of prin-
> ciples and by an exchange of promises to uphold and advance certain
> commitments among ourselves and throughout the world. Those prin-
> ciples and commitments are the core of American identity, the soul of
> the body politic. They make the American nation unique, and uniquely
> valuable, among and to the other nations. But the other side of the
> conception contains a warning, very like the warnings spoken by the
> prophets to Israel: if we fail in our promises to each other, and lose
> the principles of the covenant, then we lose everything, for they are
> we.[38]

Covenant defines politics as a moral enterprise. The polis is not
constituted by the pursuit, exercise, and distribution of power. That is
a means, not an end. It is about the pursuit of certain goods—freedom,
dignity, justice, and compassion—that honor human independence in
and through the modes of human interdependence. Covenant is about
the construction of human relationships not through dominance and
submission but in the conscious acknowledgment of the integrity of
the other. That is why, searching for a metaphor to describe the covenantal bond, the prophets repeatedly turn to the image of marriage, the
partnership that turns love into law and law into love, based not on
power but on the word given and received, the word honored in fidelity and loyalty.

Covenant is an answer, one of the most majestic in the history of
civilization, to the fundamental question of politics: How are we to
establish relationships of trust that alone make collaborative activity
possible, without coercion of, and thus indignity to, one of the partners? The strength of the covenant idea is to see that this can only be
achieved through the sharing of a moral vision, one that emerges not
through abstract and wholly general principles but through the concrete history of a people and its reflection on the past from which it
was born and the future it strives to create. Covenants are not the
product of philosophy—timeless, universal truths—but instead emerge
from a narrative, the story of a particular people set among other particular peoples.

Thinkers of early modernity—among them Hobbes and Locke—did
not differentiate, in the way we would now, between covenant and

contract. Nonetheless there is a fundamental difference between them. Covenants create societies, contracts create states. The people of Israel received their covenant in the wilderness, long before they had a land, a king, any army, and the other accoutrements of statehood. Political philosophy, from Plato to today, has been preoccupied with the concept of the state, sovereignty, and the justified use of power. The biblical narrative suggests that the state as community is prior to society, and the family to community itself. Beyond the state—and this too is part of the Hebrew Bible's continuing salience—lies humanity itself considered as a single moral community bounded by a covenant. This, in biblical terms, is the role of the covenant with Noah, made after the Flood.

Looking Forward

There is much else to be said about a Judaic politics. A fuller account would pay attention to the covenantal virtues: *mishpat* (retributive justice), *tzedakah* (distributive justice), *hessed* (the loving obligations between covenantal partners), and *rahamim* (compassion, or the primacy of the person over his or her acts). It would deal with the dual ontology of the covenant, the complex order that emerges from a sense of the universal imperatives of humanity as a whole, and the necessary particularities of the specific moral communities. It would analyze the rabbinic concept of *darkhei shalom* ("the ways of peace") as a way of structuring obligations of citizenship in a pluralistic society, the idea sometimes described as modus vivendi liberalism. There is much to be said about the biblical conception (different from, but not unrelated to, Montesquieu's) of the separation of powers, and about prophecy as a paradigm of social criticism. Much, too, remains to be said about biblical concepts of time (neither cyclical nor linear but narrative) and its relationship to politics as the time-bound realization of ideals.

It is my hope that this chapter has said enough to suggest that the Hebrew Bible and its later commentaries and codes represent a resource for political thought no less rich than its Greek or post-Enlightenment counterparts. The Bible is not a political code. It never was fully implemented. Much of biblical literature is an extended reflection on the difficulties Israel faced as it sought to live by its demands amid the vicissitudes of history. In particular, no suggestion is being made that in order to recover its message the liberal democracies of the West should return to religious modes of governance. To the contrary: one of Tocqueville's greatest insights was to see that what made religion in America an ally rather than an enemy of freedom was that it practiced a form of self-limitation. It sought influence not power. It operated at the level of society, not the state. It helped sustain the institutions—families, communities, and voluntary associations—in which citizenship and its attendant virtues were nurtured. It was, to that extent, prepolitical rather than political in the narrow sense of the word.

That said, Lord Acton's judgment remains insightful, namely that:

[T]he example of the Hebrew nation laid down the parallel lines on which all freedom has been won—the doctrine of national tradition and the doctrine of the higher law; the principle that a constitution grows from a root, by process of development, and not of essential change; and the principle that all political authorities must be tested and reformed according to a code which was not made by man.

By contrast, the Greek experiment had fatal flaws:

[T]he possession of unlimited power, which corrodes the conscience, hardens the heart, and confounds the understanding of monarchs, exercised its demoralising influence on the illustrious democracy of Athens. It is bad to be oppressed by a minority, but it is worse to be oppressed by a majority. . . . The philosophy that was then in the ascendant taught them that there is no law superior to that of the State—the lawgiver is above the law. It followed that the sovereign people had a right to do whatever was within its power, and was bound by no rule of right or wrong but its own judgment of expediency.[39]

The Jewish political tradition, neglected for several centuries, has begun to be revived by such scholars as the late Daniel Elazar, Michael Walzer, and others. The time is right for such a renewal. This author does not believe that Jews should enter the public square as mere members of an ethnic group with parochial interests. That is what they are but not all they are. They are bearers of one of the formative political traditions of Western civilization, one that in my view is deeper and richer than that of the city-states of ancient Greece from which much of our current political vocabulary derives. It is unique in its ethical rigor and its insistence on human dignity as the ultimate aim of the political enterprise and of the moral basis of a free society. Many aspects of Jewish life, which enabled it to survive and flourish throughout a history of exile and dispersion, have become prominent again in contemporary discourse. That is not surprising. What Michael Sandel calls "democracy's discontent"[40] has to do with the shortcomings of liberal individualism, to which no answer can be given from the repertoire of collectivism, source of many of the twentieth century's most egregious tyrannies. The result has been a fresh interest in the third space that stands between the individual and the state, called by some "community" and by others "civil society." If there is one respect in which the Jewish experience is unique, it is in the fact that it was able to sustain community and civil society in the absence of a state for almost two thousand years between the destruction of the Second Temple and the rebirth of Israel in 1948.

More than half a century has passed since the Holocaust and the founding of Israel. Today Jews enter the public square as equals, no more endowed with political authority but no less so than other groups. In Israel and outside—albeit on somewhat different terms—they face a challenge not posed in quite this way since biblical times, namely, to play their part as equal citizens in constructing a social order. In Israel they are a majority, elsewhere a minority. In Israel Jewish culture predominates, elsewhere it does so only in the interstices of family and community. Yet both Israel and the diaspora are set in the reality of cultural pluralism, global connectedness, and the overarching forces of the international economy and world politics. It is easy to overstate the differences between Israel and the diaspora; the commonalities remain. In both, the question asked of Jews is not simply what best serves Jewish interests. It is also what contributes to and what impedes the realization of the Judaic vision of a gracious society. What should be the next chapter in the continuing narrative of humanity's attempts to structure a collective life that does justice to our independence and interdependence, self and other, our uniqueness as individuals, and our embeddedness in networks of kinship, friendship, memory, and hope?

The Hebrew Bible is the story of a particular people, small, vulnerable, and not otherwise distinguished, who underwent a series of transformative experiences which they attributed to a divine intervention in history. Of one thing their visionary leaders were sure. That history had significance not for themselves alone. Ancient Israel had happened upon universal truths which they were called on to live out in a particular way. There is no equivalent in Judaism of *extra ecclesiam non est salus* (outside the church there is no salvation). There are many ways of creating a just and compassionate society just as there are many languages in which to describe the world, and many genres in which to create beauty, none of which precludes or excludes others. There are universals whose expression is always and inescapably particular, yet they remain universals. It is no accident that the great con-

cepts prefigured in the Hebrew Bible—human rights and responsibilities, freedom and dignity, covenant and constitution—resurfaced after
the Reformation and prepared the way for the liberal democracies of
the West. There is something compelling about these ideas that suggests that they speak to enduring features of the human condition.

The twenty-first century will confront mankind with the most difficult choices and fateful decisions it has ever faced. Globalization,
fragmenting families and communities, growing inequalities within
and between nations, the eroding biosphere, genetic intervention, international terror and the prospect of weapons of mass destruction in
the hands of extremist groups all herald a future of grave uncertainty,
one in which we will need all the cumulative wisdom at our disposal.
The Judaic heritage claims no monopoly of wisdom but it remains one
of the great and distinctive voices in the conversation of mankind.

Notes

1. Alasdair MacIntrye, *After Virtue* (London: Duckworth, 1981), 206.
2. Michael Walzer, *Exodus and Revolution* (New York: Basic Books, 1985).
3. See Daniel J. Elazar, *Covenant and Constitutionalism* (New Brunswick, N.J.: Transaction, 1998).
4. Os Guinness, *The American Hour* (New York: Free Press, 1993), 52.
5. Elazar, *Covenant and Constitutionalism,* 18.
6. Paul Mendes-Flohr and Jehuda Reinharz, eds., *The Jew in the Modern World* (New York: Oxford University Press, 1980), 104.
7. See Robert Bellah et al., *Habits of the Heart* (London: Hutchinson, 1988).
8. See Richard John Neuhas, *The Naked Public Square* (Grand Rapids, Mich.: Eerdmans, 1984).
9. John Rawls, *A Theory of Justice* (Oxford: Clarendon Press, 1972), and *Political Liberalism* (New York: Columbia University Press, 1993).
10. Rawls, *Political Liberalism*, 212-53.
11. For the argument I used at the time—invoking the concept of the Sabbath as the shared space of citizenship—see Jonathan Sacks, *The Politics of Hope*, 2nd ed. (London: Vintage, 2000), 198-202.
12. See Stephen Carter, *The Culture of Disbelief* (New York: Doubleday, 1993).
13. Quentin Skinner, *Liberty before Liberalism* (Cambridge: Cambridge University Press, 1998), 116-17.
14. *Troilus and Cressida,* Act 1, scene 3.

15. John Calvin, *Institutes of the Christian Religion*, Gilbert Meilaender, ed., *Working: Its Meaning and Its Limits* (Notre Dame, Ind.: University of Notre Dame Press, 2000), 107.

16. William Perkins, *A Treatise of the Vocations of Callings of Men*, in Meilaender, 111.

17. I Samuel 2:8.

18. Norman K. Gottwald, *The Tribes of Yahweh* (London: SCM Press, 1980), 692-933.

19. Micah 4:4.

20. Genesis 2:23.

21. John MacMurray, *Persons in Relations* (London: Faber and Faber, 1961).

22. Michael Sandel, *Liberalism and the Limits of Justice* (Cambridge: Cambridge University Press, 1982), 179.

23. Deuteronomy 6:7.

24. Genesis 18:19.

25. Leviticus 25:35.

26. Babylonian Talmud, *Sanhedrin* 27b.

27. Johannes Althusius, *Politica*, Frederick Carney, trans. (Indianapolis, Ind.: Liberty Press, 1995).

28. Mary Ann Glendon and David Blankenhorn, eds., *Seedbeds of Virtue* (New York: Lanham, 1995).

29. I Samuel 8:11-18.

30. Zvi Hirsch Chajes, "Torat hanevi'im," ch. 7, *Kol Kitvei Maharatz Chajes* (Jerusalem: Divrei Hakhamim Publishers, 1958), 43-49.

31. Judges 21:25.

32. Zechariah 4:6.

33. On the role of the prophet as social critic, see Michael Walzer, *Interpretation and Social Criticism* (Cambridge, Mass.: Harvard University Press, 1987).

34. Exodus 19:4-6.

35. Exodus 19:8, 24:3, 7.

36. Deuteronomy 31:12.

37. Philip Selznick, *The Moral Commonwealth* (Berkeley: University of California Press, 1994), 478.

38. Selznick, *The Moral Commonwealth*, 481.

39. Lord Acton, *Essays in the History of Liberty* (Indianapolis, Ind.: Liberty Classics, 1986), 8-14.

40. Michael Sandel, *Democracy's Discontent* (Cambridge, Mass.: Harvard University Press, 1996).

Index

321

About the Contributors

Michael J. Broyde is an associate professor of law at Emory University School of Law and the academic director of the Law and Religion Program at Emory University. He was ordained as a rabbi by Yeshiva University, is the founding rabbi of the Young Israel Congregation in Atlanta, and is a member (*dayan*) of the Beth Din of America, the largest Jewish law court in America.

Erwin Chemerinsky is Sydney M. Irmas Professor of Public Interest Law, Legal Ethics, and Political Science at the University of Southern California. He is the author of *Constitutional Law: Principles and Policies* (Aspen Law and Business, 2nd ed., 2002); *Constitutional Law* (Aspen Law and Business, 2001); *Federal Jurisdiction* (Aspen Law and Business, 4th ed., 2003); and *Interpreting the Constitution* (1987).

Marc Dollinger holds the Richard and Rhoda Goldman Chair in Jewish Studies and Social Responsibility at San Francisco State University. He is the author of *Quest for Inclusion: Jews and Liberalism in Modern America* (Princeton University Press, 2000) and co-editor, with Ava F. Kahn, of *California Jews* (Brandeis University Press, 2003).

Elliot N. Dorff, rabbi, Ph.D., is Distinguished Professor of Philosophy at the University of Judaism in Los Angeles and visiting professor at the UCLA School of Law. His most recent books are *Matters of Life and Death: A Jewish Approach to Modern Medical Ethics* (1998); *To Do the Right and the Good: A Jewish Approach to Modern Social Ethics* (2002); and *Love Your Neighbor and Yourself: A*

Jewish Approach to Modern Personal Ethics (2003), all published by the Jewish Publication Society.

Mickey Edwards is the John Quincy Adams Lecturer in Legislative Politics at Harvard University's Kennedy School of Government. He was previously a member of Congress for sixteen years and a member of the House Republican leadership. In the House of Representatives he served on the Appropriations and Budget Committees and was the ranking Republican member of the Subcommittee on Foreign Operations.

Jean Bethke Elshtain is the Laura Spelman Rockefeller Professor of Social and Political Ethics at the University of Chicago. She is the author of many books, including *Just War against Terror: American Power and Responsibility in a Violent World* (Basic Books, 2003).

William A. Galston is Sol I. Stern Professor at the University of Maryland, director of the Institute for Philosophy and Public Policy, and founding director of the Center for Information and Research on Civic Learning and Engagement (CIRCLE). His six books include *Liberal Purposes* (Cambridge, 1991) and *Liberal Pluralism* (Cambridge, 2002). From January 1993 until May 1995, Professor Galston served as deputy assistant to President Clinton for domestic policy.

Michael Gottsegen, Ph.D. is a senior fellow at CLAL—The National Jewish Center for Learning and Leadership. He received his Ph.D. in political theory from Columbia University and is currently completing his Ph.D. in religion at Harvard University. He has taught at Columbia University and at Brandeis University. He has written *The Political Thought of Hannah Arendt,* published by State University of New York Press, and is currently at work on a study of the relationship among politics, ethics, holiness, and law in modern Jewish thought.

Kevin J. "Seamus" Hasson is president of the Becket Fund for Religious Liberty, a nonpartisan, interfaith public interest law firm that protects the free expression of all religious traditions. He has defended the legal rights of people from many different faiths, including Jews, Christians, Muslims, Buddhists, Sikhs, Native Americans, and Zoroastrians. He holds a J.D. magna cum laude, and an M.A. in theology from the University of Notre Dame.

Gertrude Himmelfarb is professor emerita of history at the Graduate School of the City University of New York. She has written extensively on Victorian England and intellectual and cultural history. Her most recent book is *One Nation, Two Cultures* (Knopf, 1999).

Alan Mittleman is professor of religion and head of the Department of Religion at Muhlenberg College. He served as director of the Jews and the American Public Square project and edited *Jewish Polity and American Civil Society* (Rowman & Littlefield, 2002) and *Jews and the American Public Square* (Rowman & Littlefield, 2002).

David Novak is J. Richard and Dorothy Shiff Professor of Jewish Studies at the University of Toronto. He is also vice president of the Union for Traditional Judaism. He is the author of eleven books including *Covenantal Rights: A Study in Jewish Political Theory* (Princeton University Press, 2000).

Carl Raschke is professor of religious studies and chair of the department at the University of Denver. He is author or editor of eighteen books and several hundred articles on topics ranging from religious thought and philosophy to religion in contemporary American life. He is senior editor of the *Journal for Cultural and Religious Theory* and codirector of Res Publica, a national organization of citizens and scholars working on issues involving faith in American public life.

Jonathan Sacks is chief rabbi of the United Hebrew Congregations of the British Commonwealth. He is an honorary fellow of Gonville and Caius College, Cambridge, and the author of many books, most recently *The Dignity of Difference: How to Avoid the Clash of Civilizations* (Continuum International, 2002).

Kenneth D. Wald is Research Foundation Professor of Political Science and director of the Center for Jewish Studies at the University of Florida. He is the author of *Religion and Politics in the United States* (4th ed.) (Rowman & Littlefield, 2003) and coauthor of *Politics of Cultural Differences: Social Change and Voter Mobilization Strategies in the Post-New Deal Period* (Princeton University Press, 2002). He is currently working on a book about contemporary Jewish political behavior.

Alan Wolfe is professor of political science and director of the Boisi Center for Religion and American Public Life at Boston College. His latest book is *The Transformation of American Religion* (Free Press, 2003).